James A. Dombrowski

# JAMES A.
# DOMBROWSKI

An
American
Heretic,
1897–1983

## Frank T. Adams

With a Foreword
by Arthur Kinoy

The University
of Tennessee Press
Knoxville

Library of Congress Cataloging in Publication Data
Adams, Frank T., 1934–
    James A. Dombrowski : an American heretic, 1897–1983 / Frank T.
Adams.
        p.   cm.
    Includes bibliographical references and index.
    ISBN 0-87049-741-3 (cloth: alk. paper)
    ISBN 0-87049-742-1 (pbk. : alk. paper)
    1. Dombrowski, James A. (James Andersen), 1897–1983.   2. Civil
rights workers—Southern States—Bibliography.   I. Title
E185.98.D66A66   1992
323'.092—dc20
    [B]                                              91-30565
                                                        CIP

# Contents

Foreword, by Arthur Kinoy   ix

Acknowledgments   xiii

Introduction   1

1. From the South, Not of the South   5

2. Making a Name for Himself   18

3. North toward Home   27

4. Conceiving the Kingdom of God   44

5. The Reformer as an Artist   57

6. Learning from What Was Lived   81

7. Growing Acclaim, Growing Trouble   104

8. War, Race, and Conscience   132

9. Battles on the Homefront   148

10. Warring after the War   163

11. The Psalmist's Dream Is Dashed   178

12. For Another South, Another Mobilizer   186

13. Separate and Unequally Bad   203

14. On the Street, Politically Homeless   222

15. New Hands Helping with an Old Burden   239

16. A Chilling Effect   262

Epilogue: Striving for Worthwhile Ends   277

Appendix A: Chronology   289

Appendix B: From a Mill-Town Jail, by James A. Dombrowski   291

Notes   295

Bibliography   335

Index   351

# Illustrations

1. Jamie Dombrowsky   6

2. William John Dombrowsky   8

3. Isabella Elizabeth Dombrowsky   8

4. Airman Dombrowsky   16

5. "The Brotherhood" at Emory   21

6. Dombrowski after Arrest in Elizabethton   35

7. A Gentleman with Extreme Radical Social Views   58

8. Ethel Clyde on her 85th Birthday   75

9. Ellen Krida on Vacation with Dombrowski   98

10. Union Members Learning Poster Design   118

11. Champion Joe Louis Lends a Hand   161

12. Dombrowski Leaves Birmingham Jail   199

13. Jim Crow and Coca-Cola   220

14. Dombrowski in the First Police Precinct   264

15. Dombrowski at Last   285

# Foreword

James Dombrowski was a brilliant, courageous, powerful person, deeply committed to the vision of a truly democratic society. In such a society all people, regardless of their race, sex, age, or class, would be entitled to equality, freedom, and full participation in the material benefits of society.

Throughout his life, Dombrowski brought together the ideals of Christian morality and the goals of social justice—goals that had been put forward by the Socialist leaders of radical struggle against systematic oppression both in Europe and in the United States in the early days of its history. This merger of ideals became a powerful weapon giving Jim Dombrowski the fortitude to stand courageously for many years as an active participant in the intense and bitter struggles to achieve the most elementary rights for the African-American peoples of the South. These rights were two: equality, and freedom from the remaining chains of the slave system, a system which the white power structure utilized to perpetuate its control over not only African-Americans but all the working people of the South, white as well as black.

From the early 1930s on, Jim's entire life as a white southerner was dedicated to the inflexible conviction that, if political, social, and economic progress for all the people of the South and the entire country was to be achieved, white people and African-American people had to work together on an equal basis. The entrenched power structure, locally and nationally, devised attacks upon him and the organizations he was helping to build, attempting to frighten him and paralyze his efforts to build effective unity among all working and oppressed peoples. His responses to the Red-baiting assaults, the character attacks, and the viscous criminal and civil proceedings devised to destroy his effectiveness were powerful and courageous. In a manner which inspired the people working with him, who faced the same waves of persecution, Jim Dombrowski's answer to these attacks was simple and direct: "Stand up and fight—don't retreat—and if we stand together, we can win!" Jim Dombrowski was a role model for all of us involved in the intense struggles against racism in all its forms in the deep South in the early 1960s.

As a civil rights lawyer, I had the privilege of working closely with Jim during the height of efforts by the white power structure in Louisiana to utilize the Cold-War machinery of the 1950s and the state's antisedition statute to institute criminal proceedings against him and two courageous young white lawyers, Ben Smith and Bruce Waltzer. The charge was that the three men's activities—in support of the campaigns of African Americans throughout the South, for the right to vote and against all segregation—were seditious and treasonous.

Jim Dombrowski's response to this attack taught us a powerful lesson which goes to the very essence of the continuing struggles in this country for the preservation of the fundamental liberties of the people. He urged us to launch a counterattack, in the form of a sweeping federal lawsuit against the conspiracy of Louisiana state officials, aided by southern Congressional forces, to bury the most elementary constitutional promises of freedom and equality for African-Americans. In so doing, the suit would argue, these forces were attempting to destroy the basic constitutional rights of freedom of speech, freedom of the press, and freedom of assembly that had been promised to all Americans by the First Amendment. Jim Dombrowski's fervent belief in the intimate relationship between the battles for civil rights and those for civil liberties lay at the very heart of the legal counteroffensive he had urged us to institute. I, together with other lawyers, had the honor of fighting this battle through the federal courts and finally of arguing this case before the United States Supreme Court. The result was a sweeping victory for Dombrowski, Smith, and Waltzer, and for the organizations of African-Americans and their white sisters and brothers throughout the South. In the landmark opinion in which Jim Dombrowski's name has gone down in legal history, known as *Dombrowski v. Pfister,* Justice William Brennan wrote into our basic constitutional law a mandate that Jim had fought for—that where governmental forces, state or national, institute activities designed to have a "chilling effect" upon the exercise of fundamental constitutional rights by American citizens, these aims of the establishment must be repudiated and rejected by everyone, including the national government itself.

The lessons to be learned from James Dombrowski's life are essential for all of us. To be sure, they offer critical insight into the past, helping us to understand the incredible experiences of the peoples of this country during the thirties, forties, fifties, sixties, and seventies. But these lessons also are essential for all of us to grasp as we face the intense struggles for dignity and a better world, which the people of this country will be involved in the nineties and the decades to follow. Frank Adams' book on the life of James Dombrowski is essential, enabling us not only to learn about the past but also to prepare ourselves for the future.

ARTHUR KINOY

# Acknowledgments

This book has been a long time coming into print. In one way or another, I have worked on it since 1973. The story of James Anderson Dombrowski's life needed telling, that much was clear, and that necessity helped keep me at the task even when it seemed that I'd never find a publisher who agreed. *Who* insisted that I keep going is another matter, but should be made clear: Margaret, my dearest friend, and Joe Logsdon, a real historian who believed, as did Margaret, that someday . . . As a writer caught between a story as good as Dombrowski's and faith as strong as theirs, I could do little but persist.

Others weighed in at crucial moments with equally valuable support, skill, facts, or time: Mike Clark, a friend who also believed that Dombrowski had influenced importantly and positively; Marc Miller, a sharp editor with a gentle pencil; John Egerton, an esteemed man of southern letters, who knew the importance of Dombrowski's history and always believed my telling of that story would be published; Jane Becker, a cultural historian who had never heard of Dombrowski until she read one version of this work; and Jim Green, a labor historian who saw merit in my manuscript and commended it to Tana McDonald. She found Dombrowski's story worthy, offered ways to improve its telling, and said she would try to steer it to publication. It would be an understatement to say that each of them, along with the University of Tennessee Press's several readers, including James A. Hodges, Michael McDonald, and Peter Wood, have the gratitude of this writer. I am indebted also to Mavis Bryant, who got the editorial kinks out of the manuscript.

Why did I devote so much of my lifetime to this obscure man's history? The issues of central importance to Dombrowski have been matters of profound concern to me, as, I believe, they have to most North Americans of my era. What lessons could he teach? I have tried to answer that question in the pages that follow. But there is another reason, also generational in nature. Margaret and I have two children. They were in high school when the idea of this book captured my imagination. Now they are at the work of their own lives and are making us very proud. The social ills that Dombrowski tried to remedy remain very much a part of their times, perhaps glaring evermore uniformly across the nation, even though Dombrowski's sort of heresy is not much evident. So I kept on for Sam and Mary Thom, and I dedicate this book to them and to their generation.

# Introduction

"Every peg is made to fit some hole and every hole needs a peg to fit it," Asa G. Candler, founder of the Coca-Cola Company, frequently told high school graduating classes in and around Atlanta during the 1920s. "The cry always in the business world is for first class pegs to fit first class holes."[1] In 1923, Candler had his eye on just such a first-class prospect, a young Methodist he had watched progress through Emory University. S. Frank Boykin, Coca-Cola's treasurer, agreed. The soft drink they wanted to sell worldwide could profit from Jim Dombrowski.

Dombrowski graduated *cum laude* that spring, earning other honors, too, having engaged in one successful church or charitable activity after another. He had organized and managed the Emory Glee Club's first European tour, a smashing success that paid its own way with sold-out houses and introductions to wealthy benefactors who had musical interests. The young man had helped found Emory's Sigma Chi Fraternity chapter, which had grown out of an informal group of students calling themselves "The Brotherhood." Most of these men had intended to serve humankind as medical or spiritual missionaries, and they had held regular prayer meetings together. Dombrowski, who had been orphaned young, had clerked in a retail jewelry store to pay his way through Emory and used a small inheritance for loans to less fortunate fellow students. During one summer break, he had organized a Southern Methodist church in his native Tampa, Florida. And he had served his country in World War I as an aeroplane mechanic in France. Emory University's administration wanted Dombrowski to be the college's first secretary of alumni affairs.

Dombrowski was exactly the sort of man Candler hoped to see emerge from Emory University—an exemplar, living proof that the millions Candler was investing in higher education would pay off. Moreover, Dombrowski had the practical advantage of speaking two languages; he had a foreign name. He was a perfect fit. The Coca-Cola Company wanted him to organize its European sales network, starting as early as possible in 1924. Candler and Boykin offered Dombrowski the highest starting salary they ever had dangled before a recruit.[2] Dombrowski turned them down.

Six years later, Coca-Cola's bright prospect was jailed in Elizabethton,

Tennessee, charged with being an accomplice in the murder of a police chief and accused in newspaper accounts of being a Communist. Dombrowski avowed his innocence, declaring that he was a Christian Socialist who believed that the ethics of Jesus Christ should be applied in everyday life, especially in business. His arrest opened a career spanning four decades as a teacher, organizer, fundraiser, pamphleteer, or administrator in one controversial southern cause after another. He worked first with impoverished Appalachians, then with labor unions, and finally in the American civil rights movement.

Dombrowski, along with Myles Horton and Don West, two equally visionary southerners, was a founder of Highlander Folk School. Besides being the school's businesslike administrator (he was called "the Skipper" by staff), he taught, raised money, and defended the school against constant attacks by ideological foes and former friends. He was the first of many social historians who would find unique oral history among the people who came to Highlander, and he recorded many of their recollections, especially those concerning the upheavals resulting from the use of convict labor in southern mountain coalfields. Dombrowski helped Depression-stricken mountain people invent a curriculum through which they learned to take some charge of their economic lives, and that they used in trying to take control of government. The idea of "education for empowerment" infused his teaching, although that pedagogic term had not yet been invented.

Later, between 1942 and 1946, as executive director of the Southern Conference for Human Welfare, Dombrowski sought, almost alone, to unite white liberals, especially in labor unions, with the growing, unmistakable passion among African Americans for political and social freedom. His was a singular call for full integration in every sphere of southern life. President Roosevelt's patronage helped spawn the Southern Conference for Human Welfare; the organization furnished a regional counterbalance to the southern opposition to Roosevelt in the Democratic Party. But as that coalition started to come unglued after World War II, the energy for a "Southwide awakening" disintegrated, often into bitter political fights. Dombrowski did not escape this discord. Well before the Southern Conference for Human Welfare passed, on November 12, 1948, its last resolve—a motion to disband—an offshoot, the Southern Conference Education Fund, led by Dombrowski and Aubrey Williams, made the attack on segregation their organization's sole priority. Williams had fought relentlessly for inclusion of African Americans in the New Deal. For over two decades following World War II, Dombrowski, together with Williams, marshalled the South's most militant integrationists under the SCEF banner, so that these individuals—a handful, really—could speak and act forcefully. When Williams' health failed, the Reverend Fred Shuttlesworth joined Dombrowski to prosecute the same causes. And when the rallying call for black power was issued in 1965, the SCEF, with a largely white membership, was unabashed; with renewed vigor, it worked to focus the civil rights movement on parallel social and political issues, among them civil liberties.

Dombrowski's career ties together three crucial periods of southern history and three equally central southern organizations. These periods and organizations usually have been studied separately. A study of Dombrowski's life illuminates the patterns of class, labor, and race from the mid-1930s well into the 1960s. It also suggests the impact of ideological debate and government and reactionary harassment, the role of strong-willed personalities, and especially the powerfully diverse nature of communism as a national issue. Dombrowski was not a Communist, but he embraced communist associates and even more radical tenets. Communists, in fact, were angered by him, or wary of him, as often as were Socialists or moderates. Newspapers in 1929 were mistaken when they labeled him a Communist, but it is no mistake to suppose that the issue of communism is crucial to his life's story, and to events which eventually resulted in a civil rights movement.

Throughout his life, the self-effacing Dombrowski, who had an aristocratic passion for privacy, remained an obscure figure. Few knew him then; fewer know about him now. His predilections were for art, plants, and letters, rather than protest. Nevertheless, he was a pivotal figure, remembered for deeds and words that kept alive a radical vision of social change. His arrest for subversion by Louisiana authorities in 1963 eventually gave this unobtrusive person an irrevocable place in American legal history as well. In *Dombrowski v. Pfister*, the United States Supreme Court decided that the arrest had had "a chilling effect" on his First Amendment rights, leaving civil libertarians with an evocative phrase and a "quaintly styled" principle in law. Since then, the decision has been cited in more than 1,300 cases in defense of civil rights and liberties.

Had he bothered to follow the Emory graduate's career, Asa Candler no doubt would have sighed with deep relief that Dombrowski had not signed on with Coca-Cola. Until his death, Boykin did keep up with Dombrowski and said he was embarrassed by his own misjudgment and embarrassed for the university and for the Sigma Chi fraternity.[3] Nurturing heretics was not what Candler had had in mind for Emory. While he was at Emory, Dombrowski had not fit neatly into categories; he fit fewer as the years went on. Not many Methodists, southerners, or Americans of any faith or region shared his unyielding expectation of a Kingdom of God on earth. While he was from the South and confronted the great issues of his lifetime in the South, Dombrowski really was an American heretic. He gave his name to the great tradition of heresy in America.

# 1

## From
## the South,
## Not of
## the South

James Anderson Dombrowsky was born at home on January 17, 1897, in Tampa, Florida, the fourth child of William John and Isabella Elizabeth Dombrowsky.[1] The Dombrowsky household was filled with excitement. A healthy boy had been born without unusual incident and would carry the family name—a Polish name which William had anglicized slightly, changing an ending *i* to *y*.

The child was handsome. Light brown hair accented striking brown eyes. Long lashes made his eyes even more noticeable. Isabella, although suffering chronic tuberculosis, had delivered the baby easily and was herself well. She called her son Jamie, and she was proudly touched to think that his two sisters, Daisy and Rose, agreed that their brother favored her. William celebrated with his business associates, generously sharing the Dom Special hand-rolled cigars made particularly for him by Tampa's Amelio Pons Cigar Company.

Dom and Belle, as the parents were known, had grown up and married in Newark, New Jersey. His mother and father, Mathilde Harmon and Herman Dombrowski, had come to the United States from Adansk, Poland. William, the youngest of four children, had been born in Newark in 1865, the year the American Civil War ended. The family spoke German, not Polish, and, moreover, were Lutherans. Once settled in Newark, they earned a living as a family, selling ice and coal. Belle, born in London in 1866, had

Jamie Dombrowsky, aged four months. Frank T. Adams Collection.

been the third child of Annie Sully and James F. Skinner. Her family had moved to the United States to open a stationery shop and newsstand on busy South Orange Avenue in Newark.

Shortly after being married in 1884, the coupled had moved to Sanford, Florida, starting out on their own. Their reasons for choosing Florida have been obscured by time. Family memories are vague. Perhaps they, like hundreds of northerners, were attracted by land speculators who touted Florida as a balmy region of unlimited opportunity for the energetic. Typically, the Florida Investment Company was proclaiming in advertisements about the time of their marriage, "Here is a land of open pine forests, studded with crystal-clear lakes, and marked by an absence of fever, mosquitoes and negroes."[2] Maybe Belle's health prompted their decision; while a beautiful young woman, she always had been frail, and the curative myth of the Fountain of Youth still circulated when people spoke of Florida.

Dombrowsky set up a jewelry store in Sanford and prospered. His wife traveled north each summer for vacations with her family and in-laws, to escape the punishing Florida heat. Their first two children were born in Newark—Daisy in 1887 and Albert in 1891. With Albert, the couple had their first brush with sorrow. The child never spoke or walked. The exact nature of his illness was never diagnosed, despite repeated visits to doctors in New York City, who could find no cure, and eventually he died. This must have made the birth of an apparently healthy boy even more important for the couple. Beyond the family itself, there was no extended network of kin in Tampa. Their children were from the South, not of the South.

The young Dombrowsky coupled had faced other difficulties just after a third child, Rose, was born in 1894. In the midst of a nationwide depression, a hard winter freeze destroyed the citrus crop in northern Florida. A disastrous fire in the business district ruined what remained of Sanford's economy. The outlook for retail jewelry sales there looked bleak. The family moved to Tampa, a port town on the Gulf Coast that was growing even faster than its most avid civic boosters claimed.

In 1880, Tampa's population had been under a thousand, consisting mostly of cattlemen, who, along with citrus growers, used Tampa Bay's deep, sheltered waters as a convenient port for shipping to the lucrative northern and Cuban markets.[3] The few small businesses mostly sold necessities. Ten years later, the population passed five thousand. In the decade between, enterprising businessmen had persuaded the Cuban cigar industry to relocate in Tampa from Cuba and from Key West, Florida, where

William John Dombrowsky, father
of James A. Dombrowsky (no date).
Frank T. Adams Collection.

Isabella Elizabeth Dombrowsky,
mother of James A. Dombrowsky
(no date). Frank T. Adams Collection.

Cubans earlier had established a manufacturing foothold. The cigar-makers brought a new culture. Tampa had a decidedly Latin air about it when the Dombrowskys moved there. Half the population spoke Spanish. In a dozen or more factories, Cuban love songs and ballads eased the tedium of rolling cigars and flowed over into nearby streets.

Dombrowsky, an expansive man who sometimes sported a flowing handlebar mustache, opened his store in the Hayden Building on Franklin Street, Tampa's still unpaved main commercial thoroughfare. He built a flourishing trade with the Cubans from nearby Ybor City and West Tampa, where most Spanish-speaking citizens lived, often in squalid housing, and with his own neighbors in affluent, prestigious Hyde Park, the "high-toned" residential community across the Hillsborough River from downtown Tampa.[4]

The Dombrowskys bought a large Victorian home between Platt and Azeele Streets on Hyde Park Avenue. The family of T.C. Talleferro, president of the First National Bank, lived next door. H.L. Knight, half owner of the town's largest retail and wholesale hardware store, and his family lived across the street. Peter O. Knight, a lawyer who counted the owners of several cigar factories among his clients, lived on the opposite corner. Oak trees shaded the Dombrowsky home. Honeysuckle climbed the front porch bannisters. "Mother especially loves roses, and there was a rose garden in the back yard," Rose remembered.[5] Inside the house, patterned, heavily-upholstered furnishings with flowery carving, wicker and bentwood chairs, and solid oak tables underscored the family's middle-class respectability.

On February 15, 1898, just after the family marked Jamie's first birthday, the American battleship *Maine* was in Havana's harbor, supposedly to protect Americans and their property from Cubans battling over the issue of independence from Spain. The warship exploded, killing 260 persons. Even before the tragedy, William Randolph Hearst and Joseph Pulitzer had demanded on the editorial pages of their many newspapers that American troops be sent to Cuba. The deaths and the battleship's loss stirred chauvinistic passions, providing patriotic Americans with a fiery slogan, "Remember the Maine!"

By April, President William McKinley and Congress, unable or unwilling to forget the *Maine*, declared war on Spain. Soon, over fifteen-thousand foot soldiers and dashing officers on horseback poured into Tampa, the port of debarkation. A Washington correspondent reported that city shopkeepers were making so much money local banks could hardly contain the flood. "Even a lemonade man, equipped with a bucket and two tin cups, can make $25 a day," he wrote.[6] Dombrowsky, like his colleagues, prospered. Before the troops embarked for Cuba, he joined other businessmen to host a banquet at the Tampa Bay Hotel for the officers, including a young lieutenant colonel, Theodore Roosevelt, who, rumor had it in Tampa's political circles, had a bright future. The glittering event was complete with rattling sabres, gold braid, and patriotic speeches.

As wars go, this one was short. Congress declared war on Spain in April. By August, an armistice had been signed. Spain gave up Guam, Puerto Rico, and the Philippines in return for twenty million dollars. Teddy Roosevelt rode up San Juan Hill to fame and the presidency. He had been president one year when Belle Dombrowsky died on July 10, 1902, at the age of thirty-six.

"She had been an invalid for all the years I could remember and, when not bedridden, she was lying on a couch most of the time." Rose, who was then eight, recalled.[7] The Reverend William Wilson DeHart, who was rector at Saint Andrew's Episcopal Church, christened Rose and Jamie at home the afternoon before. Daisy had been confirmed at Saint Andrew's earlier. "Jamie would go upstairs to visit mother every morning after breakfast. It was a habit with him. I remember very clearly how little Jamie cried and carried on because the nurse wouldn't let him in mother's room the next morning. Mother was gone. Of course, the whole family was crushed when mother died, and it was a terrible blow to our father."

Jamie Dombrowsky was five and living in Newark, with an aunt and uncle, Florence and Will Cox, his mother's sister and brother-in-law, when he refused to answer to Jamie any longer, and declared he would be called Jim or James. Already he was a sober youngster.[8] The Coxes lived modestly compared to the Dombrowskys of Tampa. But they were comfortable in a sturdy home. They had two children, Helen and Roy, who got along famously with Daisy, Rose, and Jim. Albert, the invalid child, was cared for by his Dombrowsky grandparents; his condition remained undiagnosed and unchanged. From Tampa, their father sent money to pay for whatever the children needed in the way of clothing, books, or food. They never wanted. Nor was there among them a feeling of self-pity at the loss of their mother. Belle Dombrowsky had sensed, if not realized, the certainty of her death. Besides attending to her children's spiritual needs, she insured that they would be surrounded by loving relatives. The jeweler came north on buying trips at least twice a year, and always for his mother's birthday on October 12.[9] He stayed in New York at the Astor Hotel but would come to Newark often, taking his children to Broadway shows in New York or to dinner at famous restaurants. They saw performances at the Hippodrome. His children adored him.

Jim's first memories of his father formed at this time, mostly during family parties. His father and uncle sang *lieders*, drank beer, and ate for hours. Years later, he would remember his father fondly, perhaps because they were around each other for short spells and there was seldom any reason for the father to discipline his well-behaved son.[10]

Within a year after moving to Newark, the Coxes, Daisy, Rose, and Jim moved into a roomier house. While the children were there, their brother Albert died. Within weeks of his death, the Dombrowsky patriarch, Herman, died. Once again a death in the family changed the boy's circumstances. Dombrowsky rented a brick duplex not far from his cousin Eugene Dombrowsky's home and business. Grandmother Dombrowsky moved in with her grandchildren. Daisy assumed duties as head of the household; she was in her final year of high school and was planning to marry her beau, William Hansberry. After school every day, Jim fetched his bedridden grandmother a tin of homemade soup from one of several aunts living in the neighborhood. Her health declined seriously after her husband's death. Her grandson sat for hours on a footstool at her feet listening to her reminisce.

Despite the upsetting loss of loved ones and their frequent moves, the Dombrowsky children were, by all accounts, happy in Newark. Jim was earning high marks at South Street Elementary School. He was selected to give the graduation speech. In his teachers' eyes, the quiet child had only one flaw, but it was one they were determined to correct. He was naturally left-handed. They insisted he do lessons with his right hand. To practice, he started drawing, spending hours every night copying the patterns in lace curtains, or sketching chairs, pots, or the people around him. Without encouragement other than his own desire, Jim persisted in this solitary way of expressing himself. Drawing became more than a way to learn how to use his right hand or to while away a few hours. The cosmos could be understood, if only in small parts. His hand and eye learned to work together. Relationships he had not yet found words to describe, but which were on his mind, could be stated through lines.[11] He thought about being an architect.

Jim joined the Young Men's Christian Association, where he took up swimming, leather crafts, and Bible study. In a Bible-study class run by J. August Wolfe, the "Y" secretary, Biblical events, the people, their problems, and their land came alive for young Dombrowsky. The Bible told a story that actually had taken place. Palestine was still there. Years later, Dombrowsky remembered Wolfe as a formative source of his social imagination. Through the Bible-study class, the boy learned that history was one way individuals struggled with their inner lives in the society around them. "I may have picked up some ethical ideas out of that class," he reflected.[12]

At South Eighth Street School, Jim took up track, running dashes and relays. One summer he competed in a citywide athletic meet, winning first prize for the fifty-yard dash. He got a gold medal. Unexpectedly, his picture appeared in a rotogravure section of the *New York Times*. In Tampa, his father got a copy from his family, and wrote proudly congratulating his son. The next year, Jim entered another citywide meet. Dombrowsky, who was on his annual buying trip at the time, came to see his son. The boy lost. After the race, Jim remembered his father saying, "Well, anyway, you beat the nigger."[13]

At the time, the racist remark did not seem to have made a hurtful impression on Jim; it became, however, an indexing moment as he matured to sort out his own social values. His father and his family shared the prejudices of their times, were no more or less ignorant about race than other businessmen, or their neighbors. Jim never forgot the cutting epithet. His father, a typical southern businessman, was redeemed in his son's eyes only by the love the man gave his son and family, and by his gregariousness.

The Dombrowsky family had a flair for business, and, in James, as they had gradually come to call him, they saw promise for the third generation. In Tampa, Dombrowsky had opened a second jewelry store, including a thriving pawn shop. In Newark, the family's coal and ice company flourished. A cousin, Eugene, ran a sewing factory making embroidered children's and infants' clothing. He farmed out garments to neighborhood women for embroidery. While the embroidering was done by machine, edges and extra material had to be cut away by hand. The women were paid by the piece. His niece Rose did scalloping handwork, too, and was paid the same pittance for each piece, her family relationship notwithstanding. Cousin Eugene lived in the largest house in the neighborhood; his factory was behind it. To young Dombrowsky, Cousin Eugene was refinement. He dressed and lived elegantly.[14] The family assumed that the bright boy would take up a business career.

In October 1912, as was his custom, Dombrowsky came north for business and for his mother's birthday. She had lost her eyesight during the summer. Daisy and William Hansberry had been married without family fanfare earlier. The ailing grandmother's birthday, the wedding, and Dombrowsky's return were reasons for a festive celebration. "All of our relatives came, the women for coffee and cakes in the afternoon, and their menfolks for dinner—chicken, potato salad, fresh ham, and things that could be prepared ahead," Rose remembered.[15] "We always set two tables—grownups first and the second table for the children. Grandma had a lovely time." The next Sunday, Eugene, who had recently bought a Cadillac and hired a chauffeur, invited Dombrowsky and his children to motor with him for a picnic in the mountains. It was a cloudy, damp day, and chilly for the time of year. Even so, the trip was exhilarating. No one seemed to notice the weather. Evidently, however, Dombrowsky caught a cold, and the next day he came home from New York with a raging fever. Four days later, on October 25, he died of pneumonia. Two months later, on Christmas eve, Grandmother Dombrowsky died. "The death of our father was like the end of the world to Jim and me," Rose recalled.[16]

His father's death destroyed a large part of the self-centered teenager's secure world. Dombrowsky had been too young to remember his feelings at the time of his mother's death.[17] Two loving sisters and a big family had taken her place. His father, however, had given the boy anything he wanted, such as a bicycle or clothes, almost always accompanied by expressions of love and esteem. He had protected the boy from the need to work. The boy could and did dream of what he'd like to be, rather than thinking of what necessity forced him to do. Before the year was out, however, his study at Newark's Central High School and his dream of becoming an architect ended. Eugene Dombrowsky, appointed executor of his cousin's estate, and Daisy's husband, William, went to Tampa planning to sell the Dombrowsky business. However, a banker there persuaded them to keep both firms going. Hansberry was to run them. Rose graduated from high school in February. By March, she and Jim left for Tampa, taking a Clyde Steamship Company boat, the *Lenape,* out of New York harbor. Daisy took Rose and Jim into her home on South Boulevard, in Tampa's Suburb Beautiful just off Tampa Bay. Dombrowsky enrolled at Hillsborough High School. Each Fourth of July, the Hansberrys hung the American flag on their front porch. Dombrowsky got a canoe and kept it in a boathouse on the Hillsborough River. He canoed often, finding the sport more exhilarating than competition where winning was the only aim.

As his love of physical exertion grew, so, too, did his interest in religion. The Reverend L.M. Broyles was pastor at Hyde Park Methodist Church when Jim returned to his native city. He and Rose, Episcopalian offspring of Lutheran ancestors, became Methodists. The young Dombrowskys were not overly concerned with a particular church's rituals. Hyde Park Methodist was conveniently near their new home. Rev. Broyles befriended the teenager. They often went fishing or canoeing. Soon Dombrowsky was teaching Sunday School classes. The friendships he made through church flowed naturally into high school and the yacht club, where he was gaining renown as a graceful dancer. Methodistism would encircle him for years to come; religion, rather than family or region, would provide a sense of community and belonging.

By 1915, when Dombrowsky graduated from high school, he was "the most dignified boy" in the senior class, an honor roll student four years.[18] A flair for writing surfaced. He had been editor of *The Red and Black*, a literary magazine. The 1915 *Hillsborean* said, "Jim has shown us that he is an excellent editor as well as a scholar."[19] Hillsborough's principal, a graduate of Yale University, urged Jim to apply for a scholarship to the Ivy League school.

Jim didn't think he was ready for college. Instead, he clerked fulltime in his father's first store. Business proved to have no appeal; only the precious stones caught his imagination. He spent hours arranging them to catch the light in differing glistening patterns, and enjoyed arranging displays in the store windows. He questioned the business world's values. He became acquainted with the cashier of the Exchange National Bank, not far from the store. Once, while making a deposit, the earnest young man told the banker that charging 10 percent interest for loans was unethical. The banker laughed, asking, "What do you think would happen to the banking world if interest was unfair?" Dombrowsky had no answer, except to say people should share any extra money they had, or at least loan it without interest.[20] Business violated his sense of fairness, for him an increasingly compelling but still unarticulated instinct. Fairness, rather than profit, would drive Dombrowsky the rest of his life. Shortly after the episode at the bank, he began searching for an alternative to business, and soon he enrolled in the Bowman School of Watchmaking and Engraving in Lancaster,

Pennsylvania, to study engraving. On April 2, 1917, as he worked to learn the delicate art of engraving jewelry, President Woodrow Wilson told Congress that American neutrality was no longer feasible or practical. "The world must be made safe for democracy," Wilson declared.[21] By June, the first soldiers to finish training gave up singing "Oh, How I Hate to Get Up in the Morning," and instead were eagerly chorusing the "Mademoiselle from Armentieres" at troop-ship railings. They were heading for war in Europe. That fall, before school started again, Dombrowsky enlisted in the Aero Service. "It was considered a good thing, a patriotic thing, to contribute to the war effort in some way," he said.[22]

The young recruit was sent to Fort Screven, Georgia, outside Savannah. At the cantonment, Dombrowsky learned how to wind on putees, and to march in step with other equally enthusiastic newcomers to military life. Eight weeks later, when he finished basic training, he was sent to Kelly Field, near San Antonio, Texas, to learn aeroplane instrument repair. American aviation was so young that the nation didn't have enough flyers to train recruits. Among his instructors, only the commanding officer was American. The rest were from Great Britain, members of the Royal Flying Corps, who provided sound training in the theory of flight, in what made a plane fly, and in how to keep it flying.

Learning to repair planes fascinated Dombrowsky. He got plenty of opportunity to learn. The army only had fifty-five planes when President Wilson declared war. Those few had to be maintained until the new British DeHavilands could be gotten off production lines. Dombrowsky quickly won his rating as a repairman and thought of little else. "I never thought at all about killing and the deaths in the trenches," he said years later.[23] He had never been exposed to any criticism of war, or of the policies which resulted in war. War was inevitable; his history books had been filled with war. It never occurred to him that people could believe that a world without war was possible.

Dombrowsky's squadron went to Issoudun, an airfield well inside the Allied lines, about 150 miles south of Paris. He never fired a shot but was never far from death in the abstract. Artillery could be heard in the distance at all times of the day and night. While the flyers were largely confined to reconnaissance flights or to observation of German trenches, an occasional flight would be made to bomb behind enemy lines. Most losses resulted from aerial dogfights over the battlefields. Lt. Eddie Rickenbacker flew out of Issoudun to fame, downing twenty-six planes. He became America's first

Airman James A. Dombrowsky, Newark N.J., 1918. Frank T. Adams Collection.

air ace. Quentin Roosevelt, son of former President Teddy Roosevelt, also flew out of Issoudun. He died in a dogfight. Dombrowsky, despite his rank, knew them both. Before the war ended, every pilot in the squadron he trained with in Texas was killed.

Unlike enlisted soldiers in the muddy, cold, and deathly trenches, Dombrowsky enjoyed warm meals, good company, a dry bed at night, and time to think about what was happening around him. For once, he was not the master of his own destiny. He had never been ordered to do anything before, only asked or encouraged. He was thrust into a social life from which his comfortable, Victorian childhood had kept him sheltered. Many of his fellow soldiers had grown up through experiences he never imagined. An Irish mechanic boasted that he had been born in a whorehouse. At first, Dombrowsky was ill-at-ease working beside the man. Gradually, however, they got to be buddies. For the first time, too, he associated with African Americans. In his father's world, in the neighborhoods of his youth, certainly in the churches he attended, and even in the YMCA, African Americans were elsewhere, at best seen in cheap religious art as abstractions demonstrating Christ's love of all the little children.

Dombrowsky was struck by how the military separated soldiers into distinct social or racial units. Authority, jobs, mess halls, bunks, even entertainment were based on visible or invisible distinctions. Uniforms marked off differences. As instrument repairman, Dombrowsky did his job in the hanger, while African-American airmen swept the floor or hauled away trash. A few of them, he learned, were from the South. For them, the war was not simply "the patriotic thing to do," it was a way to eat three meals a day, to get away from the South where every future seemed bleak. The war redirected Dombrowsky's life. Engraving lost its allure. He decided to go to college, although he had no idea which college or what exactly he would study, save perhaps the ministry or teaching. He had in mind doing something to help people. War put that thought into his head.

Unexpectedly, on November 7, 1918, the routine at Issoudun was interrupted. News reached the airfield that Germany had signed a truce. "There was a spirit of rejoicing and of great relief from the satisfaction that we were not dead, and that we would be going home," Dombrowsky remembered.[24]

# 2

## Making a
## Name for
## Himself

Dombrowsky's homecoming passed lazily. There were good times with his family, dances at the yacht club, and fishing trips up the Hillsborough River with Rev. Broyles. On one of these trips, the minister persuaded Dombrowsky to apply to Emory University, a new institution being created from an older Methodist school in Oxford, Georgia, and relocated to Atlanta. He applied and was accepted to enter with the first class admitted to Emory's new campus in 1919.

Dombrowsky was an anomaly almost from the moment he arrived. He was, as a friend, G. Raymond Mitchell, recalled, a "different kettle of fish from the other boys who came."[1] Diffident and reserved, he made friendships slowly. He was diligent about his studies. Some students took him as aloof.[2] He was fastidious about his appearance, which, together with his bearing and good looks, caused others to think he was putting on airs. However, to John Knox, a Methodist minister's son from Baltimore, Dombrowsky's quiet manners bespoke the opposite. To Knox, he was openhearted, warm, and down to earth, with values resting on strongly felt religious convictions. Dombrowsky was stoutly loyal to friends. Knox had the persistent feeling that Dombrowsky had a longing for human warmth and contact, which had not yet found full expression.[3]

Emory had been located some thirty-eight miles from Atlanta in Oxford. During the war, the college—through Bishop Warren Akin Candler, a Methodist leader and brother of Asa Griggs Candler, founder of Coca-Cola Company and one of Georgia's wealthiest men—had arranged to relocate on seventy-five acres of land six miles from downtown Atlanta. Atlanta Medical College merged with the college, and schools of law and theology were to be added. The college, on paper, became a university. Dombrowsky's first impression of the school, however, was mud. Roads were being built, and bridges connecting knolls of the wooded, hilly landscape were being hammered together. The campus was remote and, when it rained, all but inaccessible. To a veteran, the place had the feel of battlefield trenches.[4]

Dombrowsky worked to pay for tuition and other expenses, first in a downtown Atlanta jewelry store, using his considerable experience, if not his interest, in retail sales. Later he delivered morning newspapers, too. Campus gossips had him inheriting $250,000, and, they added incredulously, he loaned money in generous amounts, without record, promise of return, or any mention of interest, to needy outstanding students.[5] That unfounded rumor persisted long after Dombrowsky graduated.[6] Actually, he inherited $5,000 from his father's estate, a princely sum at the time, and did lend his friends money without interest when they were in a pinch. But he kept careful records and expected everyone to repay him. Noone let him down.

Some new faculty with even newer ideas moved to Atlanta that September. Dr. Howard W. Odum, a sociologist who would become one of the South's most famous teachers, was elected dean of the new School of Liberal Arts. He was thinking about opening the college's doors to women. While Odum eventually would influence an entire generation of southern leaders, he had scant influence on Dombrowsky's experience at Emory, chiefly because his role as an administrator took precedence over his love of teaching.[7] However, another faculty newcomer, Dr. Malcolm H. Dewey, professor of romance languages, right away started a glee club. He and Dombrowsky became friends. They shared interests in art and music; Dombrowsky enrolled in his French class.

The Emory Glee Club became one major focus of Dombrowsky's student life. When Dewey started the group, many of the all-male chorus members had never sung; most could not read music. Yet, almost overnight, they were a much-applauded campus success, singing a broad range of classical choral music but "specializing in Negro spirituals."[8] Dewey's choice of spirituals was curious, even to Dombrowsky, especially since Emory had no African-American students or faculty. If they devoted serious thought to race at all, Southern Methodists at the time, like most southerners, figured racial issues centered on the fair and proper treatment of inferior and subordinate persons. Paternalistic fairness had nothing to do with religion. Without qualm or twitch of conscience, Southern Methodists made distinctions between African-American brothers and sisters in Christ and white brothers and sisters in Christ, founding such ill-funded institutions as Paine College in Augusta for African Americans while heavily endowing an Emory or Duke for whites.[9]

Beyond noticing the apparent contradiction, Dombrowsky made no attempt to penetrate the labyrinth of religion and race, however. There were too many other attractions, not the least of which was administering the Glee Club's affairs. "To keep me from singing, they made me the manager," Dombrowsky recalled.[10] He remained manager throughout his four years, increasing his responsibilities each year. He arranged a trip through Georgia and Florida and then on to Cuba, to show off Emory's musical talent. The Coca-Cola company had a strong interest in Cuban markets, and the Candlers were delighted to support the Glee Club tour as a way to recruit to Emory Cuban students who eventually might become part of the soft-drink company's network. The tours became an Emory tradition.

Jimmy Dom, as the intense young man was known, established himself socially and academically by the end of his first year. His marks placed him near the top of his class. He had a few close friends, despite the fact that he was older than most; his friendships centered chiefly around Methodist church activities. The thought of teaching religion appealed to him. He entertained the notion of becoming a parish minister. But none of his close friends could see him in the ministry. "He was too urbane, too intelligent to be a preacher," one said.[11]

During summer vacation, Jimmy was Rev. Broyles' assistant pastor, regularly teaching Sunday School and sometimes giving sermons in place of Rev. Broyles at Hyde Park Methodist Church. One summer he organized a new Methodist congregation, getting them on the way to finding a minister. He spent a lot of time proselytizing, either for Hyde Park Methodist Church or Emory University. On one such excursion, he and James B. "Jimmy" Mitchell, another Emory student home in Tampa for the summer, found two prospects reading the Sunday papers in the lobby of the YMCA. Ernest C. Colwell, and his older brother, Edwin, were reading the "help wanted" ads. Edwin had worked in the offices of a Tampa cigar factory until a strike closed the plant down. He was out of work. Ernest had come to Tampa from their home in Pennsylvania expecting to work with

The "Brotherhood" at Emory. *Left to right:* Perry Mullinax, Homer Allen, J. Foster Barnes, James Dombrowsky, James Ellis, John Ruskin, Lavens Thomas, Henry W. Blackburn. Frank T. Adams Collection.

his brother. When Dombrowsky came on them in the YMCA, their spirits were low, their funds lower. It was July and sweltering. Ernest recalled:

> We were accosted by two well-dressed young men who invited us to go along with them to their Sunday School. We went—along with two carloads of those politely called the "disadvantaged." Our two hosts and their well-to-do friends welcomed us into their social life. Moreover, they began almost at once urging me to change universities and return with them in autumn to Emory University in Atlanta. I finally agreed to switch for three reasons: (1) I liked them; (2) one of them promised to get me a job in Atlanta; and (3) I didn't have enough money to buy a ticket back home.[12]

At Emory and later, Colwell was known as "Pomp." Dombrowsky found him a job delivering Atlanta newspapers. He became part of a circle of Dombrowsky's friends who named themselves "The Brotherhood." They were determined to express their religious convictions in the service of humankind. Most wanted to go to Africa as medical or spiritual missionaries. Students outside their circle, with more than a hint of racism, derisively called them "the Congo group."[13] The Brotherhood jelled after the famed Methodist evangelist, Plato T. Durham, held a revival on campus. "He was an eloquent, forceful, and appealing speaker who captured the attention of the students, and won their hearts by the challenging way in which he presented the Christian life," recalled Henry W. Blackburn, one of the Brotherhood's members.[14] Dombrowsky was no less impressed.

With evangelistic fervor, the Brotherhood met on call for prayer or to plan youth revivals in Florida's leading Methodist churches. They provided speakers for weekend youth retreats and raised money for the American Orphans Relief. The Holy Club at England's Oxford University was their immediate guiding model. Dombrowsky was the Brotherhood's administrator. He answered mail, compiled contributor lists, and made certain that speakers arrived at their destinations and got back to campus. Consistently, according to friends, Dombrowsky saw to it that others won credit. When group photographs were taken, he would appear on the back row, if at all. A philosophy professor told Dombrowsky he'd make a good organizer.[15]

For him, the Brotherhood was almost a family. The members saw salvation in very personal terms. Christian charity began within their own select group, then extended, usually paternalistically, to less fortunate persons who evinced some spark of promise. In this way, good works succeeded, and benefactors could point to the wisdom of their Christian investment.[16] Loans made within this circle assuredly would be repaid.

Christian individualism shielded Dombrowsky from much of the life around him. Riding the streetcar in Atlanta to work, he passed some of the South's largest cotton mills, among them the Fulton Bag and Cotton Company. Lint from the looms usually billowed from the windows. Hundreds of people worked in those mills for pennies an hour. He never noticed or wondered what lint did to the workers' eyes and lungs, or speculated on how the few dollars they earned put food on their tables. Earlier, In Newark, he'd never given any thought to the source of Cousin Eugene's wealth.

There is no evidence that Dombrowski knew, or cared to know, about the government's repression of so-called radical aliens, repression which reached spectacular proportions the fall he entered Emory. Several thousand political activists, many of them foreign-born, were arrested in raids around the nation between June and November 1919. Attorney General A. Mitchell Palmer was determined, he said, to deport "thousands of aliens . . . direct allies of Trotsky." In December, on one raid alone, nearly 250 were sent packing, having been arrested and deported without charge or hearing.[17] Some Emory students began to wonder, however, "about a person with the name Dombrowsky, which was uncharacteristic of southern family names."[18]

Dombrowsky's political and social views were unobtrusive. He subscribed to the religious values dominating Emory; they provided moral sanction for the prevailing economic organizations or were largely indifferent to economic matters. Churches in the South and their larger affiliated bodies supported the emergence of industry, especially cotton mills. Parents sent their boys to Emory to become Christian gentlemen. To be a Christian gentleman meant to honor God, to live the good life, and to give wise, loyal support to those institutions which served the good life—church, business, family, and state.[19]

Dombrowsky knew only one student, Mercer Evans, who questioned these verities. He was the campus radical. Although Dombrowsky's contact with Evans was sporadic and casual, being limited chiefly to a few economics classes, through Evans Dombrowsky began wondering about those accepted Christian truths. Evans was studying economics. He entered Emory in 1919 also, at age eighteen. He did not belong to any of the Emory fraternities nor to the Brotherhood, but instead was the leader of campus independents. He openly questioned religious thought and practice and made no bones about his abhorance of racial segregation. Older students, including one from the newly organized School of Theology, brutally hazed Evans one night, then stripped him naked and tied him to a campus telephone pole. The next morning, a startled but compassionate passerby set the exhausted, humiliated youth free. Emory's administration did not let on if they knew about the episode. No-one was punished, although most students knew who was involved. For Dombrowsky, the attack on his classmate was his first encounter with violence spawned in reaction to deviation from social norms.[20] He never forgot Evans, or what happened, or what did not happen. Evans recovered, continuing without letup to challenge the social conventions on campus and off. Not long afterward, he asked Dombrowsky to accompany him on a visit to Eugene Debs in the United States penitentiary in Atlanta. The socialist was running for president while jailed. "I had no idea who Eugene Debs was, or what he thought, or what an opportunity this was," Dombrowsky said later.[21] "And I didn't go. I was so ignorant." Debs polled 923,000 votes in 1920.

Eventually, Evans became an economist and shared in shaping southern history. He helped author the influential *Report on Economic Conditions of the South,* used by President Franklin D. Roosevelt to "do something about . . . the Nation's No. 1 economic problem."[22]

Dombrowsky was a founder of the Emory chapter of the Sigma Chi, a fraternity with a white cross centered in its heraldry, which for founding members, most of whom were members of the Brotherhood, symbolized the spirit among them which accepted no lesser Lord than God and no meaner law than brotherhood. The fraternity was an elite schoolroom within an elite school for leadership, service, and Christian ideals. They used the home of S. Frank Boykin near the campus for meetings and social events until the chapter house was built. Boykin was treasurer of the Coca-Cola Company. On one congenial evening there, Dombrowsky asked Boykin for some financial advice. "I had gotten a little additional money from my father's estate," he said, "and I asked him what to do with it."[23] Boykin told him to buy White Motor Company stock. Dombrowsky did. Several weeks later, Boykin recommended he sell the stock. "I did and doubled my money. I was flabbergasted. I may have made five hundred dollars or so. I hadn't lifted a finger and was suddenly five hundred dollars richer. This was one of my earliest lessons in the capitalist system and how it works. It gives to those who have."

Every Sunday evening before visiting Boykin, Dombrowsky and his friends dined at the Biltmore, Atlanta's poshest hotel. "We dressed in dinner clothes for the occasions and gave ourselves noble titles—Jim was 'the duke'; I was 'the count'," Knox recalled.[24] His fraternity brothers ignored the sneering references Sigma Chis from Georgia Tech made about Dombrowsky. One asked, "What the hell is that Russian named Dombrowsky y'all got over there?"[25] He was unaware of the ethnic hatred evoked by his name, only learning about the frequent questions much later in life. The Brotherhood shielded him. So, too, did his own social and academic accomplishments.

Early in February 1923, not long before he was to graduate with honors, Emory officials, including President Cox, called Dombrowsky to a meeting.[26] They told him of plans to organize an alumni association and to publish a magazine. The idea was to cement ties between the young university and its graduates. They wanted to know if he would be interested in becoming the association's secretary and editor of the magazine. He accepted on the spot, even though, only a few weeks before, he had been offered a handsome salary to organize the European sales market for Coca-Cola. That was business; the work for Emory was service. He arranged a meeting with Candler and Boykin to tell them of his decision.

As alumni secretary, Dombrowsky proved to be a trailblazer.[27] He set a frantic pace: before February ended, he had written and edited the first alumni newsletter; by May he had the organization's by-laws and constitution adopted; in June he graduated *cum laude;* in July he left Atlanta for Europe to canvas the possibilities of a Glee Club tour in 1925; and by September he had opened an office and hired a secretary and two parttime student employees—William "Wee Willie" Wilkerson and Hollis Edens; that fall, he organized Emory Clubs throughout the South. In the meantime, he enrolled in the Candler School of Theology and was taking a full course load in philosophy. He was twenty-six, with boundless energy.

Dombrowsky's work showed bottom-line results. Money started pouring in. "It was a year so high in school spirit that the students and faculty in one day over-subscribed their own $75,000 quota by a third," the *Alumnus* reported.[28] Asa Candler personally gave the university a million dollars, and his Druid Hills Company deeded the school another fifty-five acres of land. By 1926, the money had become a virtual flood: $215,000 was given to build a church and auditorium, $150,000 for a nurses' home, and $32,000 to endow the medical library.

Dombrowsky linked Emory with wealth and social prominence elsewhere, too. The Glee Club's European tour in 1925 opened with a concert at the Waldorf-Astoria Hotel in New York City attended by Mayor Jimmy Walker. They sailed for Europe to spend a week each in France, Scotland, Wales, and England. Crowds everywhere were large and enthusiastic. Lady Astor, the Virginia native who was the first woman in the British Parliament, entertained them at her home and struck up a lasting friendship with Emory. All expenses were met through ticket sales; Lady Astor became an Emory donor.[29]

At Emory, Dombrowsky could write his own ticket. From all appearance, he was enormously successful in his work and satisfied with life.[30] He had established files on 6,500 of the university's 7,000 graduates, complete with personal histories, and was the first editor of the alumni magazine. Graduates and undergraduates alike were giving money in ever-increasing amounts. He regularly hobnobbed with Atlanta's wealthy and powerful. He'd met Nell Buchanan, the alumnae secretary at Agnes Scott College, a daughter of a Virginia State Supreme Court justice. They made an eye-catching couple, seen together frequently at musical evenings in Atlanta, having dinner, or motoring on warm Sunday afternoons.

"I guess anyone looking at the situation would have decided I had a very good future," Dombrowsky reflected later.[31] "But, in truth, I knew so little. I had missed so many opportunities. So I resigned when we came back from England to enter graduate school at the University of California in Berkeley, and to take a job as assistant pastor and secretary at Epworth Methodist Church there."

# 3

## North toward Home

"Johnson City, Tenn. (AP) James A. Dombrowski, alleged communist leader, was arrested near Elizabethton late Tuesday, and is being held for Gastonia, N.C., officers in connection with the fatal shooting of the chief of police of Gastonia."[1] Hunter Bell, The *Atlanta Journal*'s city editor, stared in disbelief at the report. "There can't be but one James A. Dombrowski," he thought.[2] "It's got to be Jimmy Dom." He asked the Associated Press to look further into the story, requesting they double-check how the prisoner spelled his name. The wire service did, filing a longer story on June 12, 1929, which noted that no charges had been placed against Dombrowski, and that the jailed man spelled his name with an *i*. He had graduated from Emory University and was 32 years of age.

Five years earlier, Bell and Dombrowski had toured Europe together with the Glee Club, and, as the *Atlanta Journal* noted that afternoon, "Dombrowski was well known in Atlanta, having attended Emory University, where he was prominent in all phases of college activities."[3] The news report astonished Dombrowski's friends at the Sigma Chi house, at the Alumni Association office, and in Emory's administration. They shared the disbelief expressed by Bell. Mercer Evans, who had earned his doctorate at the University of Chicago with a dissertation on the history of labor in Georgia and now was on the Emory faculty as a junior professor, "couldn't believe his eyes."[4]

The next day, Rose, Dombrowski's sister, read about the arrest in the *Tampa Times*.[5] "I was so mad," she remembered.[6] "It was right at the top of the page. I called up the editor. He had been one of Jim's best friends in high school. I said, 'Aren't you ashamed to print such a thing?' He said, 'Well, it's news.' I told him, 'You know Jim. You know he couldn't commit a murder.' He said, 'Well, you know, some people lead a double life.' I was furious." Meanwhile, in Elizabethton, Dombrowski wrote in his journal, "Well, this begins to look serious. About 4:30 p.m., a deputy sheriff served a warrant on me, charging me with being an accomplice in the murder of the chief of police of Gastonia, N.C., which occurred, I am told, on Saturday."[7]

Dombrowski had gone to Elizabethton as part of his graduate studies at Union Theological Seminary in New York City, where he had enrolled in fall 1928. His stay at the University of California at Berkeley and his work as an assistant pastor had been brief and mostly disappointing, except that he had been introduced to Dr. Harry F. Ward, professor of christian ethics at Union Theological Seminary in New York City. Ward, visiting his friend Alexander Meiklejohn, who was teaching at Berkeley, lectured on "Why I am a Radical."[8] Dombrowski was taken with Ward as a person and with his views. Having been a street preacher in Chicago's packinghouse districts before taking up an academic career, Ward argued forcefully that clergy should actively engage with social and economic issues, particularly on the side of working men and women. In 1907, Ward had written a treatise arguing that industrialism was incompatible with the humanitarian concerns of religion. That same year, he had organized what came to be called the Methodist Federation for Social Action, which became a rallying place for Methodist liberals for many years. Later, in 1920, Ward had helped organize the American Civil Liberties Union and served as its national chairman until 1940. Throughout, he ceaselessly backed the causes of labor unions.

Dombrowski heard Ward's lecture by chance. The minister's religious radicalism challenged the soothing Christian truths of Dombrowski's childhood and of Emory's Brotherhood. For Ward, the Bible authorized revolt against an "obsolete" economic system that fostered "greed, distrust and injustice to workers." His gospel called for "regeneration of communities" and "democratic control of industry, both process and proceeds."[9] Ward and Dombrowski started corresponding. When Dombrowski next registered for classes at Berkeley, he spelled his name with the original *i*, not *y*, restoring its Polish origins. "I was trying to get to the root of things."[10] He kept that spelling for the rest of his life.

Intellectually and emotionally, Dombrowski was changing—indeed, had been changed—but he wasn't ready yet to be plunged by Ward into the baptismal waters of revolt. He fulfilled his responsibilities as assistant pastor and left Berkeley for Harvard University. There in fall 1927, he took six courses, including one on general metaphysical problems with Albert North Whitehead.[11] He roomed with George A. Morgan, who had been a Sigma Chi at Emory. Morgan was studying for a doctorate in philosophy. "Harvard philosophy and Jim didn't hit it off very well together," Morgan remembered.[12] "I don't think what Harvard had to offer was what Jim was groping for." Ward, through letters, urged Dombrowski to read R.H. Tawney, Thorsten Veblen, Henry George, or Max Weber—authors not assigned by Harvard's dons. Dombrowski left Harvard on November 16, 1927, for Union Theological Seminary to study with Ward. W. Aiken Smart, dean of men at Emory, in a letter of recommendation written on February 8, 1928, told Seminary President Henry Sloan Coffin, "Mr. Dombrowski . . . will accomplish great things."[13]

Hardly more than a year later, Dombrowski was in jail. Ward urged students to immerse themselves in the troubles of the times. And there were troubles aplenty in 1929. The Great Depression gripped much of the nation. Across the South, a wave of spontaneous strikes closed one textile mill after another. In the Appalachian coalfields, miners waged bloody fights for better wages and safer working conditions. In New York, dock workers and retail clerks were organizing unions. Ward thought seminarians needed to learn directly from the experiences of working people or from those persons trying to correct social ills, such as Jane Addams of Hull House in Chicago. Those lessons were best learned firsthand, the professor said, adding that the time for reflection, discussion, debate, or systematic reading came after direct exposure. In this light, Dombrowski was reading the Scriptures and Karl Marx. Dombrowski hitchhiked to Elizabethton to learn what caused over five thousand men and women to shut down two huge rayon factories. The strike was three months old when Dombrowski got there on June 11. A year earlier, Herbert Hoover, campaigning for the presidency, gave his single southern speech to an overflow crowd in Elizabethton. The town built a tabernacle for his campaign. Hoover praised industry and outlined the special blessings of industrial development for the South. He won Tennessee's electoral vote that fall, and, in the doing, shook the confidence of many southern African-American leaders in the Republican Party. They were excluded from industry's blessings.

Elizabethton thrived on commercial trade and especially on its rayon mills. Small farms, tilled by independent individuals, belied its growing industrial economy. Most strikers, Dombrowski learned quickly, still lived on farms, but hard times had forced them "to take public work." Unions were new to them. Piece-rate pay, twelve-hour shifts seven days a week, and stretch-outs taught the need for unity. They called their union "God's union."[14] Dozens of people had been jailed for picketing. Water mains had been dynamited. Businesses were going bankrupt.

The night Dombrowski arrived, the Chamber of Commerce had arranged a meeting to organize a league for better law enforcement. Over one hundred business and civic leaders turned out. Dombrowski listened to one emotional plea after another to halt the strike with force. A silver-haired Presbyterian minister stood to say, "The time for prayer is past. When the devil is in your midst, fire upon him."[15] His remarks were applauded enthusiastically. The men had worked all day, and the meeting had been going on nearly four hours. They wanted action. As their applause quieted, the chairman recognized Dombrowski, who had raised his hand for a chance to speak. From toe to head, his appearance was ludicrously at odds with the businessmen crowding the hall. They wore dark suits and neckties, and most had on bowler hats. Dombrowski wore walking oxfords, argyle knee socks tucked over neatly pressed plus-fours, and a red and white Scotch plaid pullover sweater. He was dressed for golf at a country club.

A hush fell over the audience as the tall, spare stranger began speaking. His voice was loud enough to be heard throughout the room. The man had a southerner's accent, but he was not saying what they expected to hear from a southerner. He talked about a vision of the world when women and men could seriously apply the ethics of Jesus to rationally order society, particularly industry. It was, he said, a vision of the Kingdom of God on earth. There was hope, he continued, that the South, known for its gentler ways of living, would pioneer the spiritualization of industry. The emphasis of Christ's teachings, he said, was on the sacredness of human beings. Applied to Elizabethton, this biblical teaching meant that human values and life must be considered above all other values. He sat down.

My training as a student had not prepared me for what happened next. I was cross-examined until my life history had been told, without allaying their suspicions. That a student should make a trip at his own expense from New York to Tennessee merely in the interest of his education was incomprehensible to men for whom profit was the only legitimate incentive for the expenditure of time and effort. They must have taken me for a spy, a Red, perhaps a "dangerous agitator." At any rate, following adjournment, I was threatened with personal violence.[16]

Cooler heads kept Dombrowski from harm that night. Some men wedged Dombrowski through the businessmen he'd angered to the hotel where he had booked a room. Safely there, they warned him to leave town when the sun came up. He took their advice, and by dawn had hitched a ride with a farmer, heading for Gastonia, where another strike was in progress. Dombrowski was thinking about "the lessons that Elizabethton offered for the advancement of my education," when several carloads of armed men stopped the farmer's truck. At gunpoint, Dombrowski was ordered out of the truck and told he was under arrest but showed no warrant. He was pushed into a car, then driven back to Elizabethton and jailed. Later that day, he was charged with "aiding and abetting in the murder of the chief of police of Gastonia."[17]

The telephone wires in and out of Elizabethton were hot. John Paty, a company doctor at one of Elizabethton's struck mills, had been at the Chamber of Commerce meeting. He telephoned his brother, Raymond, who had graduated from Emory, asking if he knew a man named Dombrowski. Raymond Paty had been a Sigma Chi brother. "Raymond urged him to go help Jim and assure authorities that he was a fine gentleman," his widow, Adelaide, recalled.[18] The Paty family was prominent in East Tennessee commercial affairs, and, privately, John Paty interceded on Dombrowski's behalf. A lawyer, A.C. Tipton, who had been Dombrowski's chief inquisitor the night before, became Dombrowski's counsel once formal charges had been filed. He, too, began checking on Dombrowski, speaking with U.S. District Judge Dozier Devane, a neighbor in Tampa. He wired Dr. Ward at Union Theological Seminary, who immediately wired that, as president of the American Civil Liberties Union, he had asked two ACLU lawyers from Memphis to leave for Elizabethton immediately to defend Dombrowski. No hearing was held on the charges against him. Dombrowski was released the next morning. He wrote in his journal: "Well, I can now appreciate what makes lawbreakers, breeds contempt for courts and nourishes pessimism. If it were not for the foul-smelling tobacco-stained cell with its filthy and reeking blankets, I would not mind so much this additional period in my education. It seems to me I have learned more in the last twelve hours than I did for four years of college."[19]

Despite his brush with vigilanteeism, his resulting notoriety, and what he imagined to be ahead in Gastonia, Dombrowski left jail and again headed for a strife-ridden milltown. He was determined to fulfill his academic obligations, but a deeper motive pushed him to North Carolina. He had experienced the outcome of education at Emory. He was determined to see where another educational road would lead. One Methodist, Plato Durham, had quickened Dombrowski to develop a businessman's Christian charity. Another Methodist, Harry Ward, had ignited his long-smoldering aversion to profit, and to the Christian ideal of the virtuous person as one who increased wealth, an end in itself. Dombrowski was face to face with the same spiritual dilemma that confounded John Wesley, the founder of Methodism, who himself had a genuine compassion for the poor and who worried:

> I fear wherever riches have increased, the essence of religion, the mind that was in Christ, has decreased in the same proportion. For religion must necessarily produce both industry and frugality, and these cannot but produce riches. But as riches increase, so will pride, anger and love of the world. So although the form of religion remains, the spirit is swiftly vanishing away.[20]

What happened to Dombrowski in Gastonia was even more disturbing than Elizabethton's mob or its jail. Workers at the Manville-Jenckes Mills had been out on strike since April 1, 1929, demanding twenty-dollar minimum weekly wages; a forty-hour, five-day week; an end to the piecework system; and that the company, which owned the houses they rented in Loray Village, add window screens and bathtubs.[21] Workers on their own secretly had organized within the Loray mill, then gotten help from National Textile Workers' Union (NTWU) organizers who were working in nearby Charlotte. The workers wanted union recognition.[22] From the outset, the strike had stirred violent passions. Will Truet, the worker who secretly had been organizing other workers and who contacted the NTWU, had been fired. More workers had been threatened. When Fred Beal, the NTWU's organizer, arrived, secret meetings became public, almost revivals with workers picketing the mill singing a song learned from Beal, "Solidarity Forever," to the tune of "Glory, Glory Hallelujah."

Beal and some other organizers who initially flocked to Gastonia were Communists. For the NTWU, a strike was more than a struggle for unionization; it was an opportunity to "bring out the political nature of the conflict."[23] Gastonia provided the NTWU with an opportunity to challenge both the local power structure and the conservative American Federation of Labor. For the owners of Loray Mill, and for others in surrounding Gaston County, which, with 112 similar mills, called itself "the Combed Yarn Center of the South," the stakes were high. Before the walkout, they had freely "stretched work," giving workers more and more machinery to tend while paying the same or lower wages. A citizens' Committee of One Hundred, many of whom were local ministers, was organized to denounce the strikers and the Communist organizers who arrived in growing numbers.

On April 3, after a minor scuffle between striking workers and sheriff's deputies, North Carolina Gov. O. Max Gardner, himself a mill owner, ordered state militia into Gastonia, first the Gastonia Howitzer Company, then the Shelby Infantry, and finally the Lincoln Cavalry. Threats were made against workers and NTWU organizers. Workers and their families got eviction notices.[24] Many were living in tents gotten together through NTWU appeals. But no violence occurred until June 7. During a melee on the picket line, bottles, rocks, and eggs pelted both strikers and militia. Fists and blackjacks bloodied heads. Pistol shots were fired, scattering strikers, who fled to their makeshift union hall. That night, Gastonia's chief of police, O.F. Aderholt, was shot to death. Beal and sixteen others were quickly arrested and charged with "complicity in the murder of Aderholt."[25]

Eventually, charges were dropped against most of them; but Beal and six others were in jail waiting to be tried when Dombrowski reached Gastonia. He talked with whomever he encountered. He didn't try to reach any of the strike leaders, in jail or out. Just the ordinary people. Like the strikers in Elizabethton, most had lived on small farms, working the land as crops demanded or as hunting seasons came and went. In the mills, they worked twelve hours a day, seven days a week. The mills ran two shifts a day. Men were bringing home under ten dollars a week. Women were paid less, even though they worked the same hours. Children left school in the fifth or sixth grade to take jobs on the looms. They had to work. For the families who left farming altogether, the company provided shelter in row upon row of cigar-box houses set up on high piles on brick-lined unpaved streets.

Each house had an open privy. "Gastonia was the incarnation of drab monotony, a sanitary menace, an aesthetic nightmare, a living hell," Dombrowski wrote.[26]

Dombrowski learned about this conflict from mill workers and their families. He became so depressed hearing what one family suffered that he tried to give them ten dollars, half of the money he had with him. They wouldn't take it. "The father told me they didn't need charity; they had a union," Dombrowski remembered.[27] He left Gastonia immediately, hitchhiking to his sister Daisy's home in East Orange, New Jersey. For the rest of the summer he relaxed, read, kept up his diary, and commuted into New York, enrolling in his first formal art course at Columbia Teachers College. And he reflected on the meaning of having his charity spurned.

Ward's lectures gave Dombrowski an intellectual framework through which he could make sense of the class basis of society. His father's remark after the foot race, his experiences in Issoudun, and his memories of Mercer Evans began to cohere. Never again would he be able to ignore the meaning of Cousin Eugene's wealth or Atlanta's Fulton Bag and Cotton Company. Yet, as his behavior in Elizabethton and Gastonia demonstrated, he was unable to quit acting with individualistic compassion in the face of misery. Dombrowski was unable or unwilling, at this moment in his transformation, to put his ability as an organizer to work for the political values brewing in him. He had learned and honed those organizational skills at Emory. The Brotherhood's patronizing solutions still surrounded his response to social ill. Dombrowski had been part of a brotherhood which never had experienced the liberating outcomes of solidarity.

In the wake of Elizabethton and Gastonia, as he had done since childhood when his natural pattern of life was upset, Dombrowski turned to art. Left-handedness had been abandoned in this way. He commuted daily from his sister's house to Columbia Teachers College for his first art course. On the train back and forth, he read William James and John Dewey. Sketching and drawing reordered his world. He delighted in seeing how life's forms could look; drawing gave him a feeling of well-being and contentment. He could work with his hands, creating an existence which had not existed previously. Innately, as an artist, and intellectually, through his mentor Ward, Dombrowski was coming to fit easily within the tradition of American pragmatists, especially James and Dewey, who sought to verify truth through the correlation of experience, concept, and inquiry.[28] "Art

Dombrowski after arrest in Elizabethton, 1929. Frank T. Adams Collection.

helped me get at some of the roots of questions I had about the meaning of life. Often I could see things visually before I could see them concretely."[29]

Indeed, art and social change, particularly socialism, were becoming one in his mind. Beauty and justice were differing aspects of the same quality for Dombrowski. The aesthetic side of life could be recognized and nurtured if an equitable distribution of work and goods was assured. He had come to believe that a socialist economic order would unfold new persons and a new world, releasing the creative powers of every individual. Free of want, he reasoned, everyone could become an artist, a person who did something—no matter what—which had a useful, fulfilling function. "The artist is not only the painter, but the artist makes shoes, or machines, or bridges so long as they are artistically done," he said.[30]

While the artist in him could civilize society with comeliness and taste, Dombrowski remained unsure how to act in the real, stunting world he had seen in Elizabethton and Gastonia. The experiences of his privileged life contradicted his emerging beliefs and values. He had learned to savor the good life at Emory. His conspicuous jailing in Elizabethton and his spurned charity in Gastonia were moments of profound change for Dombrowski's concept of himself, not unlike the biblical Paul's. Dombrowski's transformation was equally irrevocable, but not lightning swift. Gradually, he was coming to believe that he was at odds with his Christian heritage. The bits and pieces he'd gotten as a child in Newark or Tampa were fitting into a pattern that seemed to conflict with the very institutions which offered the lessons. In the YMCA Bible class, he had learned from J. August Wolfe the unequivocal intent of Mosaic law, as declared in Deuteronomy: "To the end that there be no poor among you."[31] In the Hyde Park Methodist Church's Sunday School, he had learned that the Bible admonished in Leviticus, "Take thou no usury or increase of him; but fear thy God, that thy brother may live with thee. Thou shalt not give him thy money upon usury nor lend him thy victuals for increase."[32] The biblical authors were addressing the economic issues of their day.

Eventually, Dombrowski recognized that Emory University had schooled him to raise and administer money for the poor, without reminding them to be content with pitifully small wages, as John the Baptist had advised Roman soldiers. Education, in the mind of Asa G. Candler, Emory's greatest benefactor, "must be permeated with the type of Christianity that makes for a wholesome conservatism politically and socially and for a blessed civilization crowned with piety and peace."[33]

Dombrowski had lived without thought to the human source of wealth which made Emory, or his own comforts, possible. Only Mercer Evans, the campus independent, had questioned that poverty was an institution ordained by God. Only after leaving Emory did Dombrowski examine church history.

In 1844, the first of several splits among American Protestant denominations over slavery was touched off by the fact that Emory's board president, Bishop James O. Andrews, owned a woman slave. Southern Methodists, a preponderance of whom were Georgians, argued that the bishop could not break the civil law which forbade freeing slaves. Therefore, they told Northern Methodists who were upset about slavery, the bishop should not be asked to give up his ecclesiastical office, or be faulted.[34] The northerners disagreed, going their own way.

After the Civil War, Methodist philanthropy flourished in Georgia, chiefly funded with Northern Methodist money. An orphanage in Decatur was completed in 1869, and neighborhood centers operated for the poor in Atlanta. These good works were too liberal for most Georgia Methodists, who were indifferent or hostile to spending money for such ends. Hoping to train freed slaves for "proper responsibility" in white society, however, they energetically supported drives to build Clark College and Gammon Theological Seminary in South Atlanta during the early 1880s.[35]

Bishop Candler's own son-in-law, Andrew Sledd, was fired from his Emory professorship for publicizing his antilynching views in 1902. On the campus, still in Oxford, Georgia, sides were passionately drawn over the issue. The bishop defended his son-in-law, saying the young teacher was opposed to mob violence, not in favor of equality. Lynching became a prevailing social issue among Methodists throughout the 1920s and 1930s, with many Methodist women leading efforts to curb the savage violence.

Nevertheless, while Dombrowski was at Emory, the commanding view of Christian charity and benevolence defining the college's universe was expressed by Asa Candler, who, as he poured money into the college buildings and professorships, said that Jesus did not and does not propose to remove the inequities of life. On the contrary, those inequities are a part of the divine order, ordained by him to promote the brotherhood of man and to bind together the members of God's family by the tenderest ties of service and gratitude.[36]

The Methodist Harry F. Ward disputed the views represented by Candler. Ward taught that capitalists used human beings as tools for their own profit. Jesus was a carpenter, a worker, as all persons should be, he said. Working people and their labor unions "were the most advanced point at which the divine energy was operating in the higher evolution of man."[37] Also Ward argued with then-prominent advocates of the Social Gospel, Methodist or otherwise, including Josiah Strong, Washington Gladden, and Walter Rauschenbusch, with whom he debated and corresponded for years. There was no social gospel, Ward declared, only one gospel deriving from the life and work of Christ and the prophets. The key to salvation, he told students, was active involvement in reform and social change. Always demand to know, he said, "What is the social situation? What are the facts? What do they mean? What can we do about them?"[38] Each spring, his students put their books aside to join working-class struggles.

Dombrowski was still an innocent when he got to Elizabethton and Gastonia. He had gone West to California and then North to Boston and New York searching for an intellectual or spiritual home. He returned to the South prepared to declare, as John Wesley, the founder of Methodism, had in 1739, "The Gospel of Christ knows no religion but social, no holiness but social holiness."[39] Instead, he learned about God's union, and about workers who preferred to care for themselves through solidarity rather than be cared for by the well-off.

For Ward, the problem for the teacher was how to enlarge the experience of his students. What students thought about the world was only important as it is related to those forces which sustained life: how to put food on the table, how to be clothed, and how to have shelter. "For him," Dombrowski remembered, "everything else was luxury. This, of course, was news to me, having been brought up in Hyde Park Methodist Church, and having gone to Emory."[40]

Ward, born in England the son of a butcher and lay preacher, had graduated from Northwestern University in Chicago, having gone there on a scholarship.[41] At Northwestern, Ward had caught the attention of George A. Coe, the famed pragmatist, and John Gray, who taught philosophy. Together, they helped the young Englishman embrace the American Progressive tradition. He read Richard Ely's *The Social Aspects of Christianity* and John Dewey. Gray introduced Ward to George Herbert Mead of Harvard, and Ward spent a year there reading William James and Josiah Royce. After graduation from Northwestern, he took a Methodist pulpit in Chicago's stockyard district and, through his experiences, soon became convinced that socialism and Christianity were linked. He and his wife lived in the neighborhood. He preached on street corners and in settlement houses, as well as from the pulpit. His sermons attracted attention. He agreed with Karl Marx that religion was used to divert people's attention from cruel injustice, hunger, and war with promises of a better life in the hereafter. This use, Ward felt, distorted Christ's message. The Kingdom of God offered hope to an oppressed Jewish people, who were urged to liberate themselves from Rome so as to establish the economic justice proclaimed by Old Testament prophets and the peace promised in the three synoptic Gospels of Matthew, Luke, and Mark. The same message was relevant in Chicago.

Those ideals were summed up, in Ward's thinking, by the Sermon on the Mount, the eloquent vision of the new age Jesus sought to introduce; and by the parable of the Good Samaritan, with its entreaty to end human suffering without consideration of religion, conviction, origin, or nationality. Ward formulated his Christian Socialist views into "The Social Creed of the Churches," a document later declared to be a Magna Carta for church and labor. Under its tenets, other Methodists organized the national Federation for Social Service to put those views into action. Ward wrote books and lectured, indefatigably crisscrossing the country urging church and labor to pursue common goals.

In 1913, Ward accepted an invitation to become the first professor of social service at Boston University School of Theology, where "he swept across religious skies like a meteor" before resigning under fire from mounting numbers of "Christian employers" who demanded that Ward be denied tenure.[42] Friends got him an appointment at Union as professor of Christian ethics in 1918. Henry Sloan Coffin, president of Union when Ward commenced teaching at the New York school, chiefly wanted the seminary to provide students ministerial training for large urban ministries. The majority of the student body came with such a goal in mind. A smaller group revolved around the heady atmosphere provided by Ward and, following shortly, Reinhold Niebuhr.

Socially, when he enrolled at Union, Dombrowski was closer to Niebuhr, who often ate with students in the refractory and would sit talking with them for hours afterward in the social room. Intellectually, however, he was increasingly drawn to Ward, who lived on the Palisades across the Hudson River in New Jersey and who traveled frequently, and who consequently associated less with students. Behind the lectern, Ward was a small, wiry, intense figure. Ward, to a greater degree than Niebuhr, accepted Marxism as an analytical tool to help understand the causes of economic and social injustice. Students remembered how Niebuhr took the academic stage with wit, logic, and locution. He was soon to publish his famous *Moral Man and Immoral Society*, in which he accepted a large part of the Marxist view of history and of political strategy. The book was to make him a celebrity but drive a wedge between him and Ward, Coe, and others who were dedicated to social reconstruction, which would never heal.[43] Ward, on the other hand, was remembered as a Socratic teacher, inclined to permit students to argue among themselves before interjecting his views or supplying some fact they'd missed examining. "Reinie was always a theologian," J. King Gordon recalled.[44] "He would bring under rigorous Lutheran review any action he took, weighing it against certain absolutes. Those absolutes never bothered Ward at all. Christianity to him was social action. Christian ethics demanded socialism."

Dombrowski established himself at Union and in New York quickly.[45] He developed a circle of close friends, including Franz Daniel, a giant with enormous shoulders who was given to oratory and flamboyance, and J. King Gordon, a Canadian and the acknowledged leader among Union's student activists. He met two southerners, Myles Horton and John Thompson, both from Tennessee. They, too, were on roads which would eventually lead back south. The Morningside Heights Branch of the Socialist Party invited him to join, and he accepted. Socialism seemed reasonable and logical.

Dombrowski won the President's Merit Scholarship that fall. During the Christmas holidays after his experiences in Elizabethton and Gastonia, he shared the platform with A.J. Muste, then dean of Brookwood Labor College, at the League for Industrial Democracy's Intercollegiate Conference on "The Textile Industry—the Battleground of Social Forces."[46] Dombrowski's essay, "From a Mill-Town Jail," was published in *The New Republic*.

Throughout the fall, the conflict in Gastonia intersected with Dombrowski's conscience and his reality. The strike continued, its tensions unrelieved, despite the jailing and sensational trials in nearby Charlotte of Beal and the other defendants. After a first trial, the seven defendants were acquitted. But in subsequent court proceedings, Beal and the others were convicted of murder and sentenced to years of hard labor.[47] On September 14, tragedy in Gastonia again made headlines around the nation. Union

activists had organized a rally to bolster flagging spirits.[48] As supporting
workers from neighboring mill villages arrived, they were met by armed
citizens and militia at every road coming into Gastonia. One truck carried
Ella May Wiggins, who worked in a Bessemer City mill and mothered nine
children, four of whom had died of whooping cough. She was to lead singing during the rally. Wiggins had become a legend among strikers for the
way she turned familiar church music into songs about their strike. The
truck carrying Wiggins and nearly two dozen other unarmed supporters
was stopped at the Gastonia town line and turned around. As they headed
back to Bessemer City, a carload of men sped behind and began firing
pistols. Wiggins was shot in the throat and killed. Dombrowski did not
know Wiggins, but he felt as if he'd met the dead woman while in Gastonia;
she assumed mythic dimensions in his mind, becoming a working-class
heroine he would never forget.

About the same time, he got a letter from Mercer Evans, who wrote from
Emory: "Dear Dombrowski: From various sources I have heard of your
exploits. I congratulate you. I would consider it a matter of prestige to have
incurred the Elizabethton experience."[49]

Mercifully, play sometimes interrupted Dombrowski's relentless se-
riousness. His Canadian friend, King Gordon, was a hockey enthusiast and
frequently went to matches in New York. Once Gordon prevailed on
Dombrowski to quit the books for a game. Gordon brought a companion,
Ellen Krida, a striking brunette he had been dating. "I confess to have been
less interested in the game than in Ellen," Dombrowski remembered.[50]
"She was the most beautiful woman I'd ever seen. Her eyes left an impression on me. They were luminous. She encouraged me ever so slightly."
Some days later, during his regular afternoon walk along Riverside Drive
and the Hudson River, Dombrowski again met Krida, this time by accident. They did not have much to say, Dombrowski recalled. She was an
extremely shy person, finding it difficult to relate to most people easily or
quickly, if at all. That chance encounter gradually became habitual.
Dombrowski was in love.

The young woman lived alone in a flat on Riverside Drive not far from
Union. Like Dombrowski, she had been left an orphan at an early age. Her
father had been born in Ludz, Poland, of Austrian and Polish parents. Her
mother was from Strasbourg, Alsace, of German and French parents. They
emigrated to the United States in 1893.[51] An older brother, Arthur, who
had become a prominent, highly acclaimed orthopedic surgeon, lived in

New York City. Another sister, Helena, had married a successful medical doctor, Robert MacTaggart of Schenectedy. Ellen, a year older than Dombrowski, spent summers in Schenectedy and winters in New York. Ellen loved music, especially opera. She was supported by her family.

Late afternoon walks together soon extended to dinner and drinks in quiet restaurants, then to evenings at the Metropolitan Opera during the season. At thirty-three, Dombrowski wanted to be married. He spent hours sketching her. She, however, was reticent; her family had misgivings about Dombrowski. When they met him, he devoted most of his conversation to social issues of the day, expressing views that put him at variance with them.[52] And, as Dombrowski remembered: "We were all very much aware of the poverty, the bread lines, of people selling apples to survive. This was, of course, the Depression. Most people were in desperate circumstances. We were all young, and full of talk about changing society, and presumably dedicated to doing something to contribute to that change."[53]

Increasingly, Dombrowski's views were associated with communism. A great fear of "Bolshevism" was developing among liberals throughout America and seemed especially severe in Union's intensely intellectual atmosphere. Socialists were particularly enraged at what they frequently charged were dogmatic tactics used by Communists. Any means did not justify the end, they argued. Not since the Palmer raids in 1919 had debates been as bitter. "It was a tense time," recalled John Bennett, who also was studying with Ward and Niebuhr.[54] Secular organizations on the liberal and left end of the political spectrum argued endlessly, it seemed to many, including Dombrowski, against Communists, who, they alleged, used unfair tactics to control unions or church groups. In this regard, Ward left an indelible mark on Dombrowski. The professor refused on principle to disfavor Communists or Russia. This infuriated many of Ward's Socialist allies and alienated him from fellow church leaders who otherwise supported his Social Creed. Ward believed that people of the Soviet Union would overthrow Stalin and fulfill the corrective reforms which prompted the revolution in 1917. Nevertheless, others branded Ward as a rigid Stalinist and since have ignored him in their histories of Christian Socialism.[55]

Further, as a civil libertarian, Ward stood firm in asserting that Communists, like anyone else with a political opinion, had the right as Americans to express and act on their political beliefs. On the other hand, Ward's persistent attacks on American laissez-faire capitalism enraged others, including some Union trustees who were wealthy businessmen or substantial churchmen. Pressure mounted on President Coffin to fire Ward, but he stood fast. Dombrowski took up this same baggage, carrying the principled load for the rest of his life. It was a matter of ethics and logic.

Dombrowski, well aware of the schisms springing up among friends, busied himself with study and his love affair, thus avoiding, for the time being, confrontations. He was taking eight courses in religion, ethics, and philosophy. He had been named a Fellow of the National Council on Religion in Higher Education. He devoted several hours weekly to the Morningside Heights' branch of the Socialist Party, usually distributing leaflets at some strike. On Saturday nights, he supervised public forums at the Church of All Nations in the Bowery. Most days some time was spent visiting Krida.

Among Union's most active students, Dombrowski had formed another brotherhood. This fraternity, unlike that which bonded at Emory, was preparing to challenge any traditional doctrine, religious or secular, which reinforced capitalism. King Gordon, Franz Daniel, John Thompson, and John Bennett were honing intellectual skills which they felt would make them useful in the working-class revolution that all were certain was coming soon. Myles Horton was bent on finding a way to bring that Socialist revolution to powerless rural Americans. The rest were concerned with industrial society. Daniel finished Union and immediately began organizing for the Socialist Party in Philadelphia. Horton left to study in Chicago, then went to Denmark to learn about the folk-school movement.

Before the seminary reopened in the fall of 1931, Dombrowski learned he had been selected as Union's Traveling Fellow, one of the school's highest honors. He could study at any university in the world, with all expenses paid. Most of those chosen went to England and Oxford, or Scotland and Edinburgh. Dombrowski stayed at Union. Dr. Ward had asked him to be his teaching assistant, an invitation which, to him, carried the most honor. To his fellow student, Myles Horton, even years later, Dombrowski was "the most thorough-going radical among us."[56]

# 4

## Conceiving
## the Kingdom
## of God

In 1929, on the eve of an extended trip to the Soviet Union, Harry Ward and his wife Daisy were given a farewell party by his seminarians. The couple was going to learn firsthand what the Russian revolution had accomplished in twelve years. Earlier, on similar study tours, the couple had lived in China and in India, each trip intensifying Ward's views about "the egregious sin of private profit."[1]

Many attending the party that evening were writing the epitaph of capitalism. Thousands of Americans were looking for jobs, and, even though the stock market crash still lay ahead, whole regions, especially the South, were economically depressed. Socialism was the alternative; the Soviet Union was the model. Besides Moscow, Soviet officials had approved visits to Sochi, Baku, Odessa, and other places not on the usual traveler's itinerary. The Wards were to talk with Soviet workers on agricultural communes, in oil refineries, and in tractor plants, and to students, as well as to Ward's academic peers. One of Ward's former students lived in Moscow and would translate for them. Ward intended to work on the Lenin Commune as a carpenter, a skill he practiced during vacations. Dombrowski and King Gordon gave their teacher a carpenter's tool kit.

After his first visit to the Soviet Union in 1919, in a published article Ward lauded Russia for being the first nation in modern history to establish a socialist economy. "The beginning of a new order is upon us," he wrote, praising the revolution as the expression of a new religious ideal: "From each according to ability, to each according to need."[2] He also expressed misgivings about a central tenet of the Soviet revolution:

> I am against the theory and practice of dictatorship by the proletariat not only because I believe it is unethical, but also because I believe it to be unscientific. You cannot carry out the change to economic democracy that way, for the simple reason that you cannot control economic production efficiently in the transitional stage by means of one class alone. You have to have the co-operation of everybody that knows how to manage industry if you are going to democratize it.[3]

Methodists around the nation, even some in the activist federation he founded, were shocked by the views expressed in his article. Some wanted him dismissed "as a teaching force within the church." Close friends urged him to write a fuller explanation, which he did, critiquing Soviet Marxism for "crass materialism," "Bolshevik atrocities," and "mechanistic science." Again, he underscored opposition to any religious repression.[4] He said again, however, that the stay in the Soviet Union had convinced him that an "economic theology not unlike predestination" gripped the Russians.[5]

His faith in that conclusion had been hard to shake, no matter what he learned subsequently. His second visit was hardly casual. Upon his return, he scored the Soviets' disregard of civil liberties, reporting that abuses were not fabrications of opponents to the political regime. Stalin's use of force to build the socialist state, he felt, contained seeds of its own destruction.[6] On the whole, however, his criticisms were muted, no matter how balanced. He continued to praise the lofty ideals of the Russian nation, thus reinforcing his reputation as a Stalinist.

Dombrowski, absorbing Ward's reports of his Russian experiences, unexpectedly got a letter from Dr. Sherwood Eddy, the renowned missionary and reformer, who was international secretary for the Young Men's Christian Association. He tried to foster improved international relations by taking influential Americans abroad to European capitals. His next trip would include Moscow and Warsaw. He was casting about for an assistant. He asked Dombrowski: "Supposing you take guidance of this tour. . . . would that have any bearing on your future?"[7] Dombrowski, still unclear about his future, nevertheless spared no effort to persuade Eddy that he was just the man. He wanted badly to visit Russia. He opened a campaign to get his reclusive sweetheart to go if he were selected. He won the position, despite the fact that the missionary's own son-in-law applied. But he was unable to prevail on Ellen Krida, who stayed in New York, certain that she'd get a letter from him daily.

Thirty-five tour members gathered in New York City in June 1932. Mercer Evans and his wife, Eva Knox Evans, the sister of Dombrowski's friend at Emory, John Knox, were among them. Evans continued to teach at Emory but was under fire from the Candler family for having invited Ernest Gruening, the controversial editor of *The Nation,* to speak on campus. Eva Knox Evans taught at Atlanta University, an African-American college, a fact that scandalized some Emory leaders. Reinhold Neibuhr's sister was in the group, as were several college teachers, a few businessmen, newspaper and religious magazine editors, and several writers. Many were socialists; all were in positions to influence public opinion.[8]

The first stop was London, where they put up for ten days in Toynbee House, the settlement house. Through Eddy's influence and Dombrowski's organizing ability, they met with several dozen governmental leaders, union officials, political figures, students, and workers. Lady Astor, remembering Dombrowski, arranged for them to have tea with George Bernard Shaw at her London townhouse. The famous writer admired British Christian Socialists. "Ethics were the basis of their protest against social and economic injustice," he said.[9] "Christ, not Marx, founded modern socialism. Marx was the last of the Old Testament Prophets, an Amos or Micah." While *Das Capital* had exposed the evils of the British economic system as no other book before it, Shaw, the Fabian, argued that Marx's theoretical assumptions had been wrong. Over three million British workers were out of work. James Ramsey MacDonald's Labor Party, a fragile coalition with the Conservatives and Liberals, was failing to end the depression. The government raised taxes, abandoned free trade policies, and cut its own spending, but no matter what steps were taken, the depression ground on. Moreover, the British worried about Germany.

In Berlin, the tour group found that Germany, like much of the rest of the world, was bogged in depression. Business ruin was commonplace, as were suicides and gloom, everywhere heightened by despair of any improvement. Adolph Hitler's National Socialist German Workers Party was the most powerful political force in the German Reichstag. Thousands of Germans were out of work, and when the unemployed voted, they backed political parties openly advocating the overthrow of the Weimar Republic.

Hitler was promising prosperity, rearmament, and repudiation of the hated Treaty of Versailles.

Next Eddy took the tour to Leningrad and Moscow. The Soviets were as hard pressed economically as neighboring capitalist nations. Despite industrial expansion, farm production was woefully inadequate. In was a starvation year. The first of Stalin's five-year plans, begun in 1928, was coming to an inconclusive end. Opposition to Stalin was on the rise; to curb dissent, the dictator was launching a bloody purge of unprecedented dimensions. Secret police were arresting anyone who had opposed Stalin during his relentless ascendence. Countless thousands of peasants were being sent to labor camps in Siberia or Central Asia. "Eddy went over and over how we were to act in Russia," Eva Knox Evans remembered.[10] "He was worried." Stalin refused to meet the tour.

The Americans spent ten days in Moscow, talking with workers, managers, political leaders, and students; visiting nurseries and museums; and going to the theater. They went to homes for retired prostitutes and aging professors. At a rest home which had been the residence of a former rubber magnate, Dombrowski, through an interpreter, spoke with an elderly woman. As they talked, she looked about at the handcarved oak chairs and tables, tapestried walls, and other remaining symbols of luxurious living. "To think this is all ours," she said.[11]

The possessive pronoun, with its undergirding political concepts, resonated in Dombrowski for years.[12] His notes on the interview reveal a level of thinking beyond surface politics:

> The Russian worker and peasant looks upon the factories, the farms, the power dams, all of the wealth of the nation, as the people's very own. Naturally, they gladly defend it with their lives. In Russia, as soon as you stepped over the border, you felt a different atmosphere. The prevailing mood was one of laughter, confidence, hope for the future. One had the impression that youth were in control, and were the masters of the situation. To travel from Berlin to Moscow in the summer of 1932 was like stepping from a funeral parlor into the spontaneous gaiety of a mountain square dance.[13]

Was Dombrowski blinding himself to reality, seeing and hearing only what reinforced his hope for a socialist society? He stood amid evident poverty, in a society rife with suggestions that a pogrom was under way.

Religious freedom, such as he practiced and took for granted, was not allowed. Dombrowski was convinced that socialization of a nation's wealth, along with central planning, could lead eventually to full flowering of both individual and collective wellbeing. This principle had become an *idee fixe* in Dombrowski's Christian Socialism. The fact that living standards of skilled Russian workers were low compared with those of American workers could be explained. Russia was building industry upon a near-feudal agrarian economy; short-term sacrifices could be expected. The society, however, was in transition to improvement; continued stagnation and hopelessness could be expected through capitalism. History demonstrated as much. About central planning, covering every phase of the social and economic life, Dombrowski wrote:

> This permitted intelligence to cope with the problems and to insure that the most was made of the resources at hand. Under such circumstances, hardships and low living standards were endurable. Life was rational and dignified for it was under control. Everywhere in Russia that summer we met enthusiastic, singing, and joyous bands of youth who told us confidently that the future belonged to them.[14]

Even a three-day visit to a collective farm outside Moscow did not change his mind. Farm workers lived in huts heated by open wood fires. Under communism as under the czars, ownership of land and a share in deciding what crops to plant or when to till eluded the peasants. Dombrowski spent an afternoon listening to the workers gripe about mismanagement and production problems. The situation was the same in factories.

More than a decade was to pass before Niebuhr concluded that, although "Marxism is nearer to the truth than liberalism on the property issue, the socialization of property as proposed in Marxism is too simple a solution to the problem."[15] Ward's own optimism apparently never failed. Judging by the careful notes he made documenting his experiences, Dombrowski's senses were not impaired; yet to mature, however, was faith in his own independent political judgment.

Back in Moscow, Dombrowski visited a bookstore with a huge selection of books and posters on art and education before heading back to the United States. At the time, the Soviets circulated roughly two kinds of posters. One sort was inspirational, an artistic presentation of some aspect of the revolution. The other, while artfully done, would spell out what people could do for certain practical problems—inexpensive ways to keep flies from their food, or birth control methods. The information was very specific, aimed at people who often couldn't read, and who had very few newspapers. Dombrowski bought a few posters in each category, along with several books, and had them mailed to New York City.

Warsaw was the Eddy tour's last stop. Much to everyone's surprise, a large delegation was waiting at the train station to welcome Dombrowski, not the internationally known Eddy or the tour itself. "It turned out Dombrowski was the name of a great Polish revolutionary family, a fact that I hadn't learned from my family," Dombrowski remembered fondly.[16] " 'Here's the long lost son of a great hero,' they thought when they saw the passenger list before we arrived. To their utter dismay, they discovered this long lost son's ignorance of their history. He couldn't speak a word of Polish, and, further, he was not a person of real standing in the group of visitors! They were crestfallen."

Dombrowski's reunion with Ellen Krida was delayed several hours after the tour reached the Port of New York. A U.S. Customs agent had seized the posters Dombrowski mailed from Moscow, declaring they were "seditious."[17] Hours after his tour companions departed, Dombrowski debated customs officials. Eventually, he was given the package.

Krida delighted in Dombrowski's Warsaw and dockside adventures. Her man, the descendent of a revolutionary, ensnared by a government's revolutionary posters! Those were parts of the trip she wished she'd experienced. Otherwise, politics held no interest for her; immersion in groups large or small, or junketing about was even less appealing. She was a private person, deeply in love with Dombrowski, especially the gentle, artistic man. Dombrowski devoted what remained of his semester break entirely to her, mentioning only in passing politics or the worsening depression.

He could afford to catch his academic breath. Union was behind him. He had been awarded the bachelor of divinity degree *magna cum laude* on May 19, 1931, shortly before he left for the Soviet Union.[18] His thesis analyzed how the Christian church (chiefly Anglican) in Colonial Virginia had supported slavery with ethical canons. As he traveled further from Emory, the racial doctrines of his Southern Methodist heritage became clearer, and more important. He had not forgotten his father's stinging, bigoted remark, or the commercial motives which had influenced his family's decision to move to Florida in the first place. His virtually all-white seminary and Socialist circles were daily reminders that racial dogma persisted, antithetical to his own values. He found no trace of Christian Socialists in early Virginia church history.

Dombrowski started looking for positive southern examples of interracial harmony. He combed *The Christian Socialist,* a yellowing publication collected by the Columbia University library. The Reverend George Washington Woodbey, a Baptist minister who had been born a slave in 1854 and set free after the Civil War, regularly contributed to the paper. In one essay Rev. Woodbey said, "When you show the church member how the Bible, in every line of it, is with the poor as against their oppressors . . . you have made the first step toward converting him to the idea that it [Christian Socialism] cannot be done in its entirety without the collective ownership and operation of the industries."[19] Biblical expressions of socialist ideals might have escaped the notice of southern whites, but not of some African Americans.

Browsing in another Columbia collection on a wintry day, Dombrowski, seeking an original topic for his doctoral dissertation, came across *The Social Gospel,* a magazine published during an ill-fated attempt between 1896 and 1900 to found the Kingdom of God in Georgia. Reminded immediately of his own improbable audacity in Elizabethton, he spent the next several hours going through each copy, forgetting supper arrangements with Krida.

Initially, some thirty persons, calling themselves Christian Socialists, founded the Christian Commonwealth Colony on an old plantation of about one thousand acres—half upland and tillable, the rest swamp—about twelve miles east of Columbus, Georgia. The settlers welcomed anyone, unemployed or well off; they were not trying to withdraw. During the colony's existence, between three hundred and four hundred persons lived there. Jane Addams visited. Luther Burbank sent flowers and fruit trees from his Santa Rosa, California, home. Leo Tolstoi corresponded, suggesting once the much persecuted Doukhobors might settle there from the Soviet Union. *The Social Gospel* was the colony's voice, a way to recruit and persuade. It circulated throughout America.

The colony was to have been a rallying place for the nation's religious radicals. A statement of purpose declared, "We have been drawn together by a common passion for individual and social righteousness and for what we conceive to be the Kingdom of God. We make straight the way for the surely coming reform of the twentieth-century which will be a reform of propertyism and industrialism."[20] At the colony, all property except an individual's clothing was held in common. Dombrowski found one quotation with special appeal: "Selfishness is the basis of social wrong, and the chief bulwark of selfishness is private property."[21] The colony had also been influenced by George D. Herron, a spellbinding preacher. Its members took the job of revolutionizing society as their primary task, believing, as Herron once declared, "The worst charge that can be made against a Christian is that he attempts to justify the existing social order."[22]

Reading the magazines, Dombrowski realized that the colony was but one example of a rich, largely unexplored history of American Christian Socialism. The short essays, letters, and speeches that filled the magazine's pages had been written by persons whom history had forgotten, or was forgetting. The aging pages suggested an earlier social movement among American Christians with a decidedly antitheological basis, one in which ethics, not dogma, were given precedence, and the Kingdom of God meant the transformation of this world, not the hereafter, into a just society.

For the next eighteen months, Dombrowski used the history he unearthed to write a dissertation attacking the widely popular Social Gospel on two grounds. First, he contended, depending on good will as a technique for social change was futile. Doubtless his experiences in Elizabethton and Gastonia were still fresh in his mind. But his research in labor archives had revealed a pattern of criticism by union leaders during the last three decades of the 1800s. In general, the officials criticized religion on four counts. First, churches were conservative, viewing society with its class distinctions as a result of an unalterable edict of Providence. Second, ministers taught meekness and submission to authority, rather than revolt in the face of oppression and injustice, proffering the rewards of a life in the next world as compensation for the lack of well-being and happiness in this world. Third, religious pretensions to brotherhood were steeped in hypocrisy, since churches offered charity rather than advocating economic equality and justice. Finally, churches, with their vested interests and dependence upon wealthy donors, inevitably were instruments promoting the ends of bourgeois society.[23]

Dombrowski concluded that the Social Gospel had failed to acknowledge the impact of economic power on either politics or religion. Regular contact with Ward, and with the several dozen passionate students around the professor, almost assured that Dombrowski would conclude that individual salvation and social ethics were one and the same, not differing metaphysical entities. The social, ethical self arose out of experience—but experience examined critically, with an eye to taking action rather than passively accepting "the what is of life" as the immutable result of original sin. Dombrowski supported his argument by showing how labor historians had ignored the influence of Protestantism on the American labor movement, especially between 1850 and 1900, a period of vast industrial expansion. Theologians, too, had overlooked the impact of working people on Protestantism during this so-called Gilded Age. Ordinary workers, most of whom were deeply religious, through rapidly growing unions, provided the pivotal demonstration of the social gospel's inherent flaws.

Dombrowski argued that it was false to assume that the chief impetus for the prominence of the Social Gospel had been the denominational social service commissions which had sprung into being at the turn of the century. There had been many antecedent factors, chiefly within the industrial working class. The Civil War impelled both industrial expansion and the labor movement. By 1870, there were thirty-two national trade unions in the United States. Virtually every city had its trade union assembly, labor newspaper, and workingman's library. The economic panic in 1873 hurt the union movement, but during the 1880s, spurred in part by the aggressive Knights of Labor and by the bloody Haymarket riot, more than 600,000 persons had been involved in 1,600 strikes.

By 1892, these social forces had coalesced around the Populist Party, signaling widespread dissatisfaction with unemployment and poverty in the industrial East, high transportation rates, crop liens and watered stocks in the South, and mortgages in the West. "During this period," Dombrowski wrote, "criticism of religion by labor leaders, socialists and reformers, as well as the alienation from the church of large numbers of workers, put religion on the defensive."[24]

Most labor leaders, like thousands of ordinary workers, were professed followers of Jesus, but only a handful of allies in the church world shared labor's view. Dombrowski examined the personal histories of some leading churchmen who did take labor into account, including Stephen Colwell, Henry George, Richard T. Ely, Edward Bellamy, W.D.P. Bliss, Henry Demarest, and George D. Herron. He also looked at the role of seminaries; two radical religious publications, *The Kingdom* and *The Dawn;* and the Christian Labor Union, one of the first efforts to join unions and religion in the struggles of labor, founded in Boston in 1872. Of course, he examined the Christian Commonwealth Colony's four-year history.

Dombrowski was surprised to find Colwell to be critical of churches. He was a wealthy Philadelphia manufacturer and trustee of Princeton Theological Seminary. In 1851, Colwell published *New Themes for Protestant Clergy*, a book heavily influenced by Saint-Simon, Comte, and Sismondi, which declared that agitation for justice among workers was a natural reaction against both economic and social indignities. Christianity, he said, had become so overlaid with theology, critical studies, vested interest, and tradition that it was no longer entitled to be called by the name of its founder.[25]

Henry George, who as a compositor and journalist often bartered printed labels for food, wood, or milk for his family, offered specific proposals labor could use to recapture the value of property. George conceived every problem in the political economy first as a religious problem. Dombrowski learned that George judged ideas instrumentally, according to their efficiency in assisting labor to achieve a more just society. His single-tax idea was one example. Virtually all land would be owned by society as a whole. Taxes would equal rental values, with those revenues applied to social services. "This program," Dombrowski wrote, "not only commends itself to reason but it is just, conforming to the eighteen century principle of 'rights'."[26]

Another early ally of working people was Richard T. Ely, whose first book, *Social Aspects of Christianity*, influenced Ward during his ministry in Chicago's stockyards. A founder of the American Economics Association, Ely wrote part of its first formal platform, including a section Dombrowski found important to quote: "We hold that the conflict of labor and capital has brought to the front a vast number of social problems whose solution is impossible without the united efforts of the church, state and science."[27] Ely assumed that the controlling economic groups would relinquish power voluntarily, or that they could be moved by moral arguments to improve the lot of working people. In what Ely said was his "final word to workingmen," labor was urged to "educate, organize, wait."[28] This advice, Dombrowski concluded, contained "all of the fallacies of liberalism that have made radical religion and the labor movement in this country so impotent for the past fifty years."[29]

Few of labor's clerical friends during the period were as dramatic, even fiery, as George D. Herron, who, in one of his more restrained speeches, declared, "Our economic system is organized social wrong. Competition is not the law of life, but a contradiction of every principle of Christianity."[30] No-one appealed more to Dombrowski.

Herron had little formal education. He entered the Congregational ministry in 1883 and eight years later came to nationwide prominence after delivering an address entitled "The Message of Jesus to Men of Wealth," in which he declared that workers themselves had to organize to secure their own demands, and that they would not secure justice without a fight. At the time, this strategic suggestion was new to Dombrowski. He was more familiar with Herron's assertion that all religious people were duty-bound to destroy capitalism, without regard to their own welfare. "We must lay the axe at the root of the tree of social wrong," he thundered.[31] In city after city, Herron stirred listeners as if "a dynamite bomb had exploded in the square."[32]

Herron influenced Ralph Albertson, the principal founder of the Christian Commonwealth Colony. In 1893, the young Albertson, an Oberlin College theology graduate, was pastoring a Congregational church in an industrial section of Springfield, Ohio. He invited Herron to deliver a series of lectures. The older minister apparently was no less passionate in Springfield than elsewhere. In a few months, many of Albertson's parishoners were on strike. Their young minister was firmly on their side. Later, in the midst of the Pullman strike, Albertson went to Chicago to talk with Lucy Parsons, Eugene Debs, Joseph Altgeld, and others.

Two years later, in 1896, Albertson left the Springfield pulpit and, with two other men, trekked on foot over three hundred miles searching for a site for their dream of a gathering ground for religious radicals. Soon after the group located land in Georgia, others followed. They lived in self-imposed poverty, determined to express their belief in an egalitarian ethic. Land was cleared. Rugged, unadorned houses went up. So did a school. The mayor of Toledo, Ohio, presented the colony with a power plant for a sawmill. They started making their own cornmeal and peanut butter, as well as growing sweet potatoes and other crops. By 1898, the first issue of *The Social Gospel* had been published and the colonists had built fourteen cottages, a sawmill, bachelors' hall, cotton mill, farm buildings, and blacksmith and print shops, as well as expanding the school. Dombrowski, with a businessman's care for details, meticulously reconstructed the colony's diet, noting that rations for sixty-four adults and thirty-six children cost three cents per individual per meal, and included 600 pounds of cornmeal, 100 pounds of wheat flour, 150 pounds of wheat middlings, 100 pounds of pearl grits, 7 gallons of cottonseed oil, 30 gallons of milk, 5 dozen eggs, and some pork and fish. Dombrowski found and recorded the colonists' spending during six months in 1898: $512 for agricultural supplies, $217 for mechanical equipment and repairs, $276 for the cotton mill, $405 on food, and $66 on clothing. Eventually, they had a large nursery, planted a thirty-five-acre orchard, fenced in three hundred acres of pasture, and put two hundred acres under cultivation. Dombrowski's census ended with an inventory of the livestock: eight cows, six mules, two horses, twenty pigs, a small flock of poultry, about fifty rabbits, and a few beehives.[33]

Two years later, however, the colony was weathering sundering ideological fights, including ones over whether or not to incorporate under Georgia law to protect the colony's property. A heavy snow and hard freeze in the winter of 1899 damaged fruit trees and winter crops, leaving the colonists, who had never gotten beyond a primitive, sweat-labor economy, with scarce rations. A dozen members tried to throw the colony into bankruptcy. Published accusations about "free sex" further demoralized colonists. An epidemic of typhoid fever was the final blow. The colony closed.

In all, Dombrowski demonstrated that religious working people had a formative role in American religious and labor history. The dissertation, later published as a book, was favorably reviewed by *The Nation*. In effect, its author wrote about working-class Christianity rather than the better understood and more frequently described middle-class religious life. But he could not escape the fact that failure threaded his history of Christian Socialism in American. Colwell was scorned by his intellectual and business contemporaries. Ely was rejected by the working class. Single-tax colonies had sprung up, suffered, and then died, like the Christian Commonwealth Colony. There was no Christian Labor Union, only Christians in labor unions. Only a handful of Christians had ever heard of Herron; even fewer acted on his advice. Time had obscured the memory of most early Christian Socialists. The Kingdom of God had not been established. In conclusion, Dombrowski wondered aloud, "By what standards shall we judge a human achievement to be a success or a failure?"[34] His answer, particularly its last sentence, while rhetorical and evincing a minister's embellishment, reveals the yardstick by which he would eventually measure his own life:

Is it merely the material evidence of activity—so much cement, stone, and wood assembled in more or less pleasing patterns? Is it the time element which is important—that is good which endures? But everything eventually must perish, and only in death is there life. Are there other quantitative standards? Certainly when the rod of the acquisitive society is applied to the record of Commonwealth is must be judged a failure. But perhaps it should be judged by a standard in quite another category, the functional one, for example. How adequately does an event fulfill its essential purpose? Yet even when tested by this formula, the colony must be judged a failure. Its avowed purpose was to demonstrate that the absolute ethic of love is an adequate rule of behavior in an industrial society. And their experience indicates that a society which rigorously follows the logic of such an absolute ethical standard must eventually face extinction at the hands of a world in which individuals may be redeemed by love, but which is still too weighted down and calloused by brutality and selfishness for the multitudes to yield to the spiritual appeal of vicarious suffering. Does the striving after a high-flung ideal become a worthwhile end in itself?[35]

Through Union and Columbia, Dombrowski journeyed into his own religious past to examine deeply compelling questions, some encountered as a child, others in adolescence, and still others as a man facing the prospect of a promising career with Emory University or Coca-Cola. Class and race connected early and uniquely in Dombrowski, bonding over time, not in sudden revelation. Looking at a man of Dombrowski's aristocratic bearing, people saw no evidence to suggest that social heresy coursed passionately beneath his calm exterior. The road he took from Tampa to New York City—like most life journeys, especially the journeys of examined lives—was circuitous. With the dissertation completed, and with his doctorate of philosophy awarded in spring of 1933, Dombrowski finally felt prepared "to make straight the way for coming reforms."

# 5

## The
## Reformer
## as an
## Artist


At thirty-five, for the first time in his life, Dombrowski faced the necessity of earning a living, and his immediate prospects were dim. It was 1933. The Depression continued, with no end in sight. Having graduated from Union Theological Seminary *magna cum laude*, he had no academic haven. His years of theological training notwithstanding, he did not consider the pulpit. His closest friends and teachers at Union could not see Dr. James Anderson Dombrowski ministering to a congregation. Ellen Krida thought the idea preposterous, probably because she too had come to know the private man. He considered going back to Atlanta, where, briefly, between stints at Harvard and Union, he had apprenticed with L.W. Neff, a printer and former Methodist minister with radical theological views. Neff ran Banner Press, located in a piney woods on the edge of the Emory campus. Dombrowski had made a small investment in the business, thinking that his love of books could be turned into a career with another dissident Methodist. "At the time," Dombrowski recalled, "I worked through the courtesy of my partner, for I was not worth that much to the business."[1] He corresponded with Neff, who still had a place for him. Editing and publishing fine books on religious subjects, particularly Methodism, appealed to Dombrowski. His fiancée could envision married life in Atlanta. In the end, however, a genteel suburban existence held little

A Gentleman with Extreme Radical Social Views. Frank T. Adams Collection.

appeal. He did not pursue the opening. The experiences in Elizabethton and Gastonia had honed Dombrowski's conscience too sharply.

Other friends wondered if Dombrowski could ever find employment, but not because jobs were scarce. One, writing to a mutual acquaintance in Atlanta, said, "I am anxious about our mutual friend James Dombrowski. He is an unusually well qualified man along certain lines. I do not know where he is going to get a place and yet he ought to be used. I think he is so much of a gentleman that he will keep his rather extreme radical social views in check and do his work quietly as leaven rather than dynamite."[2]

As he pondered the future, Dombrowski got a letter from Myles Horton, who had left Union in 1930 to study with famed sociologist Robert E. Park at the University of Chicago. Eventually, Horton had traveled to Denmark to learn about the Danish Folk High School movement. Dombrowski knew that Horton was back in the South trying to start a folk school. In the letter, Horton told him another southerner, Don West, shared a similar dream; they had a place at Monteagle, Tennessee, in the Cumberland Mountains, and they wanted Dombrowski to join them at what they had decided to call Highlander Folk School. Horton described his idea:

> Our task is to make class-conscious workers who envision their roles in society, and to furnish as well, technicians for the achievement of this goal.
>
> In other words, we must try to give the students an understanding of the world in which we live (a class-divided society) and an idea of the kind of world we would like to have. We have found that a very effective way to help students to understand the present social order is to throw them into conflict situations where the real nature of our society is projected in all its ugliness. To be effective, such exposure must be preceded, accompanied by, and followed by efforts to help the observer appreciate and digest what he has seen. This keeps education from getting unrealistic. While this process is going on, students need to be given an inkling of the new society.
>
> This is where our communal living at the school comes into the picture as an important educational factor. The tie-in with the conflict situations and participation in community life keeps our school from being a detached colony or utopian venture. But our efforts to live out our ideals makes possible the development of a bit of proletarian culture as an essential part of our program of workers' education.[3]

The opportunity to "live out" his ideals struck several chords in Dombrowski. He expected the South to be the scene of stirring change. Poverty was widespread; somehow, he was certain, people would rise against the causes of their deprivation. Unions were certain to expand as industry grew. Churches might take on new roles. At a less political and more personal level, Dombrowski envisioned the school Horton described as a microcosm of what society ought to be, an example of the Kingdom of God. He had one reservation: "It was to be a worker's school. I had never worked. My exposure to industrial work was nil. So I felt it would be an imposition for me to turn up expecting room and board in return for doing what teaching I might be able to do."[4]

Ellen Krida didn't agree with his reasoning, urging him to postpone a decision to return South. He obliged her temporarily by setting out to raise five hundred dollars, both to cover his expenses for one year and to give him more time to persuade her otherwise. There was always stiff competition for liberal dollars. He knew that it would take several months, if not longer, to raise the money. "I didn't want to take money away from any worthwhile projects," he recalled, "so I set out to find a hundred new contributors who would give five or ten dollars for the dubious privilege of supporting me for a year."[5] To start, he asked Norman Thomas for three names and, if he would give it, his personal card with a note introducing Dombrowski. One of the three, Ethel Clyde, was among the few wealthy Americans who gave to liberal causes and was well known to most socialists who raised money to support their causes. She had a standard defense against prospective solicitors, usually saying her calendar was full. Nevertheless, Dombrowski telephoned saying he would appreciate the privilege of meeting her and telling her about this new workers' education venture, and he promised that he would not ask for a contribution. "She invited me to her home at Huntington, Long Island."[6] Ethel Clyde was a widow. Her husband's grandfather had founded Clyde Steamship Lines, the company whose ship, the *Lenape*, years earlier had carried Rose and Jamie Dombrowsky south to Tampa after their father's death. Later, as the Clyde-Mallory Lines, the firm prospered as the principal means of transportation in and out of Florida. Her home on Long Island, where she spent the summers, was a spacious estate. Clyde took sociology courses at Columbia University, mostly to satisfy an easily bored, inquisitive mind. A liveried chauffeur drove her to classes in a limousine flying the Clyde Line flag on its fender.

Through these courses, Dombrowski learned from her later, the heiress had concluded that inherited wealth was morally wrong when poverty was widespread throughout the world. "Her conscience began to hurt, and she asked Dr. Leroy Bowman, one of her professors, for advice," Dombrowski remembered.[7] "He sent her to Norman Thomas." Thomas suggested that she go to the West Virginia coalfields to see for herself the conditions people endured to provide coal for industry, including the Clyde steamships. She went and was profoundly moved by the poverty and living conditions she saw. When she got back to New York, she joined the board of the League for Industrial Democracy. She was not a Socialist, but she gave generously to socialists for years after her West Virginia trip.

Dombrowski knew nothing of her background when he arrived at Clyde's Long Island estate. Thomas had given only her name, address, and telephone number. She had heard about the Danish Folk High Schools from a neighbor, she told Dombrowski, and she was intrigued with the idea of trying to fit those techniques to modern industrial society. She was sympathetic to helping workers, especially miners, organize. "We became very good friends," Dombrowski said.[8] She offered Dombrowski no money. As promised, he asked for none. However, before leaving, he asked if she would give him the name of another person who might be interested in the school, and also, if she would arrange an appointment. She telephoned the neighbor she'd mentioned earlier, Dr. John Dewey, who, she said, often advised her about where "she could be useful." Dewey and Harry Ward, Dombrowski's mentor, were political friends. They rejected revolutionary approaches to social change. For Dewey especially, education, rather than violent upheaval, was the means of social reform.[9] Dewey argued that the American mobilization during World War I had demonstrated that the effort to remedy social ills need not wait for an "unconscious, natural law to accomplish anything serious and important in the way of reorganization" and that "intelligent, organized and cooperative action" could attain commonly held goals for social reorganization.[10] Despite the fact that Dewey taught at Columbia, Dombrowski had not taken any of his courses. His first encounter with the famous and controversial Vermont-born philosopher became a seminar on social change, as well as a solicitation visit.

Dewey and Ward held differing views on the critically important matter of economic control. Ward advocated democratic, but absolute, state control of the economy. In Dewey's mind, the state should assume responsibility for the welfare of workers only "if the ordinary economic machinery breaks down through a crisis of some sort."[11] In those historic moments, the state should "come to the rescue," seeing to it that individual workers had productive, worthwhile work, "not breaking stone . . . or something else to get a soup ticket with."[12]

Industrial democracy, a concept which Dewey championed through lectures, prolific writings, and the League for Industrial Democracy, rested on his belief that political democracy was impossible without economic democracy.[13] His social arrangement did not "involve absolute state ownership and absolute state control, but rather a kind of conjoined supervision and regulation, with supervisors and arbiters . . . to look after the public interests."[14]

Dewey supported a minimum wage, health and old age insurance, and subsidies for housing and sanitation. Industrial democracy implied that the wage earner, not the state, would have a greater share "in controlling the conditions of his own activity."[15] The state's role, Dewey said, was to assist, or adapt, the economy so that workers "in any particular trade or occupation" collaborated to control work instead of laboring under conditions "of external control of where they have no interest, no insight into what they are doing, and no social outlook upon the consequence and meaning of what they are doing."[16] Not unlike other liberal critics during the early 1900s, Dewey supported a range of alternative educational efforts aimed at giving the working class the knowledge and skills needed to reorder society.[17] Among these were the unique Work Peoples' College, founded in 1903 in Minnesota; the well-known Brookwood Labor College in New York State, started in 1921; and the controversial Commonwealth College in Arkansas, which opened in 1925.

Dewey spent several hours with Dombrowski. The professor proved to be down-to-earth and approachable; he explained that the origins of these workers' schools were in what Danes called "the people's high schools." Dombrowski had as much to learn about this unusual approach to education as he did about industrial work.

Inspired by Bishop N.S.F. Grundtvig, the original purpose of the folk schools had been to awaken oppressed rural peasants to take pride in their nation and to rejuvenate the country economically and socially, from the bottom up.[18] Denmark had been defeated decisively in a war with Prussia and Austria in 1864–65. In the wake of the conflict, the country's agricultural economy hardly sustained life; much of the culture was being abandoned in favor of Germanic language and culture. Bishop Grundtvig wanted to rebuild the nation's patriotism and prosperity by bringing Danes together at the schools for short periods, mostly during the long winter months, so they could share their cultural heritage and learn technical information which would add value to their labor.

The bishop never realized his educational dream. Later, however, a shoemaker, Kristen Kold, through a school he founded on the island of Fyn, gave life to Grundtvig's idea of "the living word." Kold tied education to the daily lives of fellow townspeople. There were no books; there was no money to buy them. So they talked a lot, sharing thoughts about cooperation or ways to improve crops; and they cooperated to keep the residential school going, preparing their own meals, cleaning, or cutting firewood together. They sang songs or hymns handed down through families. Poetry, traditional crafts, and art were equally important elements in the curriculum. Kold saw no need for grades, class rankings, or tests. The cobbler's school championed islanders' causes against landlords, the nobility, and even Grundtvig's church. The teacher's motto was "First enliven, then enlighten."[19] His school worked. Life improved for the people on Fyn. Within thirteen years, by the end of the 1800s, twenty-six similar folk schools operated, each with its own "emotionally charged" purpose. By the 1920s, folk schools operated throughout Denmark and were being copied in other Scandinavian countries. They were widely acknowledged to be the reason that agricultural production had improved, cultural life had taken on new vitality, and Socialist influence in government had grown.

One of Dewey's academic colleagues, Joseph K. Hart, was among the first of many American educators who traveled to Denmark during the 1920s to learn what might be applied back home.[20] Before Dombrowski left, Dewey gave a small donation for Highlander and took time to write an endorsement: "It is one of the most hopeful social-educational plans I know of."[21] Eventually, Dombrowski collected money from well over one hundred persons, and, with Dewey's endorsement, he left for Monteagle in Grundy County, Tennessee, on October 1, 1933. Ellen Krida was disappointed, but not bitter, that Dombrowski left New York City.

Highlander Folk School had opened November 1, 1932, nearly a year before Dombrowski arrived. Horton and West, its founding staff, like Dewey and other progressives, saw education as a weapon in the defense of the working class and as a means of advancing their ends. The two had met

through Will W. Alexander, executive director of the Commission on Interracial Cooperation in Atlanta, whom Horton had visited after returning
from Denmark. While in Denmark, he had told Alexander, after months of
study and hesitation about his half-formed ideals for social change, he had
visited a Workers' Folk School at Esbjerg. There, his vision crystalized
when the school's director told him, "We try to evoke among our students a
picture of reality not as we have met it in our surroundings, but as we ourselves would have formed it if we could—a picture of reality as it ought to
be."22 He was determined to adapt the folk high school concept to life in
southern Appalachia. Alexander only half-understood Horton's purpose.
But he knew of another young man, Don West, who was talking about a
similar idea. West was preaching in a small Congregational church near
Crossville, Tennessee, while he looked for a place to open his own folk
school. Like Horton, West had been to Denmark to study the folk school
movement. A native of rural Georgia, West had worked his way through
Lincoln Memorial University in Harrogate, Tennessee, and then had enrolled at Vanderbilt University to study with Alva W. Taylor, professor of
Christian social ethics, who was another friend of Harry Ward.

Taylor, a Disciples of Christ minister, had been teaching at Vanderbilt's
School of Religion since 1928. Some theologians viewed Taylor and his
course with suspicion. He had been involved actively with one Social-
Gospel cause after another, believing that science, combined with religious
passion, possessed the power to make the world over into the Kingdom of
God. He had taken charge of relief efforts during several strikes, always
gathering up food or clothes for striking workers. A generation of southern
activists met in his classroom, and West was among them.

West also had studied with Joseph K. Hart, who encouraged the Georgian
to go to Denmark, which he did in 1929. He returned to Vanderbilt convinced that the Danish schools were a model for the way mountain people
could improve their communities and also learn "to see the advantages of
cooperation—Socialism."23 West finished his bachelor of divinity degree
in 1931 and started looking for a place to start a school.

He and Horton arranged to meet at the Blue Ridge Assembly in North
Carolina in the summer of 1932. West was twenty-six, Horton a year older.
Both were Socialists, talkative, from the rural South, and passionately de-
termined to start a school where small groups of working men and women
could "learn how to take their place intelligently in the changing world."24
They wanted their school to be financially self-sustaining. Beyond those

similarities, the "two young Galahads," as Professor Taylor called them, were quite different.[25] West was tall and hard to miss in a crowd; Horton was short and could go most places unnoticed. West was plainspoken, if not blunt, about his political values. He was given to writing poetry, especially about southern Appalachia or workers, which expressed these values. In one poem, he called himself an agitator. Horton had mastered a capacity for political ambiguity early, refining this ability as he matured. Meetings, more than the written word, were Horton's forte, and in them his keen sense of what could spark humans to act was masked by a disarming rural charm. One had studied almost exclusively with respected southern scholars, the other with renowned northern teachers. West roared into the countryside on a powerful motorcycle. Horton took the bus.

The pair spent several days at the Blue Ridge Assembly getting to know each other. They agreed to be codirectors of a folk school for "Highlanders," the cultural label given southern Appalachians in the 1920s. West knew a place the folk school might be located. Horton had $1,300 that he had raised that spring from New York socialists and religious activists. They set off to convince Dr. Lillian Johnson in Monteagle, Tennessee, to let them use her property.[26] Johnson was a singular southern woman. Her family was composed of wealthy Memphis bankers and merchants. She had earned a doctorate in history from Cornell University and had studied with John Dewey. She served as president of Western State College at Oxford, Ohio, and then played prominent roles as a suffragist, an influential member of the Women's Christian Temperance Union, and as an advocate of agricultural cooperatives.

Johnson's interest in the European cooperative movement had been kindled during a trip to Italy to study how cooperatives worked. Impressed, she returned to her native Tennessee determined to spread the cooperative idea.[27] She bought land in Summerfield, outside Monteagle, a fashionable vacation resort at the time, and in Tracy City, a coal-mining town. In 1915, she built a house, both for her own use and for service as a cooperative center. The place was Summerfield's finest. Plain, unadorned lines marked the sturdy, two-story frame dwelling. A vine-covered porch stretched the length of the house, level with a well-kept lawn. Her living room was used as a lecture hall to which she invited farmers to hear about new stock-breeding methods or ways of farming.

Most of Johnson's efforts failed; the distance was too great between her life and ways, and what she wanted her neighbors to learn. Horton later said she worked out a program that tried to do good for her neighbors, and that she was "a little bit elitist."[28] By 1932, at sixty-eight years of age, she was disappointed, tired, and ready to donate the property to some good cause when West and Horton showed up. She met with them several times, eventually agreeing to let them use the property for a year, provided they would operate the school themselves, show some tangible results, and establish good relations with neighbors.[29]

The day after Thanksgiving, less than a month after setting up in Monteagle, Horton was arrested in Wilder, Tennessee, about ninety miles to the north, and charged by the National Guard with "coming here, getting information, and going back and teaching it."[30] Coal mines in Wilder had been closed by striking miners since the summer. As winter set in, events had turned against the strikers. Fentress Coal and Coke Company, based in Nashville, owned the mines, the workers' housing, and the town's grocery store. Deputies hired by the company had taken doors off some houses or had evicted other miners outright. The company store refused to sell strikers food; other merchants couldn't afford to give them credit. The county's Red Cross chapter, headed by the mine superintendent's wife, gave food she collected to strikebreakers, lured to work with promises of high wages, room and board, and "a woman at night."[31]

The miners had struck for better pay. They had earned two dollars for a sixteen-hour shift, but had had to buy picks and shovels, drills, detonators and blasting powder, and to pay bathhouse fees. A house, if they wanted one, or burial insurance, was extra. They took home pennies a day. Wages had been cut twice since the stock market crashed in 1929, and a third cut was set for 1931. Led by Barney Graham, the men secretly organized a United Mine Workers local and, surprisingly, won a contract. When that first contract expired in June 1932, the company announced a 20 percent pay cut, and started firing union members.

The United Mine Workers ordered its Wilder local to put down their picks; it was the international's first authorized strike in Appalachian coalfields since the Depression commenced.[32] Miners in two nearby communities also walked off their jobs in solidarity. Violence erupted when the quickly recruited labor arrived to reopen the mines. Strikebreakers traveling to work were ambushed. A tipple was set afire, two power stations were dynamited, one with such force that books were knocked off shelves in Wilder. Nearly two hundred National Guardsmen were posted to Wilder, but, for the next seven months, a bitter, bloody conflict raged, and families starved. Wilder was exactly the sort of conflict situation Horton had imagined when he wrote recruiting Dombrowski. He went there to see how the four students he and West had gathered to study at Highlander could learn from the conflict. Horton had taken Thanksgiving dinner with Graham and his family—a meal, he remembered, of turnips and sweet-potato pie. "It was the biggest meal they had in days," Horton said.[33] The next morning, as he waited for a bus, National Guardsmen arrested Horton. He was held overnight at the mine superintendent's home, which served as headquarters for the National Guard, then released the next morning with orders to leave town.[34] He took a bus to Crossville, the home of Rev. Abram Nightingale, a Congregational minister, who had befriended Horton in 1927, when, as a young Presbyterian church worker, Horton was organizing daily vacation Bible schools. Nightingale, who knew West, too, had urged Horton to study with Ward at Union. They wasted no time trying to turn Horton's arrest to the advantage of the strikers, and to cause Tennessee newspapers to give "attention to a sorely neglected industrial struggle, and further investigations and relief work."[35]

They telephoned Alva Taylor in Nashville, who contacted several friends, including Albert Barnett, a Methodist minister and professor at Scarritt College, and Howard A. Kester and his wife Alice. Kester had studied with Taylor and was southern secretary of the Fellowship of Reconciliation. The Wilder strike set the Kesters off on long and important careers as activists. They started a Wilder Emergency Relief Committee to collect food or clothing for the strikers and their families.[36] Meanwhile, Horton was in Rev. Nightingale's pulpit the next day describing for the congregation the situation in Wilder. By chance, and unbeknownst to Horton, a Knoxville newspaper reporter was in the congregation and reported the young teacher's remarks.[38] Newspapers around the state picked up his story. Horton was depicted as an outside agitator who was using the Wilder strike to promote Communist subversion.[37]

Her tenants gave Lillian Johnson another jolt three weeks later. On December 12, West was barred by the Grundy County Board of Education from using any public school building.[38] He had been holding neighborhood meetings in the schools to discuss local problems. Some residents got upset when he likened Jesus Christ to Karl Marx, saying their aims were the same. Highlander, he declared, "educates for a socialized nation" with "human justice, cooperation, a livelihood for every man and a fair distribution of wealth."[39] A small booklet of his poems, "Between the Plow

Handles," was circulating about the county, adding more controversy. In powerful populist images, West's poetry made much the same plea as his exhortations in the school meetings. He and Horton thought the poems could raise funds for Highlander by exemplifying the cultural traditions they wanted to enrich. Instead, the booklet increased the furor over West and Highlander.

During the folk school's first winter, the founders contended with Wilder, their neighbors, and life at the margins. Barney Graham, the union leader in Wilder, was shot and killed.[40] Nevertheless, the strike continued. Support for the strikers continued, chiefly because the Kesters worked tirelessly to find money, clothing, and political allies. No amount of cajoling could persuade the Grundy County school board to change its mind. The poet remained quarantined. With good reason, West and Horton feared that Johnson would oust them from her property. They had attracted a handful of residential students, none of whom paid much, if any, tuition. The intellectual climate was nourishing, but the food was mostly beans, turnip greens, and potatoes. Both strong-willed, West and Horton clashed, often in public view. Horton felt that West was too easy with the school's few dollars, and that the Georgian paid too little attention to administrative affairs. West charged that Horton made decisions unilaterally, and that his foray into Wilder had accomplished nothing "except to stir up a lot of hell."[41]

Fears about their landlady proved unfounded. On the contrary, she publicly defended the school but privately warned Horton not to teach divisive theories, "socialist slogans neighbors could associate with the worst kind of trade unionism," or "loose living."[42] However, tension between "the two Galahads" continued to mount, and on April 1, 1933, West left Highlander. He and Horton divided up their assets—a few books, the unsold copies of his poems, a sack of beans, some flour, and two hundred dollars. West moved to Atlanta, where he headed a defense committee for Angelo Herndon, a Communist organizer who had been charged with violating a Georgia insurrection act.[43] The next month, despite her family's opposition, Johnson agreed to a five-year lease. Highlander had $5.57 in cash.

Horton launched into recruiting Union students to fill the hole left by West's departure. John Thompson, another Tennessean who had studied with Niebuhr, joined Highlander after finishing his degree at Union. His sister, Dorothy, had been teaching piano almost since the school opened. Elizabeth Hawes arrived. Known as Zilla, she had spent a year at Brookwood Labor College and a summer at the John C. Campbell Folk School in Brasstown, North Carolina. The daughter of a Unitarian minister in Massachusetts, she was to be Highlander's link to unions. The handful of students was growing, too. However, despite having Johnson's signature on a lease, Horton believed Highlander was going to have to relocate.

For one thing, the school had drawn more attention to itself by helping the Kesters arrange for Norman Thomas to speak to over seven hundred cheering miners at Wilder, and afterwards to another large crowd at Crossville. Using contacts within the fledgling Tennessee Valley Authority, Horton and West had helped several dozen Wilder miners find jobs in that new but already controversial agency. Dorothy Thompson had gotten Highlander embroiled in a spontaneous strike of Grundy County bugwood cutters. Grundy County was on the southern tip of the Cumberland Plateau and once had been thickly forested. The most valuable lumber had been shorn already. In 1933, Tennessee Products Corporation was the county's chief employer, paying seventy-five cents a day for cutting bugwood, knotty crooks of trees found in cut-over timberland. Bugwood was used in distilling wood alcohol. Beyond cutting bugwood, few other jobs existed. Grundy County's poverty was extreme, even by Depression standards. Horton described its 9,700 people as a "stranded population."[44] The crop land was exhausted. A few family-run wagon mines still operated, employing one or two men each; most other coal mining operations had shut down. Rich coal deposits had been mined there since the 1850s.

One bugwood cutter, Henry Thomas, had made good money as a logger before the Depression. By July 1933, however, he was barely feeding his family. "I got to figuring that my pay amounted to two-and-a-half cents a meal for the members of my family," Thomas said. "So I went around to the other woodcutters and said to them, 'It takes a sharp axe, a strong back, and a weak mind to cut bugwood at seventy-five cents a day. Let's strike!'"[45] They did, and again Highlander was in the midst of conflict—right at home, and not in distant Wilder. Men, women, and even children set up picket lines in the scarred forests for miles around Monteagle, Tracy City, and Altamont, the county seat. No bugwood was cut. After efforts to affiliate the strikers with the American Federation of Labor came to naught, Thompson helped strikers form the Cumberland Mountain Workers and Unemployed League. Ten days later a majority of the county's woodcutters had signed the organization's statement of purpose: "To be loyal to one another and to the purposes of the organization, which are: (1) to prevent the wholesale destruction of our forests; (2) to better the conditions of the community by raising wages."[46]

The strike stretched on into May 1934. Horton was approached by several bugwood cutters about starting an employment agency for Grundy's unemployed. "At first," Horton recalled, "it seemed like a pretty good idea. It came from the people. If it worked, it would be of help. But we refused, and told them our goal was to help workers unite with other workers for common strength and not to help individuals rise above others."[47]

While the strike caused no major economic change, in part because of the strikers' contradictory goals, the bugwood cutters had given the young staff its first opportunity to promote a collective solution to social ills suffered individually by Highlander's neighbors. Horton could talk about some accomplishment when trying to raise funds. Among some union leaders, Highlander was beginning to be seen as a school for southern labor.[48]

Gradually, Highlander attracted students. One, Walker Martin, whose father was a coal miner, organized weekly meetings in nearby coal camps teaching labor history and union organizing tactics. Another, Dee Farris, who had been a member of a plasterers' union, worked on a road crew encouraging his fellow workers to think and talk about unions. Elsie West, Don West's sister, taught youngsters dramatics, and her group was writing a labor history play. Dorothy Thompson said in one appeal for funds, "Our social room is the only place where many local youngsters ever hear good music or find opportunities for wholesome recreation."[49]

In November, when Dombrowski arrived, eight young men and women were enrolled for the winter term. The faculty—Thompson, Hawes, Horton, and Dombrowski—were expecting Rupert Hampton, another Union graduate, to work as music teacher and bookkeeper. Dombrowski set right in to establish a financial base for the school, figuring their budget at $2,000. "Considering that this includes the living expenses of four people, this is rather an amazingly economical budget," he wrote in a promotional letter.[50]

During the first year, Horton and West spent $1,327.30 to keep the school going.[51] They did not pay themselves salaries. Volunteers helped cut some costs. Everyone—students, teachers, visitors—shared in boiling clothes in iron pots outdoors or cooking. Labor was in ample supply; it was cash that was scarce. To generate revenue, Dombrowski solicited staff for names of friends; no acquaintance was spared an appeal letter. Elizabeth

Duncan, the Emory Alumni Association secretary whom Dombrowski had hired, got one. The list he had collected through Norma Thomas, Ethel Clyde, John Dewey, or others in New York got appeals. Dewey's letter of endorsement circulated widely and got donations. Individually written thank-you notes were promptly dispatched hours after contributions arrived. Dombrowski commenced the process of getting Highlander chartered as a nonprofit education center. The school soon had a prestigious advisory committee, including Reinhold Niebuhr, Sherwood Eddy, Norman Thomas, Alva Taylor, and W. W. Alexander.[52]

"Highlander was a group of dedicated, would-be liberal adult educators until Jim got here," Horton said years later.[53]

> I did a lot of running around talking with people, but he did the solid work of coalescing the whole thing. He was the head of the school. He did the administrative chores, wrote promotions, raised funds, wrote the newsletter. He taught labor history. He organized workshops away from the school. He brought people together who, while working on their own programs, provided support for the working-class struggle and for Highlander. I had the ideas; he had the vision and the strategy.

Dombrowski came to be called "the Skipper."[54] He laid the school's administrative foundation, finally putting his business experience to use for a cause he fully believed in. He was as careful preparing reports or typing up minutes of a meeting as he was putting together budgets, a newsletter, or appeals to donors. "But," Horton continued, "this didn't detract from his creativity as a teacher. He was no bureaucrat. He always wanted to be where the action was, but never tried to get out front and tell people what to think, or be a teacher. He never argued his beliefs with anyone. He was not a speech-making radical."[55] No job was beneath him.

Confident appearances and their lease notwithstanding, the staff remained uneasy about the school's situation in Monteagle. The school's finances were dismally low; Dombrowski's energetic appeals hardly raised enough to cover expenses. Horton's early dream of self-sufficiency was fading. Reinhold Niebuhr was urging the staff to turn to foundations. On December 11, 1933, a cold, rainy day, Horton, Hawes, and Dombrowski left for Fentress County, fully expecting that they were going to look at the future home of Highlander. They had been invited to the home of Joe Kelly Stockton and Kate Bradford Stockton. Horton had known the Stocktons since the 1920s. Joe Stockton was secretary of the Tennessee Socialist Party and had been dreaming for years about building a worker's school on his property. "I have a thousand acres more than I can use," Joe Stockton told his enthralled visitors.[56] "We don't really own the land. We only rent it from the state. No man ought to have more land than he can use. My idea is to turn it over to the school, as much as the school can use, and when I get ready to wind up my contract on earth, I'll turn it over to the school to use for all humanity."

Joe and Kate Stockton, joined by Alec Beaty, a neighbor, welcomed the Highlander staff with a huge meal in front of a kitchen fireplace. For the first time since his visit to the Soviet collective farm, Dombrowski felt as if he were with authentic revolutionaries. There was nothing metaphysical about his hosts' aspirations to bring down the *ancien regime*. Beaty and Joe Stockton vied to assert their political fervor. As he listened, Dombrowski's pencil worked at a furious pace, sketching their faces and recording their words.

*Beaty:* Socialism means for every man to be a free man. There's Joe Young sold nine thousand feet of lumber and works people ten hours a day for a dollar a day. No government ought to allow that.

*Stockton:* I'm a strong individualist when it comes to every man having as much land as he can use, and a home.

*Beaty:* Every man in the United States ought to have a living. And there's enough natural resources in the country for every man to do it.

*Stockton:* All these millionaires that got their living made. They don't care whether you and me live or not. When Andrew Jackson could take his buggy and drive to Washington to represent the people, people were fair and honest. In those days, if people didn't find a living, they could move West. But now we ought to change the system and stay where you are. Those rich people are talking about Roosevelt and about him ruining the country. All they want is to keep things like they are.

*Beaty:* Well, they'd just have to be put to death. Now these rich people that got their living made, they say, "Um, umh. These Socialists. They want to come along and take all we got away from us." Now that's the very height of ignorance. There are folks right here now that can't own their own home for the high taxes. The system's got to be changed. And right now. Not sometime later.[57]

The next day Stockton took them to his farm on Crooked Creek Road, near Allardt, Tennessee. To reach the farmhouse, a long, rambling structure with a barn nearby, they forded a small creek. The house had been built from hand-hewn timbers some fifty years earlier, and looked its age. Immediately, they laid out a plan to settle Highlander there. Dombrowski figured that a new residential center could be built for about $3,550, large enough for fifteen students, and include a furniture shop, along with a cottage for teachers.[58] They would use volunteer labor and get some northern architects he knew to draw up plans free.

With hardly enough money on hand to operate their school in Monteagle, Horton, Hawes, and Dombrowski started "an outpost," as Horton called it, the next day, driving to Armathwaite, six miles off, to a secondhand furniture store run by Socialist friends of the Stocktons. They bought a dinette for $4.50, a bedspring and mattress for $4.00, nine tin cups, some putty and glass to repair windows, and lumber for bookshelves.[59] Later that week, Horton and Dombrowski went to Knoxville to buy blankets and a tire for the school's secondhand car, a vehicle bought with Hawes' dowery. Horton and Hawes returned to Monteagle; Dombrowski moved in to take charge of reconstruction. "We scrubbed it, painted one room for a living room, plugged the largest holes and managed to survive. . . . when it got down to 40 below zero, one could stand with his back to a roaring hickory log fire and break off icicles from his beard. Water in the buckets froze solid ten feet from the hearth," he wrote.[60] Dombrowski left Allardt for a less spartan Christmas holiday at Monteagle. Christmas night Dombrowski wrote to King Gordon: "The job at Allardt is a much more primitive affair than Monteagle. . . . It is going to be a hard job, but a lot of fun. A gorgeous country and perfectly fascinating people, many of them ready for revolutionary action."[61] Dombrowski told his Canadian friend that the separation from Ellen Krida was the only difficulty his work at Highlander presented. "Ellen has become more and more an indispensable part of my life," he wrote.[62] "Things are so rough and primitive that I could not ask a girl to chance it at present. And the whole undertaking is so precarious and insecure that it is exceedingly dubious as to whether it would be wise ever." As he wrote, Krida was trying to reach him by telephone at Highlander. Two days later, she wrote from Schenectedy, "I tried to call you on Christmas night, thrilled with the anticipation, but, honey, they said no phone in H.F.S., a horrible shock because I knew you had no Xmas message from your girl."[63]

The winter of 1933–34 was a low point in Highlander's early history. Telephones were not the only missing ingredient. Horton fell ill, mentally and physically exhausted, and was admitted to a sanitarium where rest and quiet were his medication. He recovered within weeks. Dombrowski and Hawes had been involved in two bitter but losing union organizing drives in Knoxville and Harriman. A five-month residential term especially for miners and mill workers, which had been planned to start December 1, opened in March and lasted only ten weeks. Four students enrolled, paying tuition of $75 each. When the unsuccessful term closed, a bitter argument ensued about rebating some tuition. Work on the Allardt outpost was frustratingly slow; needed tools, materials, or money seemed never to be on hand at the right moment.

Gradually the staff began to define both an effective curriculum and clearer roles for themselves as teachers. They agreed on criteria for screening students, and encouraged students to come as official representatives of union locals. Their aim was to teach new union members the ropes of union work. Some students had been dressing, drinking, or behaving in ways the staff knew upset neighbors, even some who otherwise appreciated Highlander because of its support of working people. They set down the school's social expectations.

Hawes had been organizing for the Amalgamated Clothing Workers of America (ACWA) in Knoxville and succeeded in organizing the union's first southern local in that East Tennessee city. She opened a Highlander extension school in Knoxville, holding weekly classes either in an ACWA office or in a rented hotel room. Horton, Dombrowski, or Hawes offered courses on labor history or on religion and labor, but only a few students participated. Before they decided to close the extension, a union official who had been dismissed for misconduct blamed Highlander for strikes labor unions lost in Knoxville and Harriman. Books he took from the reading room proved, he said, that Highlander's staff were "Communists and atheists."[64]

For the most part, however, despite setbacks, threats, allegations, and scarce funds, Dombrowski was turning initiatives taken by Horton and Hawes into educational programs and collective social action. The handful of persons who would become long-term contributors was growing. "It was his steady hand," recalled Ralph Tefferteller, another Union graduate who came to Highlander, "together with his managerial and developmental abilities, which made it possible for Highlander to survive those early, turbulent years."[65]

Twice a year, Dombrowski went North searching for money in Wash-

Ethel Clyde on her eighty-fifth birthday, August 5, 1964. Frank T. Adams Collection.

ington, New York, or Boston. These pilgrimages later were expanded to include Chicago and Los Angeles. No systematic effort to raise funds had been made until Dombrowski arrived, partly because Horton and West had their hands full, but also because fundraising appealed very little to them. "Some people detested the idea," Dombrowski said.[66] "I always felt that I was doing a person a favor when I asked for a hundred dollars or ten dollars." For him, fundraising was another way to redistribute the world's wealth. If a person had more than they needed, in a capitalist system there were always others who had less. "The problem was how to properly redistribute those extra goods," he said.[67] "We had a perfect answer at Highlander." He developed a network of loyal supporters. Some, like Ethel Clyde, visited Highlander from time to time and contributed generously throughout their lives. For others, especially some who never went south of Wall Street, Dombrowski became a trusted link between northern philanthropy and southern radicals, a role he played for years.

Dombrowski, in a way, envisioned Highlander as a pulpit from which he could minister, and not just to the poor. Shortly after arriving in Monteagle, he and Howard Kester, a Virginian who had earned a bachelor of divinity degree at Vanderbilt under Dr. Taylor, started discussing how they could organize liberal southern ministers. Kester, on top of his relief work at Wilder, was crisscrossing the South on behalf of the Fellowship for Reconciliation and preaching the need for interracial working-class action. After a talk by Kester on the economic relationships between white and African-American workers, several students asked to learn "the Negroes' side since the problem was important to the working class."[68] Reluctantly, the faculty decided against inviting African Americans, fearing "the harm it would do in the community would more than offset any sort of value."[69] A few months later, however, figuring they could prepare Monteagle neighbors through friendships established during the bugwood strike, Hawes and Dombrowski invited Dr. J. Herman Daves, who taught at Knoxville College.

No African Americans lived in Monteagle; a few miles to the south, in Sewanee, where the University of the South was located, African Americans worked as maids or janitors but left town at sunset. Hawes and Dombrowski had made contact with a few African-American union members in Knoxville, and with Daves at Knoxville College. Daves, undoubtedly an adventurous person, accepted the invitation and spoke about the need for interracial solidarity among union members. Within hours, the staff received threats warning that the school would be dynamited. For several weeks during the early spring of 1934, armed men guarded Highlander at night.[70]

Since 1931, Howard Kester had been organizing integrated conferences, the first in Birmingham, Alabama, and the second at Paine College in Augusta, Georgia. The event in Birmingham had been attended by more than eighty persons who shared sleeping quarters and dining tables while talking about racism and peace. Both gatherings had been unprecedented. In 1933, Kester joined Mrs. Ada Wright, the mother of one of the Scottsboro Boys, and Dr. Benjamin B. Goldstein of Montgomery, Alabama, for an Easter Sunday defense committee rally in Birmingham. He and Dombrowski believed that the time was ripe to organize a radical political party of both races.[71] Ministers, they agreed, would be their first recruits.

To this end, Dombrowski and Kester wrote to every theologian, church worker, or minister they knew inviting them to the Monteagle Assembly for a three-day meeting beginning May 27, 1934. The agenda called for discussions on prophetic Christianity and the New Deal, and speeches by Reinhold Niebuhr and Kirby Page, editor of *The World Tomorrow,* a progressive tabloid. The event was Dombrowski's first major initiative at Highlander.

Some forty church workers, mostly ministers, from five southern states attended. Each believed devoutly in the potential of the South's Protestant proletariat.[72] They took as their motto St. Luke's injunction, "To preach the gospel to the poor, to heal the broken-hearted, to preach deliverance to the captive, and recovery of sight to the blind, to set at liberty them that are bruised, to preach an acceptable year of the Lord."[73] Most agreed with Dombrowski and Kester that the day was at hand when the biblical prophecy of a violent revolution would be fulfilled. "Those of us who attended will never forget Niebuhr's mind-kindling talks, his dialectical skill, his prophetic probing of our social order and the Church," wrote Thomas B. Cowan, who added, "Reinie is Judgment Day in britches."[74] The group decided to organize, as Dombrowski had hoped, taking the name Younger Churchmen of the South, a name that would change twice, first to Fellowship of Southern Churchmen, and finally to Committee of Southern Churchmen. Kester was elected secretary and charged with keeping the organization going.

In addition to listening to stirring oratory, the churchmen critiqued the New Deal. They approved of President Roosevelt's objectives "to abolish poverty, and child labor, recognize the right of the workers to bargain collectively, move in the direction of a planned economy, and provide a more equitable distribution of wealth."[75] However, the administration's attempts to end poverty "with the economics of scarcity" or the free market economy were insufficient, they declared. The churchmen also faulted relief to the unemployed, the failure to protect the bargaining rights of workers, and what they considered unjustifiable discrimination in the wages paid northern and southern workers.

Dombrowski and Kester pushed a resolution on racial issues and got a strongly worded statement condemning "the manifest injustices done to the Negro, as evidenced by discrimination by employers and trade unions and in the matter of wages . . . and in the courts, in the disproportionate sums expended for education, in restricting the right of suffrage, in the operation of Jim Crow laws, and the inadequacy of housing, recreation, and health facilities."[76] Their last resolution called for the establishment of "a radical political party of all races . . . which shall recognize the revolutionary tradition of America and the higher values of a patriotism and religion."[77]

The day after the meeting ended, a newspaper headline trumpeted, "Politics Needs Radical Party, Churchmen say. Program of Socialism Urged by Young Ministers at Monteagle."[78] The committee held its next meeting at Chattanooga, this time with black religious leaders present, including George Streator, managing editor of *The Crisis*, voice of the National Association for the Advancement of Colored People. Delegates from all eleven southern states attended. Again a flurry of headlines resulted: "Social Justice Cry Is Sounded at Conference. Younger Churchmen Denounce Economic System that Leads to Dictatorship. George Streator Speaks . . . Sees Exploitation of Masses in South."[79] Dombrowski and Kester had struck a responsive chord.

In April, Dombrowski signed another call for revolutionary action; it, too, was stirring passions, but inside the Socialist Party. He joined eighty-three other Socialists who called themselves the Revolutionary Policy Committee for Socialists. They urged fellow Socialists to "act as a militant working-class party."[80] The appeal's millenial rhetoric was born, no doubt, from genuine fear of emerging fascism in Germany and Italy and at home. The signers also seem to have been frustrated with the party's gradualist policies which, as the resolution charged, resulted in small growth in membership and poor showings at the polls. Dombrowski and Hawes signed the call; Horton did not. "There is no longer a middle road," the statement said, "it is necessary to acquire possession of state power so as to transform capitalist society into socialist society by means of the dictatorship of the proletariat."[81]

The appeal, printed and widely distributed at five cents a copy, infuriated "old-guard" Socialists such as David Dubinsky, Algernon Lee, James O'Neal, and many trade union leaders, all of whom were opposed to any endorsement of violent class struggle. In 1933, after years of effort under their close-handed but democratic guidance, the party claimed fewer than nineteen thousand paid members.[82] Suppressed bickering between the wing of the party they controlled and the wing loyal to Norman Thomas, who perhaps more than any other American Socialist had spread the message of how socialism would work, broke into the open. In June 1934, two months after the appeal was issued, Dubinsky's "old guard" was ousted from the party convention in Detroit. The Revolutionary Policy Committee said, in effect, that only a militant working-class political party would unite the divided masses. The appeal was not the first, or the only, or the last ideological split among Socialists. But insofar as Dombrowski and Highlander were concerned, his signature and that of Hawes on the revolutionary call planted seeds of mistrust and eventual attack. Persons who otherwise might have been allies never forgot nor forgave Dombrowski.[83]

Why did Dombrowski sign the inflammatory appeal? Normally a prudent man, as his cautious academic journey away from Emory showed, he thought twice before doing anything. He knew the broadside would cause political mischief at least. The seasoned Dombrowski of Monteagle and Allardt in 1934 certainly was not the innocent Dombrowski of Elizabethton and Gastonia in 1929. His most influential mentor, Ward, spurned the Marxist tenet of a dictatorship of the proletariat. Dewey, too, argued that education and not militancy was the correct tool for social change. As a minister, albeit one without a traditional pulpit, Dombrowski believed that conditions in America were fulfilling the biblical prophecy of the Second Advent. He was surrounded by human beings who were determined to change society—most out of desperation, others out of ideological commitment. The injustices he saw daily outraged his spirit, awakening an obligation to disobey his instinctive caution. Dombrowski the scholar was calm, reflective, always appearing to be in full control of the moment's political passion; Dombrowski the preacher, by contrast, seethed, often acted impulsively, and was intensely radical. By training or by trait, Dombrowski, like many preachers, seemed able to manage everything but his tongue. The appeal was his sermon to out-of-touch elders. It was significant, perhaps, that Myles Horton did not sign the appeal.

The Stocktons and Beaty, who struggled to build a Socialist society where they lived, paying little heed to party infighting, also influenced Dombrowski. They wanted no national attention; none came their way. Two Monteagle neighbors, Will L. Brown and Alf Kilgore, shared home-made blackberry cordial with Dombrowski nearly every evening and talked for hours about their dreams of a new society and about the revolution required to reach that end. In Dombrowski's mind, Brown and Kilgore, like his friends in Allardt, were the chosen who would lead the nation out of the economic wilderness. They were the mythical, Messianic folk—the poor or captive of his biblical imagination. They wanted action.

Too, Dombrowski was living as he imagined an artist would live during a revolutionary moment. He was sketching historic persons during historic events at Highlander, at Wilder, at the meeting of Younger Churchmen. He molded, shadowed, and shaped historical reality in the dozens of penciled sketches he drew on the backs of envelopes, or in his diaries and countless notebooks. Hilda Hulbert, who joined Highlander as librarian after graduating from Wellseley, remembered that he told her, "Organizers are the greatest artists, especially if they are radical organizers with a socialist goal and vision. They do what any artist does. They use the material they find in the community or some little spot in the world and reorganize that environment into a more rational and pleasing environment. That's really what the artist does. Great artists are great reformers."[84]

# 6

## Learning
## from What
## Was Lived

The Progressive Education Association invited Highlander to send a speaker to its annual convention in Washington, D.C., in February 1935. The staff decided that Dombrowski should give the talk and afterward try to raise money from the school's growing number of supporters in the nation's capitol. At the time he left Monteagle, Highlander staff or union friends were involved one way or another in a flurry of strikes and the inevitable anti-union reaction to them.

Mean things were happening in the Arkansas Delta.[1] Tenant farmers on cotton plantations were joining the Southern Tenant Farmer's Union, stirred to attend swelling interracial meetings, and even sit-downs by their desperate lives and by H.L. Mitchell and J.R. Butler. One union organizer, Ward Rogers, a Texan who had attended Vanderbilt with Howard Kester, had been teaching tenants how to read, write, and do arithmetic. He had been jailed in Marked Tree, Arkansas, and charged with trying to overthrow the government.[2]

On Sunday, February 10, in Rossville, Georgia, Pink Miller, who had led a successful strike against the Richmond Hosiery Mills, had been shot dead. The shotgun blast which killed him ripped apart military discharge papers in his coat showing that he had been cited five times for bravery in World War I.[3] At home, the Grundy County welfare director, who administered the Works Progress Administration (WPA), chastised the unemployed for organizing a Relief Workers' Union and announced that wages would be reduced from twenty-five cents an hour to fifteen.[4] Horton had been in Arkansas recruiting prospective students from the tenant farmers' organization, and had left only a few days before Rogers' arrest. Franz Daniel had been the Amalgamated Clothing Workers' organizer in Rossville. Dombrowski had organized Grundy County's WPA workers.

In two hectic years, Highlander had established itself among activists south and north, as a place to gather, a reputation it cherished over the years. As a school, however, Highlander was only starting to fashion a clear, sustained program. Dombrowski brought a unique perspective to the audience of educators in Washington. Most of them taught in traditional classrooms at one grade level or another. The adults he was teaching pushed him farther and farther away from the traditional classroom.

"Rural schools, and particularly mountain schools," Dombrowski said, "are training students for a world which does not exist. They are concerned with the past and even there do not have an understanding of how the achievements of the past were effected. There is little attention to the present, or to the social forces at work in contemporary society on which the future is built. The emphasis is on the old one of 'individual success' which has little significance in a world of monopoly and finance capitalism, and of socialized production. Thus, education, instead of contributing to a peaceful solution to the pressing social problems, functions as a conservative drag on progressive tendencies. In a revolutionary age, there is no neutral education."[5]

Highlander, he continued, was a modest experiment attempting to use education to build a new social order. The school tried to avoid the trap of teaching people to endure poverty and hardship, or to believe their problems could be resolved by heroic individual enterprise. Highlander's purpose, he said, was to help southern mountaineers, farmers, industrial workers, and others understand the world they lived in and how to collectively change that world for the benefit of themselves, their families, and society. To accomplish these aims, he added, Highlander had developed a program with three phases which often overlapped.

To make the Highlander Folk School an integral part of the life of the little community of Summerfield, a settlement of about 75 families surrounding the school, we are open night and day as an educational and social center. We have started a library with over 4,000 donated volumes, and it is in constant use. We have helped form a gardening and canning cooperative to lower food costs by cutting out the middle man, but, as well, to teach methods of mutual aid. We have helped form the Cumberland Mountain Workers and Unemployed League, and the Relief Workers' Union, as a means of demonstrating how unity might solve economic problems.

Each summer and fall, we hold a six-week long residential program for carefully selected students from industrial and farming communities. They are given intensive course work in economics and philosophy, labor history, dramatics, music, public speaking, how we think, religion and social problems, journalism, cooperative techniques, weaving and handicrafts. The idea is to equip them to go back into their communities or unions and carry on educational work for the new social order and to occupy places of leadership.

Finally, an extension program has been created. Residential students and friends from the community take regular weekly trips to hear lectures in Nashville or Chattanooga, to give assistance to striking coal miners, textile workers, or farm groups. Study groups have been organized by our students in several dozen communities and are led by former students or by local labor leaders. The school's library loans books regularly to more than twenty-five community groups within a 145-mile radius. Our traveling chautauqua gives plays, lectures, puppet shows or teaches local leaders how to present dramatic productions or lead group singing.

Thus, theory and practice are closely related. Fresh material for class discussions comes from the student's own experiences, or from their visits to local communities and the situations they see there. There is a dynamic for social change. Philosophy is used to change the world as well as to understand it.[6]

Even by the standards of progressive educators, Highlander was a radically different school. John Dewey was the patron philosopher of the Progressive Education Association and an influence obvious in the Tennessee folk school. But, for the most part, Highlander fell outside the scope of their child-centered classroom interests. Education for adults was not their major focus. Nevertheless, lasting ties were established between Highlander and teachers at three northern colleges—Antioch, Smith, and Goddard.

Their students and faculty, over the years to follow, were frequently in and out of Highlander.

While Dombrowski captured the outlines of Highlander's educational program during the mid- to late 1930s, he did not describe the intensity or the pace of students and staff alike. Nor did he acknowledge how much the staff itself was having to learn, not just about managing a school but, of greater importance, about how to teach adults. An unsigned, undated letter in Highlander's files, typical of many student accounts written at the time, provides a glimpse of the school from a resident's perspective:

> As the sun peeks over a mountain ridge high up in the Cumberlands, you see students in twos and threes coming from the cabins near the main building of the school, and within a few minutes, a group of young men and women are gathered around the huge fireplace in the living room ready for a hearty breakfast.
>
> Thus starts the day at Highlander Folk School. Now at 7:30 there is quite a scramble about washing dishes. . . . At 8:30 the "Bell," which means Labor History class by Jim Dombrowski, where we have a discussion on the split between the AF of L and the CIO. At 9:20 we have Economics conducted by Bill Buttrick, and at 10:15 Dramatics. We are practicing our mass chant, "Tom Mooney Lives Again," which we are going to give to the Textile Workers Organizing Committee (TWOC) convention next week in Chattanooga. Now a short walk to the gate and back, just for a breath of fresh air.
>
> At 12:30 dinner is served. Now that we have had dinner we will wash dishes and do our cleaning. At 2:30 we have Union Problems, taught by Myles Horton. Today we had Edna Lamb, John Pate, and Bill Flanagan answer questions on Union Problems.
>
> At 4:30 everybody is out for volley ball. Boy! What a game. Darkness has arrived and there goes the supper bell, and after this game everyone is hungry. Now, after eating for thirty minutes, Zilphia [then Johnson, a student from Mena, Arkansas, who later married Myles Horton] passes out song books and it's likely we will start with "Arise You Workers" and finish with "Whirlwinds of Danger." Well, it's dishes again but we don't mind them this time. When we have finished, we will have our speaker of the evening, Tommy Burns of the Rubber Workers, who, by the way, is a very interesting speaker.

Now at 10:30 things are getting quiet as the students slowly wander off to their rooms for a good night's rest. Ho! Hum! Guess I'll turn in too. Good night.[7]

When he arrived at Highlander, Dombrowski, like the other staff, taught as he himself had been schooled. Knowledge was transferred from teacher to student, like pouring water from a kettle to a cup. Most of what he tried to teach came from textbooks and was not necessarily related to the situations which prompted students to come to Highlander. He would dwell on facts or abstractions far removed from their interests or experience. There were courses with grand titles, including "Socialism and Christianity" and "Technology and Socialism." Once, for instance, to explain economic theory, Dombrowski used pots and pans in the kitchen and a blackboard over the sink. While his classroom was markedly different from those at Hillsborough High, Emory, Harvard, or Union, the assumptions of his teaching differed hardly a bit. Learning was a one-way street; he knew what others needed to know. But Dombrowski and especially Horton, who did more teaching and recruiting, soon learned, often with embarrassment or emotional pain to themselves, how to value the experience of students and how the students' perceptions of their own problems could become the starting point of education for political action. Problems of social justice and political power, along with solid, factual information about those problems, not courses, became the school's educational focus.

As a problem-centered curriculum evolved, Highlander's staff discovered that teaching methods had to change. Stimulating lectures and compulsory reading gave way to a dialogue among equals. Dombrowski figured, probably correctly, that pedagogic analysis rather than anecdote was called for at the Washington meeting of progressive teachers. So he did not mention the contrast between one of Horton's early methods and how Horton was teaching by 1935. Shortly after opening the school, Horton had been teaching a course on psychology. When the students asked him how "to think straight," Horton launched a discussion of the nervous system.

Horton and Dombrowski began to convene groups—some of whom might be in contention—to talk about common problems. Thinking and talking together in groups helped individuals overcome their sense of helplessness or isolation. Dombrowski realized that he had to respect individual autonomy while helping individuals develop the ability to act collectively. Transferring expertise or knowledge became a group's responsibility, in collaboration with a teacher. Democratic political action resulted when groups came to agree about the nature of their problems and why those problems existed, and formulated their own solutions. Years later, Horton described this crucial distinction which he and Dombrowski learned during Highlander's early years:

> It's very important that you understand the difference between your perception of what people's problems are and their perceptions of them. You shouldn't be trying to discover your perception of their perception. You must find a way to determine what their perception is. . . . they haven't learned to analyze their experience and learn from it. When you help them to respect and learn from their experience, they can know more about themselves than you do.[8]

Still, not all life was synonymous with learning. Some experiences, especially demeaning poverty, did not necessarily result in the kind of learning that enabled individuals to act together or to believe in what they knew. Not every political action resulted in political change or did much to unmask who really controlled the institutions managing or causing poverty. The strike at Wilder was educative. Conflict and controversy were part of the process at Highlander.

During one of Dombrowski's labor history classes, students suggested that Highlander invite John E. Egerton, a woolen manufacturer from Lebanon, Tennessee, to speak. Egerton was president of the Tennessee Manufacturers Association and a vigorous opponent of unions. The invitation was posted. Egerton responded promptly. No, he said, he wouldn't come to Highlander. And the next day, June 28, 1934, he wrote every member of the state's manufacturing association:

> Yesterday, I received a letter from Mr. Myles Horton, one of the promoters of the so-called HIGHLANDER FOLK SCHOOL at Monteagle, Tennessee, inviting me to have a representative of the Tennessee Manufacturers Association to appear before the student body and present our views. . . . Assisting Mr. Horton in operating the school is Mr. Dombrowski, who is armed with Russian posters collected during a recent visit, Miss Hawes, organizer for the Amalgamated Clothing Workers in East Tennessee, and two or three others. . . . the students

are trained as labor organizers. . . . Mr. Dombrowski, "who has traveled in Russia," will tell all about his impressions of the Soviet and its accomplishments. . . . I declined the invitation in courteous, but vigorous terms. This enterprise of destruction requires no comment from me. It is about the boldest and most insulting thing to the Anglo-Saxon South that has yet been done.[9]

Egerton's letter proved to be Highlander's first serious encounter with Red-baiting, and the first attempt to cast a fear-evoking shadow of foreign intrigue on the school by using Dombrowski's surname. Targeting the Soviet Union had become a convenient means of masking ills at home. For several years, Egerton skillfully exploited the issue, saying later, when he became president of the Southern States Industrial Council, that Highlander was a thoroughly Communist enterprise.[10] Nor was his attack on Dombrowski's name the last. In the political climate Egerton and others were creating, the name Dombrowski, by its sound alone, marked him as a radical, no matter what his political or social views.

The Russian posters, previously a bone of contention with authorities, as we have seen, were viewed as further evidence of Dombrowski's menace. In fact, "the posters were valuable aids," he recalled.[11] "The students were eager to learn what was going on in the world. Working people always are interested in the problems of other working people—especially about a country where there was no unemployment and everyone had something to eat, even if it was not fancy."

Eating also posed educational problems for Highlander's staff, nor could that problem be explained easily in a brief talk to the Progressive Education Association. Few in the audience would have understood. Food was scarce for most Highlander students and often for the staff. A diet of greens, fatback, cornmeal and molasses, or flour gravy was a common way to keep the body alive, but one which hardly nourished or gave much energy for collective action. For example, Dombrowski was driving a member of the Relief Union's steering committee home one night after a meeting. The man lived twenty miles from Tracy City, where the meeting had been held. It was 10:30 p.m. He had walked to the meeting.

"Brother," Dombrowski asked as they drove along, "what have you eaten today?"

"I haven't eaten yet," the man replied.

"What did you have yesterday?" Dombrowski asked.

"Bread."

"How long has it been since you had some real food?" Dombrowski continued.

"About a week."[12]

Isolation, too, posed difficulties. Roads were poor. Feet or mules provided the chief means of transportation, especially in the hollows, where there was a marked absence of social life.

Religious views which sternly frowned on dancing, music, or singing save for hymns at church curbed the Highlander staff's desire to use music to "first enliven." By the 1930s, a rich mountain folk culture was washing away. Around Summerfield, Ralph Tefferteller, a Union graduate who had joined Highlander to put his musical abilities to use in the Socialist cause, began searching for invitations to be taught the beautiful old mountain reels and jigs. A native of Blount County, Tennessee, Tefferteller played the fiddle and was an affable man. Slowly some neighbors saw him often enough so they felt they could entrust to him songs they themselves were beginning to forget. First he learned some children's singing games; later Sacred Harp or shaped-note hymns; then more personal ballads.

Gradually reluctance to sing or act in plays was overcome. On the eve of Dombrowski's trip to Washington, Dorothy Thompson's dramatics class— fifteen youngsters from Summerfield—presented an operetta, "Strike Me Red," to a full house in the Highlander living room. While he was in Washington, five Summerfield adults and two staff members presented a one-act play, "We Ain't A'goin' Back," written by the cast and based on a strike in Ohio's onion fields. A Highlander student had been a leader in the struggle to organize a farm worker's union.

Just before Dombrowski went to Washington, Horton took eleven students to Nashville to hear Dr. Toyohiko Kagawa, a well-known Japanese Christian Socialist active in organizing cooperatives and labor unions in Japan. The field trip was part of Highlander's way of teaching critical thinking. After the public lecture, they talked with Kagawa personally at the home of Dr. Taylor, the Vanderbilt professor who was a member of Highlander's Advisory Committee. Later they wrote in "Our Verdict," a one-page mimeographed newspaper that each group of residential students published:

The value of Kagawa's remarkable achievements in building cooperative and labor unions in Japan likewise was questioned. Japan is ruled by a military dictatorship. The chief opposition to this regime comes from the royal families, the old traditional ruling class. The terrible conditions of Japanese workers, taxed heavily to finance a top-heavy program of military expansion and conquest, has resulted in a rapidly-growing left-wing movement. Is the military dictatorship using Kagawa and his anti-Communist Christian cooperative movement as a tool to split the working class?"[13]

Who were these questioning, "straight-thinking" students? Sam Amburn had been sent by Local 188 of the Mine, Mill and Smelter Workers from the zinc mines at Mascot, Tennessee, to learn how to keep his union strong. Odean Enestvedt and Charles Prouty came from the Farmers Holiday Association, a Socialist cooperative in Minnesota, to study the economic policies of the Farm Home Administration. Taylor Payne of Cowan, Tennessee, was learning how to organize tenant farmers like himself. Local 145 of the United Garment Workers of America sent Angel Prior, their president, to learn how to organize sweatshops. The Amalgamated Clothing Workers sent Charles Handy, who had taught school in Norfolk, Virginia, before being fired for union activities, to learn how to establish a workers' education program. Edna Champion, a member of the International Garment Workers' Union Local 122 in Atlanta, was studying American labor history. Benton Prugh wanted to learn how to strengthen his cooperative in Gladden, Missouri. Only Eugene and Margaret Sutherland of Louisville, Kentucky, were not already working for either a co-op or a union. They came "to learn more about producers and consumers cooperatives and to share the social adventure of cooperative living at a folk school."[14]

Dombrowski didn't stay in Washington long after the conference. He made a few solicitations, then caught a train back to Chattanooga. He and Howard Kester had locked themselves into a dispute over invitations to a southwide conference they had been organizing. Kester asked Highlander to join him in circulating a call for a "united front conference for mapping out ways and means to struggle against the growing reaction in the South."[15] Kester, Dombrowski, and Horton agreed that attention should be focused on the widespread brutality being unleashed in the South against organizing drives and organizers. Dombrowski had been assigned to represent Highlander and help put together the Southwide conference on trade unions and civil rights. There would be calls to repeal sedition and antilabor laws, prohibit lynching, and abolish the poll tax.

As work on the conference got underway, Kester insisted that only Socialists should be invited. Dombrowski was equally determined that invitations would be sent to any group or individual regardless of political stripe. The two young clergymen, who agreed on so many radical issues, were not able to reconcile their differences during the planning meeting in Chattanooga which Dombrowski hurried to attend. Kester quit the effort, agreeing, however, to let his name appear on the call. Dombrowski got a reputation among some southern activists as one obdurately fixed in his ways and difficult to work with. His insistence that the region's few Communist Party representatives be included in meetings rankled friend and foe alike.[16]

The echoes of the Kester argument were still reverberating in late March 1935, when Raleigh Crumbliss, a Chattanooga insurance agent, got wind that Highlander's staff was arranging a meeting in his town on April 14. As chairman of his American Legion post's Americanism Committee, Crumbliss, a civic-minded man, swung into action. He assembled fellow Legionnaires on April 6, afterwards telling reporters from the town's two newspapers, "During the war, the Germans were in uniform and we knew where to find them. In the present situation, we can't always locate the people back of these movements in America."[17] Here, though, Crumbliss had some clear targets, the eight men who had signed the conference call: James A. Dombrowski, director of Highlander Folk School; Lee Burns of the Bessemer, Alabama, Trades Council; Rev. Howard Kester, secretary of the Committee for Economic Justice, Nashville; Gaines T. Bradford, publisher of *The Birmingham World;* Rev. L.T. Baptiste, of Birmingham; H.L. Mitchell of Tyronza, Arkansas, head of the Southern Tenant Farmers' Union; Robert C. Wood, secretary of District 17, International Labor Defense Committee, Birmingham; and Myles Horton, education director at Highlander Folk School.[18]

Nearly two hundred delegates were expected from trade unions and religious and civic groups, including the Committee of Younger Churchmen, the Socialist and Communist parties, reform-minded Democrats, and the Interracial Commission headed by W.W. Alexander. Roger Baldwin of the American Civil Liberties Union was to be a featured speaker. The Chattanooga Odd Fellows had one of the few buildings in town large enough to hold a meeting of the size envisioned, and Dombrowski had a contract with them to use the space. Within hours after Crumbliss made his charges, the Odd Fellows canceled the agreement.[19] Dismayed, Dombrowski turned to

Bradford for help. As publisher of one of the South's most influential African-American newspapers, Bradford had contacts in virtually every southern community. He persuaded the Pythian Lodge of Chattanooga to let Highlander use their hall. Again Crumbliss attacked. The Pythians canceled. Ellen Krida wrote from New York, "I'm sorry to hear about your conference mess. . . . doesn't your being a Legionnaire have some value?"[20]

Dombrowski, who had joined the Willard Straight Post in New York City while at Union, acknowledged the irony but told her the Legion membership meant nothing. Concerned for Dombrowski's safety in the increasingly hostile city, she wrote on May 15, "Pretty hot stuff was handed out to you in print. Honey, is there any sympathy for you from any quarter down there? Isn't there some other place you could hold the conference of 'Reds'? Darling, I think you should change your name. It smacks too much of the Russian for these people's digestion."[21]

Dombrowski finally arranged to hold the meeting on May 26 in a room over the Villa DeLuxe beer garden. That Sunday morning dawned warm. Delegates began assembling over the beer hall about 10:30 a.m. Their numbers were reduced to barely a hundred as a result of the postponements and the fear aroused by the insurance salesman's allegations. They were settling into their seats when suddenly over fifty uniformed Legionnaires, some with sticks of dynamite and others with drawn pistols, charged up the stairwell into the hall. Crumbliss led the assault. A few city policemen and several local political figures followed the Legionnaire. They demanded that the delegates clear out immediately. Taken aback, Dombrowski and the other conveners huddled quickly, deciding to quit the place but to send their tormentors on a false chase. As the Legionnaires glared, the shaken delegates were told that the meeting would reconvene at a roadhouse in Summit, not far away. Directions were given. Privately, as delegates filed downstairs back into the sunny morning, the leaders whispered that they should head for Summit but to go instead to Highlander, not the roadhouse. Highlander, they figured, was a safe haven.

Fletcher Knebel, who later became a famous author, was a reporter for the *Chattanooga News* at the time. He covered the flight from Chattanooga. The Legionnaires, he wrote, were determined that the meeting wouldn't be held in Summit either.[22] Summit was in Hamilton County. They jettisoned their city police escort, located a half-dozen Hamilton County sheriff's deputies, and made a final stop at the city's Labor Hall to add reinforcements before boiling out onto the highway for Summit. The roadhouse was empty when they arrived. Some of the vigilantes, Knebel reported, "mulled about in the hot sun, questioned miscellaneous Negroes and laid worried plans for further quest."[23] Others reconnoitered surrounding roads. Innocently, Henry Sprinkle, a Methodist minister from Nashville, with three other persons in his car, late but heading for Chattanooga and the All-Southern Conference, stopped at the roadhouse when he spotted the crowd. The Reverend Mr. Sprinkle, who was secretary to the General Board of Christian Education, pulled his car up to the gathering and asked, "What's all the fuss about?"

"We're looking for Reds," replied Wiley Couch, a towering Hamilton County official.

"You mean the All-Southern Conference for Civil and Trade Union Rights?" asked Sprinkle, playing into their hands.

"Red is the word we use," Couch said.

"But what's the objection?" Sprinkle asked. "It's just a conference for . . ."

Couch reached inside the car and whacked the minister across the face, yelling, "Don't give me that!"[24] Sprinkle wasn't seriously hurt. Wisely, he drove off; his three passengers were African Americans.

The Legionnaires were getting ready to head back to Chattanooga when a second car stopped. The driver told them that a crowd of suspicious-looking people was gathering near Cleveland, Tennessee. Couch and five carloads of men headed for Cleveland, only to learn that the doubtful company was the graduating class of Bob Jones College, the fundamentalist Bible School, attending commencement exercises. The Red hunt ended for the day.

In the meantime, the ousted delegates, their number shrunk to seventy-five, reached Highlander. After a hastily prepared lunch, they took up the matters which had brought them together. Resolutions were debated and adopted: lynching must be outlawed; African Americans must be seated on grand juries; the Scottsboro defendants, still in Alabama jails, must be unconditionally released immediately; the rape convictions of two young farmers from Blytheville, Arkansas, must be reversed; charges of sabotage against six Burlington, North Carolina, textile workers and union leaders must be dismissed; charges of anarchy and battery against Rev. Claude C. Williams and Horace Bryan of Arkansas must be dismissed; a Florida union leader was told to stop breaking up efforts by tobacco stemmers to build a democratic union; the Federal Emergency Relief Administration was urged to release a grant to the Highlander Folk Cooperative; and, lastly, all anti-union legislation previously adopted or pending before southern legislative bodies must be repealed.[25]

Originally, Kester and Dombrowski had hoped to spawn a durable, united front organization as an antidote to the fearful violence raging across the South. The success of the Committee of Southern Churchmen had spurred their confidence. In this respect, the ill-fated conference failed; it was, however, one of the few attempts in the 1930s to form a united inter-racial coalition of southern political, religious, and labor organizations.

The American Legion's campaign against Highlander did not end in Summit. Later that summer, several hundred Legionnaires convened at a statewide rally in Monteagle. Speakers railed against the Communist men-ace to America. Again, Highlander's neighbors guarded the school.

Clearly, Highlander's ideological foes were increasing in number. Howard Kester was but one among many. Philosophical differences kept Commonwealth College in Mena, Arkansas, and the John C. Campbell Folk School in Brasstown, North Carolina, from productive collaboration with Highlander as either a labor college or a center nourishing cultural heritage. Although he taught at the Southern Summer School for Women Workers near Asheville, Dombrowski thought its program too academic.[26] Horton taught at several Southern Tenant Farmers' Union workshops and, during that organization's early days, worked closely with Mitchell. But a nasty argument between STFU leaders and Commonwealth College ended with lasting suspicion in that interracial organization of labor schools gen-erally. Mitchell and Horton clashed, leaving both embittered against each other throughout their lives.[27] Personality differences cut Highlander off from leaders emerging from the South's most successful interracial union organizing. Likewise, the STFU, always strapped for money, itself was un-able to develop an appropriate, sustained educational program, and it re-fused to use Highlander.

Kester's departure from the All-Southern Conference for Civil and Trade Union Rights furthered Highlander's reputation for cranky independence. Both Dombrowski and Horton were dogmatic in their belief in freedom of speech and association. The more they learned how to teach, at least at Highlander, the more important those democratic Constitutional princi-ples became. Unfettered discourse was the stuff of learning and their stu-dents had "boundless faith in the government's willingness and ability to assist in a struggle against a rich and powerful corporation."[28] Dombrowski would repeat over and over, to friend and foe, that Highlander's policy was to remain nonpartisan in fact and in spirit.

Dombrowski knew that, in early 1935, Communist Party policy had shifted from building unions such as the one in Gastonia toward building united fronts. He figured that any call for a united front against violence against unions and African Americans would be branded as Communist-inspired. He reasoned that the attacks would come from industrialists or trade associations. He hoped that historic differences between Socialists and Communists would not filter south, rupturing the unity needed if unions were to thrive and segregation was to be challenged. "I was willing then, and am willing now, to work with anyone who was going my way with a socialist philosophy," Dombrowski would reflect years later. "I believe Socialists and Communists can work together for a decent society. As far as the opposition is concerned, they don't make distinctions. In their minds, Socialists and Communists were Reds. Anyone working for social change was a Red."[29]

In the wake of the Chattanooga meeting, Dombrowski got a letter from Franz Daniel demonstrating exactly how heretical his views were. Daniel, since Union Seminary days one of Dombrowski's closest personal friends, had been beaten twice by Communist Party members for his Socialist views. He wrote Dombrowski a stinging letter from Knoxville, where he'd been organizing a suit factory:

> I'm returning the letter about the conference. Thanks for letting me see it. I'm afraid that it hasn't convinced me of the wisdom of such affairs. Liberals have no business messing in labor affairs until such time as labor is facing an actual problem—that it understands to be a problem, and then invites liberals' support. That can be the only basis for effective work. As it is you got a group of liberals run out of Chattanooga, you got the school in bad with the AF of L. You aren't in a position to do anything effective about defying fascist forces in Chattanooga—because you don't have and can't get mass labor support there. I'm afraid I think that the school played the C.P. game—that of 'social workers' coming into a labor situation from the outside and attempting to give leadership to the poor dear workers, who are too dumb to know what is good for them. I hope I'm wrong.[30]

Dombrowski was heartsick. Kester's departure had been a keen disappointment; Daniel's rebuke was a blow, causing Dombrowski to reconsider his almost obsessive opposition to sectarianism. He puzzled through the issue for weeks. In the end, however, nothing had happened to change his mind: collective action, not debate over political purity, generated genuine social change. For Dombrowski, the issue was not how to exclude, but how to include.

Had the clamor raised in 1935 by Egerton or the Legionnaires come a year earlier, Highlander might have been devastated.[31] The school had jelled, with no collective sense of purpose and no history of accomplishment. In the minds of many cautious southern liberals, Highlander was a fool's errand, precariously impermanent, with one foot in Summerfield and the other in Allardt. But in one sense, Egerton and the Legionnaires helped Highlander to forge its own agenda, giving it recognition among the poor and the persecuted as a school that would stand on principle. "People have to believe that you genuinely respect their ideas and that your involvement with them is not just an academic exercise," Horton said later.[32]

Lillian Johnson helped, too. She ended months of indecision in January 1935, writing to Dombrowski that she would deed the house and two hundred acres of land to the school. "I have made these last years a sort of test of your experiment," she said.[33] "Don't worry about the property because none of my family would contend any wish of mine and they know that I want it all for the good of the community." Her decision ended months of stressful speculation. The costly, physically draining operation at Allardt came to an end.

After Chattanooga, Dombrowski again turned to art as a means of returning himself to harmony with the world, as he had when events in Elizabethton and Gastonia unsettled him. He bought a box of watercolors, plunging for the first time into a medium other than pen or pencil. "I knew nothing about color but I went to work," he said later.

> My first paintings were really drawings in watercolor. The first was a thumbnail-sized—a tiny thing—of an amaryllis bud. The second was my own hands in my lap looking down toward the floor. That was quite realistic, too. Then I did a salad bowl and what I had around— onions, carrots and some apples. I did my fireplace with my cocker spaniel sprawled out in front of it. That was a semi-abstraction. They were simple studies and very primitive.[34]

Dombrowski started a rock garden near his cabin, which he wrote Ellen Krida about, hoping her own love of flowers would lure her South for the first time. As added inducement, he sent the watercolor of the amaryllis. Shortly, she wrote back:

> It's true, darling, that I am not happy in the present state of separation and indecision. However, I have never seen things as clearly as you, and still don't. While the love is apparent, the drawbacks to its fulfillment are likewise in evidence. I made a mental note of agreement with a sentence I heard someone utter recently—"That's the trouble with the labor group, they lose sense of proportion." You seem, dear, to be slipping so far away from the actual world in reference to your own life—our lives—more so than others even. Perhaps, I'm wrong, tho.
>
> I'm sad at the idea of your making a rock garden for some seemingly unappreciative gal. I'm sure its a dream and I'm anxious to look it over; perhaps, even yet, I may have an opportunity, that is, of course, if you can redeem me.[35]

Reared in an urbane if not a chivalrous society, Ellen was hardly prepared for a life in the Cumberland Mountains, much less the tumult of Highlander. She feared, based on the evidence before her, that living in New York City she saw Dombrowski as often as she might were she married to him and living at Summerfield. The demands of meetings, fundraising, and recruiting students were constant. He had hardly a free moment. There was danger sometimes and stress constantly. After a textile worker had been beaten to death in Harriman, Tennessee, she wrote to Dombrowski, who had been running a workshop there, "How are you standing the fray? Has anyone else been murdered yet? That killing has been on my mind nearly every minute with you in the midst of it."[36] Carrying out the routine administrative work required long hours. Visitors coming and going added to the responsibility. Horton fell ill again, this time contracting pneumonia. When Krida learned he was sick, she wrote with foreboding concern for Dombrowski: "I'm frightfully sorry to hear about Myles. He seemed like such a husky fellow . . . If that life wears out a good native, what is it going to do to you?"[37]

Ellen accepted Dombrowski's views and adored him for being "different," but his zealousness far outstripped her own. In a letter explaining why she had decided against visiting him in 1934, she said, "It is perfectly natural, and quite alright in the case of Z (Zilla Hawes), a rip-roaring socialist throwing everything into the hat for the cause. But I don't claim any such pretensions. I have only sympathies."[38] Too, as far as Krida could see, New York's theater, varied musical attractions, film, and tempting restaurants, all of which she greatly enjoyed, had no counterparts in Monteagle or Chattanooga. The folksinging, labor plays, and square dancing which filled recreational needs at Highlander failed to arouse her cultural interest. "I saw Gorky's 'Mother' at the Acme," she wrote.[39] "Do you have the book? Revolution of 1905. It was beautifully done—the stark brutality of those people—grand massed action—human emotions and marvelous photography. I was quite stirred. It was such a decidedly revolutionary thing tho. I marveled that it finally passed the censors. I so wished you might have seen it."

Dombrowski filled his letters with news about working people's winning union recognition or giving their first plays, or the rousing songfests after evening meals. "There is nothing here or anywhere to compare with your crazy tales," she wrote. "I'm bad, as you know, not to write more often, but there are no glamorous tales such as yours to enthuse about and you would hardly be interested in the everyday pettiness that surrounds me."[40]

In Schenectedy, life at Krida's sister's home was dominated by her brother-in-law's talk of the stock market, his opposition to the Roosevelt administration, or his friends' influence on the city's political life. By loving Dombrowski, Krida risked being repudiated by her own family. She gave up trying to explain Dombrowski or what he was doing. Her relatives were unable to fathom why a man trained for the ministry would be working for board and room at a school which seemed constantly threatened. Dombrowski arranged one fundraising trip annually to New York, usually while Krida was there. His visits would be preceded by eager anticipatory letters planning every minute together. When he left, her letters would be touching but recriminating. "Retribution and remorse for mein kleiner Jimmie—what a mix I have been. . . . It's a strange house with only half of me in it. I'm beginning to look around all the corners for the rest of me."[41]

Krida had no job to occupy her, and apparently wanted none. She attended Russell Sage College almost as a matter of family duty. No intellectual curiosity sparked her interest. Her brother Arthur, prospering as an orthopedic surgeon, frequently scolded Krida for not finding employment. He supported her, nevertheless, hoping she would take an interest in someone other than Dombrowski, who "utterly failed," in his view, as a prospective husband for his sister.[42] Her family insisted that appearances and

Ellen Krida on vacation with Dombrowski, 1938. Frank T. Adams Collection.

standards of propriety be maintained. In 1934, as Krida vacillated over a decision to go south for a visit, she wrote:

> Darling, your letters are becoming increasingly impatient and I am be-
> coming increasingly doubtful. You know, my dear, how much I want to
> be with you and see for myself just what you are doing. But there are
> several considerations jeopardizing my best plans. One is that my sister
> is rather unhappy at what seems to her a cheerless prospect ahead of

me. And as for going down on this jaunt and living in that vague fashion unchaperoned, it is distasteful to her. And, of course, it might be questionable to any average person outside your own group. And while I don't apparently appear to, I do have lots of regard for my family.[43]

Dombrowski had hoped to go north in May 1935. Events in Chattanooga precluded that trip. Krida, disappointed, wrote, "I realized you were needed there but all things are possible. . . . There are no recriminations at this late date but I've been so tremendously let down. . . . About marriage, tho, darling, I am no nearer a solution of that problem. And you seem to be burying yourself contentedly within the glories of nature and that spot. I'm afraid for you—you're getting too far away in another world."[44]

Behind Dombrowski's cabin, through woods, the mountain plateau Highlander rested on suddenly dropped into a Cumberland valley. Many evenings, after work in Highlander's office or after classes, Dombrowski headed to the cliff's edge to relax in solitude. He planted daffodils along the path to the cliff. Sometimes he would cook a meal there. Increasingly, the natural beauty of his surroundings and the fulfillment he experienced in his work imparted an aura of contentment unlike any he had experienced. Dombrowski was growing away from any possibility of a return to a traditional academic career. He found peace in his cabin's simplicity, in the quiet at the cliff, and with his watercolors or rock garden. For the first time in his adult life, Dombrowski felt at home, easy and supremely happy. Only Krida's companionship would have improved his lot. His contentment caused no little trepidation for Krida. Obviously, he was not on a lark which would soon end. Twice, at the last moment, she canceled plans to visit Tennessee. Each time her family intervened, insisting that she not go. Dombrowski's patience with them grew thin.

Their views prevailed until August 1935; then Krida wired Dombrowski to meet her in Knoxville. The couple drove from Knoxville to Allardt first. Dombrowski wanted her to meet the Stocktons, and to see the old farmhouse. It was even more weathered than his description. Joe Kelly Stockton, brusque, barrel-chested, and in galloused overalls, greeted Dombrowski and Krida equally with crushing hugs. Kate Bradford, or "Madam," as Stockton called his wife, read Krida poetry she had written on birth control, on Socialism, and on life in the country. She sang ballads which had been handed down through generations of her Cumberland Mountain family. She planned to run for governor of Tennessee in the 1936 election campaign.

Krida stayed for six weeks, seeing the people and the sights which had become Dombrowski's life. She loved his cabin and worked in the rock garden, determined to leave her mark. The nights had turned decidedly cool when Krida in late October left for Schenectedy. Her spirits were high, expecting Dombrowski to spend Christmas with her in New York. On November 5, safely home, she wrote, "I've hardly unpacked my bags and packing is again on my mind. . . . I'm expected to be in New York by December 7. But I'm getting impatient to see you so, please don't tarry, my dear."[45]

Dombrowski did not spend the Christmas holidays with Krida. The long hours demanded at Highlander and the Cumberland's piercing cold laid him low with a vexatious cough. By mid-November, doctors, fearing he might develop pneumonia, ordered him to Florida to rest. Remembering how suddenly his robust father had died, he agreed, arranging with sister Daisy to stay at her home. Rose lived in Tampa, too; there would be a family reunion, the first since 1929.

Tampa, he learned, was no longer the charming small town he had left after World War I. By 1935, the city's population was 100,000. Many citizens earned a living shipping citrus or phosphates through the thriving port. The cigar industry had grown, and now made world-renowned tobacco products.

Tampa had a new, thriving business, too—*bolita,* an illegal numbers game taking in over one million dollars monthly and employing nearly a thousand persons, according to estimates in a Junior Chamber of Commerce report.[46] Some local authorities were on the take, according to the Jaycees. Political campaigns had become bloody fights between rival factions hoping to control and profit from *bolita.* On election day in fall 1935, fifty persons were arrested for stuffing ballot boxes. Two men were wounded with gunshot. The incumbent was re-elected. Tampa was regaining its civic composure when Dombrowski arrived to rest and to enjoy a visit with his sisters.

On November 30, police, without warrants, raided a private home and seized six men who called themselves Modern Democrats. They had formed an interracial political party after the September primary, and had run an unsuccessful slate of candidates in the November general election. The Modern Democrats advocated Socialist ideas. Four of the six were members of the Socialist Party.[47] They were questioned briefly at police headquarters that night about their alleged "Communist activities" and their views on "racial equality."[48] Then police released them. Outside police headquarters, three of the men, Joseph Shoemaker, Eugene F. Poulnot, and Sam Rogers, were greeted by a gang of men who ordered them into waiting cars. They were driven to woods outside Tampa, stripped naked, brutally flogged, then tarred and feathered. Their tormentors left the bloody men with the warning "to get out of town in twenty-four hours or we'll kill you."[49] Hours later, Poulnot and Rogers were able to make their way for help. Shoemaker had been beaten until he collapsed unconscious. His friends left him "under a tree, where the dew would not be so cold."[50] His brother and other friends found him the next morning, mutilated and partially paralyzed. He was taken to Centro Español Hospital, where doctors amputated one leg in a vain attempt to save his life. Nine days later, Shoemaker died.

Tampa's attention was fixed on the political murder and floggings. The newspapers were full of the story. Dombrowski, his sisters, and their families talked of little else. Daisy and Rose were dismayed by the violence but said little else to indicate their political leanings. Their husbands, however, declared that the Modern Democrats had gotten what was coming to them as Socialist agitators. Dombrowski moved to the YMCA.

Dombrowski telephoned Mary Fox at the League for Industrial Democracy in New York City to alert that organization. She told him that other Florida Socialists had made similar calls. Norman Thomas was sending telegrams to Tampa's mayor and the Hillsborough County sheriff demanding a full investigation. She told him that Frank McCallister, southern director of the Worker's Defense League, was en route to Tampa from Atlanta. She asked Dombrowski to work with McCallister setting up a defense committee. On the back of a letter he'd received from Zilla Hawes with news of Highlander, Dombrowski, in his cribbed handwriting, listed individuals and church leaders he felt might form a local defense committee. Through his contacts, McAllister was introduced to religious and civic leaders who proved helpful. A defense fund was started and a support letter campaign organized.[51]

A memorial service for Shoemaker at the municipal auditorium attracted one thousand persons. The Reverend Walter Metcalf, pastor at the First Congregational Church, told the audience, "These victims did not like the looks of our infamous primary election with hundreds of armed men at the polls. They did not like to think of nearly half the population of Tampa on relief rolls. Such men were branded as 'Reds.'"[52]

The Shoemaker case, as the crime came to be known, made news long after Dombrowski returned to Highlander late in January. The *New Republic* reported on the floggings. The American Civil Liberties Union posted a one-thousand-dollar reward for the arrest and conviction of the perpetrators. Eventually, five policemen were arrested and charged with premeditated murder; later the charges were amended to include kidnapping and assault. The trial of the policemen opened in March 1936. For six weeks a jury heard prosecution testimony. The prosecutor appealed for a conviction, saying it would signal that freedom of speech and assembly would be guaranteed in Tampa. The defense attacked Poulnot's credibility, charging that the real issue in the trial was the Communist threat to Anglo-Saxon civilization. Defense lawyers rested their case after twenty-seven minutes.[53] The jury deliberated less than three hours before returning a guilty verdict, a surprise to most observers. The policemen were sentenced to four years in prison. They appealed, and eventually the state Supreme Court overturned their convictions on technicalities. They were tried again, but the second jury found them not guilty.

And Dombrowski? Did Tampa hold any further lessons for its native son? Class and race, his preoccupations since early manhood there, had proven to be insurmountable barriers between Dombrowski and his kin. Either issue, class or race, in and of itself, upset his sisters and alarmed their husbands; when the two issues were joined, as they were by the Modern Democrats, family harmony disintegrated. Hearing Dombrowski in their own homes question accepted truths, no matter how dispassionately, was beyond their tolerance. He understood their views, but his understanding made the estrangement was no less painful. Dombrowski longed for the intimacy of a family. But he also remembered Rose's reaction to the news of his arrest in Elizabethton, and her angry exchange with the Tampa newspaper editor. Dombrowski knew there would be no escaping allegations of Communist meddling so long as he or anyone else persisted in linking the issues of class and race. Such a connection was antithetical to the American way of life. Tampa convinced him, too, that both political and moral force had to be applied if change were to be secured. One without the other was not sufficient. The All-Southern Conference for Civil and Trade Union Rights failed, in part, Dombrowski believed, because of Kester's angry departure. In Tampa, however, when Socialists and Christians united, some measure of justice had been secured.

Ideology, fear, homesickness, estrangement, discouragement, the need to make a living, threats, blacklists, violence—all were good reasons why reformers, one after another, abandoned the path Dombrowski walked. Tampa, during the winter of 1935, deepened his resolve to struggle with the questions which first had surfaced for him there years earlier.

# 7

## Growing Acclaim, Growing Trouble

Between 1935 and 1940, while the Great Depression continued without letup, Highlander was making its mark both as a source of competent union leadership and as a waystation for controversy. The school's staff, and especially Dombrowski as "the Skipper," was dosed regularly with praise or calumny, welcome or ostracism; one day staffers might celebrate students' accomplishments and the next brace themselves for retaliation.

On May 2, 1938, a zenith of sorts was reached. Eleanor Roosevelt invited guests to the White House for a private screening of *People of the Cumberlands*, a film about coal miners fighting for a union and a decent life, a fictional depiction of the cruel strike at Wilder, Tennessee, of Highlander's role, and of the New Deal. The president's wife was visibly angered by the events depicted.[1] Afterward, Highlander's Ralph Tefferteller and four Smoky Mountain musician friends—Long John Trentham on fiddle, Ashley Moore on banjo, Harvey Oakley on guitar, Sam Maples on ukelele, with Tefferteller filling in as needed on banjo or fiddle—furnished a program of folk music and square dancing. Between songs, Harvey Oakley's father Wiley enthralled the audience with folk stories, outrageous tales, or plain lies.

The entire production had been midwifed by Dombrowski, still a fundraiser as he had been earlier for Emory but now one with serious political purpose. He had recruited Elia Kazan to write and film the movie; persuaded Ethel Clyde to underwrite its costs; and, finally, through Highlander's growing number of friends within the Roosevelt administration, many of them southerners, arranged the White House showing.

The night before, *People of the Cumberlands* had premiered at the New School for Social Research in New York City to an equally enthusiastic audience. Among the intellectual *avant garde* attending were Leo Huberman and Max Lerner, both influential promoters of workers' causes. Both declared the film a cinematic first, an authentic made-in-America proletarian movie. The Highlander Folk School was gaining in appreciation among the nation's many-hued Socialists.[2] Elsewhere the movie played to mixed reviews.

Militant unionism had been revived during the mid-1930s by the Great Depression.[3] Strikes and vigorous organizing in mass production industries, and especially in the coalfields, steel mills, and auto factories, enjoyed widespread public support, forcing the Roosevelt administration and Congress to produce the Wagner Act, the Fair Labor Standards Act, the Social Security Act. The turnout for elections in 1936 was 65 percent larger than that in 1924. Millions of voters pushed a Progressive reorientation of the Democratic Party, especially in many northern cities where recent immigrants and African Americans were organizing politically.

During the 1920s, many labor unions, following the lead of the American Federation of Labor, had spurned the idea of a political party for labor and had limited labor's role in politics. By 1933, union membership had shrunk to 7 percent of the nonfarm workforce, and interest in a labor party rose within the unions.[4] Many unions were actively involved in city or state politics. The Congress of Industrial Unions, organized in 1936, gave its political support to Franklin Roosevelt, putting an end to talk of a third political party; American labor reached a short-lived political high point.

Dombrowski was in fine spirits after the successful evenings in New York and Washington. He believed that the film would continuously bring favorable attention to Highlander. And he was certain that having friends in the White House would pay off in terms of both donations and powerful political connections.

In Grundy County, where Dombrowski headed after the film showings, a union-based political campaign was hitting its rambunctious stride. A coalition of Grundy County unions was running candidates for three key local offices. Leaders in the Works Progress Administration locals—

birthed at Highlander—had taken charge of the political campaign. The primary was less than a month off when Dombrowski got back. The coalition called itself Labor's Political Conference and was an outgrowth of organizing by Dolph Vaughn, a Grundy County coal miner who had been blacklisted in 1925 when he joined a strike against Tennessee Coal and Iron. The business, a subsidiary of United States Steel Company, was Grundy County's largest employer. Vaughn came to Highlander in 1934 asking if they had a class on "how to organize a union."[5]

Vaughn had a WPA job, one in which he felt he needed labor's voice. He told Dombrowski that safety regulations were ignored, wages were not paid uniformly, foremen bullied workers, and if workers got mad, they were fired immediately. "I figure we need a union," he told Dombrowski, "but we need the $19.20 they pay us every month, too."[6] Dombrowski got a copy of the WPA's regulations through friends in Washington, including its safety and administration guidelines. He and Vaughn learned how the WPA was supposed to operate, and the ex-miner was soon on Highlander's payroll. Throughout 1935 and 1936, Vaughn brought small groups of WPA workers to Highlander.

At first, the going was slow, even though Vaughn had discovered that nearly every Grundy County WPA worker was being paid unskilled wages for jobs classified as skilled. The fear of being fired for "talkin' union" was widespread, and the need for any available income, even shortchanged wages, was real and present. Vaughn's efforts got an unexpected boost, however, when a Nashville citizen's improvement group, the Tennessee Taxpayers Association, reported after careful study that Grundy County's government was corrupt.[7]

Vaughn, Dombrowski, and Tefferteller redoubled their efforts, bringing WPA workers to Highlander to hear about the report and to discuss their ideas for correcting the political situation. WPA workers soon voted to affiliate with the International Hod Carriers and the Builders and Common Laborers' Union of America. Vaughn was elected business agent. One local won the right to elect timekeepers and supervisors, and to rotate all higher-paying jobs. Within days, county WPA officials reclassified every job from unskilled to skilled.

Vaughn's accomplishments caught the attention of the director of the WPA regional office in Nashville, Col. Harry S. Berry.[8] At first union grievances were ignored; but before long, Grundy County's WPA administration began an all-out counterattack. Projects employing nonunion workers were given overtime. At union work sites, hours were cut. Union men were laid off without explanation. Supervisors started ribbing Vaughn for not protecting union jobs. Union membership dropped. By winter 1937, Vaughn and Dombrowski watched the gains of nearly two years slipping away. Word spread through the county that the union was done for.[9]

On February 6, 1937, the union was dealt another blow. In a story headlined "Folk School is Held 'Immoral,' Dangerous," the *Chattanooga News* reported that the chairman of Chattanooga's American Legion Americanization Committee, Lyle C. Stovall, had evidence that Highlander was an "immoral and dangerous institution" and a Communist front.[10] Stovall said folk-school classes opened with "students singing the Communist 'Internationale'." Stovall said that the Tennessee State Highway Patrol had investigated Highlander and had given him their evidence.

Dombrowski telephoned highway patrol officials in Grundy County and Nashville, who denied knowing of any investigation. Trying to limit the damage, he kept the telephone wires hot, calling several dozen supporters, including Alva Taylor and John Dewey, and urging them to write strong protests to the newspaper. Taking another tack, he asked several dozen other prominent persons, including Reinhold Niebuhr and Norman Thomas, to write letters supporting Highlander to the newspaper's competition, the *Chattanooga Free Press*.

In Grundy County, Dombrowski and Vaughn got a petition drive going. Over four hundred persons signed, demonstrating, Dombrowski felt, proof of the school's worth to its neighbors. Nevertheless, the Red-baiting article, along with similar reporting which followed, caused the union to lose members; some kept their union affiliation but stayed away from Vaughn and Highlander. The campaign consumed hours Dombrowski needed to devote to growing administrative chores.

In the meantime, more union men were laid off. Vaughn watched helplessly. In March, at his urging, the remaining members voted to strike nine of the fifteen WPA projects, demanding that no other union man be laid off and that the county's WPA administrator be replaced by someone "more honest and more human."[11] To dramatize the strike and to secure publicity, they wired President Roosevelt, who was vacationing in Warm Springs, Georgia:

A man died a few days ago of starvation. The doctor said after an examination that he had never seen a man with less in his stomach. Scores of families in these mountains are in similar condition. We are desperate men forgotten in these mountains. For weeks we have attempted by every peaceful means to show the WPA district administrators we want to deal with this situation without violence, but it is difficult to restrain hungry men when they see WPA funds squandered illegally by officials.[12]

The next day in Nashville, Colonel Berry called a news conference, telling reporters, "A communistic organization has for months been feeding muscovite hops to relief clients in Grundy County."[13] He defended the county's WPA officials, saying job classifications and pay scales were fixed in Washington. WPA officials from Washington were sent to Grundy County. Some irregularities were corrected; the union members won reclassifications and pay increases. Interest in the union revived, and by spring 1938 Vaughn had eleven locals functioning.

Vaughn had no trouble organizing Labor's Political Coalition. Urging workers to vote, he argued that they had enough votes to take control of the county's political apparatus. On June 4, 1938, over 1,700 citizens turned out for the Democratic Party primary, an unusually large vote. Union members barely nominated Charles Adams, Jim Fults, and Bob Crouch for road commissioners, the board which controlled WPA funds. By a wider margin, 964 to 769, they nominated Roy Thomas, who had run once unsuccessfully for sheriff. J. Lewis Rollins was nominated for school superintendent. If the union slate won in the August 4 general election, then, in theory, union members would have representative control over their jobs, the county's law enforcement, and the public schools.[14] Over 80 percent of the county's population depended on the WPA for work or was on relief.

Before the primary vote count was complete, Phil McGovern, who opposed Thomas for sheriff, declared himself an independent and vowed to "run against the Reds in Monteagle" who had engineered the union slate's victory.[15] Between the primary and general election, McGovern contested Thomas for every vote. County officials refused to let the union hold rallies in the courthouse. But voters turned out in record numbers; the union coalition held. Thomas and the other union-backed candidates won. Candidates for governor and the U.S. Congress who were backed by the Labor's Political Conference won neatly, too.

The next day, Dombrowski wrote to Ethel Clyde, "In Tracy City last night there was considerable joking as the returns were marked on a bulletin board. 'How do you like them red votes?' Roy would ask. It was thought the 'red scare' raised by McGovern cost Roy some votes in the districts where neither he nor the school was known. The WPA workers and miners were feeling cocky."[16]

History was not on their side. That much Dombrowski knew. He had won a prestigious Rosenwald Fellowship to record the oral history of Grundy County during the coalfield wars. Julius Rosenwald, head of Sears, Roebuck and Company of Chicago, gave some of his considerable wealth to improve the lot of workers, particularly African Americans and Appalachians. The $1,500 Rosenwald award paid Dombrowski's Highlander wage. His research had revealed that the county's working class never had had much time to cheer a victory, or many victories to savor. Tennessee Coal and Iron Company dominated the county, running it in its own interest. Eventually, his research became a book-length labor history manuscript titled "Fire in the Hole."[17] Longtime Grundy citizens told Dombrowski how the militant but secretive Knights of Labor had challenged Tennessee Coal and Iron in 1871, and how the company had broken that show of resistance. Miners struck to protest low wages and intolerable working conditions. The coal company, rather than negotiate with the Knights of Labor, convinced Tennessee lawmakers to lease convicts to it as strikebreakers. Dombrowski found company records, newspaper clippings in Nashville, Chattanooga, and Tracy City which confirmed their memories.[18] The convicts worked from sunup to sunset six days weekly. They were paid twenty-four and a half cents daily. Free men were used parttime, if at all, and paid two cents a bushel for coal dug and hauled to the tipple. A willing, strong man could earn as much as $2.50 daily. Convict and free alike worked in ill-vented, dark, wet shafts, often in water up to their waists, picking coal from seams which sometimes were no more than eighteen inches wide.

Coal mine operators quickly adopted convict leasing, as the practice spread from Grundy throughout East Tennessee and into Alabama. Convicts were plentiful, the supply endless. Their wages and upkeep were low. There was no reason to fear union organizers. Countless "free" miners were thrown out of work throughout the Appalachian coalfields.

Among the several dozen persons whom Dombrowski interviewed were men and women who had lived near the company's first stockade. One said he'd seen men being whipped until the flesh sloughed off their backs and hips in hand-sized pieces. Another told him:

> Me and a widow woman used to carry pies to the stockade and sell 'em to the convicts. They were treated cruelly. With my own eyes I saw where they wus buried. Their thighs or shank bones were not buried deep enough or something. They used to stick out of the ground. They used to cry out to my daddy to let 'em out. The lice and the chinch bugs were eatin' 'em up. Convicts would be punished for not gettin' their tasks. The warden and the deputy warden would do the whippin'. The whippin' wus done with a two-ply strap as wide as your three fingers, tied to a staff. The convicts wus face down with their pants off. They wus whipped on the hips and legs five to twelve lashes. Ordinary offenses wus punished with a few lashes.[19]

In 1891, miners around Briceville, Tennessee, fed up watching their families starve, seized the convict stockade, burned it to the ground, and set the inmates on a train to Knoxville. Similar revolts quickly followed, and a running gunbattle raged throughout the Cumberlands among state militia, coal company gunmen, and the miners. The revolt hit Grundy on August 13, 1892. Over 150 armed miners marched on Tennessee Coal and Iron's grim stockade. They quickly seized control of the mine, then sent representatives to the company demanding employment on equal terms with the convicts. Company officers refused to talk. Miners then loaded convicts on a train, sending it to Nashville. They burned the stockade to the ground. In response, Tennessee's governor immediately posted militia to Grundy County, promising to send "fifty thousand troops if the sheriff asked."[20] Many convicts were recaptured. Under watchful militia, they rebuilt the stockade. Others, however, along with fugitive miners, hidden by friends or relatives, eluded militia posses. A granddaughter of Basil Summers, the pioneer who gave the Grundy County community of Summerfield its name, told Dombrowski, "I fed men right off my table without seeing a face. Miners were lying out in the woods hunted by the company. I called 'em to the table by a white flag run up on the fence. I fed eight to ten men a day that way."[21] Meanwhile, Grundy's miners secretly drilled for another raid on the rebuilt stockade. They attacked on the night of April 19, 1893. Fearful of being recognized, the miners threw coats over their heads and blackened their faces with gunpowder. One participant described the raid to Dombrowski only after being assured of anonymity. Despite the years that had passed, he feared that the company would learn he had been a raider:

I knew there would be killing that night. Good heavens and earth. There was about twenty shot and Bob Erwin was killed. Shot from the left-hand corner of the stockade. I shot a guard. Put a load of number three buckshot through the boxwood, and some of it caught him right here between the eyes. He did not die. We had two boxes of dynamite planted under the corner of the office building on the corner of the stockade. But a heavy rain come up and we could not get it to go off. We used up two boxes of matches.[22]

The miners withdrew about 3:00 a.m. with heavier than expected casualties, the assault frustrated. At dawn the militia arrived from Nashville. Again the coal company prevailed. However, three years later, when Tennessee Coal and Iron's contract with the state expired in 1896, state officials, aware of intense, widespread sentiment against the convict leasing system, refused to renew the contract. For twenty-five often-bloody years, Grundy miners had competed with slavery. The strength of the Knights of Labor gradually diminished as miners replaced convicts. Emboldened, the coal company first cut wages, then opened a company commissary, or what the miners called the "pluckme." Workers got paid in script good only at the commissary. In 1898, the United Mine Workers organized a local in Grundy County, which represented miners until Tennessee Coal and Iron won an injunction against it during a strike in 1905. A second UMW local formed in 1917. Seven years later, the company broke that local too, using a lockout and blacklist. Dolph Vaughn's name was on that list. In 1933, just before Highlander opened its doors, Grundy miners for a third time organized a UMW local. While its strength had grown in proportion to the WPA workers' militancy, both unions maintained only fragile opposition to the powerful coal company.

Dombrowski considered this history during the celebration of the labor coalition's election sweep. He feared that the victory might be hollow, its results shortlived. Nevertheless, he savored the moment and hoped. Apprehension had little time to foster paranoia. On August 20, 1938, Horton attended a meeting of miners' wives in Coalmont, near Tracy City. The night before, he learned, *People of the Cumberlands* had been shown at the Dixie Theater as a part of the union auxiliary fund drive. Friends of the coal company were in the audience. They demanded that the manager stop the film. Angry miners' wives insisted the movie continue. A fistfight was narrowly averted. Eventually the movie was shown, but the fundraiser was a bust.[23]

Six weeks later, as the sourwood and black gum trees reached their vivid October hues, Roy Thomas was sworn into office as sheriff. Within days, the State of Tennessee, acting at the request of the Grundy County clerk of court, cut the new sheriff's annual salary from $800 to $600. An allowance for gasoline that was customarily an additional part of the sheriff's funds was eliminated. He was given no money to hire deputies.[24]

Next the road commissioners came under attack. Federal WPA guidelines stipulated that local road commissioners administer all WPA funds. After the union-backed commissioners were sworn into office, the regional WPA office, still headed by Colonel Berry, stopped all funds. The newly elected commissioners weren't paid; instead, the ousted commissioners stayed on the payroll. Officials in Washington were notified. Their investigation took weeks and came to nothing. In the meanwhile, Berry ordered the locks on Grundy County WPA equipment sheds replaced. He vowed to end every WPA job in Grundy if the new commissioners didn't resign. "The highway commission (has) attempted to build roads by the hammer and sickle rather than pick and shovel," he declared.[25]

Thomas stayed on as sheriff. Adams, Fults, and Crouch refused to quit. By January 1939, all WPA jobs under their control had been terminated. Berry ordered nonunion men from outside the county to be trucked in for work. On January 28, unemployed WPA workers marched into Tracy City to hear Paul Christopher, a leader of the Textile Workers Organizing Committee who was coming to prominence as a Tennessee labor leader. He defended labor's right to back political candidates and lauded the Highlander staff for its role in the election effort. "Only Hitler would try to force elected representatives of the people out of office," he told a cheering crowd.[26]

Two days later, despite a cold rain, miners and their families streamed into Tracy City, filling the courthouse and occupying the WPA office. By noon over seven hundred persons, many of whom had not eaten for days, filled both buildings. A relief committee was organized to canvass merchants for food or cash to buy food. Another committee was selected to maintain order. Pleas were sent to WPA officials in Washington. Newspaper reporters were notified.

By late afternoon enough food had been collected for an evening meal. One merchant gave a second-hand, six-burner kerosene stove. "Tonight,"

Dombrowski wrote in his journal, "a stew will be our first meal. The people are hungry. It is pouring down rain but they are not complaining."[27] Dombrowski brought Highlander's mimeograph machine to the occupied buildings to produce a daily newssheet called "We, the people." Highlander's residential term students reported, printed, and circulated the newssheet.

The largest workers' term in Highlander's experience opened on January 10. Thirty-five students sponsored by union locals throughout the South were learning firsthand from Highlander's neighbors about labor and politics. The students organized daily discussion groups on union rights, economic problems, and the worsening world situation. After the spare evening meals, fiddling contests or songfests were held. Every night, the crowds sang "We Shall Not Be Moved;" it was everyone's favorite. As Sunday approached, Highlander's residential students helped arrange church services for the protesters. Three ministers agreed to speak after holding services in their own churches. The first minister came and went without event. A second, never identified in Dombrowski's notes, rose and, without a line of scripture to preface his remarks, attacked communism, a subject no-one had mentioned.

"Do you mean to tell me if I make a little more than the other man that I don't have the right to spend it?" he asked the near penniless crowd. "Do you tell me you are going to make me equal to everyone else?"

He was interrupted and put on the spot by one of the workers. "What do you mean by communism?" the worker asked. He hemmed and hawed. "Webster says it's equality in production," the worker continued. The preacher was plainly ill at ease. He was used to laying down the law and the truth without retort.

"Do you think it's wrong to feed hungry people?" another worker shouted. "Read the signs," someone shouted. "That's what we want. Our children are starving. We want bread. We demand jobs. Read the signs."

He tries to leave, becoming very ill at ease before these angry, hungry men who did not act like his obedient flock on Sunday morning. "Let 'em go back to Italy or Russia!," he shouts, trying to leave.

The preacher makes it to the door. A fiery textile worker rises to speak. Words pour forth. "If you had hungry children, if you did not know where your next meal was coming from, you would know what we want. Christ said let everyone come together in one organization to help one another. I don't know what the organization here is called, but we're trying to help each other."

The preacher tries to get a word in . . . he holds out $2.60. "That's all the money in the world I got," he said. "If anyone is hungry, I'll share it with him!"

"We don't want your money! We want jobs!" chorused the people. The preacher fled. The crowd cheered and stomped the floor.[28]

Memories of Elizabethton and Gastonia rushed into Dombrowski's consciousness. His earlier, similar embarrassment drowned out the tumult around him. He understood the minister's confusion, having traveled the same charitable road himself. Church services ended.

Nels Anderson, director of WPA's Labor Relations office in Washington, arrived in Tracy City to begin negotiations between the unemployed and Berry. By February 21, he had worked out a compromise, and at dusk that evening the occupation of the WPA offices and courthouse ended. The union men got their jobs back. Berry promised Anderson that no-one would be laid off in retaliation. In return, however, Berry and not the road commissioners was to control what the WPA did in Grundy County.[29]

Anderson went back to Washington. Almost immediately, union men were laid off, two and three at a time. By April, nearly every union man had been fired. By summer's end, Labor's Political Conference had disbanded, signaling that workers had lost yet another battle for political and economic control. Again starvation became a real possibility for many people, especially the elderly. During one meeting which Dombrowski recorded, a desperately angry WPA worker said,

The first question is food. What do they give out for commodities? A pound of butter, a 10-cent can of milk, 10 cents worth of dried fruit, 25 cents worth of greens to a family of ten for one month's rations! I got a feist dog that kin eat that and still go hungry.

I been here longer than anyone in this room. In the convict days we went along for a few years and finally we give 'em a good fight. We burned the stockade and turned the convicts loose. Then things got better. We need food. The first thing is to stop our children cryin' for bread.[30]

Highlander, no less than its neighbors, was financially pressed. Time Dombrowski spent on county politics could not be spent raising funds or recruiting unions to send paying students. Revenue dropped sharply that winter and spring. Dombrowski realized that his temper had gotten short; he was exhausted by the ceaseless Grundy County political fight.

Even with a growing list of prestigious northern contributors, including Eleanor Roosevelt, Dombrowski worried if he'd find money to run the school into the fall. Rations for Highlander's students and staff, as for their neighbors, got scarce. Eventually Highlander's 1939 income reached $14,000, about $1,600 below operating expenses.

There were other problems. At 42, Dombrowski was questioning his future. For the first time, long days sapped his strength. Sharp aches in his knees and hips were diagnosed as arthritis; doctors predicted that the disease might cripple him. He was no longer thin and dashing. His hairline was receding. He and Krida remained in love but at odds, unwilling to compromise their lifestyles. On April 15, 1939, as the WPA compromise was falling to pieces, Dombrowski was resting before cooking his supper. His back was hurting. His mood was somber. Horton knocked on the door of his cabin.[31]

With him was an agent from the Federal Bureau of Investigation (FBI), Richard Barker, who showed Dombrowski his credentials, as he had Horton minutes earlier. He was an investigator for the Dies Committee. Martin Dies, a Democrat from Texas, as chair of the House Special Committee on Un-American Activities (HUAC), had made headlines on Thanksgiving Day, 1938, with allegations that leading New Deal figures, including Frances Perkins, Harold Ickes, and Harry Hopkins, were purveyors of class hatred. Barker wanted to know if Highlander got money from the Communist Party, or if the school was directly or indirectly connected with the Communist Party. Evidently he had spent considerable time on the case and was thoroughly familiar with the staff. He had been in Hardin County and seen Horton's birthplace, a log cabin. He had questions about Zilla Hawes Daniel and Franz Daniel and wanted to know if students "were taught how to strike." He asked to see Highlander's list of contributors. "We said it was quite a job but would attempt it," Dombrowski recalled.[32] Strategically, he and Horton agreed that to be less than forthcoming would only feed rumors about Communist subversion and might even spark new attacks by local vigilante groups. They assumed that the Roosevelt administration could be counted on to check any constitutional transgression by HUAC. Their fears focused on Grundy County, not Washington. The school had nothing to hide. Barker spent most of the next morning making notes from the list of nearly six hundred names. Before leaving, the agent bought a copy of Dombrowski's book, *The Early Days of Christian Social-ism in America,* asking for the author's autograph, and then said, "I want to congratulate you—or rather—compliment you on the frankness you have shown. You have been more than cordial. It is very unusual. This is the first time I have been given access to the books, for example. I appreciate it."

What exactly he reported to superiors in Washington may never be known. The file maintained by the FBI on Dombrowski contained no rec-ord of Barker's visit. However, Dies announced in the spring of 1940 that his committee had been probing radical activities in the South and that he had a large amount of material on Highlander.[34]

Dombrowski and Horton suspected that Tennessee Coal and Iron was behind the Dies investigation. Some company officials saw the election of Roy Thomas and other prounion officials as "the Folk School's first move in overthrowing the government of Grundy County."[35] In August 1940, Thomas was up for re-election. The First National Bank of Tracy City fig-ured in their suspicions. Eleanor Roosevelt had given Highlander one hun-dred dollars to fund a scholarship for deserving union students. Barker had gotten a photostat copy of her check from the bank's cashier, Alvin Hen-derson. Carl Roberts, president of the bank, was also secretary of the coal company. C.H. Kilby, secretary to the coal company's vice president and the company's chief bookkeeper, had written to Dies, asking him to inves-tigate the school.[36]

Another federal agency, however, the U.S. Treasury Department, gave Highlander's financial future a lift that spring. Dombrowski had applied to the Internal Revenue Service (IRS) to grant Highlander status as an exempt organization, an indirect subsidy that had become essential for the school's financial survival. Donors could deduct their gifts on their income tax re-turns. Dombrowski had sought the IRS ruling for months. That approval came in May 1937. But his second long-range effort to build a financial base did not fare as well.

Dombrowski had persuaded the staff to form an association of "gradu-ates." On the surface, the numbers were impressive. Between 1932 and 1939, over 400 persons had attended residential terms. More than 90 per-cent of them were union members, and almost as many were from the South. Another 1,800 persons had attended special institutes, and nearly 5,000 had enrolled in extension courses held throughout the South. Six for-mer students had been elected local presidents. Several had responsible jobs as staff in the growing number of union education programs. Twenty or more were union organizers.

Dombrowski kept careful track of these "graduates," figuring that an association could become a important source of financial support. Additionally, maintaining ties to activists made it possible for Highlander staff to stay well-informed. The drive yielded little, however, while demanding substantial staff time to mail letters, keep records, and change addresses. Most of the men and women who graduated from Highlander had little surplus income to give away.

Two years earlier, in spring 1937, Dombrowski had been convinced that most if not all of Highlander's usually pressing financial woes could be solved. And for a period, his prediction was realized. The Congress of Industrial Organizations (CIO) announced a two-million dollar drive to bring unions to the South. Dombrowski felt assured that the union effort would benefit Highlander.

Immediately after the announcement, the CIO started recruiting experienced organizers to bring unions to thousands of workers in the South's textile industry. Highlander's staff heard the union's bugle and enlisted. They could carry on Highlander's crusade and be paid, too. At least, that was the strategy. Top officials from the Amalgamated Clothing Workers, the United Rubber Workers, the American Federation of Hosiery Workers, and the International Ladies Garment Workers formed the Textile Workers Organizing Committee to spearhead the drive. Over 450,000 southern textile workers were unorganized, ill-paid, poorly housed, and as sickly as any workers in America. A. Steve Nance, who had led the Georgia Federation of Labor until he was impeached by the AFL for supporting the CIO, headed the TWOC's Deep South office in Atlanta. Franz Daniel was his assistant in charge of organizing. A Virginian with patrician family lineage, Lucy Randolph Mason, was recruited from her job as general secretary of the National Consumer League. She recalled going "into mill towns, among unorganized workers, to preach the gospel of organization—though I would distinctly not be an organizer, merely an interpreter."[37] Zilla Hawes Daniel was to oversee organizing in South Carolina, Zilphia Horton was sent to LaFollette, Tennessee, north of Knoxville, to continue work that Zilla Hawes Daniel and a Highlander graduate, Charles Handy, had started earlier at two shirt factories and at a raincoat operation. Myles Horton was to organize mills in North Carolina.

Union workers learning poster design with Dombrowski (*center*) in Charlotte, North Carolina, ca. 1938–39. Frank T. Adams Collection.

Dombrowski, although wanting badly to quit administering Highlander so as to organize or teach fulltime, agreed to a parttime, paying role in the campaign, editing a broadside appeal to the South's ministers. Tefferteller was to organize special musical events, also parttime, and help Dombrowski mind Highlander's affairs. Highlander had cut its labor costs without badly cutting its program. The most intense need for funds was diminished.

As Dombrowski had expected, by 1939 a majority of the persons attending Highlander's residential programs were CIO members. The common thread uniting them was the need to build and operate a local union chapter. They came from every southern state. Many were young, already local presidents, and on their way up union leadership ladders. Each six-week term cost sponsoring locals $42 per student. While well below Highlander's expenses, which Dombrowski figured totaled $100 per student, the expanded enrollment increased cash flow and opened opportunities to appeal to CIO leaders for additional support.

The organizing campaign opened with meetings in Atlanta the weekend of April 2, 1937, with nearly 200 persons, about 160 of them southerners, attending. Dombrowski, Zilphia and Myles Horton, and Tefferteller drove to Atlanta together. Dombrowski felt that he was part of the most important event in recent southern labor history, likening the atmosphere to that of a family reunion. Horton believed the campaign marked the beginning of a "democratic, radical, social movement."[38]

Except for two reservations, the CIO's agenda nicely matched Dombrowski's. He agreed with the CIO that the American Federation of Labor's goals were severely limited. The CIO, mostly industrial unions, wanted a better life for all workers, whether they were part of collective bargaining agreements or not. They backed universal medical care, a federal guarantee of education for every youngster, day care, enough WPA funds to assure productive jobs for every American, and strengthened civil liberties.[39]

Dombrowski raised the issue of race. He feared the TWOC would fail labor's cause if African Americans were not included. Race was not a secondary strategic issue for him. He had been disappointed bitterly in 1938 when Highlander's staff decided to go along with union sentiment and not enroll African-American students.[40] He believed that Highlander's students and staff gained perspective when African Americans taught courses. For five years, whenever possible, Dr. J. Herman Daves of Knoxville College taught labor courses. In 1934, Daves and his wife had been the first African Americans to violate Tennessee's Jim Crow laws at Highlander.[41] Dombrowski and Horton had spent weeks preparing their Monteagle neighbors for that weekend, and events had gone off without hitch or harm. Dombrowski's thinking was summed up by A. Philip Randolph, head of the Brotherhood of Sleeping Car Porters, who said that African Americans were "99% workers."[42]

In May 1935, at the conclusion of the National Conference on the Economic Crisis and the Negro at Howard University, a federation of socialists and African-American organizations formed to forge a closer alliance between industrial unions and African Americans. While he had not attended the Howard meeting, many of Dombrowski's friends from New York City's Socialist community had, and he was a pivotal southern ally, corresponding regularly with leaders of the federation.[43] Eventually, most whites pulled away from the federation, and it became primarily an organization of the nation's African-American Left, calling itself the National Negro Congress. A Philip Randolph was its first president. Dombrowski linked Highlander to the Congress through mutually beneficial projects and through the Rosenwald Fund. Edwin R. Embree, president of the Rosenwald Fund, and Randolph were confidantes. Clark H. Foreman, another political associate of Embree, was a key advisor to the Roosevelt administration on race and the economy.[44] He knew Dombrowski personally, both through Highlander and through the fledgling Southern Conference for Human Welfare.

Dombrowski brought speakers to Highlander whom he knew would keep the issue alive. James H. Terry, an international representative for the United Mine Workers (UMW), told winter term students, "If we raise the Negro, we raise ourselves."[45] Arthur Raper of the Commission on Interracial Cooperation (CIC) took part in seminars on race. Dombrowski also wanted the TWOC to form a united front and include churches or Communists as allies in the organizing drive.[46] He remembered the bitter factional splits in Gastonia, which played to the advantage of mill owners. Many TWOC leaders were Socialists, indisposed to any collaboration with Communists.[47] A nod toward the churches was given through Dombrowski's assignment. He was to edit a special issue of *Parade,* the TWOC's publication, on the church and labor. It was to focus on how mill owners often used evangelists to thwart union drives, sometimes even deducting money from the workers' checks to pay for preachers to hold prayer meetings on company time.

On the issue of making common cause with Communists, however, Dombrowski was swimming against the tide. TWOC leaders, particularly Daniel, argued that, if any gain was expected, the unions should only take on one social challenge at a time. Daniel and others believed that the organizing drive would yield economic benefit to all southern workers and thus set the stage for Dombrowski's agenda. In Dombrowski's mind, united fronts were the only way working people and their allies could withstand the counterattacks which could be predicted from any serious challenge to the South's industrial and political establishments.[48]

Dombrowski returned to Highlander unconvinced but willing to go along. Highlander's pressing need to cut overhead also muted his opposition. Typically, however, Dombrowski, when thwarted in one direction, tried another way. By the summer of 1939, Highlander collaborated with the Communist-led League of American Writers to sponsor a two-week program for aspiring writers and journalists.[49]

Horton left the TWOC in October 1937, after successfully organizing mills in McColl, South Carolina, and Lumberton, North Carolina. TWOC leaders saw Horton as one of the South's foremost organizers. However, fulltime organizing convinced Horton that teaching, not organizing, was his bent. The distinction, he told Dombrowski, was crucial: "If you advocate just one action, you're an organizer. We teach leadership here. Then people go out and do what they want."[50] Horton predicted that the South-wide drive would not live up to its promises; significant social change must derive from the bottom, not the top. The CIO effort was top-down organizing, he said, and did not grow from either the action or the inspiration of workers.

Dombrowski hoped that Horton was ready to shoulder some of Highlander's administrative chores. After lengthy discussions about roles and responsibilities, the two men reached an agreement. Horton was to raise funds and recruit students; Dombrowski would do essential organizational housekeeping—bookkeeping, correspondence, and maintenance. This permitted both men time to teach or to follow up on students' work after they left Highlander. Soon after, during a recruiting trip in Arkansas, Myles and Zilphia were in an auto accident, leaving both slightly injured and destroying their car. When Horton was able to work again, he arranged several fundraising trips but balked at any fundraising planning or administration. Dombrowski never forgave this breech of agreement.[51]

A year later, on a warm October day, a man who identified himself as John McDougal, a Texas school teacher, arrived, saying that he was interested in unions and Highlander.[52] He stayed several days. His endless questions raised staff suspicions. Soon after he left, two photographers from the *Nashville Tennessean* arrived, saying they wanted to take photographs for a Sunday feature. A few days later, six articles under the name John McDougal Burns appeared in the *Nashville Tennessean*. Among many charges, Burns asserted Highlander "is a center, if not the center, for the spreading Communist doctrine in thirteen southeastern states."[53]

The last article disclosed that Mrs. Roosevelt had donated funds to Highlander, showing photographs of her cancelled check. Burns reported that Mrs. Roosevelt had "earned only contempt in Grundy County" and that he could find no-one there with a single good word to say about Highlander.[54] The articles cheered Highlander's foes; once again, friends were asked to issue denials. Predictably, after the last article appeared, a carload of men drove up to the school's office, shouting, "God damn you, come out of there. We're coming back tonight and bomb you out."[55] Dolph Vaughn and other friendly neighbors immediately arranged to guard the property until passions cooled. Once again, the responsibility to defend against political attack fell to Dombrowski. He and Leon Wilson, a Californian who had joined the staff, arranged to visit Alvin Henderson at the First National Bank in Tracy City. The bank officer readily admitted giving Burns a copy of the check.

"Don't you consider this a violation of banking ethics?" Dombrowski asked.[56]

"The school is against government," Henderson said, adding candidly, "I'm going to fight it any way I can." Highlander was a public institution, he continued, and therefore its banking affairs were not private. Besides, he added, he acted as a private citizen, not a bank official.

"Does this mean you helped yourself to bank records and isn't that tantamount to a confession of conspiracy or theft?" Dombrowski asked.[57] Henderson refused to answer. Their meeting came to an unsatisfactory conclusion.

Highlander's opposition continued hammering at Highlander's links with Eleanor Roosevelt and her husband's administration. In January 1940, copies of a pamphlet, "The Fifth Column in the South," attacking Highlander as "a hotbed of communistic activity," circulated in Grundy County.[58] The author, Joseph P. Kamp, headed a New York organization called the Constitutional Educational League. The pamphlet, which contained a reprint of Mrs. Roosevelt's check, described her as a dupe of Highlander, and similarly labeled Sidney Hillman, a leading official with TWOC drive, Henry Wallace, John L. Lewis of the United Mine Workers, and Aubrey Williams, an Alabaman with the National Youth Administration.

Grundy miners were given copies of the pamphlet with their paychecks. In nearby Sewanee, students at the University of the South got the pamphlet in their mail. One Highlander supporter, a Tracy City businessman, told Dombrowski that E.L. Hampton, the coal company's major stockholder, who lived in Nashville, had mailed him a copy.[59] The booklet's circulation reached well beyond Grundy County. Franz Daniel, organizing laundry workers in New York City, wrote Dombrowski, "I got in a barroom argument last night about radicalism in the New Deal and as proof the enclosed circular was shown to me. Isn't there something you can do about the bank?"[60]

Dombrowski next heard from Henderson early in November 1940. The banker asked if he and some friends could visit the school "to see what actually went on."[61] He wanted to drop by about 7:30 p.m., Tuesday, November 12, he said. Dombrowski, on behalf of the staff, responded with a written invitation. Shortly after he'd mailed the letter to Henderson, a reporter from the *Nashville Tennessean* telephoned asking, "Is it true you have been notified of a mass march that is to be staged against you Tuesday night?" The reporter read Dombrowski a letter he'd gotten, signed by C.H. Kilby, announcing "a mass march of Grundy County citizenry to the Highlander Folk School." The *Tennessean* was invited to send a reporter. Kilby claimed to have the official backing of the Junior Order of United American Mechanics, Tracy City Local 277, the Daughters of America, the Veterans of Foreign Wars, and the Grundy Parent-Teachers Association, and Local 5881 of the UMW in Palmer.[62]

Kilby said in his letter that the coalition, called the Grundy County Crusaders, had adopted the slogan of "One Hundred Percent Americans" to spur their efforts "night and day" to run Highlander out of the county. The next morning, Dombrowski and another new staff member, Bill Buttrick, found Kilby in his office at the coal company. Kilby admitted that he was planning a march and that Henderson's letter was to serve as notification. "I'll tell you, Mr. Buttrick, we haven't strained at a gnat to be straight out about this meeting. The Highlander Folk School had done so many things which the citizenry of Grundy County didn't know about that we didn't think we needed to notify the school of everything we do."[63] The march, he said, was planned because the Dies Committee "wasn't doing enough," and he added, "It is the duty of every community afflicted with un-American groups to act." Dombrowski saw a copy of Kamp's booklet on Kilby's desk. Kilby was adamant. The march would not be cancelled.

Was Highlander a problem for the White House, or was the White House a problem for Highlander? Either way, Dombrowski faced a serious, potentially volatile situation. He and Buttrick left Tracy City determined to find some way to prevent any march, with its probable violence. For help, Dombrowski reached to personal contacts made over nearly a decade in the state. Organized labor, through Paul Christopher, who was now head of the CIO in Tennessee, wired Kilby. The state office of the Veterans of Foreign Wars publically denied that the VFW was part of the Crusaders. Dr. Alva Taylor urged local ministers to back the embattled school. Eventually, Tennessee Gov. Prentice Cooper telephoned Kilby. The march was called off.

In its stead the two sides agreed to air their differences during what Dombrowski proposed as a "genuine conference" at the University of the South in Sewanee. Dean Fleming James of the School of Theology agreed to moderate. The public and press were invited, and both groups immediately launched campaigns in Grundy County to rally support for their points of view.

About one hundred citizens came to Sewanee for the dramatic event, which began at 9 p.m. Most were Highlander supporters. Other Highlander friends stayed in Summerfield guarding the school's buildings. Dombrowski had been delegated to speak for the school. Horton was to present evidence supporting the school's purposes.

Dean James guided the meeting with a parliamentarian's decorum. Kilby, with Henderson the banker at his side, was given the floor first. He read the Crusader resolution, noting off the cuff that since Highlander had opened, Grundy County had received unwanted publicity while deriving no benefits from the school's work. The school, he alleged, taught Communism and subversion. A Chattanooga reporter observed that Kilby's remarks "rose to oratorical heights."[64]

Dombrowski spoke next. He reported that a petition had been gotten up by Summerfield neighbors urging that the school continue its work and deploring any attempt to "demolish" it. Dr. Lillian Johnson, he said, had given the property to the school only after she had been assured that her neighbors approved of Highlander. He'd brought all the school's financial records, contributors' lists, and the name of every student or visitor during seven years. He offered the Crusaders the opportunity to study those documents then and there. They did not accept.

Both groups peppered each other with increasingly hostile questions. Kilby reluctantly admitted that, despite previous claims, not one of the organizations supposedly a part of the Crusaders had resolved officially to censure Highlander. The Crusaders were especially bothered by a widely circulated statement Dombrowski made during the 1938 election, that "Highlander helped union members overthrow the power of a large coal company."[65] Kilby particularly was vexed by the remark, saying he'd worked for Tennessee Consolidated Coal for fifteen years and he'd never known the company's management to try to influence employee votes. Bodies but not passions were spent by 2 a.m., when the meeting came to an end. Another Chattanooga paper reported that there was "no love fest at the completion of the lengthy, tension-packed meeting."[66]

Press coverage surprised Highlander's staff. Both Nashville papers carried accurate, fair accounts. The *Chattanooga Times* printed an extensive, impartial report, plus an editorial stating, in part, "When a Labor School in the mountains wants to exist, it is the part of Americanism to discuss its aims with its leaders, not merely to fling the word 'communism' at it as an excuse for threats of violence."[67] The rival *Chattanooga News-Free Press* commented: "Plain country folk, true Americans, met some intelligentsia . . . who out talked them."[68] A Federal Bureau of Investigation agent present reported: "Dombrowski is a very talented orator. . . . he spoke so forcefully and convincingly that the Grundy County Crusaders were pacified and beaten at every argument advanced."[69]

Ironically, throughout the fight with the Grundy County Crusaders, which lasted twenty months, Dombrowski was casting about for a way to leave Highlander.[70] Teaching had lost no luster for him. He was delighted by opportunities to put Highlander's unique stamp on future union leaders. But the time for classroom teaching was increasingly scarce. Administration, fundraising, and constantly defending the school as its official spokesman had come to occupy most of his time. Unable to find a way to shed some of the duties which dragged on his usually even temper, as early as April 1939 Dombrowski looked for ways to leave Highlander. Only Krida and Zilla Hawes Daniel knew of his growing dissatisfaction. Dombrowski wrote to Daniel, "You know that I have been anxious for a long time to do some work in the field. It has been a long grind here in the office and I need the experience. I would prefer to do some organizing work."[71]

Ralph Tefferteller decided to join the union movement fulltime. This added to Dombrowski's disquiet. The redoubtable musician-organizer had worked for no pay. He planned to marry and needed an income. His departure created a breach hard for Dombrowski to fill. Tefferteller had remarkable skills working with people, using music in ways Dombrowski imagined would have pleased Kristen Kold, founder of the first folk school. He was one of the Skipper's closest friends, sharing ideas, values, and many of the administrative tasks.

As staff manager, Dombrowski often made unpopular choices. Once, for instance, at the height of the Chattanooga American Legion's attacks, while Dombrowski and Horton scurried to rebut Stovall's charges, Zilla Hawes Daniel telephoned needing help during a strike in Cleveland, Tennessee. No-one, Dombrowski decided, had time to lend a hand. In response, Zilla wrote stiffly, "A responsible labor school must be ready to serve at all times in spite of apparent sacrifice."[72]

Time and responsibility also figured in grumblings as Kazan and his film crew made *People of the Cumberlands*. The staff, ignorant of the time filming would take, agreed with Dombrowski's proposal that they assist Kazan in making the film. Tefferteller was assigned fulltime to the production unit; yet, almost daily, other staff members, especially Horton, were pulled away from Highlander duties. Work piled on other, already overtaxed, shoulders, usually Dombrowski's, or went undone. "Jim's style grated on some people, myself included at times," Horton said years later.[73] "He was especially careful about details and guarded principles as immutable once they had been agreed on. Oh, he'd give or take on strategies, but on a principle, you couldn't budge him."

His episodic relationship with Ellen Krida weighed increasingly on Dombrowski's mind. In her letters she worried often about Dombrowski's never-ending work and his painful arthritis. "Eight hours at your desk is ghastly, my darling. You must not. And, if everyone else could find time to write or follow their particular bents, why can't you? . . . Can't you shift part of your chores to give more free time?"[74] Krida refused to live at Highlander. Her visits had convinced her that Summerfield was not the place to share Dombrowski's life. She found Dombrowski's cabin to be lonely, no matter how picturesque. She was accustomed to and enjoyed urban amenities. Myles Horton, she felt, regarded her with ill-concealed disapproval.[75] She could not imagine how she would be happy in such circumstances. Dombrowski realized that it would be unfair to insist that she move to Summerfield. When he went to New York, their reunions commenced with joy but ended with pain. Typically, after Dombrowski had returned to Highlander after several weeks fundraising in New York, Krida wrote only half-jokingly that her lodgings were as empty as a sepulcher, adding that she could "empathize with the maidens staring into Christ's empty tomb."[76] By early 1941, their relationship, for years based on interludes, seemed permanently adjourned. Dombrowski suggested that either they marry or go their separate ways. Krida was stung, waiting several days before writing a confused, stumbling letter: "Darling, I have recovered somewhat. . . . That 'or else' business smashed me down . . . I was on the point of saying, ok, you are right, but I lacked the necessary courage. . . . The frightening picture of no you, ever, no place, is deathly."[77]

Other external forces kept Dombrowski from Highlander's central purposes, too. He devoted countless hours to trying to maintain Highlander's ties with union leaders. The relentless attacks in the press, the electoral defeat in Grundy County, and Horton's abrupt resignation from the TWOC had begun to wear thin the bond between Highlander and the unions. Dombrowski's own softly but regularly stated argument that all races and persuasions had to be united in common struggle against capitalism had frayed union nerves, too.

AFL President William Green had fought the CIO from its inception, and, as the TWOC drive got underway, his attacks intensified. On April 13, 1937, Joe Dobbs, one of Highlander's strongest union backers in Chattanooga, was re-elected head of that city's central labor council, carrying into office with him a slate of progressive officers, all of whom supported TWOC. Three days later, Dobbs was expelled from his own local. "Green sent a special representative to Chattanooga to read Dobbs out of the union by decree without charges or a trial," Dombrowski recounted in his journal.[78] During the 1939 annual meeting of the Mississippi AFL, Dombrowski heard an AFL leader attack TWOC organizers as "a bunch of paid, mercenary Hessians."[79] Later that year, during the convention of the Tennessee AFL, union leaders grilled Dombrowski for nearly four hours. They attacked Highlander for promoting the aborted All-Trade Union conference in 1934, and for backing the CIO. One union leader told Dombrowski that he had been trying to persuade Tennessee's governor to investigate Highlander.

In general, the CIO's leadership went along with Highlander's policy on race, sending members to the school knowing that they might share experiences, meals, and lodging with African Americans or Mexican Americans. Highlander's united-front policy was another matter, even for the CIO. That meant working with Communists, who were seen as the amoral agents of a Moscow bent on destroying America, and even in some cases working with union or Socialist rivals.

In December 1939, Franz Daniel wrote to Dombrowski, "I'm getting disquieting reports about HFS. There seems to be too much suspicion on the part of the labor men toward the school."[80] More and more leaders within the CIO were listening to Franz and Zilla Hawes Daniel, who had become harsh political critics of Highlander and, by extension, of Dombrowski. At first the couple regularly declared their loyalty to Dombrowski and Horton personally, while attacking Highlander's policies. The distinction was hard for Dombrowski to keep in mind.

Daniel, en route to New York from the 1941 Tennessee CIO convention, stopped at Highlander, saying that he and Zilla wanted to sever all relationship with the school. Dombrowski and Horton, he said, while not Communists themselves, were Communist stooges. He was irritated because Dombrowski had hired a secretary who, as a student at Vassar, had been active in the Communist Youth Organization. But the last straw, he said, was Highlander's cooperation with Joseph Gelders, a suspected Communist, and the coalition of interests he'd organized in the Southern Conference for Human Welfare, which allowed Communists to participate. On June 9, Dombrowski wrote to his friend of more than a decade:

> We are dropping your name from our advisory council. . . . It is now understood that you will have completely broken your official relationship with the school and in no way will be responsible for any of its policies and program. . . . We wish to assure you that we entirely agree with you that our disagreement on trade union policy need not be an occasion for interrupting the friendly personal relationship which has existed between you and the staff.[81]

Once, at least, Dombrowski's united-front strategy kept him from landing a job which might have proven a satisfactory way to leave Highlander.

J.B.S. Hardman, director of the Department of Cultural Affairs for the Amalgamated Clothing Workers, wanted Dombrowski to organize the union's education centers around the country. Dombrowski wanted the job. But in a letter formally proposing the job, Hardman cautioned:

> I think it is only fair to you to make clear the basic philosophy of the organization. I enclose a few paragraphs from my article in the last issue of *The Advance* which indicates the union's philosophy toward the Communist movement and philosophy. . . . The union's work cannot be regarded as a middle ground of activity preparatory to something 'more essential.' We do not relish split loyalties within union labor.[82]

Dombrowski didn't pursue the offer any further.

Dombrowski argued that the TWOC had made a mistake in allowing mill owners to use the Communist issue virtually without rebuttal. They had convinced many southerners that there was a Red behind every black. As evidence, Dombrowski cited a National Labor Relations Board hearing in Nashville, Tennessee, during which lawyers for a mill owner asked a union witness:

"Now this Amalgamated Union takes in members whether they are white or black, natives or what not?"

"It does."

"Can a Negro be a member, and if elected, can he attend convention as a member?"

"He can. . . ."[83]

After the exchange, a Tennessee legislator said that the hearing proved that unions stood for "race mingling," adding, "Integration is the Southern version of communism."[84] Most union leaders did not want to hear Dombrowski's argument or the evidence.

Through 1939, Dombrowski and Horton agreed that a united front was required to end economic oppression; by then, however, they had come to differ on the strategic importance of race. Horton, like the TWOC leadership, was keenly aware that large numbers of African Americans worked in textile mills. He complied with union policy during his six months as an organizer, never openly encouraging African Americans to help plan or to have a voice in organizing drives. Once whites in a plant were organized, Horton always insisted that the contract cover African Americans. Some TWOC organizers ignored African-American textile workers or brought them into the bargaining agreement only after representation elections were held and certified. Such a strategy, no matter how pragmatic, Dombrowski argued, alienated African Americans, opening the way for them to be used as strikebreakers. By balking at organizing every worker, regardless of race, unions gave mill owners the opportunity to use organizing drives to intensify racial divisions, he said. Horton took the criticism personally, still smarting at it years later. TWOC leaders blamed the nation's Depression for the organizing drive's limited success.[85]

His other differences with the TWOC campaign aside, Dombrowski found its central lessons hard, if not demoralizing. His faith that workers could play central political roles locally and regionally had been tested and found wanting, first in Grundy County and then the South. But Dombrowski never changed his mind. Years later, he said, "We were faced with the tragedy of the workers fighting against each other instead of uniting to present a solid front against the real enemy."[86] More had been lost than the opportunity to bring unions to the South's textile industry. The TWOC failed to make the case that exploitation and not African Americans was the real foe of workers, and that mistake was compounded when union leaders joined Red-baiting segregationists.

Dombrowski was dispirited. He wanted Highlander to rethink its strategy, particularly its relationship to the Roosevelt administration and to the unions. Those discussions never got very far. Horton was always too busy to take the time needed for such a crucial discussion. The tension between them over direction spilled into a contest over personal styles and authority. For all their shared intellectual values and their years of collaboration, Dombrowski and Horton presented a study in opposites. Dombrowski was quiet, cautious, always neatly dressed; Horton, on the other hand, was gregarious, an experimenter, always a bit dishevelled. As a manager, Dombrowski insisted on having funds to launch new ventures. Horton, with an evangelist's confidence, was equally certain that money would come the next time the collection plates were passed. Horton saw Dombrowski, the deacon, passing the plates, and himself, as the preacher, saying when the plates were to be passed. What Dombrowski thought was prudent fiscal management, Horton took as tight-fisted and reactionary.

By 1941, Dombrowski and Horton were near a break. A letter from Krida to Dombrowski that summer revealed what neither man would subsequently confirm or deny:

I hope, my darling, things are looking less bleak at the moment. . . . it frightens me to think of your walking out of the place that you have thrown so much into all these years, and with no prospect of anything else. . . . If you can't come to any understanding with Myles, why doesn't he leave!!!

You are pretty responsible for that two-by-four school despite the fact that Myles got there the previous year on a bag of beans. . . . I am afraid, tho, that you are too inclined to modesty. . . . Now if you had a decent gal and one with gold, she'd just say to hell, quit.[87]

# 8

## War,
## Race, and
## Conscience

History stamped the moment in Dombrowski's memory forever. Alone in his cabin beside a comforting fire, the radio droning, he was weighing the decision to leave Highlander. Unexpectedly, President Roosevelt's voice flooded his consciousness. The Japanese had bombed Pearl Harbor. Hundreds of lives had been lost; great battleships had been sunk. The president was asking Congress to declare war. For the moment, Dombrowski's conflict with Horton paled.

Five days later, on December 12, 1941, Dombrowski telephoned Virginia Durr in Arlington, Virginia. She and her husband, Clifford, often had been hosts to him during business or fundraising trips to Washington. She was leading the Southern Conference for Human Welfare's (SCHW) fight to repeal poll taxes. He was a Roosevelt appointee to the Federal Communications Commission, a lawyer and former Rhodes Scholar whose brother-in-law was Supreme Court Justice Hugo Black. Dombrowski asked if he could again stay with the Durrs for a day or so. He had some business matters to discuss with her before continuing on to New York for the holidays with Ellen Krida, he said.

Virginia Durr met Dombrowski at Union Station. "We sat in my car outside the station after he got there," she remembered.[1] "And he said, 'Virginia, I really have to leave Highlander. The situation has become impossible.' He looked tired and worn. He never told me what the situation was, or why he was having to leave. And Jim was not the kind of person you would have asked why. In the first place, he's not going to tell you. In the second, you have to respect his privacy."

The post of executive secretary of Southern Conference for Human Welfare was vacant and going begging. Dombrowski wanted the job. Durr immediately telephoned Dr. Frank Graham, president of the University of North Carolina and head of the troubled coalition. " 'Frank,' " she recalled asking, " 'what do you think about getting Jim Dombrowski as secretary?' He said without hesitation, 'That would be too great to be true!' I said, 'It's true. All you have to do is ask him.' "2

The SCHW job hardly presented attractive employment, especially with the nation at war. Dombrowski's pursuit of another probably thankless and certainly low-paying and politically stressful job underscored the depths to which his relations with Horton had sunk. Equally, however, Dombrowski was determined to press more actively on racial issues than Highlander's labor agenda permitted. Any notes Dombrowski or Horton may have kept about their relationship eluded search; nor would either say what finally ruptured their long and effective friendship and political collaboration. After the winter of 1941, however, even though their lives frequently intersected, they kept a polite distance.

The SCHW had been mired in controversy since its formation four years earlier. Three administrative leaders had come and gone, each caught in political factionalism. There was less money in this group's treasury than in Highlander's. The organization had been founded to use the potential of federal power to undo the region's economic exploitation and political oppression. With a second world war commencing, however, President Roosevelt, the SCHW's chief political patron, could be expected to postpone domestic concerns and turn his full attention to prosecution of the war.[3]

Joseph Gelders, the son of a prominent Birmingham, Alabama, family, had kindled in President Roosevelt's mind the dream of a southern New Deal coalition.[4] Gelders conceived the regional coalition and was its first secretary. Gelders taught physics at the University of Alabama between 1930 and 1935, then became southern secretary for the National Committee for the Defense of Political Prisoners. In 1936, he was kidnapped and beaten brutally as he protested the jailing of a Birmingham Communist Party leader trying to organize the Alabama plants of Tennessee Coal and Iron Company. Similar lawless acts were common in Birmingham at the time, especially against African Americans organizing unions in the city's steel mills.[5] But because of Gelder's prominence, race, and connections with activists nationwide, his case quickly drew sympathetic attention. While he recovered, Gelders began enlisting support for an interracial Southwide conference on civil liberties violations.

Among the first to back his idea was the CIO's Lucy Randolph Mason. She first met Gelders during a strike in Tupelo, Mississippi.[6] Mason arranged for Gelders to present his idea to President and Mrs. Roosevelt in April 1938. A month earlier, in a speech given at Gainesville, Georgia, Mr. Roosevelt had denounced southern senators who opposed his effort to add sympathetic liberals to a conservative Supreme Court. He accused the senators of blocking the New Deal agenda and lamented the South's dire economic plight. That August, the National Emergency Council issued a long-awaited *Report on the Economic Conditions of the South,* declaring the region to be "the nation's number one economic problem."[7] Two of Dombrowski's acquaintances, Mercer Evans, the Emory economist, and Clark Foreman, the president's advisor on race, helped write the report. Both Roosevelts urged Gelders to press ahead with efforts to bring together the broadest possible political group. The president specifically wanted a campaign against the poll tax. On his way back to Birmingham, Gelders stopped at Highlander to enlist Dombrowski and Horton.[8]

The SCHW's first meeting opened on November 29, 1938, in Birmingham's Municipal Auditorium, and, for once, as the famed Swedish social scientist Gunnar Myrdal observed, "the lonely southern liberals met in great numbers—actually more than twelve hundred, they experienced a foretaste of the freedom and power which large-scale political organizations and concerted action give."[9] Mary McLeod Bethune, who headed the Division of Negro Affairs at the National Youth Administration, was the most prominent of some forty African Americans attending.

Delegates of every political stripe aired their opinions on the convention's broad theme, the South's economic colonialism.[10] Horton joined Eleanor Roosevelt in a panel discussion on youth. Dombrowski, who had no role on the agenda, circulated among convention delegates, renewing political friendships or making new allies, among them Aubrey Williams, a New Deal administrator. What Dombrowski and Howard Kester had hoped for in Chattanooga was writ large in Birmingham. Middle-class liberals were making common cause with labor, the dispossessed, and African Americans, and finding out that those groups were articulate about their needs.

On Sunday, the convention's first day, no-one obeyed Birmingham's segregation laws banning African Americans and whites from being seated together in public places. On Monday, however, Police Commissioner Eugene "Bull" Connor notified Judge Louise Charlton, a Birmingham jurist who was chairing the convention, that he was sending police to enforce the city's Jim Crow laws. Police and firemen arrived during a session on tenant farming, threatening to arrest anyone failing to comply with the segregationist law. Judge Charlton requested that the races sit apart, shattering the convention's idealistic facade.[11]

Most delegates honored her request. Some, however, including Eleanor Roosevelt, Dombrowski, and Horton protested, eventually agreeing on condition that the issue would be debated later that night. The issue white southern liberals had avoided for years, and which they had hoped to dodge again in Birmingham, was at the center of their first big convention.[12] Away from the hall itself, of course, African Americans stayed in Birmingham's segregated hotels or with friends, and ate in the city's segregated restaurants or brought take-out meals.

Gelders had envisioned a one-time event. But, Connor's disruptive tactic notwithstanding, momentum built during the convention for a regional gathering every two years. Eleanor Roosevelt endorsed federal legislation to end the South's ills. Resolutions were adopted urging full rights for all citizens, abolition of the poll tax, and an end to wage differentials based on race. There was a plea that the men convicted in the Scottsboro case be freed from prison. Justice Hugo Black, an Alabaman, was given the Thomas Jefferson Award for distinguished service to the South. A permanent organization was set up with Dr. Graham of the University of North Carolina as first SCHW president.

Gelders left the secretary's job at the conclusion of the SCHW's birthing convention. Howard Lee, an Arkansas sharecropper's son, took his place in October 1939. He became embroiled in sectarian politics. Powerful SCHW members felt that Lee was politically naive, despite his enjoying the confidence of Eleanor Roosevelt.[13] They charged that Lee had gotten the SCHW unnecessarily linked with the American Peace Mobilization, an organization founded by Dr. Ward, Dombrowski's mentor at Union. Ward started that group to oppose conservative attacks on domestic economic reform being proposed by Roosevelt and others.[14] Lee's foes felt that the Mobilization's aims coincided too closely with the Communist Party's policies.

Socialists in the SCHW alleged that Lee had been a member of the Young

Communist League. He denied the charge. To end the dispute and save organizational face, Lee was given a permanent leave of absence. Gelders,
also accused of being a Communist, during the meeting which decided
Lee's fate, formally severed ties with the organization he had helped
found.[15]

Alton Lawrence became the SCHW's third secretary, loaned to the organization by Labor's Non-Partisan League on orders from John L. Lewis,
the powerful president of the United Mine Workers. With Dr. Graham's
prestige and Lucy Randolph Mason's arduous help, Lawrence organized
the SCHW's 1940 convention in Chattanooga. Lewis used that gathering
to air his opposition to American entry into the war in Europe. When Germany invaded the Soviet Union, however, Lewis realized that any hope of
preventing American involvement was lost. Lawrence was called back to
union duties, leaving the SCHW looking for yet another secretary.[16]

The SCHW's troubles extended beyond being broke, purges of suspected
Reds, and infighting over foreign policy. Many widely known southerners
who initially had been attracted to the SCHW dropped their affiliation or
stopped participating. Some were unwilling to be identified with an organization opposed to segregation. The fact that Communist Party members
attended the first convention kept others away. President Roosevelt's plans
for economic reform angered some. Most, however, were too busy to give
the SCHW much time. Among these latter was Dr. Graham, who stepped
down as president after the Chattanooga meetings.

A long search for Graham's successor ended with election of Rev. John B.
Thompson, one of Dombrowski's classmates at Union. Thompson was
young and had neither Graham's prestige nor his political power. His term
was to end with the convention set for Nashville in 1942.[17] No person of
prominence was rushing to take Thompson's place, a problem Durr and
Dombrowski discussed before she telephoned Graham about Dombrowski's quest for the job of secretary.

Dombrowski's appointment was felicitous for both him and the SCHW.
He could leave Highlander gracefully for an organizing job consistent with
his own ideals. He had powerful allies with whom he was at ease. He hoped
that Ellen Krida might agree to live in Nashville. The SCHW was getting a
well-known, albeit controversial, leader with proven skills. On January 3,
1942, with most of his possessions in a suitcase, Dombrowski left Monteagle. He mailed a few books, personal papers, and a set of watercolors to
his new address, a hotel near Tennessee's capitol buildings. By telephone he

arranged to have the SCHW's few office furnishings, records, and supplies moved from Birmingham to Nashville, where the third convention was to be held.

Turning again to Ethel Clyde, the heiress who so often had helped Highlander financially, Dombrowski asked for funds. Not surprisingly, Dombrowski's agenda echoed the hopes of near-forgotten heretics—Colwell, George, Ely, Bellamy, and the others treated in his dissertation:

> My appointment came two days ago. There is no money in the treasury, but a promise of help from the Marshall Fund and the Whitney Fund. In the meantime, I am going ahead on my own funds trusting that we will be able to raise the money to run the Conference. I have only $25. Would it be possible for you to loan me sufficient funds to enable me to live for two or perhaps three months? I think the investment of time and money will be well repaid.

> There are several reasons why I think it is important to keep the Conference alive. First is a purely defensive action against . . . Southern reactionaries who are seeking to take advantage of the emergency to push anti-labor bills through Congress; second, it is the only occasion when whites and Negroes get together in the South on a progressive program, and the opportunities for progress on the race issue at the moment are enormous; third, to assure labor's maximum participation in the productive efforts of the war and in the peace settlement, the unorganized South is our greatest weakness. A great mass meeting of Southern workers and liberals, who never get together otherwise, would go far to bolster our strength, keep in motion forces already at work and initiate new activity.[18]

Clyde responded, assured through past experience that Dombrowski's word was as good as any contract. Dombrowski was a responsible businessman. Largely through the CIO's Paul Christopher and Vanderbilt theologian Dr. Alva Taylor, Dombrowski rented an inexpensive office in the Presbyterian Building, "a good address," he wrote a friend, "for an organization that has been attacked as 'red,' 'Negro lovers,' etc."[19] Marge Gelders Frantz, the daughter of Joseph Gelders, lived in Nashville with her lawyer husband, Laurent. She was recruited. Her determination to keep the SCHW alive matched Dombrowski's. Together, they organized a group of prominent Nashville citizens to host the convention set to open on April 19, less than four months off. Virginia Durr, Clark Foreman, William

Mitch of the United Mine Workers, and John P. Davis, executive secretary of the National Negro Congress, joined him to complete arrangements for the Nashville gathering. Paul Robeson would give a concert, his first in the South. Eleanor Roosevelt agreed to attend and to present the organization's Thomas Jefferson award. Despite the war, the president had not turned his back on the SCHW. Other prominent Americans, including James Carey, David E. Lilienthal, Francis Biddle, Rupert Vance, and Jonathan Daniels all agreed to appear on the program or send statements.

Dombrowski scraped together enough money to pay the rent, telephone, and other expenses. Frantz was paid, and so was he, $266 a month. He sent the Emory Alumni Association a five-dollar contribution, explaining half-apologetically that this was his first paying job since graduation.

By March 10, Dombrowski and Frantz mailed over 27,000 convention calls to groups, youth organizations, rabbis, social workers, educators, unions, TVA employees, and civic groups. Dombrowski wrote personal letters to the leaders of every African-American organization in the South and several dozen in the North, including the National Association for the Advancement of Colored People, shunned at the time by most white southerners. Dombrowski had been compiling the list since he and Howard Kester organized the meeting of Younger Churchmen in Monteagle; Frantz supplied other names gotten chiefly from her father.

Dombrowski rented a one-room studio apartment in the Hotel Noel. "The furnishings," he wrote Krida, "are an affront to decency and should be proscribed by law. . . . But, my dear, it is high. Sweet, cool summer breezes will tear through the place and the town lies below . . . it reminds me of Manhattan."[20] He wanted her at his side.

"The outlook at the moment is fine," Dombrowski told Durr in a letter.[21] Before he completed conference arrangements, however, Dombrowski made two decisions which troubled his conscience and lost him political ground with radicals. He asked Jack McMichael and Rob Hall to join panels. McMichael worked with the American Youth Congress and other allegedly Communist fronts. He had organized a demonstration outside the White House to criticize President Roosevelt. Hall belonged to the Communist Party and was one of the group's chief southern organizers.

Dombrowski had failed to appreciate the passion evoked inside the SCHW by the presence or mention of Communists.[22] But he did as he was asked. Dombrowski explained his dilemma to both men and urged them not to attend. He split hairs on McMichael, citing the demonstration as a rationalization: "The demonstrators started hurling insults. They were insulting the president. So it was more than just criticism of his programs. They were shouting at him. Eleanor was very disturbed. The president called Frank Graham and objected to this person being on the program at Nashville. He asked Frank to pass along to me his request that Jack be disinvited."[23] Dombrowski had no rationalization for "disinviting" Hall. Socialist Party members objected to him for sectarian reasons, both through Eleanor Roosevelt and to Dombrowski directly. McMichael acquiesced. Hall did not. Dombrowski made no further effort to prevent Hall from coming. Dombrowski had learned that he, too, was vulnerable; he had been party to a purge, having tied his immediate future to the Roosevelts' rising political future.

On April 19, 1942, over five hundred delegates to the third biennial convention of the SCHW began assembling in Nashville's War Memorial Auditorium. Although fewer in number than at two previous conventions, they were no less committed to a liberal, Southwide common front. Inside the War Memorial, as planned by Dombrowski, the SCHW delegates sat where they would and with whomever, flaunting law and custom. Outside, however, they went their separate, Jim-Crow ways for food or shelter.

Most delegates were white, male, well-educated, and well-heeled. But African Americans registered nearly one third of the five hundred or so delegates, and they spoke out as never before, their numbers and oratorical participation attesting to their increasing passion for full emancipation and also reflecting Dombrowski's special attention to their recruitment. Eleanor Roosevelt headed the list of officials from her husband's administration. Labor unions sent delegates, although Dombrowski's appointment had been opposed by some union leaders.

Nashville had been chosen as the site of the third convention after city officials pledged that Jim Crow laws would be ignored in the War Memorial. For their part, the SCHW conference organizing committee studiously avoided direct challenges to the historic, continuing racial injustices. Before the meeting, Roosevelt himself telephoned Ed Crump, the legendary political boss in Memphis. "Ed," said the president, "my wife is going to a meeting in Nashville and I don't want us to have any trouble there."[24]

Nashville had experienced a brief period of interracial political reform for three years beginning in 1884.[25] By 1890, however, city or state suffrage laws had disposed of African-American votes. When the SCHW meeting opened, there were no African-American officeholders; jobs, schools, public places, and restaurants all were strictly segregated. In a pre-pared statement, President Roosevelt exhorted delegates to exert them-selves in wartime mobilization efforts while not forgetting the New Deal's plans to transform the South. "Victory over the Axis," he said, "demands that neither man nor wealth be wasted, and that the privilege of participa-tion in our great national undertaking be granted to every citizen. It also demands that our democracy be maintained as a vital strengthening force."[26] Aubrey Williams, an Alabaman who headed the National Youth Administration, had written the president's speech.

Eleanor Roosevelt rode into the city from the airport with Mary McLeod Bethune, president and founder of Bethune-Cookman College in Daytona Beach, Florida. She worked with Williams in the National Youth Admin-istration. Riding with them was Lucy Randolph Mason. Federal Bureau of Investigation agents guarding the president's wife reported, "There were numerous instances of intermingling of white people and Negroes, yet there were no indications that violence would result."[27] Bethune was given the SCHW's Thomas Jefferson award for 1942 "as the Southerner who had done most to promote human and social welfare in line with the philoso-phy of Thomas Jefferson." Accepting the honor, she told the audience, "As the Negro people march into battle they know that there are many hin-drances to full participation in the country's battle for freedom; but march they must, and march they will, because they do understand that every hope they have for full democracy hinges upon the outcome of this war."[28]

Baritone Paul Robeson received a standing ovation at the end of his pro-gram, which included folk music, spirituals, and ballads. Then, in his re-marks, Robeson ignited another spark in the SCHW's short tinderbox his-tory. He told the audience that African Americans must do their part "in the saga now begun" but warned of the dangers of fascism at home. "I have seen it at its roots in Germany," he declared, "and I know our task. On my way to this meeting, I stopped in Atlanta to see a great American. . . . one who long warned people of the menace of fascism, and who . . . now lan-guishes in an Atlanta prison. I hope he will be free again."[29] There was a smattering of applause. Robeson, rumored to be a Communist, or at least a Communist sympathizer, referred to Earl Browder, the Kansas-born secre-tary of the American Communist Party. The Dies Committee had charged Browder with passport violations. He was tried, convicted, and jailed. Robeson's remarks were widely noted in the region's press, again linking SCHW proceedings to so-called Communist causes.

Race, not communism or awards, however, was at the center of the SCHW's deliberations, forced there by the war. Talk among friends in the hallways or during panel discussions focused on jobs or industrial policy in war-related industries and the Armed Forces, reflecting an intense national debate.

In 1940, A. Phillip Randolph, head of the Brotherhood of Sleeping Car Porters, had publicly proposed that African Americans march on Washington to insist on an end to job discrimination in the military and in all defense industries. It was an idea he'd considered for months. Economic security and political power were inextricably entwined in Randolph's mind. Through the march, he wanted African Americans to launch a full-scale movement to pressure government, business, political parties, and unions to respond to the needs of the masses of African Americans.

During the second annual meeting of the National Negro Congress in 1937 in Philadelphia, Randolph said, "True liberation can be acquired and maintained only when the Negro people possess power, and power is the product and flower of organization—organization of the masses, the masses in the mills and mines, on the farms, in the factories."[30] Randolph was critical of the New Deal, despite the fact that the Sleeping Car Porters had benefited directly from the Roosevelt administration's labor policies. Randolph argued that African Americans should initiate their own struggle for equality rather than depend on the Roosevelt administration or white liberals. By 1942, he had set forth eight objectives, or what he called the "full works of citizenship" upon which African-American organizations could unite to build a permanent grassroots organization.[31]

Dombrowski's personal views mirrored the ambivalence of the SCHW policies, which encouraged defiance of Jim Crow law inside the War Memorial but acceptance outside. Inside, the private Dombrowski agreed with Randolph's assertion that the New Deal was "no remedy" for African Americans. The Roosevelt administration's policies placed property rights above human rights and did not seek to change the profit system. That government was trying merely to change white attitudes toward African Americans, thereby improving everyone's economic and political lot. Outside, the public Dombrowski necessarily was wed to the assumptions and actions of the New Deal. The SCHW depended on the elected Roosevelt's continued good will and the unelected Roosevelt's personal involvement. Too, Dombrowski did believe that lessening white prejudices could result in some objective improvement in conditions endured by African Americans. Generating a climate for reform and even perhaps helping to unmask "the Negro problem" as the central issue for liberal reform were worthy ends. Finally, his own experiences with Howard Kester and with the CIO and AFL, had convinced him that church and labor leaders who were liberal on race had to make larger common cause. Symbolically, these issues were linked during panels on jobs and civil rights. One delegate told how a Mobile, Alabama, shipyard hired unskilled whites recruited throughout rural Alabama rather than employ African Americans who lived in the shipyard's shadows. A Birmingham steelworker and union man, Noel Beddow, protested: "You say the Negro is discriminated against in the South. Go to Chicago, to Pittsburgh, Detroit and look at the Negro. He receives the same treatment there. What I'm interested in is the poor white man in the South who works for nothing. Let's call an ace an ace and strip this problem like a prima donna in a nudist camp."[32]

John P. Davis, the SCHW leader who headed the National Negro Congress, did not agree. He retorted, "Southern industry seems to be waiting for the right complexion to come along." Although the National Negro Congress had been started by Davis and others to foster unity and collaboration among African-American organizations, by 1940 Davis was seeking to advance the group's agenda through united action with Progressives, churches, labor, or the Roosevelt administration.

Mortimer May, a textile manufacturer who was of the few industrialists present, tried to defuse the argument, saying, "If we fritter away too much energy in trying to solve problems that are hard to solve even in peacetime, we will have little energy left to prosecute the war."

Atlanta University sociologist Dr. Ira DeA. Reid, expressing the views of countless African Americans, was not persuaded by May, saying, "We cannot promote harmony by standing where we are. We are changing the scheme of production to win the war and on a similar token, why cannot we also change human relations?"[33]

After less contentious discussion, the SCHW citizenship and civil liberties panel, chaired by Jennings Perry, editor of the *Nashville Tennessean*, fashioned a resolve stridently opposed to the exclusion of whites from voting. Almost in passing, he mentioned that African Americans were disenfranchised, too.[34]

The SCHW refused to adopt either a program or a resolution specifically aimed at racial discrimination on the job, leaving the organization's value to blacks an open question. Durr, Williams, and Dombrowski pushed white delegates to adopt positions more closely aligned with views expressed by Davis and Reid. They were, however, a minority among a minority. The views of Clark Foreman, a principal architect of the Roosevelt administration's polices on race, prevailed. In general, Foreman argued that African Americans would benefit from strong federal policies uniformly applied and should be woven into the nation's industry as part of the South's economic reconstruction. Federal programs such as the National Youth Administration and the Fair Employment Practices Commission, while not attacking racism directly, improved life for African Americans and weakened white prejudice.[35]

In 1942, the SCHW, if measured by its formal resolutions, hardly differed from the earlier Commission on Interracial Cooperation (CIC), an outgrowth of the YMCAs, which sought regular meetings between whites and African Americans as the way to overcome segregation's deep divisions. The CIC's members believed that liberal whites were the African American's best friends and that the South was the best place for African Americans to realize their dreams. Dombrowski spurned that approach soon after arriving at Highlander. He had hoped for more of a racial advance at this convention, but—new on the job, uncertain about internal political alliances, and without a solid political base of his own in the SCHW—Dombrowski acquiesced. He had a long political road ahead, with more disappointments to come.

Members of the SCHW executive committee were convening for one last meeting before departing from Nashville. Dombrowski, with Bethune on his arm, entered the lobby of the Hotel Noel, where he lived and where the meeting was scheduled. As they stepped on the elevator, the operator told them guardedly, "I'm sorry. This elevator is for whites only. Negroes use the freight elevator. You'll have to use the freight elevator in the rear."[36]

"I'm not freight," Bethune declared. "I'll walk!" She took Dombrowski's arm and they started climbing three flights of stairs to the meeting room, Dombrowski was left in her wake as his arthritic knees kept him from matching her furious pace.

Then, during the meeting itself, Frank McCallister, the Socialist whom Dombrowski had worked with in Tampa on the Modern Democrats tragedy, appeared without notice to demand that Communists, or anyone suspected of Communist leanings, be kept out of the SCHW. Two years earlier, in Chattanooga, McCallister led a successful effort to bar Communists from office in the SCHW. This time, he was peeved at Robeson's remarks the previous evening; he suspected that John P. Davis was a Communist and wanted him ousted. "Oh, what a trial Frank McCallister was," moaned Virginia Durr years later. "Why, he was even calling Mrs. Bethune a Red!"[37] The dispute was not resolved during the executive committee meeting but instead dragged on for months. McCallister supported his argument with a letter from Roger Baldwin of the American Civil Liberties Union to Eleanor Roosevelt, charging that the SCHW was refusing to cooperate with some southern reform groups. Baldwin, writing as a member of the influential Marshall Fund, said, "I have heard from representatives of all the organizations and they are of one view in declining to cooperate further with the Conference on the grounds of what they regard as undue communist influence. As trustees we are interested only in the practical effectiveness of a union of liberal forces in the South. Apparently, the Southern Conference has not been handled with a degree of statesmanship to insure that."[38] Most of the groups he referred to depended on the Marshall Fund to operate or were aligned with Mitchell, McCallister, and the Socialist Party. Dombrowski believed that McCallister had used the anticommunism ploy to gain control of the SCHW for himself, or for the Norman Thomas wing of the Socialist Party, which he represented in the South.

When the dispute reached Eleanor Roosevelt, she and others defended the SCHW. She was surprised at his allegations and noted: "Some of the delegates from these organizations spoke to me at the conference and seemed to be active. I have always understood that the Southern Electoral Reform League was somewhat Socialist and the Southern Tenant Farmers' Union and the Workers' Defense League somewhat communistic, but I imagine in cooperation with others they do effective work."[39]

Dombrowski, attacking while seeming to defend, wrote Baldwin, "I had always supposed that a man's politics, like his religion, were his personal affair, indeed as I understand the right for civil liberties, that right to hold to a conviction differing from the norm is one of the basic rights for which the fight is conducted."[40]

In the meanwhile, the convention over, Dombrowski turned his attention to keeping the SCHW afloat financially. The convention's costs were barely covered by donations and registration fees. The treasury was empty, as it had been when Dombrowski's stewardship began. Membership fees of one dollar annually totaled $2,007 in 1942, an accurate reflection of the organization's regional popularity. Much of the SCHW's financial base lay outside the South, with Dombrowski expected to provide a link between northern philanthropy and southern need, as he had at Highlander. He managed to raise $3,000 that year, mostly from northerners who had donated funds to Highlander. Ethel Clyde was especially helpful. Support from unions had increased, too. Foundations gave the SCHW $10,000. Income totaled $15,007 in 1942.

As he attended to the McCallister fight and to the SCHW's finances, Dombrowski was faced with the sudden and unexpected resignation of the man the SCHW had just elected president. Dr. Homer Price Rainey, president of the University of Texas, was considered to be among the nation's most promising young educators. He had been recruited to succeed Dr. Thompson. When he returned to Austin, a member of the UT Board of Regents, enraged that Rainey was associated with the SCHW, demanded that he resign as SCHW president or face the prospect of being fired.[41] Rainey chose the university.

With SCHW officers and members scattered across the nation and no meeting planned for another two years, Dombrowski had to arrange balloting by mail. By June, Clark Foreman had been elected SCHW president. Besides being an influential member of Roosevelt's team, Foreman was a nephew of the publisher of the powerful *Atlanta Constitution* and well-connected throughout the South. Foreman told Baldwin that he personally had no sympathy for Communists but that he saw no reason to exclude them from politics. He insisted that Communists posed less risk to the SCHW than the risk run by "following a Red-baiting, negative, and undemocratic policy."[42] He added, "Your letter goes far beyond anything I have ever heard of an American foundation doing in an attempt to control an organization to which it contributed."

Eventually McCallister's attack was turned back, but not before the debate it caused turned some potential alliances into lasting enmities. Since its inception, the SCHW had been forced to defend itself against allegations that Communists ran it or used it as a front for other purposes. Alabama's Big Mules, the state's industrial elite, had issued the first charges after the SCHW convention in Birmingham. Subsequently, the Dies Committee had launched a much-publicized investigation. Inside the SCHW itself, Socialists, particularly McCallister and H.L. Mitchell of the Southern Tenant Farmers' Union, pushed ceaselessly for the ouster of any person they claimed to be under "external compulsion."[43] Late in 1939, Frank Graham, the SCHW's first president, was sufficiently disturbed by the persistent rumors that he privately investigated the SCHW. He identified six

Communists and four sympathizers among the over twelve hundred delegates attending the founding convention.

The SCHW survived on political connections; ties with the Roosevelt administration were essential. In this respect, Foreman seemed a better choice than Rainey. He was a Washington insider, albeit, by the time of his election, increasingly controversial. He was brilliant, brusque, and determined that African Americans would have roles in the federal government's policy councils and jobs in its offices. His secretary was the first African American employed by the Department of the Interior. He brought to Washington a young African-American economist, Robert A. Weaver, who'd made a name for himself at Harvard University, installing him as advisor on African-American affairs to Harold Ickes, secretary of the Interior. Foreman pushed for the controversial FEPC order.

Earlier, Foreman had worked for Dr. Will Alexander's Interracial Commission. His doctoral dissertation at Columbia University had been an attack on the commonly-held but racist assertion that blacks were poor, ill-schooled, and often sickly because of "race" or "blood." Foreman's immediate family in Georgia stood by him, but other relatives and friends at Atlanta's prestigious Piedmont Driving Club assailed him bitterly.[44] He offended most of the southern congressional delegation, a powerful political bloc holding back some Roosevelt policies. Foreman made an unsuccessful effort to defeat Senator Walter George, who voted against most of the New Deal legislation. The president vowed to unseat him. George did not appreciate the challenge and soundly beat Foreman. By 1942, congressional conservatives, led by southern lawmakers, were successfully blocking Roosevelt's reform program. Foreman was the target of much of their wrath.

Dombrowski, worried that the congressional attacks might force the president to abandon Foreman, wrote the vilified Georgian asking if his relationship with the SCHW might cause the president to distance himself from Foreman, thus diminishing the SCHW's influence in Washington.[45] Dombrowski and Foreman shared many beliefs and ways. Their opposition to racism and fascism relied on economics to explain both southern poverty and the attendant racism. Both agreed that fascism was a function of a capitalist economic system gone wrong; democracy and socialism were its correctives. They were men who earnestly believed that action had to follow reflection. Foreman was charismatic, forceful, extremely confident, and often politically competitive.

A test of this pair's ability to work together was postponed by war. Foreman joined the Navy and was assigned to the Office of Operational Research in England. Dombrowski tried to enlist in June 1942 at the draft board in Nashville. The draft board never responded to his initiative. The Federal Bureau of Investigation was keeping a file on his work. It noted that the draft board classified him as a citizen deserving "custodial detention" in case of a national emergency.[46]

# 9

## Battles
## on the
## Homefront

Before and during the Nashville SCHW convention, Dombrowski made political decisions that nagged at his conscience. Once the last delegate was gone and the last thank-you letter written, he spent hours alone reflecting about the compromises he made and worrying about what he might yield on in the future. He'd been reading Carson McCullers' novel, *The Heart is a Lonely Hunter;* the book added to his disquiet. Her sympathies were his. She championed the dispossessed. She pictured liberal social reformers, one African-American and one white, as so utterly estranged from their own communities that the truths they possessed distorted their judgment. Was he any different? During those moments of give-and-take when he had let go of principle, Dombrowski felt, he had allowed the SCHW to pull him from the miners or WPA workers in Grundy County, and that theorizing, excusing, and resolving—not direct political action and teaching—had become his tools for social change. Was he a misguided, disaffected, ineffectual reformer, unable or unwilling to draw the line?

Dombrowski was bothered, too, by the fact that he would not be going to war, or at least that seemed the case. The Nashville draft board ignored his enlistment application. Dombrowski was hurt and not a little puzzled; he believed in the military obligations of citizenship. He was fearful that fascism might prevail, first in Europe and then in the Soviet Union, and finally overwhelm the United States. He ignored the fact that the arthritic pain which hampered his life no doubt would have rendered him unfit for military duties. He suspected that the draft board's silence had to do with his notoriety, not his health or age. But he had no evidence for the suspicion until years later.

As he typed the convention minutes for distribution to the board and to posterity, Dombrowski realized that the SCHW's African-American delegates had given him—and the SCHW, if he could bring the organization along—an agenda for change. The war probably would improve the South's economy, but was not likely to improve life for African Americans or change their segregated status unless there was deliberate, concerted intervention. Military goods were produced in stiffly segregated factories, if African Americans were hired at all. That seemed unlikely to change after the war. But why not go to war on the homefront? The war against fascism abroad provided the SCHW a nearly irrefutable moral argument to fight segregation at home. The "master-race" ideologies of Germany and Japan differed hardly a jot from the white racism of America. The SCHW, taking its cue from African Americans, could be a companion in racial change, seizing every opportunity to influence what happened as war changed the South's character. In this battle, he could enlist despite the Nashville draft board, and he could recruit others into integrated squads. Compromise might be ahead, but for the war's duration and beyond, if possible, Dombrowski decided to campaign against racism.

Dombrowski decided, too, that his relationship with Ellen Krida would change; either she would marry him or he would end the courtship eleven years after it had begun amid the tumult of a hockey game. Dombrowski went to New York late in November 1942, on SCHW business. He once again asked Krida to marry him, and to live in Nashville. Krida agreed that the time was finally right. His job, while as demanding and political as the one he had left at Highlander, at least paid a salary. Nashville, in her eyes, was an Athens compared to Monteagle. On December 5, in the First Unitarian Church of Baltimore, Maryland, with two hastily assembled witnesses, the Reverend W. Waldermar Argrow married the couple. No family members were invited. The State of Maryland issued a marriage certificate describing Dombrowski as a teacher and forty-six years of age; Krida had no occupation and was thirty.[1] The newlyweds planned a weeklong honeymoon in Baltimore and Washington, After two days, however, reclusive Ellen Dombrowski had misgivings about leaving the solitude of her Riverside Drive apartment. She took a train back to New York City, agreeing to pack her belongings and come South in a few days. Days stretched into weeks. On May 15, his exasperation showing, Dombrowski wrote, "My dear, what have you been doing for the past five months? I thought you would be all ready by now. What you don't pack, leave or give to the Russian War Relief. Remember we have only one room!"[2] A month later, Ellen had moved to Nashville.

In the meantime, African Americans weren't waiting for well-meaning whites to advance their cause. In a historic meeting, several dozen mostly moderate or professional leaders from across the South met in Durham, North Carolina, on October 20, 1942, to set forth their own agenda in what became known as the Durham Statement.[3] They declared that their "first loyalty" was to America and the Allied cause. However, the war should not distract African Americans from "working out" problems "essential to our full contribution to the war effort."[4] They asked for equal access to work, equal pay once at work, a federal antilynching law, abolition of white-only primaries, and an end to poll taxes. They condemned official segregation but did not call for an immediate end to Jim Crow laws, adding: "We are fundamentally opposed to the principle and practice of compulsory segregation in our American society; however, we regard it as both sensible and timely to address ourselves now to the current problems of racial discrimination and neglect, and to ways in which we may cooperate in the advancement of programs aimed at the sound improvement of race relations within the democratic framework."[5]

Dombrowski and SCHW president Foreman thought that the Durham Statement was an opportunity for whites to support African-American initiatives. Several signers belonged to the SCHW, including the scholarly Charles S. Johnson. Johnson was among the influential African-American leaders sharply debating postwar strategy and tactics. He believed that New Deal policies fostered economic and political changes which increasingly were forcing the South's caste structure to disintegrate. Foreman posted a series of letters to them and to others, suggesting that the SCHW and the Durham group meet to discuss mutual problems.[6]

Elsewhere, Howard W. Odum, who had succeeded Dr. Will Alexander at the Commission on Interracial Cooperation, also proposed to meet with authors of the Durham Statement.[7] Odum, a noted University of North Carolina professor, kept his distance from the SCHW. He wanted to replace the waning CIC with an interracial organization he was tentatively calling the Southern Regional Council. Odum believed that a direct attack on Jim Crow segregation was a futile quest on the part of a few powerless persons. Alternatives to improve race relations, he argued, were education and greater federal consideration of African-American economic and social needs.

Odum's argument fell on sympathetic ears among moderate African-American leaders, including Johnson; C. C. Spaulding, a North Carolina insurance agent; and P.B. Young, publisher of a Norfolk, Virginia, newspaper. The SCHW carried too many historic liabilities, in their opinion. They wanted an organization free of Communist taint and the emotional scars left by foreign policy disputes such as those provoked by John L. Lewis at the Chattanooga convention in 1940.[8]

Early in his career, Dr. Ralph Bunche, an important New Deal figure, had been critical of Roosevelt's approach to race relations. Bunche, who had graduated from Harvard University, was one of Gunnar Myrdal's assistants during the research for his classic study, *An American Dilemma*. Along with many other African Americans, Bunche doubted that Roosevelt's liberal ideology would do much more than adjust the worst outcomes of discrimination. He tried to free the debate from the mythology of race, arguing that the emotions aroused by race kept African Americans and whites from facing their common enemy, economic disparity. Eventually, however, Bunche gave qualified support to the New Deal, even working closely with Harold Ickes and Clark Foreman.

That Johnson and Bunche changed their minds demonstrated the attractiveness of New Deal efforts to reform the nation's caste and class system but also the lack of any significant alternative strategy aimed either at caste or at class. Within the SCHW, the dilemma was no less obvious. Dombrowski and Foreman differed on how the SCHW should respond to Odum's initiative. Foreman wanted to merge the SRC and the SCHW or find ways the two organizations could cooperate.[9] Alexander, who had left the CIC to join the Roosevelt administration, supported a merger. Some African-American leaders who belonged to both groups favored a merger, too.

Dombrowski believed that Odum's approach was necessary but not sufficient.[10] He was not opposed to a merger, provided that Odum gave assurances in writing that membership would be open to anyone. Odum planned to have a self-perpetuating board of directors; Dombrowski proposed that members elect the board and that the membership debate and vote on policies during annual conventions. Odum and other SRC leaders rejected these stipulations. The talks never got far.

Odum disbanded the CIC in October 1943. In February 1944, the

Southern Regional Council opened operations in Atlanta, guided by Odum and Guy Johnson, another University of North Carolina professor, and a self-appointed board of directors. Over one thousand southerners of varying degrees of liberalism joined.[11]

Some notable southerners stayed away. Lillian Smith was among them. Smith, acclaimed for her novel *Strange Fruit,* was an active member of the SCHW and was the most prominent southerner to differ with Odum's approach. She made her case in public, sparking debate in two essays, one of which appeared in the *North Georgia Review.* She wrote, "Not much is going to be done to bring about racial democracy by this group (SRC) until its leaders accept and acknowledge publicly the basic truth that segregation is injuring us on every level of our life and is so intolerable to the human spirit that we, all of us, black and white, must bend every effort to rid our minds, hearts and culture of it."[12] Smith believed that the power whites used to dominate and exploit African Americans had to be eroded, or somehow matched, if racist ideologies were to be overcome. New laws, government pressure on businesses and unions, presidential decrees, perhaps even constitutional amendments were needed. At this juncture in history, Smith and Dombrowski were going in the same direction. He redoubled SCHW's effort to end poll taxes and pushed for a permanent Fair Employment Practices Commission. He and others waited anxiously for a Supreme Court decision on the white primaries.

Dombrowski asked the SCHW executive committee for approval to publish a regular newsletter to express the SCHW's views. He aimed to convince southerners that the SCHW's policies were correct, especially on race, and thus distance the SCHW from Odum's SRC. Dombrowski's arthritis kept him from traveling to Washington in September 1942, for a meeting of the executive committee at Foreman's home. Foreman, Durr, Helen Fuller, John Davis, and Louis Burnham, along with Alton Lawrence, Dombrowski's predecessor, attended. They approved Dombrowski's idea for a publication, deciding to publish *The Southern Patriot,* a name chosen to deflect Red-baiting and to reflect the SCHW's "love of country."[13] An editorial direction was outlined and a decision taken that the paper would make no direct attempt to persuade readers to contribute to the SCHW. Propaganda and fundraising were to be kept separate and distinct.

Fred Sweet, a respected newspaperman, was hired parttime to edit the new publication. Before he moved to Washington, Sweet's own weekly in Michigan had been bombed out of business after he had written editorials backing Walter and Victor Reuther in the United Auto Workers drive to organize Henry Ford's automobile assembly plants. For the remainder of his career, Sweet worked for union newspapers.

Despite editorial rhetoric which sometimes bordered on jingoism during the war years, *The Southern Patriot* established a reputation as a reliable source of news and analysis about race relations and liberal reforms. Feature articles were culled from government reports or academic studies. Dombrowski urged the SCHW's members to send clippings from hometown newspapers. The aim was to profile racial change in the South.[14] Funds permitting, journalists were hired to report on a particular event or story. During the first years, editorials stressed victory over the Axis and reform in the South; later the pages were devoted entirely to shifts in American racism. Any legislative proposal was assessed. Economic improvements were described. Continuing contradictions were analyzed. Race-baiting politicians were described in terms matching their own stridency. In one edition, for instance, opponents of Roosevelt's domestic policies were said to be traitors.[15]

Sweet was only the first of many persons who helped Dombrowski produce the monthly newsletter. Lou Frank, Marge Frantz, and Frank Bancroft pitched in, as well as Alfred Maund, a novelist and former *New Republic* magazine staffer, who stayed the longest. Throughout its life, the publication reflected Dombrowski's conviction, repeated in countless ways, that racism was incompatible with fellowship and Christianity.

Dombrowski and Foreman wanted *The Southern Patriot* to rekindle enthusiasm for the SCHW. Circulation did grow, reaching over five thousand paid subscribers by 1946.[16] However, *The Southern Patriot* was hardly the vehicle to reach the masses, reflecting as it did the character of the SCHW's membership—a middle-class, professional, intellectual, interracial group that wanted to repeal the poll tax, institute full and fair employment practices, secure the right of unions to organize, and end segregation, *de facto* and *de jure*.[17] Even so, *The Southern Patriot* never wanted for news, especially about jobs and race. As war production increased, the demand for labor soared, opening thousands of previously segregated jobs to African Americans. The Fair Employment Practices Committee forced other doors open. Threatened, some whites protested or used violence to keep employment privileges. Frequently, state or local governments and the more conservative trade unions joined them. Work stoppages, strikes, and sabotage sparked by race hatred were reported across the South.[18]

Through its farflung membership, *The Southern Patriot* gathered news that other publications missed or ignored. Dombrowski "broke the story" when Alabama's Gov. Frank Dixon refused to let prison inmates make badly-needed Army tents because the federal contract contained a clause prohibiting discrimination in employment. The paper was the first to report that Col. Lindley W. Camp, head of the Georgia State Guard, had ordered militiamen on alert, saying, "There have been reported efforts on the part of the Negro men and women to demand certain privileges which are not granted in Georgia and never will be."[19]

In fact, clashes between the races had become so frequent and so intense that the liberal New York daily newspaper, *PM,* posted a fulltime correspondent in the South. Dispatches read as if combat had been declared. An African-American insurance agent in Memphis was beaten for trying to sell a policy to whites. In Mobile, a white bus driver shot and killed an African-American soldier who asked for help getting his duffle bag off the bus. In Beaumont, Texas, two policemen beat, then shot and wounded, an Army private for taking a bus seat reserved for whites.[20]

Dombrowski saw an African-American soldier chased and shot outside his office. Military police repeatedly slapped the wounded soldier as they waited for an ambulance to take him to a hospital.[21] Dombrowski went to the man's side as quickly as he could on his arthritic legs. Police said they suspected the soldier was an Army deserter. The bleeding soldier showed Dombrowski his pass. Dombrowski immediately wired the Justice Department asking for an investigation, saying that the incident confirmed evidence that a widespread conspiracy "existed to exploit racial prejudices for economic and political purposes, a primary objective being to alienate the South from the national administration."[22] The complaint was ignored.

Through *The Southern Patriot,* Dombrowski learned to use propaganda techniques. In the wake of Governor Dixon's rejection of the tent contract, he arranged to run a full-page ad in the *Birmingham News-Age Herald:* "Violent speech filled with Nazi ideas and phrases . . . incite race hatred and conflict." A coupon was available for "every loyal southerner" to clip and mail to President Roosevelt pledging regional unity.[23]

Later, when three African Americans were lynched during one week in Mississippi, Dombrowski again took to a local newspaper to lambaste racist violence as harmful to the war effort. A full-page ad appeared in a Jackson, Mississippi, newspaper signed by seventy-five prominent Mississippians, including Judge J. Morgan Stevens, a one-time State Supreme Court jurist and leading Methodist layman.[24] Copies of the Mississippi ad were mailed to every southern paper, causing the *Chattanooga News Free Press* to declare Dombrowski's campaign "the acme of 'crust'." The paper's editor, remembering Dombrowski from Highlander, asked, "Who then is Mr. Dombrowski that he should be appealing for American unity?"[25]

Dombrowski appears to have had strong support among the SCHW's African-American members for this work. They feared that the violence spreading against soldiers and workers would force any postwar federal administration to give secondary attention to racial issues. Most wanted race to be the South's central postwar issue. Dr. Franklin Patterson and Dr. Rufus E. Clement, president of Atlanta University, felt the SCHW should help pave the way for new federal initiatives after the Allied victory. John P. Davis wanted the SCHW to launch a massive publicity campaign "to show that the rank and file of the white South is fully prepared to see the Negro accorded a fair opportunity. This is what we mean by mobilizing the South for victory."[26]

In addition, Dombrowski wanted to expand the SCHW through state-level affiliates. In January 1944, the executive committee, meeting at Black Mountain College outside Asheville, North Carolina, adopted a resolution instructing him to establish SCHW committees across the South. The model was to be the Washington Committee. In the nation's capitol, SCHW activists gave the SCHW access to the national press corps, political leaders, and funds, and functioned as a lobby for compatible federal legislation. The Washington Committee led the fight to repeal the poll tax. They urged the Washington Transit Company, a private firm, to hire African Americans. If similarly aggressive committees were working in each southern capitol, the reasoning went, backing for progressive municipal, state, and federal legislation might swell. By March 1944, Dombrowski had groups going in Georgia, North Carolina, and Tennessee. The SCHW wanted to reach "the little people" with roots deep in the South.[27]

The fourth biennial SCHW convention, which opened in Washington, D.C., on April 3, 1944, was less ambitious than any previous gathering, being limited by wartime rationing and the lack of money in the SCHW treasury. Chiefly, the thousand or so persons who attended were clergymen or Roosevelt administration officials. Predictably, there were calls for peace and international stability, along with full employment and industrial development in the South. The poll tax continued to preoccupy the SCHW, and delegates celebrated the Supreme Court's decision outlawing the white primary in Texas. At the banquet dinner, Supreme Court Justice Hugo Black, who had had a significant voice in the court's decision, was given the Thomas Jefferson Award a second time. Although the SCHW lacked broad public support for its program, at the convention's close Dombrowski felt that "the liberal South had been heard loud and clear."[28]

Even before the convention, there had been evidence that it would be a politically significant event. Sen. Theodore G. Bilbo of Mississippi had written Justice Black, ostensibly to learn if in fact his relative by marriage, Virginia Durr, was on the SCHW board. Bilbo said he wanted the information before denouncing the SCHW in a Senate speech. Bilbo urged Black to refuse the SCHW Jefferson Award, saying, "I sincerely hope that you will honor the state of your nativity by being absent. You know that you and I are good Ku Klux brothers and to be a party to this thing would be a dishonorable thing for us to do because, as you so well know, when we resigned from the Ku Klux we had to sign our names in the Sacred Unity Book."[29] Black, from Alabama, had been a member of the Ku Klux Klan. He ignored Bilbo's advice.

The SCHW leadership and Bilbo outraged each other. Foreman denounced Bilbo's "vile prejudice" and "neofascism." Bilbo wrote Dombrowski on November 5, 1945:

> I have just received through a friend of mine in Jackson, Mississippi, two sheets that your un-American, Negro social equality, communistic, mongrel outfit is sending out through the country in your mad desire to build up a factual case against the right and prerogative of a United States Senator or Senators to filibuster any objectionable legislation that is proposed in this great body.
>
> Of course, your immediate aim is to secure the passage of the undemocratic, un-American anti-poll tax bill which is now pending on the calendar of the United States Senate by defeating the right and power of Senators to object by filibuster. In other words, you are trying to bulldoze and intimidate members of the Senate who are conscientiously opposed to this un-American piece of legislation.
>
> You may be able for a little time to fool a few decent white people with your insidious scheme that is behind the Southern Conference for Human Welfare but not for long. If I were called upon to name the

Number One Enemy of the South today it would be the Southern Conference for Human Welfare.[30]

This bluster made splashy newspaper copy and amused the SCHW's friends in the New Deal and the CIO, and the northerners who provided the SCHW with most of its finances. However, the rhetorical exchanges created an aura of inflexible orthodoxy which tended to erode support among southern liberals. During the 1946 Georgia gubernatorial race, for instance, Foreman and Dombrowski, to their dismay, were unable to persuade the SCHW's Georgia committee, led by Margaret Fisher, publicly to support the candidate backed by Ellis Arnall. In 1942, Arnall, a moderate on race, gave the SCHW hope by beating Eugene Talmadge after a campaign filled with race baiting. As governor, Arnall engineered the repeal of Georgia's poll-tax law, again cheering southern liberals. Arnall, by law unable to succeed himself as governor, backed a candidate whom Talmadge assailed as a front for "niggers" and "Reds."[31]

Foreman and Dombrowski asked Fisher to endorse Arnall's candidate, but the leader of the SCHW's best organized and financed state committee refused, saying any public endorsement would harm Arnall's forces. Talmadge won the bitter election, but died before he could be inaugurated. Outgoing Arnall named his lieutenant governor to succeed him; the Georgia legislature chose Talmadge's son, Herman. As Georgia's political life plunged into confused, clamorous animosity, Fisher and the Georgia SCHW were silent. Eventually, Talmadge became governor.[32]

Other state committees did not live up to expectations either. Most were unable to raise enough money to support paid staff; they had to be subsidized through additional fundraising by Dombrowski. As often as not, they acted in concert with the SCHW; sometimes, however, they did not, and there was virtually no way to discipline noncompliant behavior. The SCHW did not enjoy mass political appeal, or money could have been raised locally.

Meanwhile, Mississippi's second senator, James Eastland, during a filibuster against the anti–poll tax bill, denigrated the courage of blacks in the Armed Forces. Eastland declared, "The Negro soldier was an utter and dismal failure in combat in Europe . . . He has disgraced the flag of this country. He will not fight. He will not work."[33] After reading Eastland's remarks, Dombrowski and Foreman immediately rebutted the senator, who inadvertently gave them a way to soften the SCHW's failures in

Georgia. Dombrowski and Lou Frank, who helped edit *The Southern Patriot*, assembled a pamphlet, "Look Him in the Eye," extolling the accomplishments of African-American servicemen. Prominent military officers, including Gen. Dwight Eisenhower, were quoted to counter Eastland. "In the current global war the Negro has definitely established himself in the hierarchy of distinguished soldiers," Eisenhower said.[34] When the pamphlet appeared, Eastland took to the Senate floor again, where his colleagues roared with laughter as he declared the SCHW was run by a man with the "fine old Southern name of Dombrowski. Dom-Brow-Ski."[35] Foreman, in a press statement, declared that Dombrowski was "not only a better Southerner but a better American than Senator Eastland." For a man who'd been elected by less than fifteen percent of the voting-age citizens in Mississippi, Foreman continued, Eastland's behavior was "disgraceful."[35]

The Mississippi senator's interest in the SCHW seems to have derived from the organization's responsiveness to African-American demands that jobs gained during war not be lost in peacetime. Foreman had testified before the Senate in March 1945 in favor of a permanent Fair Employment Practices Commission. Other suggestions for direct federal intervention were equally offensive to Bilbo, Eastland, and others. In the midst of these bruising exchanges, Dombrowski got a telephone call from a SCHW member in Columbia, Tennessee, about fifty miles south of Nashville, relaying to Dombrowski a horrifying story.

The day before, Monday, February 25, 1946, an African-American Navy veteran, James Stephenson, 19, and his mother, Mrs. Gladys Stephenson, returned a radio to a repair shop, claiming that it had not been repaired properly. Will Fleming, the clerk, angry that the shop's work was questioned, demanded that they pay the $13 repair bill anyway. When Mrs. Stephenson refused, the clerk slapped her. The son punched Fleming, who, as he fell, struck and broke a plate glass window, shattering glass onto the sidewalk.[36] The repairman was not seriously injured. But a crowd gathered quickly, some of whom jumped the veteran and his mother. She was knocked to the ground and kicked in the face. Police arrived to arrest the Stephensons. None of the men who had set upon them, or Fleming, was charged. Fleming's brother was running in the Democratic primary for sheriff.

The small town was electrified. A hardware store sold rope as fast as clerks pulled it off spindles. Only a few years before, a mob of whites from

Columbia had broken into the Nashville city jail to grab a fourteen-year-old boy, Cordie Cheek. He had been found innocent of rape charges. The mob brought him back to Columbia and hung him in a tree outside the courthouse. After the body had been cut down, authorities left the rope hanging for weeks as a mute warning.

A neighbor of the Stephensons made bond for them, then spirited the mother and son out of town. Less than an hour after the Stephensons were released, an armed white mob stormed the jail. Their prey gone, the mob roamed Columbia's streets looking for African Americans. Some fled Columbia; most, however, retreated inside their homes in the section of Columbia known as Mink Slide. Many were armed, prepared to defend themselves and expecting that they would be forced to. When police in unmarked cars attempted to drive into Mink Slide, they were met with a volley of buckshot. Four policemen were wounded. Infuriated officials called the governor to send militia and the Highway Patrol. Angry whites built barricades on streets leading into Mink Slide. By dawn one hundred Highway Patrolmen and four hundred National Guardsmen surrounded the neighborhood. As day broke, they began moving into the community.

Eventually, police and guardsmen searched nearly every home in Mink Slide, randomly firing machine-gun bullets into houses and cars. Businesses were destroyed—embalming fluid was poured over expensive furniture in the Morton Funeral Home; chairs and mirrors were smashed in the Blair Barber Shop. Over one hundred men, women, and children were herded into the jail, where some of them were beaten. No charges were filed against anyone.

Dombrowski immediately telephoned Laurent Frantz, the lawyer husband of Marge, his assistant. Together they telephoned eye-witnesses to get a full account of the tragedy. They spoke with white officials and African Americans to crosscheck facts. They telephoned the Mink Slide story to newspapers around the nation. Twenty-four hours later, the SCHW had in the mail a broadside, "The Truth About Columbia, Tennessee," detailing the police assault. Only a few Tennessee newspapers reported the story. State officials claimed that Mink Slide's citizens were responsible for the violence. The SCHW urged readers to "let the Governor of Tennessee know that you do not want state force used as substitutes for a lynch mob. You can help by demanding the federal government intervene to protect civil rights when they are violated by state and local officials. You can help by contributing money toward the defense."[37]

Dombrowski telephoned Walter White of the National Association for the Advancement of Colored People to ask if the NAACP would join the SCHW to form a national defense committee to work on the Columbia situation. The NAACP leadership in New York, accustomed to being ignored by southern whites, agreed.[38] On March 13, the National Committee for Justice in Columbia, Tennessee, demanded that the U.S. Justice Department investigate for violations of civil rights of Mink Slide's residents. Eleanor Roosevelt and Dr. Channing Tobias, one of the few African Americans in the YMCA's leadership, headed the ad hoc committee which represented over sixty national organizations.[39]

Letters by the dozen poured into the Tennessee governor's office denouncing the violence of the Highway Patrol and militiamen, and urging disciplinary action against any policeman found guilty of violating the civil or criminal rights of Columbia's African Americans. Another support committee was organized to help victims with bail funds, or to repair homes or businesses. Over 100,000 copies of the SCHW report were printed. Dombrowski's office was the coordinating center for both campaigns. Even with the national pressure, thirteen African Americans, most of them Mink Slide's leaders, were still in jail. Bond had been set five thousand dollars each, but no charges had been filed. Police said they were being held for a grand jury as charges of leading an insurrection were "worked up against them."[40] Over one hundred persons had been arrested. All but the thirteen had been charged with attempted murder in the first degree or carrying a concealed weapon, both felonies carrying long prison terms upon conviction.

Mink Slide or the SCHW were on the front pages of newspapers around the nation. The *New York Times* sent in a reporter. Tennessee newspapers were hostile; several inferred that the SCHW pamphlet was a cause of the police riot. One editorial cartoon depicted Dombrowski with the hammer and sickle in hand. Candidates in a Tennessee gubernatorial race vied with each other to condemn Dombrowski or the SCHW. Dombrowski was summoned before a federal grand jury called to investigate Mink Slide and testified eight hours on June 3 and 4.[41]

To cast doubt on the SCHW's defense campaign, Tennessee's American Legion started discrediting Dombrowski and the SCHW. Monroe Schaff, a retired Army major and chairman of the Tennessee American Legion's committee on subversive activities, told the Columbia Kiwanis Club that the SCHW was a Communist front. "The administrator of this organiza-

Boxing champion Joe Louis, James Dombrowski, and Malcolm C. Dobbs (*left to right*) discuss drive to improve postwar race relations in the South, 1947. Photo by Al Plum. Courtesy of *The Southern Patriot.*

tion is one James Dombrowski. He is a seasoned, well-trained agitator for the Communist Party. His pet subject is 'to uplift living conditions in the South.' That, gentlemen, is a farce. Did you ever hear of any Communist who is working for the welfare of this country?"[42]

After Schaff's speech, the *Nashville Banner,* long a foe of the SCHW, reported, "At least one *Daily Worker,* American mouthpiece of Communism, is delivered daily in Nashville. Its destination is a suite of offices in the staid old Presbyterian Building, 150–152 Fourth Avenue, North, where it comes to the hands of the couple who have given Nashville the honor of being headquarters for the Southern Conference for Human Welfare."[43]

The attacks intensified in fury and number. Politicians made stump speeches demanding that the governor run the SCHW out of Tennessee. The defense campaign suffered repeated setbacks. First, the grand jury refused to indict any Highway Patrolman or Columbia policeman, on any violation of law. Next, twenty-five African Americans went on trial in Columbia, and, while twenty-three were acquitted, two were sentenced to long prison terms. Months later, on appeal, their sentences were eventually reduced. Daily the SCHW offices received threatening telephone calls. The hate spilled on Dombrowski at home. The few friends Ellen had made in Nashville stopped telephoning, visiting, or inviting her out. Never comfortable with conflict or upheaval, she stopped answering telephone calls or the doorbell. She stayed in the apartment for days, preferring isolation to the icy stares she and her husband got if they went shopping or for a walk. The elevator operator in their apartment stopped speaking to either of them. For the first time since the mob surrounded him in Elizabethton, Dombrowski feared for his life. "This was one of the three or four periods of prolonged Red-baiting and of provocation when deranged persons could come to think they would be doing a public service by taking someone's life."[44]

# 10

## Warring
## after
## the War

Franklin Roosevelt died in Warm Springs, Georgia, on April
12, 1945, and, like much of the nation, the SCHW's leadership immediately was thrown into mourning. Perplexity followed soon after. The
SCHW's place near the corridors of power became uncertain. When police
rioted in Columbia, Tennessee, Harry S. Truman was settled in office and
still shaping his administration. For Dombrowski, the undistinguished
Missouri politician's rise to the presidency forecast at least the loss of political access. And Mink Slide suggested a frightening possibility elsewhere in
the South after the war. James Stephenson could have been any African-
American veteran coming home. Columbia's mob could have assembled in
any southern town for a lynching. Tennessee's police and militia, he feared,
could have been authorities anywhere, rioting with impunity. Mink Slide
demonstrated that the SCHW was on top of events in the South, with a
committed, effective membership tucked away in places most citizens had
never heard of. Dombrowski could only speculate what the federal government under Truman might do. One of the NAACP's most promising lawyers, Thurgood Marshall, praised the SCHW in a speech before Georgia
NAACP members, exhorting them to contribute to the SCHW.[1] But
Dombrowski realized that praise from the NAACP certainly stamped the
SCHW as an outcast in the minds of many southerners.

Would the organization retain its standing with Washington's movers
and shakers? To some extent, the state committees gave the appearance
that southern liberals were forging an appealing, well-defined program for

the postwar South. The SCHW did reach people directly. During 1945, for instance, every SCHW state committee—no matter how small or inactive—adopted voter registration campaigns, including efforts to regis-ter African Americans despite stern suffrage restrictions. Most had modest success. A few made impressive gains. In Savannah, the Georgia committee organized a registration drive which raised the number of eligible African-American voters from 900 to 19,000.[2]

Dombrowski believed that the SCHW's state committees offered the one way to maintain public influence. Additionally, they kept the SCHW com-petitive with the Southern Regional Council, which was trying to edge out the SCHW in Washington's favor.[3] But the state committees posed nettle-some issues about power. For instance, Clark Foreman believed that the "national office" should direct their activities, meaning that he, as presi-dent, and the board, would control their affairs.[4] Lillian Smith believed that the state committees should be autonomous. She organized a group in opposition to Foreman.[5] At first, Dombrowski sided with Smith, but when the Alabama committee threatened to break with the CIO over Eugene "Bull" Connor's election campaign, Dombrowski switched sides, a move which was a factor in Smith's decision to quit the SCHW.[6] By the end of 1945, Dombrowski had eleven state committees in place. Some were active and employed staffs. Most existed only on paper, although they had poten-tial to help SCHW emerge as a regional political force. In part, they were responsible for the SCHW's growth. When Dombrowski took over, about 500 persons paid the SCHW's dollar membership dues. He told the execu-tive committee in mid-1945 that 1,224 southerners had paid membership dues, 25 or so fewer than had registered at the Birmingham convention. There had been a surge in African-American memberships, he said, which reflected growing concern about the postwar South. Outside the South, mostly in New York or Washington, another 1,500 persons paid dues. Foundations or unions provided most of the SCHW's budget. Income to-taled over $82,000, much of which was spent on the state committees.[7] They cost money.

Dombrowski achieved several personal goals in 1945. He won approval from the executive committee to recruit an African-American staff mem-ber. Additionally, to take advantage of the apparent interest among African Americans, he opened talks with Mary McLeod Bethune to determine if she would lead a membership drive. He believed that white membership support would hold steady or perhaps grow slightly after the war. Growth in membership, he reasoned, had to come from African Americans or northerners. No matter how scattered geographically or numerically outnumbered, such a political base, if united against Jim Crow, could maintain a presence in Washington.

The SCHW focused a lot of its attention on the nation's capitol. The Washington committee had over three hundred members and held monthly luncheons where well-known labor, newspaper, or political speakers appeared, joining in open violation of Washington's Jim-Crow restaurant laws. Eventually, the Washington committee opened a legislative office to represent the SCHW's interests before Congress and regulatory agencies. Foreman testified regularly before congressional committees, pushing for or pulling against legislation. Public housing, agriculture, minimum wages, rural housing, and, of course, the SCHW's longstanding fight to repeal the poll tax were topics the office kept close tabs on.

The SCHW's presence was not unnoticed. Senator Bilbo attacked again, describing the SCHW's members as "white Quislings."[8] Bilbo was particularly upset with Foreman. "This little peckerwood," he wrote a friend, "is a negro-lover. . . . He is just a reprobate and a black sheep in the family and he thinks he can make a reputation and get compensation by betraying the South and all the South stands for."[9]

State committees were active, and the ones in North Carolina and Georgia were adding members. But the state committees cost money, adding to the demands on Dombrowski to keep cash flowing into the treasury. During 1945, the SCHW spent $11,000 to support the Georgia committee; over $25,000 was budgeted for 1946. The slightest drop in membership or lag in foundation or union gifts pinched Dombrowski's cash flow projections. The tenuous fiscal situation was reflected in a worried memo he mailed to state committee leaders urging them "to exert themselves during the month to secure new members. . . . You will note that the total number of memberships received for November fell off considerably from the previous two months."[10]

The state committees jeopardized the SCHW's tax-exempt status. Each had a political agenda, prompting the Internal Revenue Service to rule that the SCHW was a political organization, not an educational one. Electoral politics and education did not mix if donations were to be exempt from taxes.

Dombrowski was pondering a response to the IRS ruling when he received jolting news which he expected would hurt the SCHW immediately.

On April 18, 1946, the CIO called a news conference in New York City to announce another drive to organize the South's workers. Van A. Bittner, who had been named to direct a postwar effort, told reporters that the CIO had a million dollars to invest in the campaign, and that the union drive would differ from the earlier TWOC initiative. Operation Dixie was going to be a drive for union members carried out by union members only. Bittner lashed out at Rep. Adam Clayton Powell, a Harlem minister and politician who had formed a committee to support Operation Dixie. He told reporters that he had written to Powell, saying, "We will tolerate no interference from organizations outside the CIO. No crowd, whether Communist, Socialist or anybody else, will be permitted to 'mix up' in the campaign and that goes for the Southern Conference for Human Welfare and any other organization living off the CIO. This is a CIO affair. We don't want people to get us mixed up with all these organizations."[11]

Bittner's attack shocked Dombrowski and the SCHW's leadership, perhaps as much as President Roosevelt's death. Unions gave the SCHW over $28,000 in 1945, about half of which came from CIO locals. Money was important, but the SCHW also needed union allies in its work. The CIO's annual convention in 1944 had endorsed the SCHW and asked all locals to support the group "in its efforts to abolish intolerance and discrimination." Now Bittner had delivered what sounded to Dombrowski like a death knell for both political and financial backing from the influential union. In its contest with the Southern Regional Council for national prestige and southern loyalties, winning the CIO's endorsement had been a coup for the SCHW. The union's executive committee had said that the SCHW was "the natural and appropriate spearhead of the liberal forces of the South."[12]

The apparent cause of Bittner's attack was a letter written by Osceola McKaine to Allan S. Haywood, a CIO vice president.[13] Dombrowski, operating with a $200,000 budget, had hired two staff members to help with programs and a third to help raise money. As editor of an African-American newspaper in Charleston, South Carolina, McKaine had caught Dombrowski's attention. Dombrowski recruited him to join the SCHW as his assistant. About the same time, anticipating a broader postwar program, Dombrowski hired Witherspoon Dodge, a Unitarian minister who organized for the CIO during the thirties. A third person, Branson Price, sister of the energetic head of the SCHW's North Carolina committee,

Mary Price, was hired to raise funds through the New York committee. She had no program responsibilities.

McKaine, like most southern activists, knew well in advance of Bittner's press conference that the CIO drive was in the works. As the SCHW's new field representative, he wrote to Haywood on behalf of African-American workers, praising the CIO for planning the campaign but grousing that "the attitudes of a certain number of white CIO organizers in this region . . . could be readily mistaken for AFL or Railroad Brotherhood organizers if one judged by their racial attitudes and approaches."[14] Dombrowski knew that McKaine was sending the letter. He agreed with its contents and expected a reaction. In his mind, it was the only responsible position. Dombrowski's radicalism had gotten the better of his political pragmatism. Haywood's reply was caustic. CIO organizers, he said, "in the main deal with the problems they have in a realistic way."[15]

The CIO figured in an earlier tangle between Dombrowski and the SCHW's Alabama committee. Alabama's CIO leadership decided to back Eugene "Bull" Connor's 1944 re-election bid as city commissioner. Appalled at Connor's political record and his place in the SCHW's own history, the Alabama SCHW committee opposed Connor, threatening to end its loose coalition with the CIO. When a break between the two appeared close, Dombrowski warned the Alabama committee not to disavow the union. The CIO's financial support was too important to risk ruffled feelings, he said.[16] Publicly, the rift between the CIO and the SCHW was patched over, but the harm was done. Had Dombrowski made a costly tactical mistake, or had he willingly exposed the tension between unions and African Americans? There may not be an answer; clearly, however, the SCHW was harmed and helped. By the end of 1946, union contributions to the SCHW had dropped by $10,000.[17] But Bethune had agreed to lead an aggressive membership drive across the South. By May 1946, Dombrowski and the SCHW faced a crisis. The IRS would not be appeased; it demanded changes or taxes. The SCHW's appetite for money had never been greater. Friendship with the CIO was ruptured, if not terminated. Truman, unlike Roosevelt, seemed uninterested in a southern alliance of labor, church, and African Americans—even if one had existed. The SCHW formed a special reorganization committee. Josephine Wilkins, long a power in Georgia politics, chaired the committee charged with thinking through how to reshape the SCHW. In the 1920s she had campaigned for child labor laws. In the 1930s, as president of the League of Women Voters and later as head of the Citizens' Fact-Finding Movement, she had proposed more than forty pieces of legislation which had been enacted. Wilkins presented a draft report to the SCHW executive board during a regular meeting in Durham, North Carolina.

The Wilkins committee proposed amending the SCHW's 1942 Tennessee charter. Change the organization's name, she said, to the Southern Conference Education Fund. The SCEF would devote money and energy to public education, including publication of *The Southern Patriot* or special reports such as the one on Columbia, and thereby would continue to be eligible for tax-exempt contributions. The SCHW would retain its name but secure a new charter permitting partisan political activity. The SCHW would lobby in state capitols and Washington, conduct voter registration drives, make political endorsements, and carry on related electoral activities, and not be eligible for tax-exempt contributions. Both corporations were to be administered by the same people. Foreman was to be president. Dombrowski was to be executive secretary. In theory and on paper, the arrangement was neat, legal, and similar to the way other organizations continued tax-exempt educational activities while advocating legislative and political action. The proposal won quick approval.[18]

With the reorganization out of the way, Dombrowski again asked Bethune to undertake a Southwide tour to raise funds, attract additional African-American members, and speak out on issues for the two new organizations. She agreed and plans were carefully laid. Bethune's tour was a success. In Mobile, Alabama, over five thousand people turned out to hear her, donating $1,200. In Jacksonville, Florida, two thousand came, contributing over $1,500 after expenses. She raised nearly $10,000. When the tour ended, she had added slightly over six thousand new paid members, most of whom were African Americans, making the SCHW the largest interracial organization in the South's history.[19] Foreman suggested that the SCHW hold its 1946 biennial convention in New Orleans, envisioning a meeting to express gratitude for the Allied victory and for the creation of the United Nations—which had been a dream of Frank Graham's. The board authorized Dombrowski to commence preparations. His first step was to relocate the SCHW offices, a prewar organizational custom. Large conventions couldn't easily be planned long distance. In the summer of 1946, however, other factors made a move seem sensible. Tennessee politicians and Nashville newspapers continued their attacks on Dombrowski and the SCHW. New Orleans was a hub for rail and bus connections, especially to the Deep South and the Southwest. The SCHW wanted state committees organized next in Texas, Oklahoma, and perhaps Mississippi.

The Dombrowskis left Nashville with few regrets. Ellen had become a virtual recluse in their apartment, seldom leaving even with her husband, for fear of enduring some insulting remark or act. She had been accosted verbally in the building's elevator several times. Dombrowski was apprehensive that she'd never be happy or feel secure in the South.[20] They found an apartment at 905 Gov. Nicholls Street, at the time on a less than elegant edge of the French Quarter.

Trouble arrived with their belongings. Before leaving Nashville, Dombrowski had signed a contract with the New Orleans Auditorium Commission to use the municipal convention center for the convention. He'd signed leases for his apartment and for an office loft. Soon after he had set up his home and the SCHW headquarters, the auditorium commission reversed its decision, announcing to the city's press that they had cancelled the lease before telling Dombrowski. The commissioners insinuated to the press that Dombrowski had not told them the convention would be open to African Americans.[21]

Next the Young Men's Business Club of New Orleans, led by Ivor A. Trapolin, started a petition drive demanding that the city force the SCHW to leave New Orleans. Hundreds of names were gotten up quickly.[22] In the meanwhile, despite the SCHW's departure, *The Nashville Banner* hammered away at the organization. One of the paper's reporters was told by a spokesman for the Young Men's Business Club, "The city administration is pretty well behind us."[23] Other opposition was forming, too. An FBI agent in New Orleans wired the Washington headquarters, "It has come to the attention of this office that the American Legion of Louisiana is making efforts to combat the Southern Conference for Human Welfare by trying to prevent the organization from setting up its headquarters in New Orleans."[24] "To prevent possible embarrassment to this office," the agent asked if Washington had taken any action to help the legion.

Eventually Dombrowski arranged to use the less spacious Carpenters Hall, and on November 28, 1946, the three-day SCHW convention opened there.[25] About 270 delegates registered, although nearly six hundred persons attended opening events. For the first time, Eleanor Roosevelt did not come, choosing instead to telephone her message. President Truman and Dombrowski exchanged polite letters, but Truman apparently decided the

SCHW would not enjoy his interest. The CIO delegation was smaller, too; yet many labor leaders were present.

Over half the delegates were African Americans, evidence of emerging activism and of Bethune's importance. She gave one of the convention's two principal addresses. Walter White, head of the NAACP, who came to New Orleans as a gesture of appreciation for the SCHW's work on the Columbia tragedy, gave the other. In this sector, at least, Dombrowski's long campaign for a united front was succeeding. But could he hold onto the liberals?

Only two well-known Democratic Party figures came, Claude Pepper and Ellis Arnall. Pepper's term in the United States senate did not expire for another four years; Arnall's term as Georgia's governor was nearly over. He had no further political ambitions. Arnall was given the Thomas Jefferson award, and in his acceptance speech he called for an end to economic colonialism suffered by southerners. He urged a cheering crowd, "Let us then—you and I, the little people, roll up our sleeves and make democracy live."[26]

The dream of a united popular front goaded the delegates. They resolved to increase the number of southern voters, to back progressive candidates, to lobby hard for progressive labor laws and other legislation. They demanded that housing, schools, health services, roads, and income in the South be raised to national norms. They wanted all the region's natural resources developed along the lines of TVA. They ignored another internal fight by refusing to offer a resolve on foreign policy. Margaret Fuller, her fight with Dombrowski and Foreman smoothed over, went back to Georgia on Saturday night feeling as if "any who attended . . . must have had their faith renewed and their courage increased. . . . feeling not alone, but a part of something which they believed had strength in its honesty and wisdom in its vision. . . . Yes, it was a GOOD convention."[27]

The SCHW executive committee met the next day, as was its custom during the biennial conventions. Eight persons attended, including Foreman, Myles Horton, and Dombrowski's predecessor, John Thompson. Finances were pinched, but otherwise the executive committee agenda seemed routine. Dombrowski reported that revenues had fallen drastically in recent months as obligations for state committees had risen. The strains with the CIO were beginning to be felt. Foreman and other officers were re-elected almost as a matter of routine.

Then, according to a letter Dombrowski later wrote reconstructing the events for an ally in Kentucky, Tarleton Collier, "Someone asked if there was further business. Clark said, 'There is the matter of appointing or confirming—I have forgotten the exact word used—the administrator.' Naturally, at this point, I left the room. The Board discussed the matter for a very long time. I must have been in the hall an hour, or an hour and a half. It seemed longer to me. Then I was recalled."[28] Upon his return, Dombrowski was told by Palmer Weber, a CIO official, that on January 1, 1947, he would be relieved of his duties as administrator. Branson Price, the fundraiser, was to take his place. Foreman would begin making all policy decisions immediately. If Dombrowski should decide to stay with the organization, he was to administer the Southern Conference Education Fund. The decision was unanimous and final.[29] Dombrowski's letter continued:

> Then and then only was I asked to speak. The action came with such sudden and complete surprise that I was really stunned and it took a couple of days for me to realize the full consequences of what had been done. Not one word had been spoken to me, altho I understand that certain board members had heard that some changes might take place at the Convention. Since no one took the trouble to consult with me before the action was taken, you know as much as I do the reason for it. Even when I was recalled the only reason given that it was the thought of the board that I should be relieved of some of my heavy responsibilities.[30]

Dombrowski stayed in character. Outwardly, he was calm, assured, and silent about the decisive rebuff.[31] Inwardly, he was boiling mad and hurt, perhaps as deeply as ever in his political life, by both the decision and its implied criticism.[32] The votes cast against him by Horton and Thompson were even deeper wounds. They had been his classmates, committed politically to the same ends, a brotherhood. Both men had been still as Weber broke the news to Dombrowski. They offered no explanation, rebuttal, or defense. Finally, straining to keep his anger in check, Dombrowski told the committee that, since their decision was unanimous, "anything I might say would be useless."[33] The meeting was adjourned. Everyone hurried out of the meeting after politely saying goodbye.[34]

Apparently, Foreman wanted Dombrowski out of the organization for several reasons. He felt that Dombrowski was an inefficient administrator and overly cautious as an activist. He questioned Dombrowski's judgment in permitting McKaine's letter to be posted. He found Dombrowski's insistence that funds be secured before new programs were launched no less infuriating than Horton before him had. They had conflicting visions of the role of state committees. Moreover, there seemed no possibility that Foreman would find a position of influence in the Truman administration to equal his power under Roosevelt. Foreman was far too liberal and controversial for a presidency withdrawing from New Deal domestic reforms while heading full tilt toward a Cold War with the Soviet Union and loyalty oaths for government employees. Foreman needed a political job. He had decided to throw his considerable energy and political talent fully into the SCHW's work. Dombrowski's patient, careful style loomed as an impediment to his plan. He wanted to "throw Jim out on his ear," but, fearing a serious internal fight, settled instead on pushing him aside to the SCEF.[35]

Foreman had packed the executive committee as Roosevelt had tried to pack the Supreme Court.[36] Except for Horton and Thompson, the others who voted to demote Dombrowski that Sunday morning had belonged to the SCHW for less than a year. All were Foreman's close friends. Some had met Dombrowski for the first time in New Orleans. Apparently Foreman had figured that Dombrowski would go quietly. He knew, as did most southern activists, that Dombrowski's life was predicated on idealism and responsibility, not on the accumulation of political power or status. Dombrowski's loyalty to ideals would keep him from harming in public the organization which he had fought to build, which his friends supported, and which was under nasty attack by enemies of the principles he believed in. Foreman had never heard Dombrowski utter a critical word about Highlander, or be anything but civil toward Horton after their bitter split. Foreman believed that Dombrowski lacked the spirit for a political fight.[37]

For a while, it appeared that Foreman was right. No-one heard from Dombrowski for five days. Then, on December 6, after writing Tarleton Collier a personal letter, Dombrowski mimeographed a letter than he sent to each board member.[38] He asked, as retiring administrator, to be allowed to attend the next executive committee meeting, set for February 2, 1947, in Columbia, South Carolina. For most of the SCHW's leaders, the letter was the first word they had of his demotion. In one breath Dombrowski "accepted the action of the Board in replacing me," but in the next he opened the contest to keep his job:

> I want to insure that the democratic procedures advocated by the Southern Conference for Human Welfare be meticulously safeguarded in its own operations.

For myself, I am confused about the following: 1. Should not the full Board . . . have been notified of the major personnel change contemplated? 2. Should not the matter here have been discussed with the present administrator before the action was an accomplished fact? 3. Should not the present administrator be advised of reasons for this change and given an opportunity to speak? 4. Did the Board clearly understand that the Conference Educational Fund is a separate agency, operating under its own Board, that the Board of the Southern Conference for Human Welfare had no jurisdiction over the Southern Conference Educational Fund, and that in suggesting expansion of the work and presumably of the budget of the Southern Conference Educational Fund the Board was making a proposal that was not within its authority?[39]

His letter ignited a firestorm of correspondence.[40] Within days, virtually every one of the SCHW's thirty-four board members requested that the matter be reopened.

Two of the nine executive committee members who had voted for Dombrowski's removal shifted positions, one ever so slightly, the other declaring she'd been deceived. From Monteagle, Horton wrote to Foreman saying he wanted it clear in the minutes that he had not made the motion to move Dombrowski aside, although he did vote in favor of the demotion.[41] Horton later threatened to resign from the SCHW over how the minutes were written. Years later, he also denied voting against Dombrowski. Rebecca M. Gershon wrote to Foreman, "During the morning session the impression was distinctly given that the matter had been discussed with Jim, informal though such discussion may have been, and that he would welcome relief from some of the burdens involved in the position of director. After we had taken action it became quite obvious that this was not the case."[42]

Foreman's plan hit significant opposition when Lucy Randolph Mason wrote him saying "A terrible mistake was made. . . . If the Conference is to continue as a useful agency in the South, I believe we must undo the wrong we have done. . . . In my opinion, the action itself was unsound. Further, a great injustice was done the man, who, more than anyone else, held the Conference together at its lowest ebb and brought it to its present strong position."[43] Mason was as influential as any SCHW board member. Few deliberately chose to kindle her ire.

Dombrowski's friends were urging him to refuse the demotion. Lewis

Jones, a sociologist from Tuskegee Institute and the SCHW's parliamentarian, wrote Dombrowski from Houston, Texas, where he was working.
Dombrowski, he said, should contest the decision as a violation of the
SCHW's by-laws, adding that he'd been "acutely aware of Clark's thirst for
power."[44] Virginia Durr's appeal stirred Dombrowski to forego turning
the other cheek: "If you would only realize how many people love and look
up to you. This same impasse occurred with you and Myles. In that case, I
know how badly you were hurt and how you retired without a word and
left him the field. Don't do that again. Try and be as constructive as possible. Don't simply retire into silence because you hate dissension."[45]

Passions had been stirred. The executive committee meeting was moved
forward to January 5. Half the SCHW's board members dropped other responsibilities to attend. The rest sent regrets, explaining that they expected
word about all decisions immediately.[46] Foreman seldom ducked a fight,
and he plunged directly into the controversy once the members gathered at
the North Carolina state committee's office:

> I feel we have built a two-story house. We have a roof and a founda-
> tion, but in the words of Mrs. Bethune, we have got to stop up the
> cracks. We no longer have Washington support. We have got to be pre-
> pared to have any kind of inspection and investigation without fear.
>
> On that basis, the Board meeting in New Orleans considered the
> question of the advisability of having a tax deductible organization and
> a political organization administered by the same executive. We felt in
> doing so we were giving good grounds for criticism even to unbiased
> people, but we could by a malevolent press be smeared or misrepre-
> sented to people who made contributions to us. They could even be
> made to pay taxes on some of the money they had given us.
>
> Dr. Dombrowski has had the administration of two funds. I found
> out only yesterday that Osceola McKaine was being paid from the Edu-
> cation Fund while he was organizing the vote in the Tennessee cam-
> paign to oust Crump. We have published pamphlets under the name of
> the SCHW with money given for the Education Fund.
>
> I am not impugning Dr. Dombrowski. He used his best discretion in
> this and did good work. But we are working in a different atmosphere.
> Now we cannot take chances.
>
> This was the Board's opinion. The Board then discussed who would
> be the proper people for these two positions. There was no dissent in

the feeling that Dr. Dombrowski was one of the best in the South, that
he had given courage and leadership when no one else would do it, that
he deserves the best we could give him. He deserved to be relieved from
routine duties to carry on the beacon of work of early days, and get to
people who would not join a political action group but who would join
an educational organization. The Board felt unanimously that
Dombrowski could serve the Conference best as head of the Education
Fund. Those were decisions of the Board in New Orleans. From what
has happened, I think it has been proven that we acted too hastily.[47]

When Foreman finished, George Mitchell moved that the New Orleans
decision be rescinded. Gershon seconded the motion. Foreman argued the
decision could not be changed. Debate on this parliamentary issue continued over a half hour, and flowed into other procedural disputes. Finally,
ballots were cast. Twelve voted to rescind, three to let it stand, and one abstention.[48] Immediately, Bethune suggested that the board separate the administration of the two organizations, asking Dombrowski, however, what
he thought of the idea. He said:

There is no reason why you cannot have a director of the Education
Fund who is also administrator of the SCHW. Dr. Foreman has already
pointed out how that same situation exists in other organizations. The
SCHW is primarily an action group, but action without a good education program is foolhardy. The only reason we have an educational
fund is a legal device to enable the SCHW to do its work and get funds.

Likewise, educational groups are ineffective without action. There is
nothing more important than political action. We want the services of
the Education Fund to fit and dovetail with the work of the SCHW. The
fact that an administrator of the Southern Conference has in his mind
the whole program makes certain that these two groups do remain one
and the same.[49]

Paul Christopher, the CIO leader, sided with Dombrowski: "I think if we
are investigated, we could make a better defense if the head of both was a
good man."[50]
Aubrey Williams, the most seasoned administrator in the group, interrupted Christopher, saying, "I feel very strongly that liberal organizations
in the development of these educational funds have been playing loose with
the people who have been supporting them. I think we ought to take the

law as it is written and use money for educational purposes. The problem before us has to be decided strictly on the charter under which we get tax exempt money."[51]

Modjeska Simkins from Columbia, South Carolina, agreed with Williams. There should be two administrative officers, adding, "We certainly (should) allow Dr. Dombrowski to accept the position he would prefer."[52]

After another hour's debate, the board voted twelve to five to have an administrator for the SCHW and a director for the SCEF. Foreman, still losing ground, appointed a five-person committee to negotiate with Dombrowski over lunch. Dombrowski told the ad hoc group, which included Williams, Christopher, and Bethune, that he wanted to remain the SCHW's administrator. The issue was finally joined. Either the board turned Dombrowski out, or it repudiated Foreman.

Debate resumed after lunch. It lasted five hours, becoming less and less polite. Foreman's attack became personal. Dombrowski, he alleged, had tried to cut back the Tennessee committee's budget without board approval. Alva Taylor, chairman of the state committee, denied Foreman's accusation. Dombrowski defended himself, saying,

> The most important work of the SCHW is in the state committees. I have always believed that. But I do not think that we should obligate ourselves financially when it will not allow for any of us to survive. I opened the first state committee, and approved the second and third. I opposed the fourth, fifth, and sixth because we were not in a position to finance them. We would not be in this financial position had my advice been followed. Because we have a full-time president, I deferred to him. I should have forcibly put forward my policy. My fault has been trying to give the state committees more money.[53]

Foreman charged that Dombrowski was being overpaid through a clerical error which was yet another reflection on his lax administrative style. Mason corrected Foreman's memory about the amount Dombrowski was to be paid, noting further than he had gone without any salary for two months and was presently owed $1,500.[54]

Charlotte Hawkins Brown, the North Carolina educator, summed up the quandary while paving the way for a compromise: "Right now we cannot do without Clark Foreman. We cannot do without a man such as Dombrowski. We should find a means to finance both these men."[55]

At this point, Samuel Rodman, one of Foreman's allies, moved that Dombrowski resign. Aubrey Williams spoke before a second could be gotten, fearing a vote on the motion would mean an end to the SCHW. Tempers, not reason, seemed to be dominating, he declared. "We must go ahead with you as president, Clark, and Jim as administrator. Both of you must be more careful about some of the things that have been brought out." Rodman's motion died for want of a second. The board unanimously approved William's idea.[56]

Christopher, realizing that the vote was merely a truce, suggested that the SCHW create a mediating body to temper relationships between two determined men. Three persons should be designated to keep harmony, he said. Dombrowski should name one member, Foreman another. The board would select the third. The motion carried unanimously, either because of the soundness of the idea or because of fatigue. Louis Burham was the board's choice. Foreman named Daniel Weitzman. Dombrowski picked Bethune.[57]

After the vote, Dombrowski said, "I have no question but that Clark and I can get along. I was prepared to resign if there had been any disagreement in the vote of confidence."[58] They did not get along, however. Dombrowski's integrity had been questioned, a matter he did not take lightly. Foreman's hopes for full control over the organization were undimmed. Within weeks, both men began sniping at each other. On April 10, Foreman wrote to Dombrowski, "I am a little surprised at the implication in your letter that we are not unitedly pulling together at the present time. I wonder who you feel is not pulling his load?"[59]

Dombrowski later responded to an attack by Weitzman, Foreman's ally, with a three-page defense: "Our day-to-day fight with the reactionaries and native fascists, coupled with a steady stream of invective and abuse by one of the local papers, makes our life complicated enough without having to defend ourselves from our closest friends and associates. I am sure you appreciate that a person on the firing line can do a real job when he feels he can count upon the sympathetic understanding and backing of his own officers and board."[60]

# 11

## The Psalmist's Dream Is Dashed

The SCHW board gave Dombrowski and Foreman six months to patch up their differences and get the organization back on track. The leadership arranged to meet July 12, 1947, in Richmond, Virginia, to measure relationships between the two men and to take the SCHW's political pulse.

Dombrowski and Foreman agreed on one issue, if no other. The SCHW was strapped for cash. On January 1, the SCHW had $249.71 in the bank. The two men put personalities and politics aside to push for paychecks. Immediately after the shaky compromise was struck in Greensboro, Dombrowski left for Houston, Austin, and Los Angeles, where he raised $1,500 in cash, an equal sum in pledges, and a commitment that another $10,000 would be raised in Southern California by the year's end. The money held creditors at bay. Foreman pushed the New York and Washington committees to redouble efforts to raise funds.

Dombrowski tightened the organization's belt, giving notice to his secretary and to Frank C. Bancroft, who had been editing *The Southern Patriot*. Attrition in the state committees lowered costs. Sam Carothers, secretary of the Louisiana committee, resigned. Malcolm Dobbs in Alabama was leaving in August. On April 1, during an executive committee meeting, Dombrowski and Foreman, who had not been paid since January, pledged to raise $16,650 between them by July 1. Otherwise, Foreman said, he would continue as president without pay; and Dombrowski said he would resign as SCHW administrator.[1]

A spate of resignations added to the SCHW's woes. Except for William Mitch of the United Mine Workers, every union leader resigned from the board. Mary McLeod Bethune, citing poor health and the demands of her job as president emeritus of Bethune-Cookman College, resigned. Other African Americans quit. Henry Fowler, chairman of the Virginia committee, resigned on April 27, due, he said, to the "absence of any clear and positive stand against Communism and the inclusion of Communists in the working organization and the unwillingness of my own state committee to initiate steps which would require facing this issue."[2]

Less than a week before, the Georgia committee had closed down for good. It, too, was out of funds. Mostly, however, members were smarting from a rebuke Foreman had delivered when they decided against any public opposition to the Talmadges. Only the North Carolina committee, under the leadership of Mary Price, sustained an active program.

Trying to halt the decline, Dombrowski persuaded Edmonia K. Grant, who had been Dr. Charles Johnson's assistant at Fisk's Race Relations Institute, to leave her job with the U.S. Office of Education in Washington to become the SCHW's first African-American associate director. Her job was shore up the state committees, if possible, by sparking renewed interest in voter registration. Some few political victories in the first half of 1947 offset several defeats.

Political organizing continued, the financial and organizational woes notwithstanding. In March, Dombrowski spent three weeks in Miami, Jacksonville, and Orlando, Florida, assisting leaders of a statewide drive against the white primary. Segregationist lawmakers had introduced legislation trying to curb the franchise. Similar bills were being introduced across the South. On March 22, on the eve of the legislature's vote, over four hundred lawyers, ministers, legislators, and SCHW supporters met at Winter Park's Congregational Church. Dr. Hamilton Holt, president of Rollins College, was a principal speaker. Winter Park's mayor welcomed the participants. The state legislature voted thirty-eight to four to kill the white primary bill. Florida newspapers credited the SCHW with its defeat.

In April, the SCHW issued a special report condemning the Truman administration's "mutilation of the Wages and Hours Act," the "increasing encroachment of absentee monopoly control of Southern business," and the "crippling of many federal agencies whose services are most acutely needed in the South."[3] The report reminded readers of New Deal promises to create an economic Bill of Rights after the war. Political anger toward the SCHW flared anew in Washington.

By June the Truman administration's ire raged near fury. Former Secretary of Commerce Henry A. Wallace announced his campaign as a third-party candidate for the presidency, opening his bid in the South on a tour sponsored by the SCHW. Wallace's alienation from the Truman administration matched the attitudes of many, but not all, of the SCHW's members toward Roosevelt's successor. Wallace wanted to expand the domestic social reforms of the New Deal. He was opposed to opening a Cold War, proposing instead to cooperate with the Soviet Union. He opposed any further use of atomic weapons.

Dombrowski and Foreman made common cause to ensure that the Wallace tour would be a success. His ends were theirs; his election, a long shot, to be sure, would strengthen the SCHW politically and financially. The notice sure to be given his campaign could help their ailing organization, especially since Wallace had agreed to speak before integrated audiences. Together, using southern political contacts which were as extensive as those of any two persons then alive, they easily arranged for the candidate to speak in Texas, Louisiana, Alabama, Georgia, North Carolina, and Virginia.

The Wallace tour first tested the waters on May 16 at the University of Texas. Radio personality John Henry Faulk, who had grown up near Austin, left his work in New York City for several days to help the SCHW. The audience was standing-room-only. Next, on June 5, Wallace spoke to an enthusiastic crowd of four thousand in Raleigh, North Carolina. Two days later, over one thousand heard him during an afternoon speech at Alabama State Teachers College. Regional newspapers noticed that the tour's integrated audiences were defying Jim Crow laws and commented on the SCHW's organizational abilities. Wallace was to wind up the tour on June 13 with a major address in Washington. On June 12, the House Un-American Activities Committee (HUAC), chaired by J. Parnell Thomas, issued a report condemning the SCHW as a "most deviously camouflaged Communist-front organization."[4] The committee's "professed interest in southern welfare is simply an expedient for larger aims serving the Soviet Union and its subservient Communist Party in the United States," the report continued. Later, the committee admitted that the report had been gotten up hastily and released before Wallace's Washington speech, in an effort to under cut his candidacy and to embarrass the SCHW.[5] The strategy failed to stop Wallace, dent the crowd, or prevent them from giving some $10,000 to support the SCHW. The HUAC report, however, spawned other troubles. On June 18, the *New Orleans States* published the first article in an inflammatory series depicting the SCHW offices as the hub of a Communist conspiracy.[6] The next day, the Young Men's Business Club, which for a time had ceased taunting the SCHW, unanimously resolved to ask the city to oust the SCHW from New Orleans. They had the support of the Junior Chamber of Commerce, the Knights of Columbus, and several American Legion posts.

The newspaper attacks appeared daily, causing reactions which surpassed the intensity of the outcry in Nashville. The SCHW office received more hate letters than contributions. Volunteers quit, or missed work, leaving the office unattended much of the time. Dombrowski had been in New Orleans a total of three weeks since January. Ellen answered the telephone to hear one hate caller after another promise harm. The frightening calls continued even after Dombrowski got an unlisted telephone number. Ellen found that alcohol abated her fears. Unless Dombrowski was with her, Ellen only left the apartment to shop for groceries.

By July 1, Dombrowski and Foreman had raised but $10,744.64. No additional funds were in sight. Income totaled $26,074.32. Expenses totaled $26,324.03. Foreman told his friends in Richmond that he was going "to live up to my agreement and after July 1 continue as president but draw no pay."[7] Dombrowski's word was on the line, too. He became director of the Southern Conference Education Fund, agreeing to edit *The Southern Patriot* and special reports, and to manage the nonprofit organization. "Now," declared Aubrey Williams, hoping the conflict was behind them, "we go to the people to get money."[8] In his last report to the SCHW board, Dombrowski said, "As the major progressive organization functioning on a political level in the South, we have a special obligation. . . . We must recover the spirit of unity that characterized this organization for most of its history and which made it a strong fighting organization for full democracy and practical brotherhood."[9]

Another chapter in his life had come to a distasteful, disappointing close.[10] During the two-day train ride back to New Orleans, he could hardly remember making any significant, lasting accomplishment; instead he thought about compromises, squabbles, and lost friendships. He was tired by the pace he had been keeping and by the reactionary attacks; he was exhausted by the fight within the SCHW. Dombrowski was fifty, an age when idealism usually has fallen aside or at least been tempered. He knew that the weariness would pass and that with some rest he would soon be fit. He wondered, however, as the Southern Crescent carried him back to Louisiana, if his spirit would heal. Was he as unbowed as his last words to the SCHW board suggested? Was he still up to fighting for the Kingdom of God? Was there any hope to experience, as the Psalmist said, "how good and pleasant it would be if brothers dwelled in unity"?[11]

Dombrowski and Ellen went to Bay St. Louis, Mississippi, a place that reminded him of the Psalmist's vision. One of the oldest fishing villages along the Gulf of Mexico, residents ignored the worst racial antagonisms of the day. Whites and African Americans fished together, lived next door to one another as neighbors, and, during the broiling hot summers, swam together in the evening cool. In Dombrowski's mind, Bay St. Louis was "like the dew of Hermon." A friend there, Lewis Henderson, found the couple a cottage for the rest of July. Henderson had retired as a New Deal administrator and was starting a business selling surplus military furniture. The Dombrowskis fished, sometimes with enough skill to provide a meal, or walked on the beach. Dombrowski sketched for the first time in months, as he always did when the going got tough. He took dozens of photographs.

The paradoxes of Bay St. Louis quickened his assessment of his future. He had some assets. At the SCEF he was surrounded by strong, persevering men. Aubrey Williams, with his rich lode of political contacts, was president. Dr. Alva W. Taylor, long an ardent friend of Dombrowski's, was secretary-treasurer; he linked the organization to progressive church and intellectual organizations. The president of Morehouse College in Atlanta, Dr. Benjamin E. Mays, as vice president, added his ties to African-American intellectuals north and south, and his own high political regard. These officers knew and trusted each other. They had worked with one another over the years, but never before as a group. Like Dombrowski, they were seasoned fundraisers. The organization had tax-exempt status. *The Southern Patriot* had nearly six thousand subscribers, each of whom was a potential donor. Dombrowski also had some liabilities. The SCEF was a paper organization. It had no program and no money. He seemed permanently tainted as a Communist. He had as many foes as friends, inside the two fragile organizations and outside. He admitted to idealism.

Dombrowski spent a lot of time thinking about a proposal that Lucy Randolph Mason had put forth in April. In a memorandum she posted to each SCHW board member, Mason had suggested a dramatic reorganization plan. "If the Conference's entire membership was concentrated in one state," she wrote, "it would not constitute a mass political movement in that state."[12] She called for a pared-down organizational agenda, free of broad-based, chimerical policy. She demanded that the organization live on its income and not on its prospects for funds. She proposed that the SCHW become "an icebreaker, a spearhead, a standard bearer . . . with a frontier program" working over a long period on one or two key regional issues. And she felt that staff energy and time, as well as scarce money, could be better used.[13] There would be one or two staff members, no more. One should raise funds, but in a manner less costly than that evolved by the New York and Washington committees. She wanted staffers who knew the SCHW and the South. They should be southern and live in the South. This chauvinism, she declared, would enable the SCHW to rebuff allegations that outsiders were meddling in problems they did not understand.

Dombrowski fished, sketched, strolled with Ellen, and thought about Mason's proposal. She made sense. Compared to the present SCHW, such an organization could be managed easily and would cost less to operate. Fundraising would consume less time. Political education campaigns could be targeted, allowing one or two persons to become identified with specific regional issues. A smaller board of directors, each carefully chosen and not self-appointed, could define clear-cut policy. Programs could be gotten up quickly, without time-consuming meetings. He decided that the SCEF, if not the SCHW, would take Mason's advice.

Having reached that decision, Dombrowski had no doubt about the single issue he'd press. Race had stymied his work at Highlander and virtually every reform SCHW proposed. Away from Bay St. Louis, in nearly every southern place large or small, segregation kept the Kingdom of God from being realized. The SCEF would challenge the doctrine of separate but equal, a national policy and a regional disgrace.[14]

The SCHW had placed no strictures on what Dombrowski could do. The SCHW board, unlike many businesses when experienced leadership leaves, exacted no contract that would limit competition. Dombrowski was as free to contest the SCHW's place as the region's leading proponent of reformed race relations as he was to challenge the region's racism. Dombrowski and Ellen went back to New Orleans fit and tan. He sensed that another brotherhood was bonding. He was certain that he was back in business.

A month later, a hurricane ravaged Bay St. Louis, sweeping away the facade of harmony that Dombrowski had wanted and needed to see. All the African-American men in the town—and only African Americans—were forced to clean up the debris, bury dead cattle, patch up private homes. The local constable, backed up by the guns of white Mississippi militiamen, kept them at work for several weeks, even though many of their own homes or fishing boats went unrepaired. Henderson watched helplessly after he protested to the constable. He telephoned Dombrowski, saying that the lawman had told him to keep quiet, adding that "if anyone got in his way, he would put them in jail."[15]

Foreman and the SCHW limped through the remainder of 1947 and into 1948. Funds continued to be scarce. Henry Wallace's candidacy drove additional wedges between the organization and southern liberals. Aubrey Williams, while sympathetic to many of Wallace's views, decided to stick with the Democratic Party. United Mine Workers leader William Mitch was under pressure within the union to disavow the SCHW's support of Wallace. Virginia Durr, defying both her husband and her brother-in-law Supreme Court Justice Hugo Black, ran as the Progressive Party's candidate for governor of Virginia. Both men wanted her to stick with the Democratic Party.[16] Foreman said that Wallace's Progressive Party offered the South "the greatest chance it has ever had to escape from the feudalism that has been such a curse to its people and to the rest of the country." But he failed to get the few remaining SCHW board members to agree. He resigned in May 1948, so that the board could find someone who would "give more time and thought to their problems." His resignation was the end of the SCHW.[17]

Old friends and old rivals gathered at the Phyllis Wheatley YWCA in Richmond, Virginia, on November 21, 1948, to inter the SCHW. Foreman, Durr, Horton, Williams, and Dombrowski wrote an official obituary for the press and history: "New political alignments have largely absorbed the political energies of the members of the SCHW and make its continuation unnecessary and a duplication of effort."[18] They parted politely; their mutual loss restored a degree of friendship among them. Years later, Durr assessed the SCHW, saying that her private view was shared by the others who laid the organization to rest:

> The Southern Conference was a political organization. The idea was to run candidates in each Southern state. We didn't succeed very well, but we ran 'em, and we did stir up the two old parties in a way that had

some effect. Our organization was not only the first one which allowed blacks to come to the meetings and be seated without segregation and to participate equally, but we took up the issue and cause of integration first. Certainly the Republican Party didn't touch it with a ten-foot pole. Neither did the Democratic Party at that time. But in the ordinary sense of the word politics, we didn't do much.[19]

# 12

## For Another
## South,
## Another
## Mobilizer

President Truman issued Executive Order 9835 on March 21, 1947, launching a purge of federal civil servants and establishing the attorney general's subversive organization list, an action legitimating the idea that dissent was disloyal. Throughout the nation that year, according to the American Civil Liberties Union (ACLU), there was "an atmosphere increasingly hostile to the liberties of organized labor, the political left, and many minorities."[1]

A coalition of Republicans and southern Democrats, which included Mississippi's Bilbo and Eastland, filibustered the Fair Employment Practices Commission (FEPC) to death with nineteen days of continuous talk. They bottled up most of Truman's domestic legislative program, overrode his vetoes, and attacked him for "coddling Communists." The ACLU reported, "Excitement, bordering on hysteria, characterized the public approach to any issue related to Communism."[2] Truman angered conservative politicians by establishing the President's Commission on Civil Rights. Only Roosevelt's FEPC seems to have stirred more wrath. South Carolina Gov. J. Strom Thurmond typified southern political opposition to Truman's action. "There's not enough troops in the army to break down segregation and admit the Negro into our homes, our eating places, our swimming pools and our theaters," he declared.[3] The Ku Klux Klan was enjoying a revival.

Joe McWilliams, who called himself "the Christian Mobilizer," was touring the South on behalf of Gerald L.K. Smith's American Nationalists' Committee. He was finding it easy to raise money; industrialists and workers alike were giving generously to the Christian Mobilizer's blatantly racialist cause.[4] McWilliams was peddling one of two volatile political tags gaining popular use in 1947. He was drumming for the "segregationist" label as a name standing for United States law and folkways.

Another Christian mobilizer, Dombrowski, was trying to raise money, too, but for opposing reasons and with much less success. He was attempting to make a virtue out of the label "integrationist," a stigmatizing epithet being attached to anyone who expressed the opinion that racial discrimination violated the Constitution or human decency. "Integrationist" was the SCEF's label.

On August 30, 1947, Dombrowski announced the SCEF's birth in a letter posted with *The Southern Patriot*.[5] Henceforth, he wrote, politics would be *The Southern Patriot*'s focus—meaning, of course, to most readers, the politics of race and poverty. "The September issue . . . will contain the voting record of all Southern Senators and Congressmen on about 17 important roll calls. . . . Aubrey Williams and other outstanding citizens will give the score on how the Southern worker, farmer, and average citizen fared in the 80th Congress."[6] The SCEF did not issue a call for a revolutionary assault on Jim Crow. Dombrowski remembered how far the inflammatory resolve that he had helped write and had signed in 1933 had gotten him. The Kingdom of God had not ensued. But the first issue of *The Southern Patriot* under his full command was no less a denunciation of middle-of-the-road politics on race, and set the SCEF well apart from every other southern political organization. Every reader, present or past, was urged to renew subscriptions and to give generously to the Southern Conference Education Fund.

The phrase "Aubrey Williams and other outstanding citizens" publicly signaled Dombrowski's acceptance of Lucy Randolph Mason's advice to narrow the SCEF's goals, strategies, and tactics. For a moment at Bay St. Louis, he had considered striking out on his own, abandoning his faith in brotherhood for an individual crusade. He never had had much stomach for the seemingly endless fights at Highlander or the SCHW. They diverted energy and time and left him emotionally drained. By himself, he mused, the contests would be between his conscience and his political judgment. In the end, however, his business instincts prevailed. He realized that, in the prevailing social climate, Dombrowski, as a single propagandist crusading against Jim Crow, would be easily silenced. A company of crusaders would be less risky.[7]

Williams, Alva Taylor, and Benjamin Mays were equally steadfast opponents of Jim Crow, and each was known to a loyal constituency, each gave the SCEF access to a degree of national political influence. Williams, after years as a power-wielding New Deal administrator, had personal connections with political liberals throughout the nation. Taylor linked the SCEF with the South's liberal, but largely silent, ministers and intellectuals. Mays enjoyed high regard among African-American educators, business leaders, and political figures, and in the nation's tiny but vital African-American press. Behind the four men stood a large, prestigious advisory committee and ties to the Methodist Federation for Social Action and similar small but effective grassroots groups around the nation.

Subscribers to *The Southern Patriot* constituted an even larger base of volunteer interest. In general, they shared a political and economic view of the South's ills, some of which *The Southern Patriot* reflected in the August 1947 issue. The little paper discussed two court decisions. First, the Supreme Court had struck down freight rates which gave northern industry and banks significant advantage over southern counterparts. The Supreme Court's decision was a victory in the long regional struggle against colonial status. Second, District Judge J. Waties Waring had forbidden discrimination against African Americans in South Carolina's Democratic Party primaries. Waring's decision opened the strategic way to wrestle with poverty and racism, "for it is an axiom of history that an exploited group must achieve political freedom before it can gain economic equality."[8] The decisions, Dombrowski wrote, went to the core of the region's problems and eliminated "a dead past" blocking "the road to progress in the South."

The SCEF was a small business with the single, and singular, purpose of influencing public policy on race. Its four leaders even toyed with the idea of becoming a comprehensive media business, including a regional news service reporting almost exclusively on race.[9] They considered buying radio stations to operate with interracial staffs and integrationist broadcast formats. But, in the end, *The Southern Patriot* was their only communications medium.[10] Dombrowski and Williams spearheaded the operation. They stayed in the public eye. Taylor and Mays, while no less important to the SCEF, each had less time to give, even if they could have been compensated. They were tending other careers. Williams was a genial, genteel, companionable Alabaman who brought the new organization a leavening counterpoint to Dombrowski's sober, dogged style. He added vitally important political history. Williams had been involved with virtually every major decision President Roosevelt had made on race relations, including attending a pivotal meeting at the White House among the president, Eleanor Roosevelt, and A. Philip Randolph, head of the Sleeping Car Porters.[11]

In appearance, Williams was tall and spare. In style, he was laconic, even whimsical. He was seven years older than Dombrowski and had grown up in much different circumstances. Born in Springvale, Alabama, he was the son of a blacksmith who died when the boy was young. At age nine, Williams started working as a clerk in a Birmingham drygoods store. After college and a short period pastoring in Cincinnati, he took a job with the Wisconsin Association of Social Workers, helping to reform prisons, children's homes, and reformatories. As the Depression worsened in 1932, he was hired by Harry Hopkins, a trusted Roosevelt confidant and head of the Federal Emergency Relief Administration. A year later, Williams was named Hopkins' assistant and given the responsibility of getting money into hard-pressed southern cities and towns. Through this work, Williams came to see himself as a "southern rebel," fully aware of and committed to the cause of the African American.[12] Two years later, in 1934, he was invited to speak at the NAACP's national convention.

When Roosevelt created the National Youth Administration, Williams was appointed director. He installed Mary McLeod Bethune as his deputy. Williams hired another young southerner, Lyndon B. Johnson, a schoolteacher from Texas. Along the way, Williams collected both friends and enemies in some number. Shortly before his death, Roosevelt tried to appoint Williams head of the Rural Electrification Administration. Southern senators used his confirmation hearing as a platform to attack Roosevelt's FEPC. Under questioning, Williams acknowledged that he had supported the creation of the FEPC and had helped draft the executive order establishing the agency. His nomination was killed.

Following Roosevelt's death and his own confirmation defeat, Williams returned to Montgomery, Alabama, where he bought a small, moribund farm publication, the *Southern Farm and Home*. He had the financial backing of Marshall Field, the Chicago department store millionaire, and James P. Warburg, a successful banker who gave to liberal causes. Almost overnight, the journal's circulation climbed to nearly a million subscribers using an editorial formula mixing tips, crop reports, and home economics articles with explanations of how the fertilizer and implement companies drove up prices and editorials backing the United Nations.

Williams became moderately well off. He branched into other ventures, including developing moderately-priced housing for African Americans in Montgomery. Some of his deals prospered, others lost money. But his finances never matched the wealth of good will he had stored among the nation's political liberals. Dombrowski met Williams first during the 1938 SCHW convention. He amazed Dombrowski when he delivered an extemporaneous speech advocating Socialism. "It was the only time during the convention that point of view was expressed specifically and publicly," Dombrowski recalled.[13] From the start, the two got along easily. Over the decade, as their lives intersected, Williams came to know Dombrowski; how well was reflected in a letter the former wrote to Eleanor Roosevelt. He defended Dombrowski in the wake of an attack by Atlanta columnist Ralph McGill, which associated Dombrowski and the SCEF with Communism. Roosevelt's support of the SCEF wavered. Williams told her, "His honesty and integrity is so simon pure that it gets to be a bore at times."[14]

The SCEF was less clear about which of the pervasive institutionalized expressions of white supremacy to attack first. Voting appealed to Dombrowski; education to Mays; housing to Williams.[15] The idea of radio stations or the news service suggested promising directions with the media. In the end, however, they decided to expose the high monetary costs of segregation and political disenfranchisement, the bottom line of racism in a capitalist society and, just possibly, they reasoned, segregation's Achilles heel.

Once he had gotten the subscription appeal off and sent the September issue to the printer, Dombrowski went to Mississippi to explore what role the SCEF might play in undoing segregationist politics. A heated campaign was under way to fill the unexpired term of Theodore Bilbo, who had died in the midst of a Senate committee's investigation into charges that he had prevented African Americans from voting in his re-election campaign the year before.[16]

Throughout that campaign, Bilbo was alleged to have been suggesting to appreciative audiences that violence be used to keep African Americans from the polls. In Laurel, on June 22, 1946, he had called on "every red-blooded, Anglo-Saxon man in Mississippi to resort to any means to keep hundreds of Negroes from the polls in the July 2 primary. And if you don't know what that means, you just are not up on your persuasive measures."[17] Some Senate liberals had been offended and launched an investigation, the second of Bilbo in less than a year. The first Senate committee had censured him for breaking federal laws by securing wartime contracts for cronies. His death, however, ended the second investigation. Four men were contesting for Bilbo's seat. Dombrowski arrived in Jackson on August 4, 1947, the eve of the election.[18] The temperature was over 100° F. Through Percy Green, who had supported the SCHW for years and who lived in Jackson, the Reverend William Bender of the Farish Street Baptist Church invited Dombrowski to attend a voter's school he'd organized. Bender, with bravery tempered by furtiveness, had started the state's chapter of the NAACP. To avoid detection, Mississippi's NAACP founder never held meetings in the same place twice, holding one in the "colored" waiting room at the Illinois Central Railroad's Jackson depot.[19] Green edited one of the only African-American newspapers in Mississippi.

Dombrowski was taken directly to the sweltering church, where he was introduced to some two dozen persons ready to try to have a political say in their lives. Editor Green used the Bible to outline a long-haul strategy. "Jesus and John the Baptist," he said, "accepted the rules of the Sanhedrin until they got inside the temple. We must conform until enough of us are inside and can help set the rules."[20] The sermons over, Bender and Green began teaching the details of how to mark and fold the ballot, the location of each precinct, what a precinct was, and what to do if challenged by whites who ran the polling places. This was a curriculum born from the knowledge that a mistake could mean a beating, no job, even death.

That night, by himself, Dombrowski went to a political rally for Congressman William M. Colmer, considered the campaign's moderate on race. Making his last campaign pitch, Colmer said, "It is obvious that there can be no conflict between the aspirants for this high office . . . on the question of white supremacy and our Southern way of life. My own record on this is well known. . . . As a member of the powerful Rules Committee of the House it was my privilege only last year to join with four other Southerners on that key committee to prevent the inequitous, so-called FEPC bill, from reaching the floor of the House."[21]

At 6:30 the next morning, Bender took Dombrowski with him to the church, where would-be voters went over their instructions one last time. Their precinct was a nearby fire station. Dombrowski recorded the event: "About two-thirds had two poll tax receipts in hand—from '45 and '46—

all are orderly and peaceful. . . . But ½ are challenged. . . . no whites challenged. . . . 'delinquent' written opposite some names . . . by 7:30, 21 persons voted—17 of them colored."[22]

Dombrowski left Jackson later that morning, cutting his visit short because of a severe recurrence of arthritis. When he got back to New Orleans, he was in bed for a week, after which his working day was shortened. Usually stoical, Dombrowski told friends that he was having a "rather bad siege." Ethel Clyde offered to hospitalize him in early September. On the 22nd, he declined, saying "I have too much on hand just at the moment to even consider it but it is tempting I must admit."[23]

That same afternoon Dombrowski headed north to meet with two men who had achieved renown for successfully molding public opinion. He wanted their advice about large-scale public education drives. If the SCEF was in the public opinion business, he wanted top-flight consultants. He had propaganda on his mind. His first stop was Chicago, where he met with Dr. Robert M. Hutchins, chancellor of the University of Chicago, who also headed the Fund for the Republic. Hutchins had stirred heated debate within the nation's academic circles by arguing that intellectual pursuits and not moral ones should govern the aims of higher education. Dombrowski did not agree with Hutchins, but he did want to know how he managed to spark the nationwide discussion. He also wanted to sound Hutchins out about money. The Fund for the Republic funded reform programs.

Dombrowski communicated the SCEF's assessment of the South at that moment, explaining that that analysis had suggested how the SCEF could best use its scarce resources. The South's people, he told Hutchins, were ahead of the region's political leaders. A substantial number of whites and the majority of African Americans, for either religious or economic reasons, wanted Jim Crow laws and customs eliminated. Fear or intimidation, not complacency or hatred, explained the lack of protest, the South's silence, he said. The SCEF planned to attack segregation relentlessly on the one hand and praise integration on the other.[24] Hutchins personally was supportive of the SCEF's plan but offered no concrete suggestions about shifting the SCEF's propaganda drive into high gear and no promise of funding.

From Chicago Dombrowski went to New York City to meet with the pioneering public relations expert, Edward L. Bernays, who was using public-opinion polls to determine how and where best to market products.

Dombrowski wanted to know if it was possible to graft these techniques to the SCEF's aims. Bernays explained how public opinion research was conducted, how the results were analyzed, and how to use leaders who mold opinion. He advised doing research before launching any campaign, and selecting specific target issues such as schools, housing, the courts, recreation, health care, or other social institutions, all targets where debate, once started, could flow from self-interest.[25] Dombrowski told Ethel Clyde that he'd gotten the advice he'd come north seeking. She had given him the money for his trip.

On his last night in the city, as he and Clyde were leaving her apartment at 1 Fifth Avenue for dinner in Greenwich Village, Dombrowski crumpled to the street. "I stepped off the curb at the corner of Fifth Avenue and Eighth Street and collapsed," he remembered. "There was a sudden shock in my left hip. I couldn't stir for a few minutes. We had to take a cab after I got back to my feet."[26] He spent the next day in the hospital. X-rays revealed calcium spurs growing between each hip cup and femur, and in the joints of his knees. Medication was available to blunt the pain but could do nothing about the cause. No operation had been perfected to eliminate the problem. Dombrowski limped back to New Orleans.

Bernays' influence was soon evident in *The Southern Patriot*. The campaign to demonstrate that the doctrine of separate but equal was bankrupt, and bankrupting, opened in October 1947. The basic strategy would be repeated again and again, institution by institution. Dombrowski used numbers, not moral arguments, to expose disparities. He started with public education.[27] *The Southern Patriot* reported that Mississippi operated ten one-room schools white children were assigned to attend, but 2,015 one-room schools for African-American children. The state spent $45.79 on every white student and $10.10 on every African-American student. White schools had eight-month terms; African-American schools six-month terms. The pattern repeated itself across the rural South. In Louisiana, where African Americans comprised 36 percent of the entire school-age population, their separate schools were allocated 17.6 percent of all funds spent annually. Cities were hardly better. In Atlanta, 120 of the city's 155 African-American elementary school teachers taught double sessions daily. Classes averaged forty-four students each. Not one of the city's 612 white elementary school teachers taught in double sessions. Their class size averaged eleven students. Atlanta spent six dollars on school buildings and land for every white enrolled and one dollar for every African-American child. There were 6.5 library books for each white child and 1.4 for each African American.

The statistics on graduate and professional education in the seventeen southern states and District of Columbia were equally dramatic. No public or private college in the South offered a doctorate in any subject to African Americans. Eight offered master's degrees, not including one graduate school for library science and four law schools. Any African American who wanted to become a dentist, doctor, pharmacist, or social worker had to be trained outside the South. Whites, on the other hand, had a choice between four schools of dentistry, sixteen law schools, sixteen schools of medicine, fourteen pharmacy schools, nine schools for social work, and eleven schools for library science.

Even if physical or financial equality existed in education, Dombrowski wrote, real equality would not be achieved immediately, particularly in higher education. The value of an academic degree rested in part in the eye of the beholder, he wrote, and "the community does not regard a degree from a small separate black school as highly as it does the same degree from a large state university with a long tradition and thousands of distinguished alumni."[28] Worse, he added, segregation perpetuated narrow, stultifying patterns of thought and behavior which in themselves were inadequate for a world demanding that scientific attitudes be "substituted for prejudice." Segregated schools, he concluded, could not educate for an integrated society.

The October issue was a bestseller. In a few months, over 70,000 copies were sold, good numbers by any publisher's reckoning. Schools, libraries, labor unions, churches, and civic organizations snapped up copies. Paid circulation jumped to nearly 15,000. Dombrowski wrote a friend, saying, "It was the best thing by far . . . we have ever done and about the most timely."[29] Income generated by the sales momentarily eased some of the SCEF's financial stress, raising in Dombrowski's mind the idea of additional marketable publications.

Northern contributors were especially generous after the issue appeared. One retired couple, Edith and Neth Bower, who sent five dollars from their Staten Island home, said, "We are on public assistance for our entire living. This . . . is saved out of our eating allowance by buying no flour, bread, cake or other grains, substituting potatoes, etc."[30]

Dombrowski, with help from his friends, had what appeared to be a successful publishing formula. But would exposing an evil be sufficient to end the evil? *The Southern Patriot* issue on schools was timed to appear just before President Truman's Commission on Civil Rights made public its long-awaited report, *To Secure These Rights*. The book-length study called for a "rebirth of freedom" and issued a long list of recommendations, including outlawing the poll tax, establishing harsh sentences for persons convicted of lynching, correcting voting-rights abuses, and the creation in Congress of a Joint Standing Committee on Civil Rights. The panel wanted Truman to create a permanent civil rights commission and a Fair Employment Practices Commission within the executive branch, and asked him to propose legislation prohibiting discrimination in public housing and interstate commerce and eventually eliminating restrictive housing covenants. The commission included Dr. Frank Graham and Dr. Channing Tobias, both members of the SCEF's advisory board. The report catapulted civil rights into the forefront of social debate during a presidential election year.

By letting the commission issue its report, Truman risked losing the Solid South; no Democrat since Reconstruction had won the presidency without the Old Confederacy's vote. Two days after the commission reported its findings, John B. McDaniel, chairman of the Danville, Virginia, Democratic Party, telegraphed the president one of the mildest southern reactions: "I really believe that you have ruined the Democratic Party in the South."[31] The Associated Press reported denunciations from southern politicians as "fervid as the shouts at a backwoods camp meeting."[32] The *Charlotte News* damned the document as a "bombastic demand for upheaval."[33] Dixiecrats (another new tag) were bolting the Democratic Party. Truman also knew that his advocacy of correctives to the nation's racial abuses would insure him the growing African-American vote in major cities of the North and West. African-American leaders and the northern press lauded the report. Dombrowski and Williams felt that *To Secure These Rights* was on a par historically with Roosevelt's 1938 description of the South's economic conditions. Dombrowski wanted the SCEF to pull together a Southwide conference of leaders, arguing that support for Truman by southerners "will be of the utmost importance if anything of a practical nature is to come from this."[34] Williams, Taylor, and Mays went along with his idea to bring one hundred or so respected, representative southern leaders to sponsor the conference, doubting he'd pull it off.

Indeed, finding sponsors proved tougher than Dombrowski had expected. Liberals north and south watched as gale-force political winds ripped the old Roosevelt tent. Henry Wallace's Progressive Party was in-

creasingly popular. Many Wallace supporters in the South remained loyal
to Clark Foreman and resented Williams for sticking with the Democrats.
Other integrationists were genuinely fearful of the third-party campaign
mounted by South Carolina's Strom Thurmond, who was running for president as a Dixiecrat, declaring, "The proposed American FEPC was patterned after a Russian law written by Joseph Stalin about 1920."[35] Cham-
bers of Commerce and some Catholic leaders decried "subversionists high
up in government boring from within." Representative Eugene Cox of
Georgia, echoing Thurmond, declared, "Russia is directing the civil rights
campaign to create a 'great brown race' in the South."[36]

It was not a good time to be on the liberal side of the race issue, or to be
affiliated with someone with Dombrowski's controversial history. Congress allocated $11 million to eliminate suspected Communists from gov-
ernment employment. Truman issued his executive order creating the Temporary Commission on Employee Loyalty. The attorney general got up a
list of seventy-eight supposedly subversive organizations, one of which was
the Southern Negro Youth Congress (SNYC). The future of civil liberties,
guaranteed through a constitutional democracy, seemed in doubt.

Louis Burnham, a founder of the SNYC, invited Dombrowski and Senator Glenn Taylor, the Idaho Democrat who was Henry Wallace's running
mate on the Progressive Party, to speak during its convention in Birmingham on May 1, 1948. Both men accepted. Despite its name, the
SNYC was interracial, although its membership was drawn chiefly from
the African-American middle class. The SNYC had been organized by
Communist Party activists in 1936.[37] During its seventh annual convention in 1947, W. E. B. DuBois had given his electrifying "Behold the Land"
speech. "There were all sorts of young working people there," recalled
Modjeska Simkins, who helped to arrange that meeting. She lived in Columbia, South Carolina, and was an ardent supporter of both the SCEF and
the SNYC.[38] "Young white coal miners from Appalachia found common
interests with blacks from Georgia farms."

The SNYC had difficulty finding a place to meet in Birmingham.
African-American Masons reneged on a promise to let the group use a spacious hall. The city's largest African-American churches refused space.
"The mood of that period was to rub out anything that looked like it was
going to get the masses of blacks and whites together," Simkins remembered.[39] Finally, the Reverend C. Herbert Oliver, pastor of the Alliance
Gospel Tabernacle, opened his sanctuary, a tiny church created from a neat

frame house in downtown Birmingham. He and his wife, who was seven months pregnant with their first child, lived in two rooms. Otherwise, every space was pressed into religious service. A living room had been made into a chapel. Fifty delegates were expected.

Dombrowski, Doris S. Block of the American Youth for a Free World, a New York–based organization, and Edward Forey, a member of a National Maritime Union local in Mobile, Alabama, arrived at Alliance Gospel Tabernacle by mid-morning on May 1. They came early to help the minister, and Burnham, a longtime Dombrowski ally, with final arrangements. Burnham hadn't arrived. As the others were getting acquainted, a dozen policemen burst into the church, arresting those present for violating Birmingham's segregation ordinances. A physical barrier was required in any building where whites and African Americans mingled. They were taken to police headquarters and charged. Their trials were set for May 5 at 7:30 p.m. in night court. Bond was set at four hundred dollars each.[40] Dombrowski was elated, hoping the SCEF would have a hand in a challenge to the city's Jim Crow laws, long a thorn in his organizational side. Allowed one telephone call from the jail, he reached Ethel Clyde, asking for a loan for their bonds. She wired fifteen hundred dollars.[41]

When Dombrowski and the others got back to the Alliance Gospel Tabernacle, they found several dozen policemen stationed outside. Across the street, a large crowd of robed Klansmen watched from seats on a brick wall. Inside the church, they found Burnham. He had spirited Mrs. Oliver out of the church to safety in a friend's home. He also had mustered four lawyers to fight the city ordinance: Arthur Shores, one of the few African-Americans practicing law in Alabama; Thomas Johnson of Macon, Georgia, a member of the SCHW board for years; Robert Trawich, a white lawyer practicing in Birmingham; and Emmanuel Block of the Civil Rights Congress, who was flying in from New York City.

Reluctantly, all agreed that Rev. Oliver's church should be "segregated." No-one wanted to embarrass Senator Taylor or thoughtlessly spark an episode that would hurt his candidacy or Wallace's Progressive Party. A "Whites Only" sign was hung over the front door. A side door was marked for "Colored." The pews were separated with similar signs, and a string was tied down the aisle to form a "barrier." These arrangements were being completed as delegates arrived, passing through a police cordon and jeering Klansmen. Curious onlookers lined the street.

About 7 p.m., Senator Taylor, escorted by Simkins, arrived by taxi. They walked directly to the side door, climbed the few steps, and started through the door into the church. Several policemen jumped to bar Taylor's way.[42]

"Niggers," one told Taylor, "is supposed to go in this door. White folks use the front door."[43] Taylor pushed the policeman's arm out of his way. The policeman struck back. Both men started swinging.

"They fell into the shrubbery," Simkins remembered.[44] "Glenn beat that policeman up and down. I don't know what kind of food he'd eaten—but as the Bible says, 'Upon what meat does this our Caesar feed that he has become so great?' He beat that policeman good before they got the best of him." Taylor was taken to police headquarters, and charged with disorderly conduct and interference with a police officer. His trial was set for night court on May 5, too. Taylor was released after posting one hundred dollars bond. He told the press, "My arrest and manhandling is a blatant violation of my constitutional right. The local segregation ordinance is unconstitutional and we are prepared to carry this test case to the Supreme Court."[45] His arrest made headlines nationally. But the SNYC convention's proceedings had been shattered.

As their lawyers prepared to challenge law and custom, Simkins and Dombrowski tried to build political and financial support. Dombrowski contacted SCEF supporters and others across the South, asking for contributions to pay the legal fees. He kept the press informed. Simkins had a tougher job. She tried to find African Americans in Birmingham who would publicly risk demanding an end to segregation in churches. "The town was just terror stricken," she remembered.[46] "You couldn't imagine what the atmosphere was like. It was Bull Connor's town. Even a white United States senator wasn't safe. I was invited to a social service organization made up mostly of the wives of doctors, dentists, or lawyers. They were all middle class. I told them how they would have to be strong and not relent in the struggle for justice. And one woman told me, 'Yes, you can be strong because you are going home.' I said, 'Well, that's all the more reason for you to be strong. You have to stay here.' They got down on their knees and wept, they were so afraid. They had every reason to be afraid."

Birmingham's municipal courthouse was jammed with several hundred persons on May 5 when the integrationists came to trial. The judge ordered Taylor tried first; Dombrowski, Oliver, and the others were sent into a witness room. As they left, Taylor continued his defiance of Birmingham law, first by attempting to sit in the section reserved for African Americans and, when police thwarted him, by standing in the aisle. "He stood there like a

Doris Block, James Dombrowski, and Rev. H. Douglas Oliver leave the Birmingham jail after their arrest at Rev. Oliver's church. Courtesy of *The Southern Patriot*.

rock for two hours," Simkins said.[47] The judge disposed of all his other cases, then turned to Taylor's. He was found guilty quickly, fined fifty dollars plus costs, and given a six-month suspended sentence. His lawyers appealed immediately.

The judge adjourned court after trying Taylor and reset the cases of Dombrowski and the others until June 11. Taylor's conviction was one of three reports the *Birmingham News* carried the next morning which bore directly on race. A second reported that, while the senator was in court, three homes owned by African Americans in Birmingham had been badly damaged by bombs. No injuries were reported. The third report predicted that only "a few Negroes were expected to vote in the City primary" and noted that, of 54,000 eligible voters in Birmingham, only 1,764 were African Americans.[48]

Not one to waste time, Dombrowski resumed his efforts to find sponsors for the gathering to support the presidential commission's report. The event was planned for November 20 in Charlottesville, Virginia, if he could raise the money. He went to Houston, Austin, Dallas, Los Angeles, and San Diego. Money came out of wallets slowly; sponsors emerged even more slowly. He didn't have much to show for his wearing effort by the time he got back for court.

City Judge Oliver Hall dashed any hopes for a dramatic end to Birmingham's Jim Crow laws and a stinging defeat for Eugene "Bull" Connor. Hall listened for an hour as defense lawyers argued that the case should be dismissed since the laws violated their constitutional right to peaceful assembly. Judge Hall declared that the laws were "reasonable and good."[49] However, he added, conviction hinged on whether or not Forey, the maritime union leader, had violated the city's law by sitting in an unsegregated meeting. Forey, the judge said, "was sitting in a pew by himself. The pew was at a right angle to the other benches. I believe the people who sponsored the meeting tried to create a separation of the races and abide by the law." He dismissed all charges.

Burnham told the press, "Faced with the possibility of a direct test of the constitutionality of the local segregation ordinances, the authorities ran for cover. Their action is a tacit admission that the infamous Section 359 of the Birmingham code would probably not stand the test of a legal review in the Supreme Court. . . . It is clear that they must resort to extra-legal, extra-constitutional means to maintain the Jim Crow oppression of the Negro people."[50] The SNYC did not stand the test either. The confrontation split the organization. Communist Party members left for fulltime party work, or to support Wallace's campaign. Many of SNYC's youthful members, drawn as they were mostly from the African-American middle class, quit under pressure from worried parents.[51]

Meanwhile, the presidential campaign had a curious parallel with Dombrowski's effort to organize the Charlottesville meeting. Few figured that Truman could win re-election. Thurmond's Dixiecrats were expected to take the South. Republican contender Thomas E. Dewey was thought to have the votes of the Northeast, West, and Midwest. Dombrowski's prospects looked no better immediately after the trial. By November 1, however, he told Aubrey Williams,

> We finally succeeded in getting 121 persons to lend their names as sponsors. It is a remarkably fine list, about one-third of them ministers and a similar number of college professors. Labor names are few, one AFL editor from Tennessee and four or five CIO people, all from two or three unions. A considerable number of the signers of the statement are persons not heretofore identified with progressive causes, which is one of the most gratifying aspects of the project. States from which we have no representation pledged to come are Florida, Kentucky, Oklahoma, Georgia, and Arkansas. I think we will be able to get at least one person from each state by the time of the meeting.[52]

The two hundred or so persons gathered in Charlottesville. Like many politically active Americans, they were still astonished by Truman's re-election earlier in the month. They were no less impressed by the fact that Dombrowski had gotten them together. Williams declared that Truman's victory in the face of the civil rights backlash "changed the climate of the South. We must grasp this opportunity . . . fearlessly, without shading or compromise."[53] Given the November elections, and their own numbers, the goal of integration did not seem so distant.

Journalist Jennings Perry drafted the document signed that day, "A Declaration of Civil Rights." The statement had been circulated to each person before arrival. Some editorial changes were made by the body collectively, then the document was signed during a brief ceremony in Madison Hall, the YMCA campus center. Williams read the declaration to the press at Thomas Jefferson's home at Monticello:

> Truth and justice are not bounded or divided by parallels of latitude. . . . Many fellow citizens, especially in our Southern States, are unashamedly advocating ideas of racism and white supremacy contrary

to American democracy. . . . Discrimination inevitably means lower living standards for those who discriminate as well as for those who are victims of discrimination. Although the South is one of the richest regions in the United States in natural resources, the average citizen in a Southern State has an income forty percent lower than that of a citizen in a non-Southern State. . . . We are bound by economic, political and ethical demands to abolish segregation and discrimination against racial, religious, and national groups.[54]

The declaration called for the repeal of existing segregation laws and the passage of federal, state, and local legislation "to shield . . . the civil rights of citizens." The prospects for such legislation were dim, and the signers knew it. At best, they hoped for voluntary efforts to combat legal segregation.

How the nation divided on the SCEF's single issue was mirrored in the next day's newspapers. The *New York Times* carried a full report under a three-column headline.[55] The Associated Press, which generally decided which stories to transmit after learning how the New York City newspaper was going to play the day's event, "kept the story off the trunk lines."[56]

In the face of great odds, at a time when political dissent was suppressed officially, the SCEF had proved that it could bring together often isolated individuals from across the South to fight segregation. Relieved that the event had happened and been noticed, Dombrowski declared it "the best meeting I ever attended."[57] The SCEF had come of age.

# 13

## Separate
## and
## Unequally
## Bad

Jim Crow had been born in 1896, a year earlier than Dombrowski, when the U.S. Supreme Court embedded the racist creed of separate but equal in American law and life. Legislatures in southern states during the 1890s had busied themselves enacting laws to segregate the races. Louisiana lawmakers used the creedal language accepted by the Supreme Court in 1896, saying that railroads had "to provide separate but equal accommodations for the white and colored races."[1] Another Louisiana law defined a New Orleans man, Homer Adolph Plessy, as "colored" because he had "one-eighth African blood." To test these racist laws with the support of New Orleans friends, Plessy boarded a train one day and refused to take a seat in the "colored" coach. He was arrested. Plessy was a long-time activist who was acting as part of an equally concerned citizen's committee. He went to court arguing that the state law was in conflict with the Thirteenth Amendment abolishing slavery and the Fourteenth Amendment, which prohibits some state legislative action.[2] Plessy lost. The Supreme Court voted eight to one to sanction the doctrine in public transportation, going on to note "that segregation in education was a general American practice, not an uniquely Southern one," and thereby applying their decision to public schools. The lone dissenter, John Marshall Harlan, predicted, "the judgment this day rendered will, in time, prove to be quite as pernicious as the decision . . . in the Dred Scott case."[3] Jim Crow was legal and soon influenced virtually every aspect of national life.

Dombrowski and the SCEF were crusading against a legal and social tenet which had stood inviolate for half a century. After attacking segregated education, they campaigned to integrate health care, end white primaries, and open professional services. The SCEF would spot a potential issue, identify the constituency bound to it by self-interest, poll them, gather other relevant data, release "the facts" at a moment when policy-makers or influence leaders were looking in that direction. This was Bernays' strategy. Dombrowski's office issued a steady flow of news about positive interracial actions or policies. The SCEF harped on the theme that southerners were not universally behind Jim Crow doctrine. His "clients" were citizens who wanted an end to Jim Crow badly enough to give the SCEF donations as "a fee for service." In effect, the SCEF was a public relations firm progandizing to undermine the image that the South was one in support of Jim Crow. In later years, similar single-issue advocacy organizations became the rule rather than the exception.

Dombrowski added two distinctive "services" to the Bernays' model of a public relations enterprise. First, since he felt that it was his duty to agitate, he made certain that the SCEF did likewise. Optimistic boosterism was not his motivation. His Methodism compelled him to directly confront evil. Second, the SCEF organized zestfully. To expose evil was necessary but not sufficient, only a first step. Every expose had to lead to action. To act effectively, and with force, citizens had to organize. The SCEF pulled together dissidents to protest some meanness here today, then disband, and reform a battleline elsewhere tomorrow to celebrate some defiance. They were a roving picket of militants. The organization seldom missed an opportunity to represent its "clients' " interests—at hearings, protest marches, or petition campaigns.

Throughout 1948–51, the public SCEF mirrored the private Dombrowski. He wavered back and forth on the issue of violence. Would the powerful ever give up any of their power without a bloody struggle? The SCEF's organizing style derived from America's revolutionary insurrection against British colonial rule. Dombrowski believed that integrationists were being warred upon. His principal medium, *The Southern Patriot,* had been born and named during war; he deliberately continued the name after the war. He was preoccupied with the metaphors and realities of violence. In the end, however, he concluded that constitutional guarantees rather than weapons gave SCEF's roving pickets their moral and legal force. The right to speak and to assemble were essential to his business.

Dombrowski returned to Reinhold Niebuhr's *Moral Man and Immoral Society*. His less-loved but nevertheless well-loved teacher had predicted that the emancipation of African Americans in America "probably waits upon the adequate development of . . . social and political strategy."[4] At the time of its publication, Niebuhr's prophecy had given intellectual weight to Dombrowski's growing belief that race was America's chief political problem and to his own search for a useful way to take part in the struggle for full emancipation. By the late 1940s, Dombrowski believed that the SCEF itself was at least a modest part of an emerging strategy.

As he went about his work for the SCEF, Dombrowski sensed that the wait, as Niebuhr had put it, was nearly over, a feeling that gripped him more than at any time in his career. He found evidence of powerful political stirrings within the African-American community. The NAACP's membership had soared to over 400,000.[5] African-American veterans were being organized, by both the NAACP's office for veterans affairs and the rival United Negro and Allied Veterans of America, founded in April 1946 by the Communist Party. Limited federal legislation such as the FEPC was in place; he sensed that additional openings were possible. Was he reading more into these signs than was there? Perhaps, but he was certain that the support of white southerners, however few in number, would weaken the troops of racism. The SCEF collaborated, taking its lead from those who stood to gain the most. At every opportunity, he made the overture of fraternal cooperation to a wide array of organizations, no matter what their political stripe. His business prospered through unity.

Dombrowski remained uncertain about Niebuhr's reasoning, however. With his book, Niebuhr had broken ranks with Ward, Dombrowski, and others in the Marxist camp—and with the Social Gospel camp. The political problem, as Niebuhr saw it then, was "the endless cycle" of coercion. Injustice begat violence which begat injustice which begat more violence. Niebuhr wrote: "If social cohesion is impossible without coercion, and coercion is impossible without the creation of social injustice, the destruction of injustice is impossible without the use of further coercion, are we not in an endless cycle of social conflict?"[6]

In 1932, Dombrowski had not been able to accept Niebuhr's conclusion that the "highest goal to which society can aspire is an uneasy balance of power."[7] Idealism had propelled him to look for some new social formulation, first in the history of Christian Socialism, then in the Soviet Union. He had not changed his mind at Highlander. His call for revolutionary change with his equally militant Socialist friends was more than simple dissatisfaction with an older generation.

In the Depression, Dombrowski had stood with Ward, accepting the thesis that, to achieve a new society, coercion and perhaps even violence might be necessary and was likely. He had been convinced, however, that the revolutionary society, the Kingdom of God, would create perfect justice, or at the very least set the stage for a society in which injustice was swept away. On that point, Dombrowski had found Frederick Douglass compelling: "You can't plant without breaking ground."[8]

Niebuhr believed that nonviolent resistance was the way out of the endless cycle. Nonviolence, he argued, was the means to deflate the powerful, to acknowledge an opponent's humanity, and to appeal to "profound and ultimate unities."[9] By 1948, Dombrowski was less clear about his disagreements with the Niebuhr of 1932. Experience was softening the former's dogmatism. The SCEF's only plentiful weapons were the freedoms to speak and to organize. Realism, not a repudiation of violence, compelled Dombrowski to use nonviolent agitation in the face of overwhelming odds. He realized that, no matter how strident the call, the early Christian Socialists had failed to establish the Kingdom of God on earth. His own petitioning within the Socialist community had fallen on deaf ears. Despite the protracted coalfield wars, miners and their families lived on in exploitation. Privately, Dombrowski was appalled by the Stalinist repression, although he would never repudiate the Soviets in public. The Second World War had prevented the spread of fascism abroad but left Jim Crow largely intact at home.

Dombrowski took up the trade of propagandist at a time when he was no longer sure about his readiness to justify violent tactics. He was equally uncertain that Niebuhr's nonviolent resistance would ever shake racism's grip. He straddled the problem of violence, sure of only two things: first, striving for the Kingdom of God continued as his central, propelling motivation; and second, if he and the SCEF kept on—either militantly, striking at segregation, or passively, resisting its worst manifestations—there would be a reaction. He had no doubt that the powerful would fight to maintain their privileges. He refused to back away from such a confrontation and was able to convince others to march with him in search of the crisis. Dombrowski's outlook was not unique; most of the SCEF's other activists were tugged by the same inner compulsions and dilemmas. The SCEF became "the conscience of a troubled South," in one historian's words.[10]

These intensely personal and private debates notwithstanding, segregated schooling at every level continued to be a favorite public SCEF target. There had been hopeful breeches in judicial opinion. In 1938, the U.S. Supreme Court had ordered the University of Missouri Law School to admit Lloyd L. Gaines, in a decision that found racial discrimination unconstitutional but which left standing sanctioned or Jim Crow laws. Other challenges were brewing. Herman Sweatt had a case pending before the court. The University of Texas Law School had enrolled Sweatt, then set up a "law school" in a basement for him or any other African American.

Dombrowski hammered at segregated schooling for several additional reasons. He believed that Jim Crow's coercive sanctions would fall before learning. Dombrowski had a teacher's faith that reason could overwhelm might. In this regard if in no other, Dombrowski's behavior after the breakup of the SCHW reveals him not to have been a dogmatic Marxist revolutionary. This belief also put Dombrowski at odds with Niebuhr on a vital strategic point. The theologian's book had relentlessly attacked the Progressive illusion that through education the powerful would be persuaded to relinquish power. Even in 1932, Niebuhr was writing for and teaching among the well-off and powerful, and, as the years went on, more of his considerable energies were devoted to them. Thus he knew them better. Dombrowski, however, was not free of the thrall of unorthodox adult education, despite his unsatisfying experience at Highlander and his failure to build the SCHW into a mass educational organization. He taught among the dispossessed. He had told the Progressive educators that he believed education was propaganda. The SCEF was a school with one subject, or a public relations firm with a handful of customers. By taking advantage of current events—some court, legislative, or organizational action—he made the media his textbook, and any who read or who listened became his class. Dombrowski and the SCEF got wide attention—mileage, in the language of Bernays' world—for narrowly focused civic lessons.

This operational strategy fit with Dombrowski's life at the time. The pain in his legs and back often kept him in bed. Long trips were difficult, even disabling, and when he made them, as he would, he paid a price. Ellen demanded his attention and care. She had all but withdrawn from any social contact save with Dombrowski and a pet dog. He denied growing evidence of her dependency on alcohol, unable to admit to himself that she was ill.[11] He stayed close to New Orleans out of necessity.

Managing a public relations business made it possible for Dombrowski to both stay at home and stay near the action. Williams took the SCEF's case to the public. In this way, he and Williams fought southern racism as if they were all over the South's map. At this time, the politics of race and of education were becoming deeply entwined. Schoolmen feared that the Gaines decision signaled the end of segregation in higher education. They started looking for ways to perpetuate the *status quo*. By 1947, southern governors had settled on a plan they figured would keep higher education nearly "lily-white." They proposed a regional compact "to provide or purchase those educational services that are necessary for the education of sufficient numbers of citizens to maintain the agencies and services essential to the public welfare."[12] A year later, on February 8, 1948, in Tallahassee, Florida, they created a Southern Regional Educational Board, "empowered to submit plans and recommendations to state legislatures to create, maintain and operate educational institutions," and begin hiring staff.[13]

Support for the action was not unanimous. Two states, Kentucky and West Virginia, fearing the organization would perpetuate racial segregation, delayed ratifying the pact. The *Richmond Times-Dispatch*, a conservative newspaper, editorialized against the idea. The SCEF opposed the regional compact. "There is no evidence to indicate that the segregated regional centers operated jointly by the Southern States will be any less discriminatory than the segregated institutions operated individually by the same authorities."[14] Further, Dombrowski argued, the compact thwarted the basic purpose of a university. It was "uneconomical," acting as "a brake on the present trend toward integration in existing institutions." Worst of all, the compact would make legal redress more difficult.

That spring, within days of the U.S. Supreme Court decision admitting African Americans to the University of Oklahoma, Dombrowski mailed a questionnaire to 240 members of the Southern Sociological Society, asking them to choose among four distinct plans being used or proposed at the time to desegregate public colleges and universities. Plan A, a policy operating at the University of Delaware, opened graduate schools to any African American if the courses they wanted were not taught at a publicly financed, African-American college. Plan B, a policy in place at the University of Arkansas Law School, admitted African Americans, but on a segregated basis. Plan C, the University of Oklahoma's policy, established separate graduate schools for African Americans and whites. And Plan D was the policy agreed to by the Southern Governor's Conference, preserving segregation by creating regional graduate schools exclusively for African Americans. Seventy-three sociologists responded. Fifty-two, or 71 percent, favored Plan A. Eighteen favored Plan D. Three said all four were unacceptable choices.[15]

Dombrowski followed with a sharply stated questionnaire to 14,000 faculty members in every southern state university. Would they favor ending segregation in all existing professional and graduate schools and admitting qualified African-American applicants? Only 371 returned the survey. Of these, however, 255, or 69 percent, answered yes. Eleven respondents, or 28 percent, favored segregated regional graduate schools. The polls underscored the SCEF's contention that a measurable degree of integrationist sentiment was being obscured by political rhetoric.[16]

While Dombrowski peppered away at the regional compact in *The Southern Patriot* and with scores of letters to editors, Williams took to the hustings. He joined an array of organizations that testified against the compact before the U.S. Senate in March 1948. Elsewhere, in speech after speech, the Montgomery publisher declared that the governors' plan "was a shameless attempt to beat down the efforts of all people of good will . . . trying to advance . . . an end to discrimination in education."[17] Williams had no luck persuading anyone from the new regional board to debate him. He exchanged acrimonious letters with the organization's director, John E. Ivey, Jr., telling the official in one, "You have the task of explaining to the Negro people of the South, and to all Southern people who abhor this sickness of a segregated society, how the proposal of yours is going to aid in curing it. . . . The position the Southern Conference Education Fund has taken is that segregation is wrong—period. Wrong anywhere and anytime. Now, if you can show that what you and your Regional Control Board are doing breaks down segregation, get up and say it."[18] Ivey hotly denied Williams' charges, but would not debate him.[19]

Dombrowski tried another tack, asking the nationwide radio show, "Town Meeting on the Air," to broadcast a program on the subject. The request fell on deaf ears. Determined to spur public debate on the issue, the

SCEF board announced in mid-1949 that the organization itself would sponsor a Conference on Discrimination in Higher Education at Atlanta University in April 1950, and issued a call for sponsors.

On August 1, 1949, segregationists began to act. Dombrowski was notified that the lease on the SCEF office loft would not be renewed when it expired on October 1. The building owners explained that the Better Business Bureau of New Orleans, headed by John U. Barr, a leading Louisiana Dixiecrat, had pressured them to oust the SCEF.[20] Dombrowski told board members, "Our office problem is further complicated by the biracial character of our office staff, a policy which we are pioneering in New Orleans."[20] After weeks of fruitless effort, Dombrowski found an office two doors away at 822 Perdido. He signed a three-year lease for eighty dollars monthly.

In early November, Dombrowski was notified that the New Orleans office of the Internal Revenue Service had recommended to its Washington headquarters that the SCEF's tax-exempt status be revoked.[21] The action rocked the SCEF, and for good reason. Dombrowski feared that the SCEF would collapse if stripped of the exempt status. He and Williams appealed to every New Deal friend still in office, and to many who were not. Dombrowski urged Mary McLeod Bethune to help him reach President Truman directly, saying, "It would take a considerable portion of the funds now in the Educational Fund and make its continuation very difficult. . . . What I think needs to be done is for you and myself to try to see President Truman and lay this matter before him."[22]

Six weeks before the Conference on Discrimination in Higher Education was to open in Atlanta, the SCEF was stung from another direction. On February 26, 1950, Ralph McGill, the influential editor of the *Atlanta Constitution,* who was considered the South's leading moderate on race, Red-baited Dombrowski and the SCEF. In a column titled "Not a Commie Front—Not Yet," he charged that the Southern Conference for Human Welfare "was taken over by commies" and that its offshoot SCEF "seemed to many to exist for the purpose of dividing and confusing Southerners who were trying to be progressive."[23] McGill continued, saying that the Conference on Discrimination in Higher Education had one purpose, "to stir up trouble, to agitate the race question, and to 'bait' the South. . . . A meeting on the subject announced needs to be held and discrimination must be removed. It will, in our opinion, be removed more slowly because of the Dombrowski organization."[24]

Aubrey Williams was furious and fearful. He wanted to sue McGill for falsely accusing Dombrowski. He believed that the editorial had been published to keep the timid away and would probably succeed. He and Dombrowski believed that the editorial would find its way to the SCEF's Internal Revenue Service file. Earlier, Williams and Dombrowski had sniped at McGill and his paper for ties to Georgia Gov. Herman Talmadge, who had proposed to close the state's public schools rather than desegregate them.

No suit was filed. Less passionate tempers prevailed, partly because the response to the call for conference sponsors surpassed every expectation.[25] Two hundred and twenty-five professors from 116 southern colleges or universities agreed to lend their names. Dozens from outside the region were sponsors, including Albert Einstein at the Institute for Advanced Study at Princeton, who wrote: "It is needless to say that I am wholeheartedly in favor of your attempt to organize teachers and other intellectuals in the struggle against the most serious disease in American public life: discrimination against the colored people and especially their exclusion from many institutions of learning—equally bad for the oppressed and for the oppressor."[26]

On April 8, 1950, several hundred persons braved association with the SCEF, showing up to talk with each other and to hear Dr. E. Franklin Frazier, the famed sociologist who was a SCEF sponsor, give the keynote speech. He assailed discrimination and "the concept of Negro education" as a bar to the development of African Americans: "Negro education has never been taken seriously as a form of intellectual discipline or as a part of the stream of intellectual life in the country. A Negro doctor was a doctor or engineer or what have you, but never a Negro doctor or a Negro engineer. These are the peculiar products of that American invention known as 'Negro education.'"[27] And the sociologist rebutted McGill, although not by name. He pointed to a poll Dombrowski had taken which revealed that 70 percent of the respondents favored an immediate end to the exclusion of African Americans from graduate education and professional schools. "Evidently," Frazier said, "the so-called liberals who pretend to speak for the South (but who are unwilling to attack segregated education), do not express the growing liberal opinion; they are more likely endeavoring to forge public opinion according to their own prejudice concerning what they regard as the Negro's proper place in the South."[28]

By the SCEF's measure, the Atlanta conference was worth every nickel.

"This was," Dombrowski told the board later, "as far as we know, the first time that any substantial group of southern professional people publicly stood up against segregation."[29] They had made it virtually impossible for any African-American educators to support the regional compact.

Integrationists also won something of a judicial victory six days after the conference. Judge Charles Markell of the Maryland Court of Appeals issued a writ of mandamus compelling the University of Maryland's School of Nursing to admit Ester McCready, who had been barred because she was an African American. The university argued that McCready could be trained as a nurse at Meharry Medical College through the Regional School Compact. Judge Markell ruled that "no compact or contract can extend the territorial boundaries on the State of Maryland to Nashville."[30]

A year later, on April 27, 1951, during the SCEF's own annual meeting, Dombrowski took the measure of his segregationist foes. "Since the last annual meeting, there have been some encouraging events," he said.[31] "The three decisions of the U.S. Supreme Court on June 5, 1950, in the Sweatt, McLaurin and Henderson cases have accelerated the breaking down of racial barriers in higher education and transportation." Five private colleges in Kentucky had desegregated. South Carolina and Tennessee had removed the poll tax as a requirement for voting. He concluded:

> The deep significance of what has been happening all over the South, where the pattern of segregation has been broken, is the calm, easy acceptance of the white community of a new social situation. On railway dining cars, college campuses, army camps, and athletic fields where Southerners for the first time were permitted to mix on a basis of equality with Negroes, the trouble or confusion which some people predicted did not materialize. The lesson here is inescapable that the South is relatively ready to practice democracy and when given the opportunity will respond well.[32]

He felt that the SCEF might keep its tax-exempt status. "Our case has been referred to the chief counsel of the bureau," he said.[33] Attorneys advised him that the case was a borderline one, considering the general spirit of the times, and that "we have a 50-50 chance" to keep the subsidy.

Lamed by arthritis or not, the rest of Dombrowski's report to the board demonstrated his torrid pace.[34] He had organized successful drives to desegregate the main public library in New Orleans and that city's new train station. He had gotten a twelve-panel photographic exhibit, "Children in America" by Marion Palfi, booked in twelve southern cities, indicating "what may be done in the field of graphic education if we had the resources." On Thanksgiving Day, 1950, Dombrowski joined 125 other southerners (in the coldest weather ever recorded by the Charleston, South Carolina, weather bureau for that day) in a march to honor Judge J. Waites Waring. Waring, a Charleston aristocrat and federal judge, had ruled that the South Carolina white primary election was unconstitutional. The Warings had been ostracized by most friends and even some family members. Vandals had attacked their home. Williams presented a citation to the judge and his wife expressing the SCEF's "deep admiration and respect."

Three days later, Dombrowski and Williams attended a SCEF reception in the ballroom of the Ritz-Carlton Hotel in New York City honoring Madame Jijaya Pandit, India's ambassador to the United States, Eleanor Roosevelt, and Mary McLeod Bethune. Ralph Tefferteller, now program director for the famed Henry Street Settlement house, called figures for square dancing. Dombrowski, lame but game, and Roosevelt led the dancers in a lively Virginia reel. Over five hundred persons contributed to the SCEF.

Besides publishing *The Southern Patriot*, Dombrowski got out a ninety-page pamphlet containing the major addresses given at the Atlanta conference. Copies were sold to college administrators from seventy-five schools in thirty-three states, with dozens more ordered by individual faculty members, libraries, and state government officials. A sprightly booklet, "Adam's Children," a collection of cartoons on prejudice and intolerance by artist Frank Hanley, sold out one printing of five thousand copies and went into a second edition.

On his own time, away from his SCEF responsibilities, Dombrowski was establishing personal contacts with surviving dockworkers who had been involved with a general strike on New Orleans piers in 1907.[35] Some ten thousand white and African-American dockhands had fashioned "half and half" agreements to divide work and union leadership posts evenly between the races. The resulting interracial solidarity foiled employers who encouraged competition between the races to drive down labor costs. Dombrowski wanted to know about this history and wanted the world to know about it, too. Dombrowski found reason for optimism in such southern experience, and in the lives of earlier civil rights activists such as George

Washington Cable and Adolph Plessy. He was encouraged by their accomplishments and tried to pass that experience along, through correspondence, propaganda, and conversations.

Until December 15, 1950, Dombrowski paid but fleeting attention to segregation's impact on health care and medicine. On that day, according to a report he read in the weekly *Afro-American,* a college student, Maltheus R. Avery, 24, died being shuttled from one North Carolina hospital to another after being injured in an auto crash.[36] Avery suffered fractures of the skull, cheekbone, jaw, legs, and both arms in an accident which happened near Mebane, North Carolina, on December 1. He was taken first to Alamance General Hospital. His condition was critical, but doctors would not admit him because of his race. He was then driven some fifty miles east to Durham and the Duke University Hospital emergency room. As doctors started treating his injuries, hospital administrators determined that the ward set aside for African Americans was full. Doctors stopped, ordering him taken to Lincoln Hospital, the hospital in Durham for African Americans. He died there an hour after being admitted. "In North Carolina," Dombrowski wrote, "Hippocrates' surgical gown is much like a Klansman's hood."[37]

At the next SCEF board meeting, in spring 1951, Dombrowski asked for authorization to mount a campaign focusing on segregated medical care. He outlined a plan to assemble facts on cases in which refusal of a hospital to admit an African American resulted in the patient's death. He had a poll ready for hospital administrators and doctors. Ethel Clyde had agreed to help finance the campaign. "There is no more dramatic representation of the brutalities of segregation than in the color line drawn by most hospitals in the South," he said.[38] "Less dramatic but just as important is the inability of Negro doctors to treat their patients in white hospitals, and the racial bar in county and state medical societies." He got the go-ahead.

The SCEF's friends were soon sending newspaper clippings or personal accounts detailing how African Americans had been turned away from hospitals or ignored if admitted. In Akron, Ohio, a young star athlete died after being refused admission to a hospital which had a bed empty but in a room for whites. In Kentucky, three seriously injured African Americans were placed on the hospital's floor bleeding and left there without treatment for three or four hours. One of them died.[39]

He dug cases out of history. In 1932, Juliette Derricotte, had been injured critically in an automobile accident near Dalton, Georgia. Dalton hospital authorities refused her. She died as friends drove her to Chattanooga, Tennessee, forty miles north, where an African-American hospital was located. He found similar cases, reporting on them in *The Southern Patriot*. Eventually, he accumulated enough tragedy for a pamphlet, "The Untouchables," indicting segregation in medicine. His friend Ben Shahn did the illustrations. Over 25,000 copies were distributed.[40]

Dombrowski polled 2,414 hospital administrators and over 46,000 members of the American Medical Society in eighteen southern and border states, plus the District of Columbia. Were African Americans admitted to their hospitals as patients and, if so, on what basis? Were African-American doctors allowed to practice in their hospitals? He asked the administrators to choose the one desegregation plan they felt best served the health needs of their communities.[41]

The SCEF got usable replies from 711 hospitals, a 29.2 percent response. Segregation was widespread, and there was little evidence that anyone wanted any change. Exactly 585 hospitals, or 82 percent of the sample, admitted African Americans on a segregated basis. While 32.4 percent of the region's hospital beds were assigned for African Americans, their "depressed economic status tends to increase . . . [the] need for hospitalization."[42]

Most hospitals admitted African Americans on a quota basis. Over four hundred had wards specifically for African Americans. When they were filled, other African Americans were not admitted, even if beds were vacant in whites-only hospital wings. In addition to these artificially erected barriers, in Louisiana and South Carolina hospital beds for African Americans were concentrated in one or two large institutions. "The inconvenience and health hazards suffered by persons living in distant areas can be imagined," Dombrowski wrote.[43] He found one hopeful sign. The survey revealed that 108 hospitals—not counting federal institutions or those exclusively run for African Americans—operated without segregationist policies. Most were in border states.

And how would administrators desegregate their hospitals? In general, they voted for the *status quo*.[44] A policy to admit without regard to race got 125 votes, or 17.6 percent. The proposal to maintain racially separate hospitals got 76 votes, or 10.7 percent. A plan to admit on a segregated basis got 439 votes, or 61.7 percent. Ten percent of the respondents made no choice. "Rightly or wrongly, the initiating impulse toward a more democratic use of these facilities seemingly must come from outside," Dombrowski wrote.

To encourage external pressure on hospitals, the SCEF allied with the few like-minded organizations, most of them created by African Americans. On December 28, 1950, Williams was the featured speaker at the annual meeting of the National Committee Against Discrimination of the Association of Interns and Medical Students.[44] The publisher testified before the U.S. Senate with a coalition of such groups. In *The Southern Patriot,* Dombrowski plugged the Interracial Hospital Movement based in Louisville, Kentucky, a grassroots effort to desegregate the state's hospitals. Eventually, this movement collected ten thousand signatures on a petition demanding equal hospital care for all people. Since *The Southern Patriot* was exchanged regularly with every African-American newspaper across the country, news of this and similar campaigns reached an audience well beyond the little monthly's circulation. Editors in the South's all-white newsrooms read the monthly, too, often using its reports as the basis for their own articles.

Dombrowski and Williams asked philanthropist Marshall Field, the Chicago department store owner and a backer of Williams' farm paper, to enlist the Rockefeller and Carnegie foundations in the campaign to open medical schools for African-American applicants. Dombrowski told Field that fewer than 615 blacks were in medical schools that year, and that less than 3 percent of all the nation's hospital beds were set aside for the fifteen million African Americans.

Dombrowski organized a medical advisory committee to insure that the medical evidence the SCEF developed was sound, and to give further evidence that not all southern doctors believed the creed of separate but equal. The committee furnished *The Southern Patriot* with statistics on the grim outcomes of Jim Crow medical policies, often seeing public print for the first time. The life expectancy of African Americans was 21 percent lower than that of whites; the number of infant deaths per one thousand live births was 69 percent higher for African Americans; African-American mothers died in childbirth at a rate 143 percent higher than white ones. Eventually, a book-length study issued. Long-term solutions to the health problems, Dombrowski believed, would be a function of medical education, still equally segregated. More African Americans had to enter the field as nurses, technicians, or doctors. Schools at every level had to be opened. The businessman in him found a market. African Americans wanted medical training. Two institutions trained most of the nation's African-American physicians. Howard University got over 1,300 applications annually for 74 seats. Meharry got over 800 for 65 seats. In 1948, the last year for which he was able to find data, 85 African-American students were enrolled in 20 northern or western medical schools. Of the 1,300 schools of nursing in America, over 1,200 only admitted whites. Less than 3 percent of the nation's registered nurses were African Americans. After graduation, African-American doctors and nurses faced additional Jim Crow barriers. Only a handful of hospitals permitted them to intern or to work. In 1950, Dombrowski reported that there were only 158 internships open to African Americans in all southern hospitals, including the facilities operated exclusively by African Americans. White doctors, on the other hand, could choose among 9,000 approved openings.

Since residencies were virtually impossible to find, African-American doctors were pushed into general practice rather than into medical specialties, which often were more profitable and intellectually satisfying. Finally, when hospitals permitted African-American doctors to practice in them, local medical societies barred them from membership. This practice kept them from essential postgraduate training, off policy-making boards, and off hospital staffs. "The more I learn about this situation," he wrote Ethel Clyde, "the more aroused I become."[45]

Dombrowski's own health interrupted this campaign. Ellen, too, continued her slide into alcohol dependency. In September 1950, pain in his neck and shoulders had become unbearable. For two months, Dombrowski had treatments daily at a physiotherapist's office. He'd be given dyathermy massage, then, with a halter fitted around his neck, be hoisted so that the weight of his body was suspended from the neck. Released from daily treatment, he was ordered to quit work briefly and rest. He and Ellen went to Pensacola, Florida, five hours east of New Orleans, for a week of fishing. In February 1951, the pain laid him low again, and he was forced to take another two weeks off.

Other troubles beset the SCEF in rapid succession; 1951 was not a good year. Al Maund, a Louisiana native who wrote editorials for the *New Orleans Item*, volunteered to edit and produce *The Southern Patriot* as Dombrowski coped with his pains. A few months after he started, the larger newspaper fired him.[46] He took a job with the Louisville *Courier-Journal*. During the spring and summer of 1951, contributions fell to practically zero. Sen. Joseph McCarthy's headline-grabbing search for Communists in government was reaching a nadir. Contributors were frightened. Twice that summer, newspapers carried Red-baiting attacks on the SCEF. The worst of the two appeared in the Memphis *Commercial Appeal* under the headline, "Once Branded Active Reds, Same Men Now Operating Group on South's Problems; Dombrowski, Accused of Being Communist Party Member, Is 'Mr. Big' of the Southern Conference Education Fund."[47]

On July 20, 1951, after two years of suspense, Dombrowski was notified that the Internal Revenue Service had revoked the SCEF's exempt status. Gifts were no longer tax deductible. Income would be taxed the same as a corporation's. SCEF was ordered to pay Social Security taxes for employees. The next day, Dombrowski wrote to the board:

> These conditions have serious implications for the future of the SCEF. Although our contributors have known for three years that their gifts were not deductible, this . . . eliminates all chance of grants from foundations and makes extremely difficult the solicitation of large individual contributions. The corporation tax and social security features are especially menacing . . . they could be made retroactive to 1942. This would have a disastrous effect.[48]

Dombrowski mounted an effort to widen the SCEF's contributor base. Individual contributions in 1951 averaged $13 per person. Dombrowski needed $9,100 for his own salary and the office expenses, plus nearly $12,000 earmarked for special projects that fiscal year. If he could find five hundred new contributors, the SCEF could continue despite the IRS ruling. Six months into 1952, he told the board: "It should be clearer than clear that, in the battle to preserve the SCEF and all it stands for, we are in a state of siege. Nor, as the enclosed financial reports show, do we have limitless provisions. On the contrary, for the first six months of 1952 we have an operating deficit of $3,159."[49] Three months later, Dombrowski wrote to Ethel Clyde,

> It was good to talk with you on the telephone but I am sorry I sounded so "poorly." Actually I reckon I was a little low as a result of a multitude of troubles. The office has been having hard sledding financially and that has worried me. . . . My secretary, a very bright young Negro, tells me she probably will not be with me after the first of the year. . . . My landlady told me she wanted my apartment—and on top of all that

my bad hip has been behaving badly. . . . Well, that's the tale of woe."[50]

Two weeks later, for the second time that year, Dombrowski's automobile was stolen. Neither car was recovered.

Dombrowski had to find a place to live and to find money to keep the SCEF alive. During their taxing courtship, he and Ellen had decided to avoid "all property entanglements, thinking that it gave us more freedom."[51] They changed their minds in 1952. Expecting pressures on the SCEF to continue, if not increase, title to a house, Dombrowski reasoned, offered "protection against the whim of the landlords as the going gets rougher." By chance, a house down Gov. Nicholls Street from their apartment came up for sale as they were notified to move. Even French Quarter intimates spoke of its singular charm: "There is a serenity about its face, a kind of inner grace. . . . It has irregular features and certain inconsistencies, but, as with many beautiful women, these seem merely to enhance its appeal."[52] Political necessity and aesthetics overwhelmed the Dombrowskis' earlier resolve; by Thanksgiving they were in the house. To help pay the mortgage, they rented the second floor.

The newly propertied couple vacationed during the Christmas holidays and, returning to New Orleans, stopped in Mobile for gas. The service station boasted a new Coca-Cola dispensing machine. For a dime, the machine dropped a bottle from a slot. On either side of the box, customers could get a sip of cold water from spigots marked "Colored" and "White."

Dombrowski, the man Coca-Cola had wanted to hire, snapped a photograph of the machine. It appeared in the January 1952 issue of *The Southern Patriot*, along with a report about the "color line in the Cola line."[53] The NAACP's *Crisis* reprinted the photo and article. Newspapers as far away as India reprinted the picture or carried reports on the drink machine and the firm's policies. In one of the first challenges to racist corporate practices, Dombrowski demanded that Coca-Cola mend its ways, an irony which escaped no-one who knew his personal history. In Atlanta, Hunter Bell, the newspaper editor who had been Dombrowski's fraternity brother and who had published the astonishing story of Dombrowski's arrest in 1929, had become vice president for public relations at Coca-Cola. Now he mounted a campaign to discredit *The Southern Patriot's* report and photograph.[54] His office told the *Pittsburgh Courier,* one of the first newspapers to pick up the story, that the machine was not described correctly by

Jim Crow and Coca-Cola machines. Photo, taken by James A. Dombrowski, first appeared in *The Southern Patriot*. Frank T. Adams Collection.

*The Southern Patriot.*[55] Bottlers and jobbers, he said, were independent businessmen who selected their own dispensers. Coca-Cola had nothing to do with those decisions.

Dombrowski followed up in the February issue. "Coca-Cola has stressed that there are only a few of these machines in existence. But the number is not the important point. The newspapers of the world seized upon the machine as a symbol—of the 'separate but equal' oppression limiting the hopes and well-being of American Negroes. Therefore, destroying the machines is not enough. Coca-Cola must also demonstrate that it does not participate in policies of racial discrimination."[56] Dombrowski launched one of the earliest, if not the first, corporate campaigns, hoping to pin an ethical issue onto a company's balance sheet and so make it forego racism.

# 14

## On the Street, Politically Homeless

Aubrey Williams was busy dosing fire ants on Peace Farm in Mulberry, Alabama, on March 5, 1954. He dreamed of retiring there, making the place a model farm, and pioneering new agriculture methods or raising beef cattle. To wipe out the pesty fire ants, Williams punched holes in the mounds piled up by the ants, then poured in a lethal dose of gasoline. As he went about the chore, a U.S. marshal walked into the field, interrupting his work. Williams was given a subpoena to appear in two weeks before the U.S. Senate Internal Security Subcommittee at the Post Office Building in New Orleans. The writ was not unexpected, and Williams told the marshal, "Well, you couldn't have come with it at a more appropriate time. This subpoena had to do with some other pests . . . some of us have been trying to eliminate from Southern life—and this is their way of fighting back."[1]

Elsewhere the same day, Dombrowski was served in the SCEF's Perdido Street office, and Virginia Durr was given a similar writ at Pea Level, her home in Wetumpka, Alabama. To their surprise and his, Myles Horton got one at Highlander. Since he had helped inter the SCHW in Richmond, Horton had little to do with the SCEF, being chiefly preoccupied with Highlander's expanding work with African Americans. Earlier, on January 29, 1954, Senator William Jenner, chairman of the full Senate Internal Security Committee, had announced investigative hearings into Communist infiltration of U.S. embassies and two allegedly subversive organizations— the Federal Shorthand Reporters Association and the Southern Conference Educational Fund.[2] Senator Eastland of Mississippi would conduct the SCEF hearings, Jenner said. A few days before Jenner's announcement, SCEF's campaign to air the issues of segregated public education before a national or regional audience had succeeded. Williams had debated Georgia Gov. Eugene Talmadge on nationwide radio. The U.S. Supreme Court decision in the *Brown* case was pending; the doctrine of separate-but-equal was the political issue of the day in America. Southerners waited anxiously. Williams apparently had shaken Talmadge's defense of Jim Crow education, leaving the governor smarting, SCEF's Georgia supporters told Dombrowski. Talmadge was mulling over a suggestion that he organize a Georgia commission to investigate the SCEF for subversion.[3] Taunting the governor, the SCEF met in Atlanta on February 7, an act of political bravado masking growing fear that the SCEF's days were numbered. Most board members attended, evidence of their apprehension in the face of the IRS ruling and Eastland hearings. Dombrowski was convinced that SCEF's demise was near.[4] The IRS ruling had caused contributions to drop well below SCEF's bare-bones operating costs. Dombrowski was going without pay. Revenue would rise slightly in the wake of favorable publicity successes such as the Talmadge debate, but not enough to keep the organization afloat financially or near earlier levels. Eastland's investigation, he believed, could generate sympathy and contributions, or could build a wall of fear between SCEF and the South's few integrationists, while burying the group under a pile of legal fees.

The board's deliberations opened in a genial atmosphere. These were old friends. One of their most cherished goals seemed near at hand. Although no-one had a crystal ball, all expected the Supreme Court to rule against Jim Crow schools in the *Brown* case. If that happened, they wanted the SCEF to take the offensive, spending every available nickel organizing positive political support for school integration. Dombrowski was to poll opinion and report on desegregation efforts in *The Southern Patriot*. He was to arrange compliance conferences to allow proponents to discuss how to dismantle segregated schools. Williams was to call in his political chips, sparing no effort to marshal liberal support, and to debate, testify, or cajole at every possible opportunity.

Before the day was over, however, Eastland's investigation had inflicted its first wound. Everyone agreed that the hearings were a smokescreen, a ploy by Senate segregationists to tar and feather southern integrationists with the brush of Communism. No-one disagreed with the wording of a telegram Williams proposed to send Jenner. In it, they charged that Jenner's intent was "as dishonest as it is contemptible." He was challenged to start criminal proceedings if he had evidence that the SCEF had violated any law. Williams, who signed it, demanded that Jenner step from behind "the shield of your Senatorial immunity and make your charges directly rather than by inference and innuendo."[5]

When they reached the next item on the agenda, however, harmony gave way to discord. Dombrowski, Williams, and Durr were certain that Eastland would ask them the one question which put Senator Joseph McCarthy in the pantheon of inquisitional history: "Are you now, or have you ever been, a member of the Communist Party?" Eastland sat on the same committee with McCarthy. Both men believed that "some Communist influence [was] working" within the Supreme Court decisions on civil rights and civil liberties cases.[6] In the case of Virginia Durr, a relative by marriage of Justice Black, Eastland apparently believed he had the circumstantial evidence needed to prove his chimerical case. A probe of the SCEF would allow Eastland "to hit four or five birds with one stone" and to make inquisitional history himself.[7]

If Dombrowski or the others sought protection under the Fifth Amendment to the U.S. Constitution, or were perceived to have answered wrongly, the Constitution notwithstanding, public opinion likely would brand them and the SCEF Communists. Others who had appeared before McCarthy, believing that the Constitution offered them some protection, had lost jobs, reputations, and sometimes even their families. Benjamin Mays, the widely-esteemed Morehouse College president, wanted assurances that no SCEF officer would plead the Fifth Amendment. Williams disagreed, explaining later in a letter to Eleanor Roosevelt, "I took the position that was a matter which each individual had the right to decide for himself. I did not believe that it was fair or proper to set up a priori, conditions which bound men to conformity which might be at variance with the dictates of their conscience."[8] Williams, passionate as always, vowed that he'd say he had never been a Communist but would refuse to testify about any other SCEF supporter, even if he had "to take refuge behind all the amendments there are!"[9]

Durr planned another approach. She intended to defy the committee's authority to inquire into her political beliefs or associations, except to deny she was or ever had been "under Communist discipline." Silence was going to be her answer to any other question.[10]

Dombrowski said that he would stand on the First Amendment, arguing that the investigation violated his guarantee of free speech and association.[11] He would not invoke the Fifth Amendment, but he could not insist that others spurn that defense. He would answer questions about SCEF's work, and about himself and his own political beliefs. He would not name contributors; his compliant generosity with the Dies Committee investigation of Highlander nagged at his conscience. He would not repeat that political mistake. Horton did not come to Atlanta but sent word through Clifford Durr, who was his attorney, that he would not invoke the Fifth Amendment. However, he was going to declare that he was not a Communist and try publicly to unmask the investigation as a segregationist witch-hunt. He was going to say in "the eyes of some . . . of this Committee, opposition to segregation is 'subversive.'"[12]

After several hours of debate, the board could not agree on a common defense. Mays wouldn't budge; nor could he persuade the members present to impose a rule that all must abide by. He resigned. Everyone else went home dispirited, like Dombrowski, fearing the worst.[13] At a moment when unity was needed, individualism prevailed, as had happened when Kester and Dombrowski tangled years earlier. Eventually, following Mays' resignation, SCEF support by African-American faculty on southern campuses withered, cutting off one vital element in the interracial coalition Dombrowski had been nurturing.

Finding new allies was not easy. Williams asked friendly congressmen to lobby for "some sort of White House or top Republican statement praising the Southern Conference Educational Fund."[14] Few had much time for him. He was out of political power and advocating what seemed to be a no-win cause on behalf of a suspect, powerless group. In a small way, however, his behind-the-scenes maneuvering paid off. No Republican senator came to New Orleans with Eastland.

Many African-American leaders also turned a deaf ear to Williams. He asked Clarence Mitchell, the NAACP's legislative director, to "do some heavy visiting for me." Mitchell, and others Williams approached, listened sympathetically but did nothing.[15] Williams unloaded his anger in a letter to Bethune. He wanted her to comment on the hearings in her column in *The Chicago Defender*. "John Wesley Dobbs, a Republican at that, is the

only one outside of the *Baltimore Afro-American* who has done anything. . . . I don't mind saying I am pretty burnt up about it."[16]

The rupture with Mays, along with the lack of participation by other
equally influential African Americans, disturbed Dombrowski and Williams. The SCEF strategy required two distinct voices speaking as one. If
only southern whites were active, that strategy was doomed. Less obvious,
however, was the potential harm done to the way the SCEF set its agenda.
Whites and African Americans, cooperatively exchanging political cues,
shaped organizational policy in accord with their mutual interests and
needs. Coalition was the foundation of the SCEF's agenda. In
Dombrowski's mind, the loss of this collaboration was as harmful, if not
more so, than the loss of tax-exempt status. In a painful letter, he asked
Mays to reconsider. But there was no reply. The SCEF, then, faced one of
the sternest tests of its political life without interracial solidarity intact.

Characteristically, Dombrowski kept his anger and disappointment bur-
ied. Williams did not. He lashed out later, saying, "Negroes who are so
courageous and clear sighted in the matter of Civil Rights have not always
been so clear sighted in the matter of Civil Liberties."[17] He lamented bitterly that "so few realized that their own safety is endangered" when constitutional guarantees are breached to get at any unpopular person or
group, "and that they must protect the rights of all people to obtain their
own rights." Williams believed that African Americans "do not seem to
realize they are preparing their own grave . . . by joining the witchhunt
against the Communists, the Socialists, the Trotskyists or who have you."

Senator Eastland arrived in New Orleans with Richard Arens, the committee's lawyer, and two paid informants, both claiming to be ex-
Communists. Eastland told the press that the hearing would determine if
Communists were "masquerading behind the facade of a humanitarian educational institution."[18] Eastland and the SCEF dissenters gathered with
their briefs and defense lawyers at 10 a.m. in Room 245 of the New Orleans Post Office. Benjamin E. Smith, from New Orleans, represented
Dombrowski. John P. Kohn, Jr., a Montgomery lawyer, had volunteered to
serve as Durr's counsel. Her husband, Clifford, was counsel for Williams
and Horton. Ethel Clyde rented a suite at the St. Charles Hotel and rooms
for each witness and for Kohn, giving everyone a place to meet after each
day's hearing. Dombrowski persuaded Ellen to stay with him at the hotel.
It was the first time the Durrs had met either Ellen or Dombrowski's New
York benefactress.

The hearing room was a large hall paneled in dark wood up to its high ceilings. At one end, on the wall behind an overly tall bench, was carved the emblematic scale of justice. Under the carving, looking down from the bench, sat Eastland with Arens at his side. Two low tables were placed in front of the bench, each little bigger than a kitchen table. One was for witnesses, the other was for a dozen or more reporters. "Throughout the hearings," one of them wrote, "the emblem managed stolidly to keep its balance only because it is carved in wood."[19] Spectators jammed the hall. Police were positioned at windows, at doors, and along the railing dividing spectators and participants. Eastland announced that cross-examination would not be allowed; the procedure was unheard of in congressional hearings, he said. As for other rules, he said, they would be announced as the hearing went along. Dombrowski was swept with a sense of theatrical absurdity: "It all seemed unreal. I can still remember being fascinated by Arens whose jaw, like a shark's, made a complete rotation when he spoke, almost like a life of its own. I remember thinking, 'What a remarkable production!'"[20]

Ivor A. Trapolin, chairman of the Anti-Subversion Committee of the Young Men's Business Club (YMBC) of New Orleans, and A. James Nelson, the YMBC's president, were the first witnesses. Trapolin told Eastland that SCEF had been "spotted as a communist organization two different ways."[21] The SCEF was controlled by leaders who were "either communists or followed the Communist Party line." The SCEF's "foreign policy" consistently followed "the Party line," he said, adding:

Our report that we have been asked to make a part of this committee hearing is broken down and the first man that we deal with is James Dombrowski. He has a record of continually supporting the Communist Party line. He has been the guiding light, as far as our records show, of the Southern Conference. . . . I would like to mention that Dombrowski was an original incorporator of the Highlander Folk School near Chattanooga, which was founded early in the 1930's, and it was branded as a center, if not the center, of spreading Communist doctrine in 13 states. He had trouble bringing subversive posters back from Russia.

Trapolin was followed by two Miami, Florida, men alleged to be members of the SCEF, Leo Sheiner, a lawyer, and Max Shlafrock, a general contractor. Both claimed protection under the Fifth Amendment, refusing even to say if they had ever heard of the SCEF. When Scheiner insisted on his rights under the First, Second, Sixth, Eighth, Ninth, and Tenth Amendments, Eastland accepted the lawyer's claim for protection under the Fifth, but said, "All the rest of that stuff is bunk."[22]

Dombrowski was sworn in, but Eastland realized it was lunchtime and recessed the hearing until 2 p.m. without taking testimony. Resuming, Eastland immediately asked for the SCEF's records. As Dombrowski handed him the incorporation papers, Eastland asked, "Does your organization have members?"[23]

"No, sir, we have no members other than the members of the corporation."

"How many contributors do you have?"

"I would say approximately 3,000."

"Do you have records of those 3,000 names?"

"Yes, sir."

"Why did you not supply them to the committee?"

"I complied with the subpoena to the best of my understanding and the subpoena did not mention . . . "

"Do you have those names in here, or will I have to issue another subpoena for them?"

"I do not have the names here."

"I say, will you bring them to the committee?"

"It will be necessary to issue another subpoena, sir."

The two men sparred for nearly an hour, repeating themselves. Eastland threatened Dombrowski with a contempt citation, asking rhetorically, "You do not think the United States Senate has the power to get contributors to a Communist organization; is that what you say?"

Dombrowski responded, "It is my understanding, sir, that this is a right that is precluded under the First Amendment to our Constitution, which guarantees the right of free expression, of religion, free speech, free press, free assembly, and free association."

At the end, when Dombrowski tried to offer a moral reason for his refusal, Eastland retorted, "I am interested in the legal reason. You have to stand or fall on the legal side."

Eastland changed direction, asking Dombrowski the long-awaited question. No, he said, he was not a member of the Communist Party, nor had he ever been a member. Arens called John Butler, one of the paid informants, to the witness stand. Butler said that he had been a member of the Mine, Mill and Smelter Workers Union in Bessemer, Alabama. He had been expelled from the union for embezzlement, and left the Communist Party at that time. He had met Dombrowski in July 1942, on a Sunday at the Thomas Jefferson Hotel. He said that Alton Lawrence, Dombrowski's predecessor at the SCHW, had introduced him to Dombrowski as "upper ten. He was a big boy. We were the lower class."[24] Lawrence was an official of the Mine, Mill and Smelter Workers, and had rooms at the hotel. Butler testified that the meeting was held "to discuss the party line."

Paul Crouch, identified as a consultant for the Immigration and Naturalization Service of the Justice Department was the next witness. He acknowledged that he was a "professional witness" and boasted that he had spent "more than 5,000 hours" relating his exploits as a Communist to the FBI "and I'm not through yet."[25] Crouch testified that he first met Dombrowski at Highlander in 1938, then again in Miami in 1947. When he knew him, Crouch said, Dombrowski administered Highlander on instructions from the Communist Party, and, "when we were traveling together by automobile from Miami, Florida, to Winter Haven, Florida," Dombrowski talked about "the revolutionary movement" and sang "the International"!

Dombrowski was put back on the witness stand. He denied ever having met Butler. He agreed that he might have met Crouch once during the white primary fight in Florida. "I don't remember singing the 'International' in his presence or anyone else's," he said. All told, Dombrowski was questioned for five hours. He left the hearings for the hotel exhausted.

Durr expected to be called first in the morning, and she told Dombrowski that she hoped she would be as calm, civil, and composed as he had been. "You felt like you were in Alice in Wonderland," she said. "Reason was inverted."[26] She got an unexpected start at the supper table that night.[27] Her lawyer, John Kohn, was seated beside Ethel Clyde. "She was an old lady," Durr remembered,

> but she looked like she came out of the pages of Vogue. She was a picture in a full-length plum-colored dress, trimmed with lace, and a high lace collar. I was seated across the table.
>
> During the conversation I thought I heard her ask him, "Now, Mr. Kohn, are you a Communist?" I saw him blush, and I thought, "Oh,

my dear God!" He said, "No, I've never been." And she said, "Well, now, that's something you should do. I owe my long life and my good health to this fact."

I thought, "Dear God, here's John Kohn who represents George Wallace back home! What is going to happen?" After dinner I cornered John. He was dressed in a white linen suit and looked the last word in southern aristocracy. I said, "John, what in the world did that woman ask you? Did she want to know if you were a Communist?" He laughed out loud and said, "No, she asked if I was a nudist."

The next day, after Durr was sworn and seated, Kohn read a statement that Durr had prepared which, in closing, asserted her "total and utter contempt for this Committee."[28] That was all Eastland got from her. Butler and Crouch testified that she was "under Communist discipline" and had "plotted with Reds." For Eastland's purposes, however, to have two admitted former Communists link the sister-in-law of a Supreme Court justice with "people who are connected with the Soviet espionage apparatus" was sufficient to insure the national headlines he wanted.

Williams was next. He identified himself as publisher of a magazine read by 800,000 subscribers, a former director of the National Youth Administration, deputy director of the WPA, and president of the SCEF. He asked no immunity under the Fifth Amendment and testified freely about himself and the SCEF, except when Eastland or Arens asked for the SCEF's list of contributors. He refused, risking a contempt citation. The press noticed that Williams was questioned with a degree of caution and was let go sooner than expected. Crouch was recalled, testifying that Communist Party members had introduced him to Williams. Butler declared that he had met "Comrade Williams" at a meeting twelve years before. Ordered to return to the stand, Williams branded both allegations as lies, angrily challenging Crouch and Butler to repeat their charges in the presence of newsmen outside the courtroom. "I'll sue you for everything you've got," he all but shouted.[29]

Eastland recessed for lunch. When the hearing reconvened, Eastland reversed himself. Williams was allowed to crossexamine Crouch. His attorney, Clifford Durr, asked the first question: "Can you prove that you are not a Communist?"[30]

Crouch said that he could and, as he elaborated, Arens interrupted, "Is Mr. Durr a Communist?"

Crouch said, "I do not know if he still is."

"Do you know that he was?" Arens asked.

"Yes."

Durr, infuriated, asked to be sworn as a witness, and was. Benjamin Smith, Dombrowski's lawyer, was given permission to represent Durr. For the remainder of the afternoon, Durr attempted without success to pin Crouch down to specific evidence for his claim. "It was like trying to catch an eel with buttered fingers, and Durr did not succeed," one newsman wrote.[31]

Horton was sworn in as the third day of hearings opened on Saturday morning. During a closed-door executive session the day before, he had angered Eastland by demanding that he be allowed to read a prepared statement. Eventually, Eastland had agreed, but that agreement was forgotten, or ignored, when Horton reached the witness stand. Horton got as far as saying Highlander was a school to teach "democratic living and activity to rural and industrial leaders" when Eastland interrupted, asking whether Horton knew Mildred White, saying she was a Communist who attended Highlander.[32]

"If she did, she did not attend it as a Communist Party member," Horton said, adding, to Dombrowski's surprise, that the earlier open-door policy which he and Horton had defended repeatedly in word and deed, apparently had been changed. "We do not accept Communist students," Horton testified.

"Do you know on what basis she attended?" Eastland asked. Horton explained that he did not recall White specifically but that Highlander had certain requirements "and they must have been applied to her."

Arens interrupted to ask, "Was James Dombrowski associated with your school?"

"Mr. Chairman," Horton began, "I would like to explain why I do not want to answer that question."

Eastland pounded the bench, shouting, "Do you mean to say that you refuse to answer?" Before Horton could speak, Eastland called to the marshals, "All right, take him out!"

Horton jumped to his feet, shouting too, "Mr. Chairman, am I an American citizen or not?"

"Throw him out!" Eastland ordered.

Horton protested that he could walk, but two marshals, "with evident relish," grabbed him by the arms, carrying him out of the courtroom. As the uproar subsided, Clifford Durr moved behind the railing to a seat by the jury box. "His face was drained," Dombrowski remembered. "He was fairly shaking with emotion."[33]

Eastland recalled Crouch, saying that he planned to end the hearing with his testimony. In a long, rambling statement, Crouch disclaimed any intent to link President Roosevelt, his wife, or Justice Black with the SCHW, or to "attack the patriotism of any of these people." But, he continued, "Mrs. Virginia Foster Durr, Justice Black's sister-in-law, had full knowledge of the Communist conspiracy and its works when she allegedly persuaded Black to address the organizational meeting of the Conference in Birmingham in 1938."[34]

Clifford Durr, enraged, lunged at the witness, shouting, "Talk about my wife that way, I'll kill the son-of-a-bitch!" The marshals rushed to separate the men. Durr collapsed in their arms and was carried to a bench in the corridor outside. He had suffered a mild heart attack. Eastland gaveled the hearings to a close.

The SCEF was roughed up but unbowed. In general, the national press depicted the hearings as an inquisition. An Alabama newsman informally polled nine colleagues who had been covering the explosive hearings. "On the basis of what you have seen and heard here," he asked, "who of the principals represents the greatest threat to American ideals?"[35] Eastland got four votes, Crouch got two. Arens, Dombrowski, and Shlafrock got one each. "And Jim got that vote because of his name," Virginia Durr declared later. "His name trailed behind him like a cloud."[36]

The Senate Judiciary Committee received a petition signed by over two hundred prominent persons, including Eleanor Roosevelt and Reinhold Niebuhr, urging that the Senate halt any similar hearings.[37] On Capitol Hill, Williams' friends were disturbed at the treatment he had gotten. Lester Hill, Hubert H. Humphrey, and Paul Douglas wrote him sympathetic notes. Williams was especially pleased that Lyndon B. Johnson, leader of the Senate's Democrats, "took an hour and went into everything with thoroughness."[38]

The Supreme Court's decision in the *Brown* case vindicated the SCEF, elevating Dombrowski's spirits. Contributions to the SCEF picked up. Dombrowski was honored by Lincoln University's School of Journalism as a "fearless spokesman for the rights of minorities in a territory where such voices are comparatively silent."[39] However, despite these initially favorable signs, there was evidence that the SCEF had been hurt in other ways.

The petition to the Judiciary Committee went unnoticed. Advertisers pulled out of Williams' magazine. He tried in vain to counter a flood of subscription cancellations by enlisting African-American leaders, including E.D. Nixon of Alabama, Percy Greene of Mississippi, and Modjeska Simkins of South Carolina, to help him find African-American subscribers. But the campaign produced "practically nothing." A Ku Klux Klan poster was plastered on Dombrowski's front door in New Orleans, and threatening telephone calls regularly interrupted the night.

Those danger signals paled beside the difficulties Dombrowski felt certain lay ahead. On May 17, 1954, the Supreme Court closed one painful chapter and opened another which he believed would bring suffering far beyond the demise of the SCEF. Ominously, actions of the school board in tiny Sheridan, Arkansas, epitomized reverberations coursing through the entire South. On Friday, May 21, the board voted five to zero to integrate twenty-one black students with six hundred whites in the upper grades. The next day, they voted five to zero not to integrate any students at any grade. Almost immediately after the decision, Washington, D.C.; Greensboro, North Carolina; and Baltimore, Maryland, voluntarily chose to start desegregation, but their dismantling efforts were to drag on for two decades.[40] Senator Eastland declared that the Supreme Court had been "indoctrinated and brainwashed by Left-wing pressure groups."[41] Mississippi businessmen, dissociating themselves from the KKK, formed White Citizens Councils and said that they would use economic pressure to prevent school desegregation and black voter registration. Their weapons were denied credit, evictions, and ignored calls for fire or ambulance service.

As he crisscrossed the South trying to arrange compliance conferences, Dombrowski sensed that whites universally were hostile. Voters in South Carolina and Georgia approved constitutional amendments permitting their legislatures to abolish public schools rather than desegregate them. The Mississippi legislature was preparing to close public schools. Virginia's governor had vowed, "I shall use every legal means at my command to continue segregated schools in Virginia."[42]

Eventually, Dombrowski managed with difficulty to hold public one-day compliance conferences in New Orleans and Richmond; finally, one was held in Houston on May 17, 1955, to mark the first anniversary of the court's decision. John Wesley Dobbs, grand master of the Prince Hall Masons of Georgia, and other African-Americans involved with the SCEF helped him raise the money from church congregations. But even within that particularly interested community, opinion was divided. The FBI or their paid informants traveled the South with Dombrowski as he organized the conferences. In a report on a meeting that Dombrowski held in Atlanta on the eve of Mays' resignation, the FBI was told:

> Dombrowski emphasized . . . it was necessary for each person . . . to "tie in with the NAACP, the Urban League, and other organizations like that to aid in the fight" for immediate abolishment of all segregation. . . . When subject mentioned churches one of the persons protested against "putting this issue into the churches." Subject replied, "Churches baptize you. They marry you. They bury you. They should be interested in this issue."[43]

Through *The Southern Patriot*, Dombrowski reminded school and community officials that their oaths of office "prescribed their compliance with this new system." As Mississippi's legislators laid plans to abolish public schools, Dombrowski arranged with Dr. Charles G. Hamilton of Corinth to conduct a confidential poll of all Mississippi schoolteachers to determine their views on the proposed amendment. Over 20,000 questionnaires were mailed, and 2,886 were returned. Two of every three teachers opposed the amendment. Their jobs and pensions were in jeopardy. Overwhelming, nevertheless, the teachers, voting three to one, objected to integration.[44] That fall, Mississippians voted 91,513 to 41,572 to provide state-paid tuition to private schools and to close public schools rather than comply with the *Brown* decision. Dombrowski hated to report that news in *The Southern Patriot*.

In New Orleans, Dombrowski and others presented the New Orleans School Board with a petition signed by over 180 prominent citizens, including 30 clergymen and 20 university professors, asking for an immediate end to racially separate schools.[45] The petition got no serious notice. Given the public climate, the three compliance conferences each had a sizable turnout. Some one hundred persons attended the Houston meeting. Public school administrators from Phoenix, Arizona, and St. Louis, Missouri, explained how their schools had been successfully desegregated. Dr. Rupert C. Koeninger, chairman of the Department of Sociology at Sam Houston College in Huntsville, Texas, in the keynote address, described local school boards as "the gatekeepers who can tip the balance one way or the other." He urged school boards to decide their policy early and independently, and then issue clearly worded statements.⁴⁶

Two weeks later, integrationists suffered a setback. On May 31, the Supreme Court ruled that the chief responsibility for implementing the *Brown* decision rested not with local school boards but with federal district courts and that the latter would begin to hold hearings to assure full compliance "with all deliberate speed." The court had bowed to the welling southern sentiment. Segregationists were emboldened.

By the end of 1956, an estimated 300,000 white southerners belonged to the White Citizens Councils, the American Association for the Preservation of State Government and Racial Integrity, the State Defenders of State Sovereignty and Individual Liberties, and similar groups, including the Ku Klux Klan. Mills Godwin, a rising political figure in Virginia, coined the phrase "massive resistance" during a meeting of Virginia's leading segregationists at the Petersburg fire station. "Massive resistance" became the rallying cry of a bona fide mass southern political movement, albeit one very different from that about which Dombrowski had dreamed for so long.

The SCEF conducted a poll on school integration and health but was forced to buy newspaper advertising to make the results known. Dombrowski's press releases apparently went into trash baskets, and his follow-up telephone calls went in one polite ear and out the other. Segregationists claimed that mixed schools would adversely affect the physical and mental health of children. Dombrowski persuaded the New Orleans Medical Association to ask fifty-six psychiatrists and neurologists a single question: "From a professional point of view, how would you characterize the psychiatric effect of racially integrated schools on white and Negro children?"⁴⁷ Twenty-one replied. Seventeen believed integration would either be beneficial or have little effect. The others doubted the children would be harmed, but "feared adult behavior should schools be integrated." The *New York Times* printed Dombrowski's press release on the poll as a letter to the editor. The three dailies in New Orleans refused to print it except as a paid ad.⁴⁸

By 1956, southern liberals were putting distance between themselves and the SCEF. The Montgomery, Alabama, bus boycott was in full sway, led by the veteran E.D. Nixon and an emerging young minister, the Reverend Martin Luther King. In December, the Institute on Non-Violence and

Social Change in Montgomery, Alabama, the coordinating hub of the bus boycott, invited author Lillian Smith to speak. Ill with cancer, she at first accepted but later telephoned saying she was only able to send a prepared statement which someone could read. Nixon asked Aubrey Williams to read her remarks, but Smith objected strenuously. The invitation was withdrawn.[49] A week later, after debating with himself, Williams wrote to Smith, accusing her of having "done me a grievous wrong. . . . I have an idea why you did it. I suspect it was because I was hailed by Sen. Eastland before his so-called Sub-Committee." Sadly, he concluded, "By your action . . . you have joined Sen. Eastland in his work of destroying any southern white persons who dare to stand up unequivocally in behalf of Negroes."[50]

Dombrowski and Williams accepted as a given the idea that SCEF would be alienated from the majority of southern whites; they also anticipated that it would be estranged from southern liberals and could only hope that their differences would be set aside in time. However, the fact that Nixon had been the one issuing and then withdrawing the invitation raised serious political concerns. Nixon, years later, explained that the decision had been made because Dr. King and another young minister, Ralph Abernathy, "only knew the SCEF was supposed to be Red, and they didn't want that messed in with the bus boycott."[51] The NAACP and other northern-based integrationist organizations also cooled toward the SCEF. Williams tried vainly to have the SCEF included in a newly-formed Leadership Conference on Civil Rights headed by the NAACP's Roy Wilkins.

In August, Dombrowski asked the SCEF board to form a committee on relationships with other organizations, with Dr. Albert E. Barnett, professor at Emory's Candler School of Theology, as chairman. Barnett belonged to the NAACP's prestigious Committee of One Hundred, despite the likelihood that membership in the NAACP might prove "personally costly in view of the campaign in Southern States to brand the NAACP as subversive, and on that basis outlaw it."[52] He asked Wilkins to invite Dombrowski to the next meeting of the Leadership Conference on Civil Rights set for January 1957, and to list SCEF as a constituent organization. The SCEF, he said, "would be the one distinctly Southern member of the group, and our interracial character would add some strength to the Council." Moreover, he added, an alliance would "go a long way to strengthen the hand" of liberal white southerners if they had "the confidence of . . . the NAACP and the Leadership Conference."[53]

Barnett's actions were courageous but had little prospect of succeeding. In 1950, during its annual convention in Boston, the NAACP had voted 309 to 57 to expel any local branch which the group's powerful board of directors deemed influenced or controlled by Communists.[54] Public sentiment was massively against Communists. Even the suggestion that a handful of NAACP branches might be controlled or infiltrated by Communists was an embarrassment. The January meeting Barnett hoped Dombrowski would be invited to attend convened and adjourned before Barnett got a letter from Wilkins. The Leadership Conference, he wrote, had decided against admitting the SCEF for fear of making the group unwieldy in number.[55]

Barnett was dumbfounded. He wrote asking Wilkins to explain how raising the Leadership Conference's membership from 48 to 49 groups made the organization unmanageable. The SCEF, he said, had weathered attacks from Eastland, Talmadge, Byrnes, the Klan, and other segregationists, and stated that the SCEF would provide a seasoned voice, should the conference be attacked. No-one, he added, wanted to join "to ride anyone's coattails," but the SCEF did not want to be excluded because of misinformation, misconceptions, or smears—all of which, ironically, had come from sources that had attacked the NAACP, too.

In the course of his correspondence with friends in the NAACP, Barnett learned that the SCEF had been branded "subversive."[56] And Alfred Maund, who left the Louisville newspaper for a job with the Rubber Workers Union in Ohio, learned that the AFL-CIO maintained a subversive list.[57] The SCEF was on it. Maund also told Dombrowski that the Fund for the Republic regarded the SCEF as subversive. The Fund was headed by Robert Hutchins, who had listened to Dombrowski outline SCEF's strategy in support of desegregation. Both the AFL-CIO and the Fund contributed to the NAACP. Letters to Wilkins, Hutchins, and union officials changed nothing. The NAACP's position embittered Williams, and he wrote Dombrowski:

> The SCEF cannot long survive this sort of treatment. We must find some way of asserting our efforts at critical points such as the hearings in Washington, or at meetings of a national character where basic policy is made or else we will not be able to long hold the interest or respect of the people. We should move to have a showdown and if we fail, we should move to either reorganize with new leadership, or establish a

fighting outpost in Washington, D.C., or liquidate. I, for one, do not wish any longer to be in the equivocating position of undertaking to represent the emancipated folks of the South and being denied the opportunity to do so by those selected by the liberal forces of the nation to manage the fights or conduct the battles.[58]

The SCEF was politically homeless, put out on the street by Eastland. Dombrowski's consistent refusal to disavow or condemn Communists once again had set him apart from the civil rights movement's majority. The New Orleans NAACP branch refused to accept his annual membership dues. Nearly twenty years passed before he was allowed to rejoin the New Orleans branch.[59]

# 15

## New Hands Helping with an Old Burden

During 1956, while continuing to step on as many segregationists' toes as possible, the SCEF's leaders looked for their successors. It was a prudent business decision. Dombrowski, at 59 had to use aluminum arm crutches to walk. Williams was 66 and demoralized by the demise of his magazine. Neither man thought seriously about quitting the fight for integration, but each badly wanted their enterprise to go beyond them. The SCEF needed a new generation, and they had three toughened activists in mind.

As that year came to an end, during the early morning hours of Christmas Day, a dynamite bomb exploded at the home of the Reverend Fred L. Shuttlesworth, pastor of Bethel Baptist Church in Birmingham, and his wife. The sleeping couple's bed was blown from beneath them. Falling debris crushed the beds of their four children. Miraculously, no-one suffered a scratch, although their substantial brick home was totally destroyed. The previous June, after the Alabama legislature outlawed the NAACP, Shuttlesworth had responded by organizing the Alabama Christian Movement for Human Rights. The minister may have been the most controversial man in Birmingham, a city so segregated by 1956 that it was unlawful for African Americans and whites to play checkers together.

Two weeks after the explosion, Dombrowski visited Shuttlesworth and his family to ask if there were anything the SCEF could do to help them

recover, and if Shuttlesworth would become a member of the organization's board. "From the moment I met him," Shuttlesworth recalled, "I was
moved by his gentility and humility. I knew he was the man who'd been
arrested with Senator Taylor at the church on Sixteenth Street. But he
didn't have to prove himself as a friend. I just knew he would be a friend,
and his offer to help me proved it."[1] The minister's principled stand on First
Amendment issues, and his organizing skills, appealed to Dombrowski.
Shuttlesworth had strength and staying power; he had acted in the face of
almost certain retaliation, including possible death, without flinching.
Dombrowski wanted him to replace Williams. Shuttlesworth agreed to
consider the idea.

At the time, Dombrowski was negotiating with Carl and Anne Braden of
Louisville, Kentucky, about joining the staff. Two years earlier, the Bradens
had electrified the South. Carl was a newspaperman, and Anne worked in a
dry-cleaning plant. They were active in Louisville's tiny union organizations. Dombrowski had been in touch with them during a successful drive
to desegregate Louisville hospitals. *The Southern Patriot* was one of the few
publications to give their fight any ink.

In May 1954, just after the Supreme Court decided the *Brown* case, the
Bradens sold their house to a young African-American Navy veteran, who
had tried unsuccessfully to buy a house in Louisville's white suburbs. The
Bradens bought the house, then transferred title to the man. As news of the
transaction spread, so did outrage against the Bradens.[2] The *Courier-
Journal*, the city's liberal newspaper which was published by one-time
SCHW member Barry Bingham, opined that angry whites were within
their rights "protesting the purchase of property in their subdivision by
Negroes."[3] Other whites had less polite things to say. Segregationists
feared that any breach in the wall sanctifying private property would
hasten the day when neighborhood schools would be integrated. Less than
a month later, before the veteran and his family moved into the house, a
dynamite explosion nearly demolished the property.

By September, a grand jury had been convened to investigate the
Bradens. On October 1, 1954, the Bradens, who had two children, were
jailed on charges of sedition. Anne was locked up for a week until her parents raised the bond. Carl was in jail for three weeks before bond could be
secured. The charges against Anne eventually were dropped. Carl, however, went on trial in December. Despite help from lawyers from the American Civil Liberties Union, Braden was convicted, sentenced to fifteen years
in prison, and fined $5,000. His appeal bond was set at $40,000. He served

eight months before the U.S. Supreme Court overruled the lower court and upset his conviction.[4]

"A couple of days after the trial," Anne remembered, "I got a telegram from Dombrowski, saying, 'Tell Carl I am proud to be his friend.' People in Louisville were scared to death of us. They wouldn't speak. We didn't know Dombrowski. He'd published some of our articles on the hospital fight, but we'd never met. And here he was sending $1,000 on Carl's bond. The telegram was tremendously important psychologically."[5] Once Braden was released from prison, the Louisville couple went to meet Dombrowski in New Orleans. They were in debt for the house, fines, and legal fees. Dombrowski gave them contacts throughout the South, and the Bradens traveled telling their story to pay off their debts. They were just the sort of staff members Dombrowski felt the SCEF needed. As they discussed joining the SCEF, Anne suggested that they mount a petition campaign in opposition to the increasing violence and "terrorism sweeping African-American communities in the South." Dombrowski took issue with her, saying, "That's not why we do something. We take action because we are for integration. Anyone can be against violence. Our aim is to get people to say they are for integration."[6]

The Bradens wanted to start immediately. Dombrowski insisted that the SCEF have their salary for one year on hand before going to work. They learned that he kept a six-month reserve of funds tucked away to insure that the SCEF could operate that long without a dime in contributions. He never opened a petition drive, organized a conference, or took a trip unless funds were available. Based on his experience at Highlander and the SCHW, Dombrowski felt that the penchant to spend money before it was in the bank was poor management. The Bradens learned that the SCEF did not operate that way. They joined the staff in September 1957.

The Montgomery bus boycott spread to Tallahassee, Florida; Birmingham; and other southern cities. By fall of 1956, Dombrowski had gotten a drive going in New Orleans. Several hundred persons signed a petition asking the New Orleans transit authority to end segregation on trolleys and busses and delivered it to them in February 1957. New Orleans newspapers immediately reported that many of the petitioners "are linked with" the SCEF, which had "been investigated for Communistic activities."[7] The *New Orleans Item* went a step further, firing its music and drama critic, Ewing Poteet, for signing the petition. Editors told him that he had discredited the paper.[6] The Gentilly Citizen's Council was warned by Judge Leander H. Perez, a politically powerful segregationist from nearby Plaquemine Parish, "The aim of the Communists in this country is to foment violence and strife between two races and they know this can be done by forcing them into intimate contact."[8]

In May, the *Item* ran a six-part series attacking the SCEF. Essentially, the articles rehashed the Eastland hearings and the discredited House Un-American Activities Committee report. However, three former New Orleans members of the SCHW described Dombrowski personally as the cause of their own disillusionment with the SCHW, and as the reason why the organization died.[9] Dombrowski had "made himself ineffective as a leader because of his willingness to cooperate with persons whose motives are not above suspicion," said a Tulane professor. A rabbi felt that Dombrowski was "bumbling . . . ineffective." A lawyer declared that Dombrowski harmed "the causes he professed to promote."

The SCEF was under siege. Nuisance telephone callers rang the office throughout the day and Dombrowski's home at night, even though his number was unlisted. The secretary was threatened, and Ellen was warned "something pretty terrible" was going to happen. The office was systematically burglarized, sometimes as often as three times a week. After barring the windows and changing door locks one Saturday, Dombrowski found a note pinned outside the rear window, plaintively complaining, "I could not get in this weekend."[10]

Dombrowski had not forgotten school integration, and, as the new school year approached, he launched "a new crusade" to persuade more whites that complete desegregation was "the right way."[11] Token desegregation, he argued in *The Southern Patriot,* was segregation in fact. Children had to be admitted to schools without regard to race.

During a fundraising dinner in California on October 18, 1957, Dombrowski told a large audience what he'd seen as schools opened that fall. Shuttlesworth had been beaten badly and his wife, Ruby, stabbed in the hip trying to enroll their two daughters in an all-white Birmingham school. In Clinton, Tennessee, a half-million-dollar school building was destroyed by a dynamite explosion. Federal troops were in Little Rock, Arkansas, patroling a high school ordered to admit African-American students for the first time. He told them about what he'd seen in Little Rock:

Last Wednesday in the home of Mr. and Mrs. L.C. Bates, those great fighters for human decency and leaders in the Little Rock struggle, I heard a revealing story. This was at the height of the trouble at Central High School. Segregationist white students were chanting: "Two, four, six, eight, we ain't gonna integrate."

And the Negro students were saying under their breath: "Six, four, two, 10 to 1 we betcha' do!"[12]

Dombrowski formed a 102-member advisory committee to help the SCEF push desegregation. Members lived in eighteen southern and border states, plus the District of Columbia.[13] Their job was to start desegregation petition drives, write congressional or state legislators, and help the SCEF raise funds in their own communities. He projected that the 1958 budget would total $41,230.

In October 1957, Williams was forced to sell *Southern Farm and Home*.[14] His largest advertising accounts had canceled contracts because of his outspoken opposition to segregation. Later he had to sell what had been a prospering printing business. Adding to his woe was the discovery that he had cancer. His last editorial was an uncompromising attack on segregation. It gave no hint of the shame he felt as a businessman who had failed or of his depressing illness: "It is still my belief that most people in these deep South States are loyal to the United States, they are really and truly Christians, and if it weren't for the leadership of a wrongheaded few, they would act much as people in other parts of this great land of freedom act. As it is, the life of the average southerner is one long apology for the basic American institutions of human rights, equality and freedom."[15]

Meanwhile, the exodus of whites fed up with fear and racism became so noticeable that the *Wall Street Journal* reported that whites were leaving Mississippi, Arkansas, and Tennessee faster than African Americans.[16]

Williams' valedictory editorial hinted at another decision that he and Dombrowski made early in 1956. Voting, they concluded, rather than de-segregation of public schools, would be a faster and more potent way to curb the South's demagogic politics. The region's most vocal segregationists were elected officials, and, to insure that they stayed elected, some of them were hatching schemes to keep African Americans from voting, or to purge their few names from the registration books.

Virginia lawmakers adopted a blank sheet registration law. Any citizen wanting to vote had to fill out a blank sheet of paper provided by the registrar with her or his name, address, party affiliation, Social Security number, and similar data. A deviation in the sequence, poor legibility, or a spelling mistake automatically disqualified the prospective voter. All registrars were white.

North Carolina legislators demanded that African Americans pass a literacy test in which they had to interpret portions of the state's constitution to the satisfaction of a white registrar. Alabama lawmakers required that each hopeful African-American registrant be vouched for by two white voters. In Mississippi, dozens of African Americans were shot, were beaten to death, or had their lives threatened for attempting to vote.[17]

Dombrowski was not able to turn his attention to voting issues until early in 1958, however. The campaign was forestalled by school and bus desegregation fights, fundraising, and the need to develop ways to coordinate work with the Bradens. However, by March, he and the Bradens were devoting nearly all their attention to a conference on voting in Washington. Two weeks before the event, Dombrowski left New Orleans on a swing through the South to document voting-rights violations.

In Minden, Louisiana, he talked with an undertaker who tried twice to register but had been refused. The man filed a complaint with the U.S. Justice Department, which sent six FBI agents to investigate. The local district attorney convened a grand jury to look into the case. The jury subpoenaed thirty-five persons, including the FBI agents. In the end, the undertaker was indicted for "attempting to intimidate publicly a public official."[18] From Minden, Dombrowski went to Prentis, Mississippi, where he talked with the Reverend H.D. Darby, who had brought suit in federal court seeking to nullify a 1954 Mississippi law which cut the number of African-American voters in Jefferson Davis County from 1,221 to fewer than 40 in a year's time.

From Prentis, Dombrowski traveled to North Mississippi and the Delta town of Clarksdale. He met Aaron Henry, a pharmacist and leader of the Regional Council of Negro Leadership, who explained how Coahoma County had come to be one of the few places in Mississippi where African Americans registered and voted freely. One of Coahoma County's plantation owners, a cotton planter with over four hundred tenants, opposed a proposed school bond referendum. He feared that an increase in taxes would fall disproportionately on him. He learned that his tenants opposed the referendum because none of the money would be used to improve their dilapidated, overcrowded school. The planter got every voting-age tenant registered, and, as a consequence, African Americans held the balance of power.

Leaving Clarksdale and the only inspiring story he'd found to print in *The Southern Patriot*, Dombrowski went to Weldon, North Carolina. There, James R. Walker, Jr., an African-American lawyer, had been jailed and fined for attempting to defend a woman's right to vote. A Northampton County registrar had disqualified Mrs. Louise Lassiter because she had mispronounced three words, including "indictment," as she read a section of the state constitution. She hired Walker to take her case to federal court. While preparing the case, Walker went to the registrar who had disqualified his client. She had him arrested, claiming that he shook his finger at her. Walker was charged with disorderly conduct, trespass, assault on a female, and disturbing a registrar in the performance of duty.[19]

In spite of a cold rain, over one thousand persons filled Washington's Asbury Methodist Church on Sunday, April 27. Methodist Bishop Edgar A. Love of Baltimore chaired the meeting; Williams gave the keynote address: "We must recognize the Negro's struggle for what it is. . . . the spearhead, which if it succeeds, can clear the ground of creeping fascism and totalitarianism which is inherent in the thinking of the power elite and their supporters, the conservatives and reactionaries of both parties."[20]

Conference participants from Maryland told how white politicians unwittingly had spurred a statewide voter registration drive. Both Democratic and Republican leaders had declared that the African American vote was of no consequence to their electoral plans. Piqued, African-American leaders organized a registration drive, adding fifteen thousand new voters in Baltimore alone.

Other accounts from the Deep South were less hopeful, including Dombrowski's report. The Reverend Ben F. Wyland, head of the Florida Council for Racial Cooperation in Tampa, told how white political leaders had convened the state legislature when an African American was elected a justice of the peace in northern Florida. Lawmakers declared the election illegal, upped the number of justices to be elected, and then ordered new balloting. Faced with opposition by a number of white candidates, the African American was soundly defeated.

Tuskegee Institute Dean Charles G. Gomillion outlined how Alabama officials had gerrymandered the town of Tuskegee by using white neighborhoods in surrounding Macon County to prevent African Americans from gaining political control. A boycott was underway, and Gomillion had a suit pending in federal court, *Gomillion v. Lightfoot*. He had been threatened constantly since filing the legal action.[21]

Dr. James M. Nabrit, Jr., a law professor at Howard University, concluded the meeting. He said that action was needed on three fronts: a Southwide voter registration drive among African Americans, accompanied by a campaign to raise the level of political awareness, plus immediate voting rights enforcement by the recently created federal Civil Rights Commission.[22]

Dombrowski and Williams stayed in Washington for several days after the conference to lobby the Civil Rights Commission's staff and to see lawyers in the civil rights division of the Justice Department. They visited a few friendly congressmen, urging them to strengthen the Civil Rights Act of 1957. The first such legislation to pass Congress in eighty-two years, this act authorized the federal courts to issue injunctions to force compliance with voting rights guidelines. The two men argued that the law was going unused by the Civil Rights Commission.

Southern congressmen had fought the bill for months. When it was finally enacted, their reaction was summed up by Rep. William M. Tuck, former governor of Virginia, who declared that the bill would "release upon the country a horde of political bloodsuckers and harpies clothed with the badge of power which could, and no doubt would, in instances, reduce us to a police state."[23]

Less than six weeks after the SCEF conference on voting rights, the House Un-American Activities Committee announced hearings in Atlanta to investigate Communist infiltration in the South. Richard Arens was the committee's chief counsel.[24] Dombrowski learned of the hearings while he was in Mississippi investigating the deaths of two African-American men who had been beaten to death by police after attempting to register to vote. He returned to New Orleans immediately to mobilize opposition to HUAC's trip south. A telephone call from the Bradens was waiting for him. They were in Rhode Island, vacationing with their two children. Both had been served subpoenas to be in Atlanta on July 28. "Here we go again," Dombrowski wrote to Ethel Clyde.[25]

Dombrowski wired Frank Wilkinson, secretary of the Citizens Committee to Preserve American Freedom, whom he'd met on fundraising trips to Los Angeles. Wilkinson was starting a national campaign to abolish HUAC. He had been assistant director of the Los Angeles Housing Authority until he was dismissed for arguing for policies to integrate the city's public housing. In an exchange of telegrams, Wilkinson agreed to observe the Atlanta hearing. When he arrived at the Atlanta Biltmore Hotel, where

Dombrowski had a room reserved for him, a federal marshal was waiting to serve him a subpoena. "No one except Mr. and Mrs. Wilkinson and myself knew of the telegram," Dombrowski wrote Clyde later, "no one, that is, except the wire tappers."[26] In the meanwhile, Williams tried to persuade Sen. Lyndon B. Johnson and Rep. James Roosevelt to have the hearings called off. HUAC, he said, was trying to "publicly pillory any white person, Jew or Gentile, who openly favors and works for integration."[27] Every person who'd gotten a subpoena was white and actively involved in desegregation. But his day on Capitol Hill was over.

Dombrowski sent every congressman a letter signed by over two hundred leading African Americans from the South. Why wasn't HUAC investigating the deaths of African Americans who tried to register to vote, or who destroyed African-American churches, Jewish synagogues, and public schools with unexplained bombings?, the letter asked. "It is increasingly difficult to find white people who are willing to support our efforts for full citizenship," the letter continued. "It is unthinkable that they should instead be harassed by committees of the United States Congress."[28] The text appeared as a full-page ad in the *Washington Post,* but the *Atlanta Constitution* refused to print the ad, saying that it libeled the congressional investigators.[29]

Carl Braden arrived in Atlanta without Anne. She refused to leave Rhode Island unless the committee paid to fly her children to Atlanta with her. The committee postponed her appearance indefinitely, and she never testified. During the first day, several witnesses "insisted they were being tormented for their views favoring racial integration, but they were cut short alternately by [Frances] Walter and . . . [Donald] Jackson, " the United Press International correspondent reported.[30] But there were no dramatic fireworks. The congressmen said that they were looking for Communist "nests."

On the second day, Congressman Edwin Willis was given the chairman's gavel. Walter returned to Washington. Willis opened the hearing by calling Braden to the stand. Braden gave the committee his name but little else. Fourteen times he cited the First Amendment as protection against the questions he was asked, including whether he ever had been a Communist. Willis asked if Braden had organized opposition to legislation being considered by Congress to revive state sedition laws. A 1956 Supreme Court decision had ruled similar legislation void. "My beliefs and associations are not of the business of this committee," Braden responded.[31] Arens asked Braden if he'd written the letter congressmen had just received, and if he had put the letter in the *Washington Post*. Braden would not say, but demanded to read it into the record. As he did, his voice rose at the section asking that HUAC be kept out of the South unless the committee investigated bombings, terror against African Americans, and "activities of the White Citizens' Councils encouraging open defiance of the United States Supreme Court."

Arens asked again if he had written the letter. And when he refused to say, one of the congressional investigators leaned forward to say, "Here is a communication with the strong possibility of having been prepared by a Communist. This is an example of how well-meaning people are not sufficiently advised when they lend their names to such communications."

"I'm sure," said the peppery Braden, "the people who signed this letter will appreciate your aspersions."

Wilkinson was called to the stand next. Like Braden, he gave his name, and, as he started challenging HUAC's own legality, the hearing was ended.

"Now the 'Un-Americans' have returned to Washington," Dombrowski wrote Clyde. "They left us as they found us."[32] Not quite. On August 12, 1958, the full House of Representatives, except for one African-American congressman, Robert C. Nix of Philadelphia, cited Braden and Wilkinson for contempt. On January 29, 1959, after a short trial, Federal Judge Boyd Sloan sentenced them each to a year in prison. Both were freed on bond pending an appeal to the U.S. Supreme Court.

Braden fought the HUAC as a SCEF staff member, a decision that didn't sit well with all of the organization's backers. Some longtime supporters, including Dean Barnett of Emory, wanted every cent to go directly to efforts to end segregation, not to fighting inquisitions. The Eastland hearings had proven costly, financially and politically. But Shuttlesworth and other African Americans argued that the SCEF attack on the constitutionality of HUAC itself was a direct attack on segregation. Shuttlesworth replaced Williams as the SCEF president. "Blacks," Shuttlesworth said during one tense meeting where the matter was debated, "are concerned about civil rights, having a job, and persecution. But here we are talking about what democracy means in its fullest sense, and how to persevere in the struggle to make democracy real. Civil liberties is an extra burden, but it is an extra burden we must take up."[33] Shuttlesworth's argument won the day. And for over a year, while the SCEF did not devote its entire resources to efforts to preventing Braden from being jailed, that became the organization's focus. Petitions, nationwide speaking tours, visits to congressmen kept public attention directed on the case. All the while, Braden's lawyers were preparing for a hearing before the Supreme Court.

Within the civil rights movement, the SCEF's dictum that civil liberties and civil rights were inextricably entwined gained advocates. And the group's view was shared by some justices of the U.S. Supreme Court, but not enough of them. On February 27, 1961, in a five-to-four decision, with Justice Potter Stewart writing the majority opinion, the court found Braden and Wilkinson guilty of contempt of Congress. "The gist of the offense," Justice Stewart wrote, "is refusal to answer pertinent questions. No moral turpitude is involved. There is no misapprehension as to what was called for."[34] On May 1, an overcast, drizzly day in Atlanta, Braden and Wilkinson were on their way to jail. Amid a crowd gathered to say good-bye, or to stare curiously, Dombrowski anchored himself against the post office building, making notes:

> A little before 2 o'clock Carl, Frank, Anne, and Dr. Otto Nathan, arm in arm, turned the corner of Forsyth Street and walked the half-block down to the post office. They were smiling as if this was their day of triumph. They mounted the steps and posed for the flock of photographers, TV cameramen, and reporters and made their brief statements for the press. An admirer pinned a rose on their lapels; then they disappeared into the building but not before a note of tension was struck. A large man called out, "If you don't like this country, why don't you go back where you came from?"[35]

Upstairs in the corridor outside the U.S. Marshal's office, another crowd of friends, mostly students and professors active in the integration struggle, greeted the two men. A few minutes later, they were led out in handcuffs, put in a car, and driven off. "And so they left to begin a year in a federal prison because they could not betray their consciences—two more in that long line of freedom witnesses," Dombrowski continued.[36]

Some six months earlier, on January 20, 1961, John F. Kennedy, the youngest man ever elected president, ushered in the Camelot era, saying during his inaugural speech that a new generation had assumed leadership in America who would "pay any price, bear any burden, meet any hardship, support any friend, oppose any foe to assure the survival and success of liberty."[37] The "freedom witnesses" were testing Kennedy as no other previous Democratic administration had been tested. By the time he won election in November 1960, over 3,600 sit-in demonstrators, mostly African-American but many white, had been jailed in scores of southern cities. Some had been expelled from college or high school for trying to desegregate lunch counters. Some were being sent to the military by local draft boards that were determined to stop the tumultuous social movement. There had been no letup once Kennedy had been sworn into office. In nearly every southern city's jail, exultant voices were chorusing "We Shall Overcome," the hymn born at Highlander while Dombrowski was there.[38]

On November 14, 1960, seven days after Kennedy's narrowly won election, Dombrowski watched several dozen U.S. marshals escort three children through a hall of spit, rocks, and curses into Williams Franz School, and then take another handful—four—through a similar barrage to McDonogh No. 19, another elementary school. After months of court hearings and delay by the Orleans Parish School Board, the two schools were being desegregated. They served the city's poorest neighborhoods. The seven children had been "screened" with intelligence tests and selected for "moral standing" from among 136 African-American applicants. Apparently, the school board felt that white children from tough working-class neighborhoods were the most suitable companions for young African Americans.

Only a few white children came to Franz School that day; none showed up at McDonogh. Segregationists had organized an effective boycott.[39] New Orleans was a battleground. Gradually, however, Save Our Schools, a tiny interracial parents' group that Dombrowski had helped organize months before, was able to bring a few white children to the schools. They formed a carlift to drive them to and from school each morning and afternoon. Marshals brought the African-American children. Spit and hate greeted them coming and going.

On December 9, the New Orleans White Citizen's Council circulated a list of the carlift's volunteer drivers, their telephone numbers, and car descriptions, including license-plate numbers. Their homes were stoned. Telephones rang night and day. One white child's father worked at a drugstore. A picket line was set up outside the store, and the manager was warned that every store in the chain would be picketed if the father wasn't fired. He moved his family out of Louisiana.

In March, Dombrowski had lunch with one of the carlift volunteers, the Reverend Lloyd Foreman, whose daughter, Pamela Lynn, attended Franz. Foreman, a Methodist minister, had been forced to move his family to another part of New Orleans, hiding his address and telephone number. His daughter, he told Dombrowski, asked why people shouted at her. After explaining as best he could, Foreman asked if she understood.[40]

"Yes," she said, "but I still want to go to school."

"Why?" her father asked.

As he told Dombrowski, "she thought for a minute, then said, 'I have some cards to finish.' That was a revelation to me. In the midst of all the excitement and violence, this little one had her mind on the educational process, and on what was going on inside the school."

Other, older students brought Dombrowski to Montgomery two months later. College students calling themselves Freedom Riders were riding busses through Alabama to New Orleans, challenging segregated bus seating and bus terminal lunch counters. One group had been mobbed and beaten in Anniston, then again in Birmingham. Another contingent of twenty-one students, many of them from Fisk University, set out from Nashville on May 19, 1961 "to help the cause of true freedom for all the races." The next morning, a Saturday, their bus pulled into the Montgomery bus station at 10:30 a.m., where an angry crowd waited for them.

Susan Herrmann, a Fisk coed from Los Angeles, told reporters what happened when they got off the bus: "There was a crowd standing around. A man started pushing a white news photographer who accompanied us. Then he started hitting him and yelling obscene things. Four or five other men came up and knocked the photographer down and kicked him. One man smashed his camera."[41] At a signal given by a white man standing beside the bus, she continued, a mob of two hundred or more people started after the riders. Five African-American women riders were let through unharmed. The mob started yelling, "Get 'em! Get 'em!" The only white rider was thrown to the ground and kicked unconscious. "We thought he was dead," Herrmann said. "Still we didn't fight back. But we didn't believe in running, either." Police did not try to stop the melee. The youthful riders pleaded with bystanders for help. "One woman said, 'If you're freedom riders, I hope they kick the hell out of you.' A man came up to us and said, 'Come with me. I'll help you. I'm a federal man.' The mob converged on us and he was knocked to the ground."

That afternoon, Williams, undaunted by the fact that he faced a second operation for cancer, and the Reverend Ralph Abernathy, paster of the First Baptist Church in Montgomery, telephoned Dombrowski and asked him to come up from New Orleans. The Durrs, E.D. Nixon, and other equally staunch SCEF supporters were trying to find backing for the battered students and wanted Dombrowski at their side.[42] Did this signal the possibility of rebuilding the shattered coalition Dombrowski had been dreaming of so long? He hoped so; but the irony of the moment was not lost on him.

Montgomery's airport, Donnelly Field, was in a dither when Dombrowski's flight arrived on Sunday night at 9 p.m. Moments earlier, several dozen students had been served food at the airport's lunch counter, but police had blocked them from the segregated restrooms. Several had been arrested.

Dombrowski was met by Williams and Dion Diamond, a Howard University student who had been arrested twenty-nine times at lunch counters and bus stops between Washington and Montgomery. A half-dozen police cars followed them into Montgomery, where a rally was in progress. "In town, cars were racing through red lights," Dombrowski remembered.[43] "On Madison Street we saw the mob—several hundred men, mostly in shirtsleeves, with some women—running down the sidewalks. A car had been turned on its side, and set on fire. In the morning, we learned the car belonged to the Durrs. At the church, a crowd was in front . . . the papers estimated at two hundred . . . carrying bricks and scattering before rushes of uniformed police."

The tiny group parked well away from the church where the rally was being held, then walked through side streets to reach the building. Police followed them. Inside, before an overflow audience, the Reverend Martin Luther King, Jr., who had come to national prominence as a leader in the successful bus boycott in Montgomery five years earlier, was saying as Dombrowski entered, "Alabama has sunk to a level of barbarity comparable to the tragic days of Hitler's Germany."[44]

Dombrowski spent nearly a week in Montgomery. He, Williams, and the Durrs lined up white supporters for the Freedom Riders as their buses continued to New Orleans. Attorney General Robert Kennedy sent four hundred marshals to Montgomery, calling for a "cooling-off period" and a return to "normalcy." As usual, Dombrowski looked for some morality amid the immorality. "Well," he wrote later, "there were some good Samaritans there that day at the bus terminal. I know of at least six. There may have been others unrecorded."[45] He learned that a Montgomery photographer had stopped the mob from seriously injuring the photographer traveling with the Freedom Riders. A young African-American passerby, Henry James, a bricklayer, had protected a white student and became himself a target. John Siegenthaler, President Kennedy's personal representative, was clubbed unconscious trying to keep the mob from two Freedom Riders. State Public Safety Director Floyd Mann held the mob at bay with his pistol, protecting William Barbee, who had been beaten unconscious with a baseball bat.[46]

Frederick and Anna Gach, a young white couple from Montgomery, first angered the mob by yelling, "You ought to be ashamed of yourselves. How can you cheer on people that are kicking the ones who are down!" Anna, a graduate of the University of Alabama Law School, upset police when she shouted at them for standing still watching students being clubbed: "The Police Department is a bunch of SOBs!" The Gaches were arrested. Dombrowski posted bond for the couple, hoping they might become new hands to help the old fight.[47]

Dombrowski came back to Montgomery in August, this time to stay with Williams as he recovered from surgery. They agreed that Williams should be relieved of his responsibilities as president of the SCEF, and be named president emeritus at the September board meeting. Dombrowski left Montgomery August 13 to attend a rally for the Freedom Riders in Jackson, Mississippi, wondering if he'd see Williams alive again.[48]

Williams had lost political weight long before he lost his health. A new generation had come to power in Washington. Williams' search for support on the voting-rights issue yielded almost nothing, his entreaties on behalf of the Bradens even less. Excluded by the NAACP's Wilkins from the Leadership Conference on Civil Rights, cut off from liberal foundation money, and Red-baited at every turn, he and Dombrowski concluded that the SCEF had to find new political allies as well as new leadership.

Shut out of the places where policy was made, they decided to be in the places where policy was caused. Dombrowski and Anne Braden aligned the SCEF with local groups such as Save Our Schools in New Orleans, and with newer regionwide organizations, particularly the Student Non-Violent Coordinating Committee (SNCC) and King's Southern Christian Leadership Conference (SCLC). Starting with the school desegregation fight in New Orleans and the tragedy in Montgomery, this strategy propelled Dombrowski or the Bradens into Monroe, North Carolina; Albany, Georgia; Greenwood, Mississippi; and every other place where "vitally important" groups were carrying the fight for equality into the streets.[49]

They still used conferences to spark attention to issues that segregationists preferred not be noticed. And *The Southern Patriot* was their voice.

They organized a civil-liberties workshop in Chapel Hill on October 27, 1961, to discuss the Bill of Rights and its meaning in the South. They expected fifty participants.[50] Over three hundred turned out, many of them with unreported news about struggles in their communities which found its way into *The Southern Patriot*. In North Carolina and elsewhere, the SCEF strategy shed light on grassroots activists across the South, forcing the realization that integration was no longer the ideology of a few.

This ability to organize large biracial events, along with SCEF's close ties to Shuttlesworth, made it easier for SCLC's leadership—Martin Luther King, Jr., Wyatt Tee Walker, and Ralph Abernathy—to ignore the Redbaiting innuendoes often hurled at the SCEF. The SCLC leaders heartily pushed the campaign to secure clemency for Carl Braden and Frank Wilkinson. Walker urged SCLC's affiliates to sign the clemency petition the SCEF was circulating: "We must be loyal to the courageous white friends who pay a terrific price to be companions in our struggle for full freedom," he said.[51] "We need dedicated co-workers who absolutely refuse to compromise."

In February 1962, having served ten months, Braden and Wilkinson were paroled. Braden lost no time reconnecting with southern activists, including SNCC's volunteers, who were spearheading the civil rights movement. These volunteers assembled in Atlanta in April 1962 for their third annual meeting, dangerously near being forced to dissolve their loosely knit organization. They needed money. Older civil rights groups, especially the NAACP, had recaptured financial support lost earlier to SNCC. Fearing bankruptcy, the SNCC appealed to the SCEF for help shoring up its finances. To Dombrowski and the Bradens, the SNCC was "the hope and the heart of things."[52] Despite the difficulty they had raising funds for their own work, they agreed to help, with no strings attached.

Braden, with his strong ties to labor unions, arranged for SNCC volunteers to meet with representatives of the Teamsters' Union. The union, which had been organizing without regard to race for many years, made a contribution to SNCC's treasury and arranged to send some of its most seasoned organizers to give the volunteers a short course in organizing techniques. The Reverend W. Howard Melish, who was raising funds for the SCEF in New York City, helped SNCC volunteers establish their own fundraising network. The SCEF itself gave one thousand dollars. James Forman, SNCC's leader, later wrote to Dombrowski thanking the SCEF for its help. "This conference was vitally necessary to the development of the Southern Protest Movement," he said. "Communications and coordination between the protest groups was at a low ebb—despite the fact our staff was performing miracles."[53]

Earlier, Anne Braden and Jane Stembridge, a young Virginian who had quit college to work fulltime with SNCC, had proposed to both SNCC and the SCEF that the two organizations join to recruit southern white collegians. Stembridge was one of only a handful of young white southern civil rights activists at the time. Stembridge believed that there were others like herself on campuses around the South, and that, if encouraged, they would take part. The SCEF board adopted the idea. It was, after all, a student counterpart to what they'd been trying to do among adults over the years. SNCC agreed, provided that SCEF paid for the staff position and that any organizer recruited be acceptable to SCEF before SNCC hired them. Dombrowski arranged to pay the SNCC five thousand dollars to fund the white student project.[54]

At length, Bob Zellner, an Alabama native, was selected. Zellner had graduated from the all-white Huntingdon College, a Methodist school in Montgomery. While researching a sociology paper, he attended a meeting of the Montgomery Improvement Association. College officials tried to expel him, but his father, a minister in Mobile, stood by his son. Crosses had been burned near his dormitory, the Klan had distributed leaflets smearing him, and the state's attorney general had summoned Zellner to his office, where he had been accused of communist associations. Zellner had stood firm through it all.[55]

Anne Braden, the first SCEF staff member to hear about Zellner, had met him. Aubrey Williams wrote her later, "It is my judgment that you have found something in the discovery of the boy."[56]

Zellner joined the SNCC staff on September 1, 1961, its first paid white organizer. By the end of October, Zellner visited nearly thirty college campuses. He cornered southerners attending the National Student Association meeting in New Orleans and urged the Students for a Democratic Society to undertake a southern organizing drive. During a visit to the University of Mississippi, he talked with several white students who had courageously eaten in public with James Meredith, the first African American admitted to the university in Oxford. University officials, they told Zellner, had encouraged other students to organize "the Rebel Underground." Subsequently, these white students had been beaten, their rooms had been ransacked, and they were going to quit the university.

While visiting Huntingdon in Montgomery, Governor-elect George Wallace had ordered Zellner arrested. But since Wallace had not been sworn in, his orders were illegal, and Zellner was released. Visiting one campus after another, Zellner found what he called "a cotton curtain," a pattern of obstacles fashioned by college or state administrators to prevent students from getting involved with the civil rights movement.[57] He met a young man who'd been expelled from four southern schools for his interracial activities. Among white students, he found equal doses of admiration for civil rights activists and fear of what might happen if they became active.

Dombrowski and the Bradens had advised Zellner to work quietly among the white students, making no attempt to assert himself with SNCC's leadership or to influence policy. In McComb, Mississippi, on the afternoon of October 4, 1961, however, Zellner became one among equals. SNCC volunteers led by Robert Moses had spent weeks trying to register voters in the southern Mississippi town. Several students had been arrested. Terrorism replaced repression on September 25. Herbert Lee, a farmer and the father of nine children, was shot and killed by a Mississippi senator for his part in the registration effort.[58] Determined to honor Lee's memory and to keep the registration drive alive, several hundred SNCC volunteers gathered to march on McComb's City Hall.[59]

As the line moved out Zellner joined them. As the only white in a sea of youthful African-American faces, he quickly became the target of jeers and taunts from the crowds lining the streets. As the marchers reached City Hall, several whites rushed Zellner. Moses and Charles McDew tried to protect him. Police dragged them into City Hall, leaving Zellner to the mob. He was beaten, his eyes were gouged, and he was kicked unconscious. When the mob's fury was spent, police dragged Zellner to police headquarters. When he regained consciousness that night, police drove him to nearby Magnolia, warning him never to set foot in McComb again. Moses said that Zellner gave "new meaning" to the phrase "black and white together."[60]

Four months later, Zellner and McDew were jailed in East Baton Rouge, Louisiana, and charged with criminal anarchy. They were trying to visit Dion Diamond, who had been arrested for organizing a SNCC group on the campus of Southern University. Diamond had chosen to stay in jail to protest the excessively high bonds officials were starting to use against the demonstrators. Zellner and McDew went to the jail to give their friend some magazines and a book when they were arrested. If convicted, they faced ten-year prison sentences.

McDew was thrown into solitary confinement. Zellner was put in a cellblock with sixty-five inmates who were told by guards that he was a "Communist who tried to smuggle obscene literature on race-mixing" into Diamond. He was threatened with sharpened spoons and razors. He frequently was beaten. When he dared fall asleep, he was doused with water. Jailers arranged tours for high-school students who wanted to see "the nigger-loving Communist."[61] Two weeks later, Zellner finally managed to get word to Dombrowski in New Orleans. Until then, no-one in SNCC or the SCEF had been able to learn their whereabouts. Dombrowski arranged for legal help and tried to get all three out on bond. Eventually, the charges against Zellner and McDew were dropped; Diamond was released from jail after eighty-five days. The two organizations used their arrest to focus national media attention on the way segregationist officials were using state courts, city jails, and bail bonds to stifle the protest movement.[62] In addition, Dombrowski and Ben Smith, the New Orleans attorney who had represented him during the Eastland hearings, appealed to the National Lawyers Guild to "provide legal assistance . . . to the forces working for justice and integration in the South."[63] By mid-1962, the SCEF and the Lawyers Guild had established the Committee to Assist Southern Lawyers. Only a handful of southern lawyers would represent civil rights activists. They were overworked and often harassed.

Through the SCEF, the Lawyers Guild agreed to assist southern lawyers who would defend protesters. In addition to providing direct legal assistance, the guild would send legal experts south for SCEF-arranged conferences, prepare handbooks on civil rights law for lawyers and laymen, and start an internship program under which northern law students could spend their summers helping southern lawyers. It was an ambitious program and more of a service than anything the SCEF had sponsored previously.

Meanwhile, Reverend Shuttlesworth had been arrested in Birmingham. Starting in early 1962, he and students from Miles College had organized an economic boycott of the city's downtown merchants that had reduced the latter's profits by nearly half. The boycotters were protesting hiring practices and racial exploitation and had kept the pressure on for nearly a year when Shuttlesworth was jailed for thirty-five days and forced to haul garbage cans and sacks of potatoes in and out of the kitchen. He was re-leased early in March, leaving the jail exasperated, vowing, "Where sin abounds, we must prove that Grace can more abound."[64] Birmingham, in his mind, was just "two steps from Hell." His organization, the Alabama Christian Movement for Human Rights, was among the strongest and best organized of the grassroots organizations allied with the SCLC. Time and again, Shuttlesworth had sustained collective challenges to Eugene "Bull" Connor and other equally implacable officials. In less than a month, the ACMHR and SCLC agreed on a plan aimed at dividing Birmingham's po-litical and economic power structures. SCLC needed a victory.[65]

King had suffered an embarrassingly bitter defeat in Albany, Georgia. During an economic boycott there, the chief of police had kept federal au-thorities at a distance by abstaining from open violence. Instead, a state court injunction got King off the streets, a tactic that proved more effective than billy clubs, police dogs, or fire hoses. King refused to defy the injunc-tion, leaving many troubled by what seemed to be a failure of nerve. Until Albany, King had walked only with success, unable to make a political mis-take.

In addition, the SCLC and SNCC spent hours arguing over turf, money, and who would get the credit for any accomplishment, rather than as-sessing their foes. The first demonstrations started on April Fool's Day. Shuttlesworth and King issued a five-point list of demands, including de-segregation of downtown department stores, fair hiring practices, and the appointment of a biracial commission to set a timetable for desegregation of the public schools. SCLC had its own goal—to re-assert its leadership after the setback in Albany. King felt he must demonstrate that "the prophet did not have feet of clay" and that his organization could force the federal government to stand against a racist city government.[66]

Twenty persons marched the first day. Fourteen were arrested. Sixty marched the next day. Fifty were jailed. Two hundred marched the third day. Most of them went to jail. "We are here for the duration," Shuttles-worth told a jammed, cheering church audience during one of the nightly rallies held to exhort protesters and agree on strategies. "Many of us [were] willing to die if necessary on the streets of Birmingham."[67]

As more and more African Americans joined the daily protest marches, Connor, who years earlier had disrupted the first convening of the SCHW by enforcing the city's segregation laws, turned fire hoses on protestors, shocked them with electric cattle prods, loosed police dogs on them, and arrested hundreds, until even the city's fairground was filled. The mayor ordered all relief payments to African Americans cut off, saying, "If the Negroes are going to heed . . . irresponsible and militant advice . . . then I say let these leaders feed them."[68]

At Shuttlesworth's invitation, Dombrowski went to Birmingham on April 24 to speak at one of the nightly rallies. Until that time, Dombrowski only had secondhand information about the movement his friend had organized. Over 1,500 persons filled Saint James Church to hear Dombrowski. The basement was full. Several hundred persons were in the streets outside. As Dombrowski was being introduced, police conspicuously pushed their way into the church, causing Shuttlesworth to stop his introduction of Dombrowski to invite the detectives to sit on the floor or get out. "Standing in the aisles is a fire hazard," the gutsy minister told them. As they left, and as Dombrowski was again being introduced, an alarming message reached the church. Only a few hours earlier that afternoon, William L. Moore, a mailman from New York State, had been shot and killed from ambush outside Gadsden, Alabama. He was walking from Chattanooga to Jackson to support desegregation. The press covered his lonely hike almost step by step. The crowd was stunned and silent after Shuttlesworth announced the tragic slaying. When Dombrowski finally reached the pulpit, he put aside his prepared notes, offering instead a eulogy for the dead man. "His brutal slaying is a dramatic symbol of the hate and violence bred by segregation and white supremacy. It is the logical, inevitable and natural result of the policies of Governor George Wallace and those who uphold segregation. The killer of Moore undoubtedly felt that he was a patriot ridding the country of a dangerous radical who sought to subvert the Southern way of life."[69] His own experiences in Elizabethton flooded Dombrowski's consciousness.

Birmingham was facing a social revolution. Six days later, Shuttlesworth, leading nearly three thousand marchers in the continued protest, was battered against a brick wall by a burst of water from high pressure hoses. As he was carried to the hospital, Connor said, "I wish they had carried him away in a hearse."[70] Connor notwithstanding, nonviolence was crushing segregation. Newspapers and television around the world sent reporters and camera crews to Birmingham. The city became a symbol of the South's intransigent racism. Massive demonstrations supporting African Americans were held in San Francisco, Philadelphia, Detroit, and other cities. Secretly, the merchants and steel mill executives were preparing to negotiate with Shuttlesworth and SCLC. Behind the scenes, President Kennedy was trying eagerly to forge a compromise settlement.

On May 16, after forty-five days, the city's financial leaders capitulated, agreeing to the movement's demands for the desegregation of all public facilities, the employment of African Americans in commercial stores, the immediate release of those in jail, and the creation of a biracial committee to work on the other problems. Within a few weeks, however, Shuttlesworth realized that merchants were reneging on their promises.[71] Public facilities remained closed to African Americans. Bombs exploded at the Gaston Motel, which was owned by an African American, and at a minister's home. The white reaction to the apparently successful boycott reached a tragic climax when a dynamite blast killed eleven-year-old Denise McNair and Cynthia Wesley, Addie Mae Collins, and Carole Robertson, all fourteen years old, in their Sunday School class.

The SCLC's goal had been accomplished in Birmingham, but at great cost. And the SCEF, with Shuttlesworth playing a prominent organizational role, found new respectability, at least within the civil rights movement. Few dared to Red-bait the SCEF in Shuttlesworth's presence, although some NAACP leaders did try. Gloster Current, director of branches for the NAACP, made a special trip to Atlanta trying to dissuade Shuttlesworth from having anything to do with the SCEF. Shuttlesworth was returning to Birmingham from a SCEF meeting in Norfolk, Virginia, when Current intercepted him at Atlanta's airport.[72] "I met him in the airport," Shuttlesworth recalled, "and he opened up right away trying to get me out of the SCEF. He had a Jackson, Mississippi, newspaper. It was a green paper. The top headline said, 'Negro Pastor Heads Communist Front.' He said we couldn't afford to be mixed up with Reds." Shuttlesworth stood firm. The NAACP, and some critics within SCLC as well, were stymied. The Birmingham minister commanded the largest NAACP branch in Alabama. His grassroots strength and his ability in the pulpit, made him essential to the SCLC.

In addition, Ella J. Baker joined the SCEF staff after resigning as executive director of the SCLC. John R. Salter, Jr., also joined the staff. Salter, proudly half Micmac Indian and half white, taught sociology at Tougaloo College outside Jackson, Mississippi, until being fired for his part in successful but bloody demonstrations in Jackson, that winter and spring.[73] Salter helped pull hundreds of students into the streets to challenge segregation.

The SNCC asked the SCEF to join demonstrations being planned in Danville, Virginia, to protest police brutality. A massive March on Washington was being organized, and the SCEF was included among the planners. Williams, in spite of his critical illness, wrote saying he wanted to march with the SCEF leadership. Dombrowski was making arrangements for an interracial meeting of lawyers in New Orleans, a first in Louisiana, according to his friend and lawyer, Ben Smith. And almost daily, outside his office on Perdido Street, four or five pickets marched with placards asking "Does Racial Strife Originate Here?" or proclaiming "Race Agitators Operate From Here!"

# 16

## A
## Chilling
## Effect

Dombrowski was at his desk on Friday afternoon, October 4, 1963, finishing another week's administrative chores. He was alone in the office. His secretary had the day off. He'd spent the morning at the airport hotel where the SCEF was sponsoring an interracial meeting of lawyers. Over fifty attorneys from across the nation were in New Orleans at the invitation of the SCEF and the National Lawyers Guild, outlining a program of legal assistance for civil rights workers, focusing particularly on a coordinated voter registration drive being planned by civil rights groups the next summer in Mississippi. The SCEF's lawyers, joined by colleagues in the Louis A. Martinet Society, an association of African-American attorneys, had forced the hotel to accept the conference. The society's name honored Martinet, a lawyer who'd organized the Plessy suit.

Dombrowski, as cohost, welcomed the lawyers, explained the SCEF's interest in their professional help, and then returned to his own work. He planned to join them for supper. The lawyers were there to hammer out a strategy in response to the segregationists' use of the state's array of legal powers to thwart the civil rights movement. Injunctions had been used successfully in Albany, Georgia; Gadsden, Alabama; and Danville, Virginia, virtually halting protests. Individuals by the score were being arrested by authorities who had no intention of conducting speedy trials. Their aim was to keep protestors tied up with costly, time-consuming court proceedings.

The quiet in Dombrowski's office was shattered just after 3 p.m. Sirens wailed to a stop outside on Perdido Street. Shouts in the hallway were punctuated by hammered thuds. He thought the building was on fire. By the time Dombrowski gathered his crutches and was up on his feet, the door to the office burst open. Police shoved inside with their pistols drawn. One pushed Dombrowski back into the chair, and another read a warrant arresting him for "participation in the management of a subversive organization," being "a member of a Communist front organization," and "remaining in Louisiana five consecutive days without registering with the Department of Public Safety."[1]

Astounded, Dombrowski asked to call a lawyer. The request was refused. He started recording what was happening, writing as quickly as possible. "They ordered me to sit in the chair in the middle of my office while they poked around every nook and cranny."[2] He counted thirteen uniformed policemen. Judging by the noise, others were in the hallway and outside in the street. Plainclothesmen arrived. One took his aluminum crutches, pulled them apart, peered into the shafts, and shook them vigorously. Soon twenty or so prison trustees from the New Orleans House of Detention appeared, bringing with them packing cartons and equipment to move furniture. While police supervised and listed every item, the trustees packed the SCEF's files, mailing lists, and books. Posters and photographs, including pictures given Dombrowski by Eleanor Roosevelt, Albert Einstein, and Mary McLeod Bethune, were taken off the walls and boxed.

"There seemed to be some confusion as to who was in charge of the detail," Dombrowski wrote.

> I asked carefully who was in charge. Some thought Major Russell Willie, director of the State Police Bureau of Identification and Investigation, was in charge. He certainly kept the spotlight of attention, carrying a heavy recorder every step and asking everyone to speak into the "mike" and trying to record my answers to all questions.
>
> Others thought the senior officer was Major Presley J. Trosclair, of the New Orleans police intelligence division. Still others thought Colonel Frederick B. Alexander, Jr., staff director for the Louisiana Joint Legislative Committee on Un-American Activities, was head man. They all agreed Alexander was the man who would be in charge of the records. The city and state police said they had planned the raid for eleven

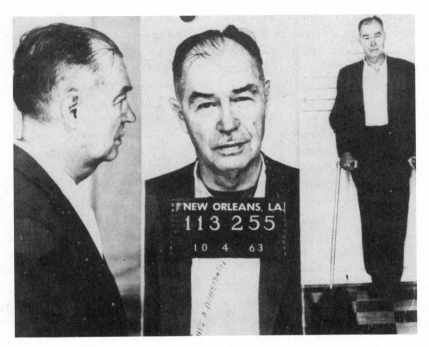

James A. Dombrowski under arrest in New Orleans, 1963. Photo taken by the New Orleans Police Department. Frank T. Adams Collection.

months, yet they arrived and used a sledge hammer and pick axe to smash down the door to the office next to ours. It was empty.

By 7:30 p.m., the SCEF's belongings had been packed in seventy-three cartons and loaded into a truck along with its furniture. Dombrowski was ordered to his feet and taken to the First Police Precinct, where he was charged with violating the Louisiana Subversive Activities and Communist Control Act.[3] After being fingerprinted and photographed, Dombrowski was allowed to use a telephone. He telephoned Ellen, but a policeman answered. She was distraught. Their home was filled with police. She was being held at gunpoint. They were searching under beds, behind pictures, in the pockets of every garment, and through books and papers. Two men were crawling in the attic searching amid the accumulation of 130 years. Check stubs, receipts, address and telephone books, and some of Dombrowski's books were being packed into boxes.

As the search continued, Ellen, frightened but infuriated by the pistol constantly pointed at her, let her pet dachshund, Wilhelmina, lunge at the policeman holding her at gunpoint. "Get that dog away, or I'm going to have to shoot her," the officer told Ellen, who put the dog on a leash.[4] Dombrowski said he'd be home shortly, expecting to make bail and be released.

Dombrowski was unable to reach Ben Smith, the SCEF lawyer who had helped to arrange the lawyers' meeting going on at the hotel, nor was the hotel switchboard operator able to find any of the other attorneys, including Arthur Shores, who had defended Dombrowski in Birmingham. His two telephone calls made, Dombrowski was taken to a cell. "I tried to make myself as comfortable as possible," Dombrowski remembered.

That was not easy. The two double-tier steel bunks were fastened to the walls and had no mattresses. The edge of the bunk was serrated at two-inch intervals, and the bed's surface had one-inch holes punched into the metal at six-inch intervals. I could neither sit on the edge lest my legs be severed, nor could I stretch out because of my arthritic hips. But I was making the best of it.

Whenever anyone entered the cellblock, a huge lever was thrown. The effect was supernatural, more terrifying than anything imaginable. It was a cacophony designed to accompany the end of the world or some cosmic tragedy. When the lever dropped, the steel walls trembled, and the cell shook like an earthquake had struck, and there was an ear-splitting series of echoes and reverberations.

The cellblock lever was suddenly thrown and the place shuddered with the horrendous sound and echoes. An officer appeared with Ben Smith. I was delighted to see him, of course. Ben sat down on the other bunk. The officer closed the cell and left. When it got quiet after the lever was pulled back into place, I asked, "How are things going at the conference?"

"Very well, when I left," he said.

We chatted for a few more minutes, then I asked, bluntly, "Ben, when are you going to get me out of here?"

And Ben asked, "What do you think I'm doing in here?"

I realized Ben had been arrested. I thought, naturally, he'd come to arrange bond for me. I thought, to be sure, he was a little leisurely, even by Southern standards, in coming to the point, and doing the business

of the moment. Also, it seemed Ben's appearance was a little casual. No
tie. Shirt open at the neck, etc. Still, it did not for a moment occur to
me that Ben was there in any other capacity than as my counsel.

Smith reconstructed what had happened to him.[5] Police had charged
him with the same three offenses as Dombrowski. Bruce Waltzer, his law
partner, was charged with being a "member of the National Lawyers Guild
and failing to register as such." Police jailed Waltzer at the Third Police Precinct. On each count, each man, including Dombrowski, if convicted,
could be fined $10,000, be imprisoned for ten years, or both. Police had
raided their homes and their law office, too, Smith told Dombrowski. No
records were confiscated, but every document related to the SCEF or to
other civil rights cases had been listed. Smith presumed that those records
would be subpoenaed later. He and Waltzer had been summoned from the
conference by their distressed secretary. By the time they reached their office, the police were gone, but the office was a shambles, with files scattered
everywhere. Table lamps had been taken to pieces, and pictures had been
taken out of their frames. Waltzer called his wife, who told him that police
were ransacking their home. His wife, a native of Germany and Jewish, had
been a child when Nazis raided her family's home. Waltzer rushed home
and was arrested. Smith was arrested at his home, too. Police were holding
his wife, their two children, and a babysitter at gunpoint while their apartment was searched.

Back at the hotel, other lawyers did not learn about the arrests until they
reconvened after supper. Then, Arthur Kinoy, the famed constitutional
lawyer, remembered, "The place exploded."[6] Jack Peebles, another New
Orleans attorney, launched a search for a judge who would release the trio
on bond. Others enlisted William Kunstler, the New York attorney who
was Martin Luther King's personal lawyer, to join them in New Orleans.
Sitting on their serrated seat, Dombrowski and Smith, while unable to relax, talked about their predicament. Dombrowski reminisced about his arrests in Elizabethton and in Birmingham.

Meanwhile, State Representative James H. Pfister, chairman of the Louisiana Joint Legislative Committee on Un-American Activities (LUAC), announced during a jammed press conference that his committee had ordered
the raids. The SCEF, he said, was "engaged in racial agitation."[7] The
SCEF's president, Fred Shuttlesworth, he said, was "a close associate of
Martin Luther King." The arrests were the result of a long investigation by
his committee and "showed the need for additional legislation."

The ten o'clock news was history when Dombrowski, Smith, and Waltzer were finally released from jail. Peebles and other lawyers appealed to seven judges before finding one who would set bond for the men. A circus atmosphere greeted Dombrowski and Smith outside the police station. A large crowd was on hand. The street was roped off. Squad cars were collected. Officers were everywhere. There were television cameras and reporters who wanted questions answered.

When Dombrowski finally arrived home, Ellen was shaking with anger and beside herself with fear that serious harm had come to her husband. Dombrowski tried to sooth her fears. Together, they made a desultory attempt to get their minds off what had happened by starting to straighten up the disarray. Reports of the raid on his office and of the arrests, complete with pictures, were played high on page one of New Orleans' newspapers the next morning. As Dombrowski sipped coffee before leaving for the hotel to confer with the lawyers, radio reporters announced that Jack N. Rogers, the LUAC's chief counsel, planned a news conference later that day.

Rogers later told the press that the SCEF was "the equivalent of a big holding company" through which "Communists infiltrated racial movements in Louisiana."[8] He said, "The SCEF has been giving us trouble all over the state." A reporter asked if the raids had been coordinated with the FBI. Rogers said that, while he "appreciated" J. Edgar Hoover, the Justice Department "couldn't be trusted with anti-communist secrets." He added, "We knew if we told the FBI about this, they would have to tell Bobby Kennedy. We cannot trust him and we expect him to tell his friend, Martin Luther King." Rogers' investigation into the SCEF had gone on for months, he said, but the raids had been sparked by Alabama Gov. George Wallace, who recently had said on national television that Dombrowski and the Bradens were "the cause of racial agitation" in his state.

That morning, the hotel's ballroom was pressed into service to hold the crush of lawyers, civil rights activists, reporters, and television cameramen who showed up to learn more about the arrests and the meetings. Smith said that not only did the "decidedly political arrests" violate First Amendment guarantees, but also civil rights workers across the South had suffered similar McCarthy-esque attacks for months. He added

The charge against me is that desegregation movements in the South are Communist inspired, and that particularly any white man who makes common cause with the Negro is a traitor to his class and to his race. The theory being that as long as the Negro can be separated from white allies in his struggle for equal rights either by selfish motives, or fear and terror, that the movement forward to a constitutional government can somehow be checked. By these prosecutions, the wider aspects of our efforts become clearer to us all. We cannot desegregate a witch-hunting society. We cannot integrate a silent and fearful nation. We cannot provide equal rights that have any meaning to citizens of a police state.[9]

Dombrowski made no speech that day. He was too tired, and his limbs ached too badly. But, as Kinoy said, Dombrowski "went to the heart of the matter" in private strategy discussions after the day's public events had ended the conference. "They're desperate," he said. "They are going back to the weapons of the 1950s."[10] The civil rights movement was a rising tide, threatening elected officials and not just storekeepers and their lunch counters. The March on Washington prompted talk of new civil rights legislation. Segregationists feared that they were losing ground, as one court decision after another chipped away at *de jure* Jim Crow. Freedom Summer was being planned as carefully as the successful assault on the power structure in Birmingham and by the same people. However, voter registration for Mississippi elections was now the target. Mrs. Fannie Lou Hamer, who had been evicted from her sharecropper home in the Delta after fearlessly registering to vote, was leading a drive to seat an interracial delegation at the national Democratic Party's nominating convention in Atlantic City. Mississippi's Democrats were infuriated; national Democrats were embarrassed. Mrs. Hamer was unfazed. "I'm sick and tired of being sick and tired," Mrs. Hamer said. At her side in the organizing drive was the Reverend Ed King, a white Mississippian who worked closely with the SCEF's John Salter.[11]

"They resorted to nullification, to interposition, to state's rights, and to force and violence," Dombrowski said to the huddle of lawyers. "Now they are digging up the Communist conspiracy theory. If they get away with this, anything goes."[12] He was prepared to draw the line. After all, what did he, or the SCEF, have to lose? No citizen, and no lawyer, would dare stand with African Americans if they could be convicted of subversion. He knew that a traditional defense against the charges would ruin the SCEF. The organization's existence was precarious at best. He feared that his health might not stand up to such stress. The costs would bankrupt him. Months of trials, hearings, and appeals would drain money and energy and, as importantly, deny or divert his purpose for the SCEF. By the day's end, Dombrowski and the lawyers had agreed to counterattack, ignoring the customary time-consuming and costly legal process—arrest, followed by trial, followed by appeals, first through state courts and then, if a constitutional issue was at stake, through a string of federal courts. They decided to do just what Kinoy the day before had theorized might work—revive remedies Congress had enacted after the Civil War, which permitted African Americans to seek immediate federal relief when state courts tried to abrogate their newly emancipated status.[13]

Dombrowski and the lawyers set out to challenge the hitherto unassailable constitutional doctrine of abstention, the legal principle which forced citizens to exhaust all remedies for enforcing their constitutional guarantees in state courts before turning to federal benches. Moreover, they would try to make the officials responsible for the raids compensate them for violating those rights and so causing embarrassment and mental anguish. Unintentionally, Pfister and Rogers gave Dombrowski a way to test on a grand scale the touchstone of the SCEF's philosophy—that civil liberties and civil rights were inseparable. "What we call euphemistically 'the struggle for integration' is not that at all," Dombrowski said.[14] "It is more accurate to speak of the civil rights movement in the South today as a fight for the right to advocate integration."

Dombrowski, Smith, and Waltzer were defended by Kinoy and Kunstler, joined by New Orleans attorneys Milton E. Brenner and A.P. Tureaud, and Walter E. Dillon of Washington, D.C. They made opening moves by asking for a preliminary hearing in Louisiana's Criminal Court. Judge J. Bernard Cocke, who had ordered the men released from jail, set Friday, October 25, as the hearing date. The LUAC was ordered to bring into court every item seized.[15]

The courtroom was packed. A policeman who took part in the raids testified that a confidential informant had supplied information that the SCEF was subversive. Under crossexamination, he refused to divulge the informant's name. Judge Cocke struck his testimony, saying that it did not constitute evidence of subversion. The LUAC lawyers did not bring the SCEF's records as ordered. When asked why they ignored the court's order, they asked to have an expert testify about their contents instead. The request was denied. Unexpectedly, the state rested. Whereupon, Judge Cocke surprised defense and prosecution alike, quashing the arrests for want of probable cause. The state, he said, had produced insufficient evidence to bring the men to trial for conspiracy. The LUAC and the police had conducted the raids based on their own conclusions, not evidence, he said.[16]

Dombrowski and his allies had won a moral victory. Their elation was shortlived. Outside the courtroom, Representative Pfister, reacting to the judge's decision, told the press, "The evidence in this matter is mountainous and could not possibly have been analyzed in so short a time."[17] The matter was far from over, he said, announcing that he and Rogers, along with the SCEF's records, were to appear before the Senate Internal Security Subcommittee at a public hearing in Washington, D.C., the next Tuesday. The confiscated records would be given to the committee, he said.[18] Until Pfister's press conference, no-one had suspected that Sen. James O. Eastland had any involvement with the case.[18] All soon learned, however, that J.G. Sourwine, chief counsel for the senator's subcommittee, had come to Louisiana the day after the raids with blank subpoenas signed by Eastland.[19] The subpoenas were dated October 4, suggesting that Eastland had had advance knowledge of the raids. Sourwine later explained that this had been a typographical error.[20] The entire truckload of materials was in federal hands, although still physically in Baton Rouge.

Astonished by this sudden turn of events, Dombrowski's lawyers filed an injunction the next day, a Saturday, to prevent the records from being moved from Baton Rouge. On Sunday, Federal District Judge Robert A. Ainsworth told the SCEF's lawyers that he had telephoned state police headquarters and determined that the records were there and safe. He set a hearing on the motion for Monday morning. By Monday, however, the question of an injunction was moot. A few minutes before midnight on Sunday, Sourwine had ordered the state police to move the records to Woodville, Mississippi, and deliver them to the clerk of chancery court there. The state police had done as they had been told. The documents thus were outside the jurisdiction of Ainsworth's federal court in Louisiana and, seemingly, en route to Washington, D.C.[21]

Ainsworth left standing, however, a second element of the complaint, which came to be known as *Dombrowski v. Eastland,* in which Dombrowski, seeking compensation for violation of his Fourth Amendment rights, was suing Eastland, Pfister, and others for a half-million dollars. The suit alleged that the raids had been a conspiracy to circumvent the Supreme Court's decision in *NAACP v. Alabama,* which prohibited southern states from forcing civil rights groups to disclose their membership lists.[22] The suit contended that federal courts had jurisdiction because Louisiana's

Subversive Activities Control Act violated federal constitutional provisions. A few days later, on October 31, a similar suit was filed in U.S. District Court in Washington, D.C., the residence of both Eastland and Sourwine.

The fast-paced legal maneuvering continued during November and December, giving Dombrowski little time to reassemble the SCEF's administration. The Bradens, Ella Baker, and John Salter kept going forward with their own program responsibilities but as often as possible traveled across the nation searching for funds and for friendly mailing lists to replace those taken in the raids.

Unsung Al Maund, the SCEF's longtime supporter, learned about the raids and took vacation time to help Dombrowski. As each new development unfolded in court or out, fact sheets issued from Perdido Street. Dombrowski and the other SCEF staffers asked for support, getting both SCLC and SNCC to send protests to the Justice Department. Some newspaper editorials expressed outrage over the raids. In New Orleans, the city's rabbinical council, the local chapter of the American Association of University Professors, the Martinet Society, the ministerial alliance, several labor unions, and even a few business organizations closed ranks with the SCEF.

*The Southern Patriot* that fall reported many important events. In Tennessee, Highlander was under renewed attack by the state. In Georgia, nine leaders in Albany were indicted as protests continued there. In Virginia, Danville activists led by Ruth Harvey Charity were starting an economic boycott. In Mississippi, an interracial coalition, including the SCEF's Salter, formed the Mississippi Freedom Democratic Party in Jackson. Dombrowski portrayed the raids as part of a segregationist plan to harass and destroy the entire civil rights movement.[23]

On November 8, Pfister and Rogers called a hearing of the LUAC, open to the press but not the public in an effort "to keep agitators out."[24] The men released photocopies of the SCEF's mailing list and other documents that they claimed proved that the organization was a Communist front. This done, the committee officially adopted a resolution declaring the SCEF "subversive . . . because it is aiding and abetting the Communist conspiracy." Besides laying the legal basis for the state's prosecution of the SCEF, the move was part of Pfister's re-election campaign.

On November 12, Dombrowski and the SCEF board courted another arrest in Birmingham, meeting openly in the tense, segregated city.[25] The board members issued blistering resolutions attacking Eastland for "stealing SCEF's records" and attacking Connor for making no arrests for the bomb explosions which had killed the four teenagers two months earlier at the Sixteenth Street Baptist Church. They demanded that the Justice Department drop its prosecution of the Albany movement leaders. They were outraged that students and ministers in Jackson had been arrested trying to attend church services with an all-white congregation, and that the Reverend Ashton Jones had been held in an Atlanta jail since June, after he'd been arrested trying to desegregate a church service; he had been unable to raise $20,000 bond. Beyond their own circle, the resolutions were hardly noticed, appearing chiefly in *The Southern Patriot*. Like the meeting where they were passed, the pronouncements were a brave front, a diversion intended to say that the raids would not keep the SCEF from its work.

Dombrowski worried about the amount of money going for legal fees. Ethel Clyde sent a check for two thousand dollars just after Thanksgiving, 1963, and Dombrowski immediately signed it over to his two New Orleans attorneys. "My N.Y. lawyers, Kunstler and Kinoy, are costing a thousand a month, a staggering burden," he wrote to his longtime benefactress.[26]

Dombrowski returned to New Orleans two days later, on November 14, as the New Orleans grand jury was being convened to investigate the SCEF for possible violations of the State Communist Control Act. Six days later, on the eve of a special three-judge federal hearing to determine the constitutionality of the Louisiana subversive law, he wrote Clyde again: "We got a real break today. Rep. Pfister, chairman of the La. Committee that started all the mess, was defeated decisively yesterday in the Democratic Party primary, receiving only about 2,700 votes out of a total of 8,400. This is a good omen."[27]

The court proceedings opened December 9, with Kinoy declaring that the Louisiana laws under which the men had been arrested "were written as if the First and Fourteenth Amendments to the U.S. Constitution did not exist."[28] Judge John Minor Wisdom agreed. Communism was a national concern, not an issue for the states to prosecute. The two other judges, E. Gordon West and Frank B. Ellis, did not see it that way. Louisiana's statute was constitutional, and they refused to hear testimony which would attempt to prove that the laws had been applied illegally. This decision opened the way for the state to resume criminal proceedings against Dombrowski, Smith, and Waltzer. Indictments were issued on January 29, 1964. District Attorney James Garrison agreed not to begin prosecution until the U.S. Supreme Court decided if it would consider the appeal of the three judges' initial ruling. This case was styled *Dombrowski v. Pfister.*[29] Later, in an unprecedented move, the court, on February 4, 1964, in a written order, reversed its ruling but invoked the doctrine of abstention.[30]

In the meantime, in the case known as *Dombrowski v. Eastland,* the motion seeking an injunction prohibiting the senator from keeping the SCEF records and asking for a half million dollars in damages, was dismissed in District Court in Washington, D.C.[31] The Mississippi senator argued that he was immune from prosecution. The constitution imposed a direct restraint on the courts, because Article I, Section 6, stated, "For any Speech or Debate in either House . . . shall not be questioned in any other Place." Moreover, he argued, he was innocently in Washington throughout the raids and only learned about them when Sourwine came to him with blank subpoenas.[32] Dombrowski's lawyers conceded that the senator was entitled to legislative immunity. However, they argued, his actions were not "things generally done in a session of the House (Senate) by one of its members in relation to the business before it," and that, in fact, his acts were of an "extraordinary character . . . an utter perversion of [his] powers to a criminal purpose."[33] They alleged that Eastland must have been aware of the Supreme Court decision forbidding the forced disclosure of an organization's membership and therefore, as a legislator, should not have attempted to obtain them. The district court found against Dombrowski. The subpoena for the records, although issued in an irregular fashion and without prior approval of the senator's subcommittee, did not put Eastland and Sourwine "beyond the pale of official legislative activity, at least for the purpose of the immunity doctrine," the court ruled.[34] The court refused to consider Dombrowski's allegation that Eastland and Sourwine actively had planned and participated in the raids. His lawyers appealed to the Supreme Court.

In that case, the Supreme Court, with Justice Black abstaining, Eastland won a victory of sorts. In a short opinion which some legal scholars since have described as ambiguous and a political compromise, Eastland's privilege of immunity was upheld, but Sourwine was ordered to stand trial, a suggestion that he was not privileged to carry out the acts alleged.[35] For the first time since 1880, a public official would be brought to trial by a private citizen.

On June 15, 1964, the Supreme Court agreed to hear the parallel litigation, *Dombrowski v. Pfister.* The American Civil Liberties Union filed supporting briefs. The NAACP Legal Defense Fund filed a brief, declaring, "If the files of our legal staff and our cooperating attorneys may be subjected to the same lawless invasion as is here alleged to have occurred, without relief being available in the federal courts, our activities and, indeed, the cause of civil rights will be most severely prejudiced."[36] On the streets, civil rights activists, knowing how important the case had become, celebrated the fact that "*Dombrowski* had gone up."

"The months that followed were trying ones for the defendants," Jack Peebles wrote.[37] "They lived, as all under a felony indictment must live, in a state of restlessness—neither guilty nor, in the eyes of their fellow citizens, unquestionably free from guilt." Smith and Waltzer tried to continue earning a living; Dombrowski carried on some semblance of organized activities for the SCEF. Each, however, in countless ways, felt the impact of the charges. Insurance was canceled. Their families were affected. Waltzer and his wife, who were in the process of adopting a child, were told that the final adoption must await the outcome of the case. Friends stopped speaking to them. Throughout, the LUAC held sporadic hearings, keeping a glare of publicity on Dombrowski and the SCEF. Not once, however, was he called to testify. Each hearing prompted a new wave of hate calls, abusive mail, or threats. The committee published three official reports on the SCEF. Mostly they consisted of photocopies of the SCEF's documents, evidence, and reports, which the committee contended demonstrated that both the SCLC and SNCC were "substantially under the control of the Communist Party through the influence of the Southern Conference Educational Fund and the Communists who managed it."[38]

The Supreme Court heard arguments in Dombrowski's case on January 25, 1965. Kinoy presented for the SCEF, arguing that the LUAC allegations of subversion were a smokescreen hiding the state's efforts to crush the civil rights movement. The joint committee, he said, intended to go after SCLC and SNCC if they managed cripple or crush the SCEF. Rogers, the LUAC's lawyer, was asked about this charge. He didn't deny it, adding, in fact, that some two hundred other civil rights organizations were being investigated. Louisiana's State Attorney John Jackson was unable to explain what Louisiana meant by subversion, or a subversive organization. "How can anyone know what a subversive organization is if you don't know?," one justice asked.[39]

Dombrowski heard the arguments in a dark mood, as dispairing as the one he had experienced in those moments after his Christian charity had been rebuked in Gastonia.[40] The pressures of the times and the persecution were telling on him. To some degree, the tone of the justices' questions pleased him and lifted his spirits. He hoped for the best, but would permit himself no great expectations. He tried to hide his pessimism, especially from Smith, Waltzer, Kinoy, and Kunstler.

Before his day in court, Dombrowski was hammered by a succession of tragedies. Bombs destroyed the automobile of a longtime friend, the president of the Louisiana Civil Liberties Union. The New Orleans Unitarian Church and the home of its pastor, another ally, were bombed. James Chaney, Andrew Goodman, and Michael Schwerner were killed in Neshoba County, Mississippi. The national Democratic Party betrayed the Mississippi Freedom Democratic Party in Atlantic City. Except for the three young civil rights workers, Dombrowski had had long friendships with the sufferers. The deaths and the constant political defeats were having a calamitous affect on him. Aubrey Williams was dying of cancer and then, on March 5, died quietly in his sleep. The next day, during a memorial service, Dombrowski said again, as he had said often before, "Aubrey Willis Williams was the most uncompromising leader for integration in the South."[41]

On April 26, 1965, after months of frustration, financial burden and anxiety for Dombrowski, the Supreme Court reached a decision. Justice William Brennen, writing for the five-to-two majority, found the Louisiana statutes unconstitutional and overbroad, and ruled that they were being used to harass and discourage constitutionally guaranteed activities. He forbid any further attempt to enforce the law. All the SCEF's belongings were to be returned immediately. Further, Brennen struck down the doctrine of abstention because of the "chilling effect upon the exercise of First Amendment rights" that "may derive from the fact of prosecution, unaffected by the prospects of its success or failure." Freedom of expression, he continued, "is of transcendent value to all society," and Dombrowski's allegations "suggested that a substantial loss or impairment of freedom of expression will occur if appellants must await the state court's disposition and ultimate review."[42] The decision, "immortalized the quaint names of the litigants . . . and gladdened—at least temporarily—the hearts of civil libertarians throughout the nation."[43] Lawyer Peebles, not without bias, declared it to be the SCEF's most significant contribution to the civil rights movement during the 1960s: "It boosted the morale of the civil rights workers throughout the South, and later was used as authority for other types of cases involving freedom of speech."[44]

The court's decision, and the justice's memorable phrase, gave Dombrowski great satisfaction. His brotherhood, one sadly absent, had a significant, lasting political triumph to celebrate. His controversial name, quaint or not, had a place in legal and social history, an accomplishment he had wanted and was proud of. He had bonded social justice and civil liberties.

# Epilogue:
# Striving for
# Worthwhile
# Ends

In the end, there was an air of melancholy about Dombrowski, and it clings to his life story. Few would dispute that he was on the side of democratic angels. He had a significant hand in the destruction of America's pernicious doctrine, the legal separation of races. He would not be cowed into silence. He spoke out and acted; as a result, the invaluable democratic doctrine of free speech is wider and can be protected more directly. As early in 1942, the Federal Bureau of Investigation believed that such a man deserved to be in custody if there should be a national emergency.

Dombrowski wanted history to note his life. He saved prodigiously for that purpose. He died uncertain that historians would find his story. If they ever did, he was sure they would have no trouble fixing him in the correct places. There was a specific period, a distinctive region, two or three vocations that knit together in service of labor, civil rights, and civil liberty. His accomplishments added to the currency of democracy, even if they could not easily be measured in dollars and cents. He hobnobbed with some of the rich and powerful of his time, but he knew the meek and cared how they lived and were governed. He had a flair for political drama, another attractive quality in history. For nearly four decades, his thinking influenced radical southern thought about social change.

Dombrowski's surname itself frequently was offered as evidence sufficient to prove that he engaged in foreign intrigue and probably in Communism. Such illogical, undemocratic thought framed his time and work, adding to the irony that he lent his controversial name to causes thoroughly American. He went to the war waged to make the world safe for democracy. During World War II, he preached the nation's patriotic ideology. Especially he practiced America's constitutional cornerstones—the right to equal treatment and the right to free speech. He paid membership dues to the American Legion and was chased from one of its halls. Even a superficial glance at the papers he saved, or which were saved by others to use against him, reveals a man convinced that slavery and its progeny were incompatible with a political democracy and with a Christian's ethical values. Racism was the central problem of his civilization. Still, before his death, as Dombrowski thought about what had gone on with him, de facto segregation remained entrenched in America and in fact seemed deeper and more thoroughgoing every day, no less a barrier to the good life and to liberty than on the day he first sensed the reality of racism. Jim Crow no longer was the law of the land, but it was the way of the land, spread throughout America and not just one region. In his mind, racism, accompanied with McCarthyite repression, remained America's unfinished business. Most of his adult life had been devoted to the dilemma of prejudice and tolerance. His father's chance remark unintentionally had given the boy a problem in social ethics that would consume much of his life. America's snarl of discriminatory law and prejudiced custom appeared to him as tightly gnarled at the end of his life as at the start. This fact whispered failure to him. In one sense, Coca-Cola baron Candler had sized Dombrowski up correctly: he was an entrepreneur. Failure did not sit well with Dombrowski, not when he was in school nor when he was in the streets trying to change society. Dombrowski was graced with a keen, quick mind and a determination to excel. He was a natural organizer, a first-rate administrator. His energy had few limits, even when he was ailing. Dombrowski seized opportunities and took risks; he made heresy his business. In the end, despite all that he invested in trying to set racism aside, the bottom-line reality was that brotherhood and citizenship continued to be thwarted by racial dogma.

Dombrowski was observant as a boy, a collegian, an activist, and an artist. He usually learned more from life around him than from teachers. Candler's Emory University had ignored the social context of thought, the way thinking can happen through the contradictions in ideology or the dilemmas of creed. Dombrowski would have been a round peg in Candler's square, profit-centered world. The spirit of equality and democracy had yet to grip many businessmen in Candler's day. Dombrowski was imbued with both throughout his life. He sensed this when he turned down Candler's offer. Later he was able to put words to those feelings.

Yet, over the years, Dombrowski himself was a square peg in the round, often tumbled business of radical social change. He refused to give in to separatist ideologies. He believed in the united, democratic front, a term and a strategy that he felt was broader than an electoral alliance of liberals, socialists, or Communists. The united front had to include everyone who was going in his direction. Harry F. Ward, his mentor, had demonstrated the profitability of such a strategy through the American Civil Liberties Union and the Methodist Federation for Social Action, organizations which had enduring impact on America and moral import for Methodism. Dombrowski was all business when it came to pushing such unity, first through Highlander, then through the Southern Conference for Human Welfare, and finally through the SCEF. The democratic front was his Christian Socialist tool for expanding democratic practices and defending against fascist reaction.

Had Dombrowski been on a fool's quest? His vision of a Christian, socialist world certainly had not been established. Once or twice, Dombrowski had experienced the grand life he had extolled before Elizabethton's astonished businessmen. Community was essential to his vision. At Emory, Dombrowski had enjoyed a brotherhood that was deep, faithful, and immature. Through this experience, Dombrowski came to suspect that good will was insufficient to eradicate social evils. As he got older, the irony that his all-white, all-male evangelical club had been called the Congo Group did not elude him. Elizabethton taught him that organized power, rather than piety, was the source of substantial economic change. Gastonia taught him to replace charity with solidarity.

Dombrowski had caught glimpses of what he was looking for through friendships with individuals at Union Theological Seminary, and with Ward, his influential teacher. He went to the Soviet Union before the Stalinist pogroms were launched and before the stultifying bureaucracies were fully in place. He saw and heard—from its beneficiaries—how socialism could be. This whet his appetite. In Grundy County, he found an effective, radical community, including contentment and a sense of place.

Friendship could and did evolve through and from social struggle. Dombrowski, Hawes, and Horton carved out a new role for education in a democracy at Highlander. The three of them collaborated to conceptualize an approach to labor education which remains unique to this day. They demonstrated modestly—for their means were modest—that workers could be trusted to find solutions to their own problems. Trusted with ideas and information, workers shaped history, even when confronted by forces dead set against them. Workers, the three believed, were a wellspring for history. The three of them used the powerful force of education to add to labor's ability to counter exploitation. Emory and schools like it ignored this approach to learning. Labor colleges, as freestanding places like Highlander have been called, came and, sometimes because of government repression, went. Dombrowski, Hawes, and Horton, their eventual differences aside, built Highlander to last. Dombrowski made a huge personal investment in Highlander. In the end, he forfeited his share in the eventual fame of that unique venture.

Dombrowski profited from Highlander nevertheless. He got over trying to teach as he had been taught. He learned how to tie knowledge with social action, argumentation with the philosophic concepts of democracy. He balanced a teacher's responsibility to impart knowledge with the learner's capacity to recover what was known already. Dombrowski told progressive educators that teaching itself was an ideological act, particularly if the act of teaching involved hard-pressed, penniless adults. The learner, not the teacher, was at the core of education. Thus, by Dombrowski's reasoning, teachers and schools could fail; students could not.

These lessons internalized, Dombrowski easily conceived the Southern Conference for Human Welfare as a cultural forum through which southerners of both races and all persuasions discussed and negotiated progressive and just social goals, along with how to achieve them through discourse, reason, or the give and take of politics. The South's collective potential, he believed, could be recognized and perhaps achieved through the exercise of organized social power and regional self-determination. To him, the SCHW was more than a regional group doing Roosevelt's bidding. His job, and the opportunity presented by the interracial SCHW, he believed, was to develop a singularly southern solution to segregation, one emerging out of the South's chaos and conflicts.

When he lost the fight for control of the SCHW's affairs, Dombrowski retreated at first, as he had after the stinging rebuke in Gastonia. His pride was wounded, as much by the rebuke as by his failure to maintain control of his business affairs. Uncharacteristically for a man of his time, Dombrowski took a woman's political advice. Lucy Randolph Mason influenced the South's history through Dombrowski, no less than through her own remarkable work. The Southern Conference Educational Fund was kindled from her widsom in his moment of despair. He listened carefully to everyone, but acted only on what made moral sense.

The SCEF was a public-relations business run by Dombrowski in part-
nership with a handful of trusted advocates. Each had a keen sense of the
South and a long history of service, as well as a knack for political words.
These friends also appreciated social unity; they shared assumptions even
if they did not always agree on the particulars concerning how to organize
an economy. They welcomed wholesome political struggle. The move to
New Orleans was Dombrowski's last relocation. He stayed put after that.
Taking a cue from successful business propagandists, Dombrowski created
a low-budget public-relations firm aimed at winning a market share of public opinion for an alternative to Jim Crow. Propaganda of the deed, often
irrational and passionate, had been a staple of radicalism since the 1800s.
Dombrowski became a propagandist of the rational and democratic deed.
In New Orleans, his discovery of the history of "half and half" solidarity
on the city's docks reinvigorated his determination. Dockhands of both
races had accomplished in New Orleans what Dombrowski believed was
possible throughout the South. The "ice-breaker" half-and-half organization he brought to life attracted and held onto, with its "frontier program,"
a handful of African-American and white visionaries who saw the crucial
link between civil rights and civil liberties. Dockhands had exemplified
how good society could be.

The SCEF's message was simple: many southerners believed that segregation was morally wrong, undemocratic, a costly burden, and certainly
unconstitutional. The SCEF demonstrated again and again (1) that whites
and African Americans—even if but a handful—would defy segregation,
and (2) that they could live and work in harmony. Interracial action was the
medium. Therefore, the freedom to speak, to write, to publish, and to organize around what was said, written, or printed took on powerful significance for Dombrowski. The First Amendment was his tool of first resort.

The confusions born of race eventually fatally wounded the SCEF and
Dombrowski. The national NAACP, which he befriended when other
whites would not, turned its back on the SCEF, refusing the heretical southerners membership in the effective lobbying coalition it assembled. In New
Orleans, the NAACP refused to accept Dombrowski's membership dues.
He was suspect, especially after Dr. Benjamin Mays and Mary McLeod
Bethune resigned from the SCEF. The false issue of Communism made any
alliance with him nearly impossible. The freedom of association, so essential to democracy, never fully recovered from McCarthyism's assault.

The issue of racial separatism tore into the SCEF with an intensity which at times exceeded the force of the Red-baiting. Even his trusted, tested successors, Carl and Anne Braden, were unable to keep the SCEF together. Bob Zellner, who in Dombrowski's mind symbolized the SCEF's future, and other youthful activists both white and African American, left the SCEF, arguing that whites had to organize whites, and African Americans had to organize African Americans.

Was disappointment always to be the fate of anyone who believed in the Kingdom of God? Dombrowski pondered that question long after the vitriolic internal struggle ended. He was less certain about the conclusion he'd reached years earlier at Union: "Does the striving after a high-flung ideal become a worthwhile end in itself?" Yes, but. Late in life, he needed to believe that some advance had issued from that striving.

Dombrowski sensed that his father had sparked the formation of his heresy at a moment when, as a boy, he was puzzling how to live a modern, complex life by an ancient, simple rule, "Do unto others as you would have them do unto you." Like his father, his friend the Tampa banker, certainly without intent, had exposed the teenager to a dilemma in economic values which forever unfitted him for slots in a conventional business. Eventually, his list of "thou shalts" and "thou shalt nots"—the admonitions of morality—was a long one, deriving more from his Methodism and Immanuel Kant than from Karl Marx. Kant was one of many philosophers who preoccupied Dombrowski on his protracted, peripatetic evolution into adulthood. The philosopher offered an exacting version of the biblical injunction: Treat everyone, yourself included, as an end; never treat anyone merely as a means. Marx offered a way of explaining the class nature of Dombrowski's society. "Do-goodism" did little to address organized exploitation and poverty which derived from a nation's social policy and cultural practices.

Dombrowski made a name for himself as a political agitator and eventually made legal history. He wanted it known that his notoriety was not an accident. He was not comfortable with the word *radical* or the concept it embodied. He believed that what he did was the responsibility of citizenship. But he feared that history's tellers, the historians, would not care that he tried to use the "ought to" of ethics to make up his mind, rather than the easier dictums of orthodox Socialism. He wanted to be known as a heretic. Even as a teenager, Dombrowski seems to have been guided by his notion of what ought to be, and ought to be done, regardless of what others thought, wished, or would do themselves. The Tampa banker was the first of many to laugh at his innocence. This was the less evident Dombrowski, the one beneath the public record. Much of the time, he managed to live by that tough standard, but not often enough, at least in his own eyes. He celebrated quietly when he made the right decision and brooded alone for long periods when he compromised, as he occasionally did. Not many knew about the compromises; he was regarded as dogmatic if not blindly stubborn. He paid a price for holding fast to his vision.

Dombrowski's search for the beloved community was full of paradoxes. He was quite happy to sacrifice his personal freedom to build trust, mutual respect, collaboration, and interracial organizations. He shied away from narrow conformity. Dombrowski thrived on the solitude of his cabin. In this and other respects, he was a loner. He could be alone in a crowd and often seemed to demand anonymity. He did not need the celebrity which came with his unorthodoxy.

Most if not all of his friends were persons he knew politically. Some knew Dombrowski the efficient manager or Dombrowski the political agitator with the unerring strategic sense. Others knew that Dombrowski would spurn an organization's traditional political power but accept considerable economic responsibility for balancing the organization's books. Still others knew Dombrowski as a propagandist against Jim Crow or as an artist. Dombrowski screened off large parts of his life, including his relationship with Ellen Krida. There were limits to the personal freedom he was willing to sacrifice for the Kingdom of God. His was the dilemma of individualism searching for democratic community.

Still, he appreciated and wanted the companionship of family, as he had since childhood. He knew his mother only from the accounts of his sisters, his father, or other relatives, and by a photograph or two. There were bittersweet memories of his father. His life and beliefs kept him a good distance from his sisters, even when the siblings made a reunion in their last years. He wanted a family. Ellen loved him and shared his life as no other person, but when he needed her companionship most—at Highlander, in Nashville at the height of the Red-baiting there, and again in New Orleans—she was the one who asked for *his* supportive embrace. She did not care to know much about his life's work, and what she knew made her anxious. Her health declined visibly after the police raid. She seldom ventured out of the house, spurning even their tree-shaded courtyard. Until the spring of 1972, Dombrowski devoted hours every day to caring for Ellen. She died on April 26, 1972. As he had for years, in good times or bad, Dombrowski wrote to Ethel Clyde, his long-distance companion:

> My sweet Ellen passed away last night. She went into a coma not long after entering the hospital and never regained consciousness, so she was not suffering from any pain. She just slowly grew weaker and gradually ceased to breathe. It was a quiet and gentle ending to an equally gentle spirit. . . . her death is a hard blow and leaves me with a sad and empty feeling. The house seems strangely quiet, although Ellen certainly was anything but noisy.[1]

Many of Dombrowski's surviving political friends came together on Wednesday, October 21, 1976. Dombrowski, Anne Braden, and Virginia Durr were honored by the American Civil Liberties Foundation of Louisiana at a benefit showing of Woody Allen's *The Front*, a film depicting the impact of McCarthy era blacklists on an entertainer's life and career. The *New Orleans States-Item*, which had pilloried Dombrowski over the years, devoted most of a page to an admiring journalistic portrait of "Dombrowski, civil rights pioneer."[2] Cedric Belfrage, who had been punished for his political views during the 1950s, chanced to be in New Orleans that day. He was going back to Cuernavaca, Mexico, where he had lived in exile since 1955. Senator McCarthy, seizing upon Belfrage's British citizenship and political views, had hounded the writer from America. Wryly, Belfrage inscribed a copy of his eleventh book, *The American Inquisition, 1945– 1960:* "For Jim Dombrowski with deep respect and felicitations on his rehabilitation by polite society."

Being remembered as *the* Dombrowski of *Dombrowski v. Pfister* was particularly pleasing. If America's worsening racism whispered failure, the famous lawsuit suggested success. He was overjoyed every time he learned that the case had been cited in defense of some heresy. His challenge to a constraining legal doctrine was the embodiment of Dombrowski's lifework, an obstinate effort to link democratic civil rights, in the broadest sense, with ever-expanding civil liberties.

A photograph accompanied the *States-Item* feature. It was one of the few ever published of Dombrowski when he was not on the cusp of conflict. He has a patriarchal appearance; a full beard is flecked with grey. He is leaning against a mantle. Dombrowski might have been a retired businessman posing to promote his post-career successes. He had been rehabilitated, as

Dombrowski at last, New Orleans, 1982. Photo courtesy of Jack Peebles, Esq.

Belfrage said. After the U.S. Supreme Court ruling, the State of Louisiana publicly apologized to Dombrowski and the SCEF for the raids, the arrests, and the allegations that they had operated a Communist front.[3] It had been years since detectives in plainclothes followed him about the French Quarter.

Dombrowski left the day-to-day responsibilities of the SCEF in December 1965, forced to by the arthritis which had impaired him for twenty years. Eventually, surgeons replaced both knees and hips with plastic joints. When he quit the daily routine, he worried more about the facts suggesting that his business had accumulated few social assets. The Kingdom of God seemed light years away. That goal seemed discouragingly distant especially during the clash within the SCEF over racial unity. Like many retired businessmen, Dombrowski worried about lost opportunities. He also continued to ponder dilemmas he had never come to terms with— conflict and violence, for instance. He never made up his mind—finally, at least—about the problem of violence. He went into World War I an innocent, never having given much thought to individual or state-sponsored violence. When World War II came, Dombrowski was hardly the politically innocent. He wanted to go to that war; it was a just war against fascism. Ironically, it seems that his opposition to racial fascism in America kept him out of war. He was on crutches when the Vietnam War boiled slowly into American life. That was a war Dombrowski opposed. He had come to suspect that violence would not, and could not, achieve the Kingdom of God; but he remained unprepared to accept the argument that violence always should be set aside. Frederick Douglass' aphorism made sense to him much of the time.

He thought a lot about the early days of Christian Socialism in America, and especially about Gladden's argument that workers must own the means of production directly, not through the state, if democracy were to endure. Examples of worker-owned enterprises were coming into existence, and they set Dombrowski's entrepreneurial imagination to work. How much value could he have added to the Kingdom of God with that conceptual tool?

Dombrowski nurtured his artistic gifts when he retired. The unfinished work of his life and those ethical puzzles carried over into his art. He poured energy into oils and watercolors that reflected his experiences: a child with outstretched arms offering a ball to anyone who would play with him; the Grundy County chairmaker who led the bugwood strike; a homage to the dead of the tragic Republic Steel strike; a Puerto Rican mother and her children amid a thorny, harsh landscape. Art became another way to search for the Kingdom of God. By spring 1976, his work had attracted sufficient critical notice and was broad enough in range so that he was invited to hang a one-man exhibit at the Earl K. Long Library on the campus of the University of New Orleans. Starting in 1973, on the second Sunday of each December and continuing until he went into a nursing home, Dombrowski invited friends to what he called an art distribution. His art was not for sale. That was the way of art in capitalism. He devised a Christian Socialist's way to share his art. Each person drew a number which determined the sequence in which they selected from among nearly a hundred of his oils, watercolors, sketches, or pen-and-ink drawings. They could keep the work for a year, then return it in time for the next art distribution. No-one owned a Dombrowski.

Dombrowski would not use the word *retirement* and did not like to hear it used to describe his status after 1965. He was too busy to be retired. Hardly a week passed without some activist, writer, scholar, or friend knocking at the door of 715 Gov. Nicholls Street. Besides dedicating two or three hours daily to his art, he produced petitions, raised funds for his favorite causes, and attended rallies in New Orleans for civil rights workers, antiwar protestors, or *causes celebres* such as the Wilmington 10, the J.P. Stevens boycott, or Gary Tyler. He would not let go and spent hours trying to help the Bradens rebuild the shattered SCEF. He suffered founder's syndrome, a malady common to the entrepreneurial spirit.

Eventually Dombrowski lost his personal freedom in a New Orleans nursing home. His spirit remained free, but his body was imprisoned, albeit by caring people who provided for his every immediate need. It was a dialectic he had not considered much until his own near-total confinement. He considered suicide, wondering how long he would last if he diminished the food he ate and the water he drank. He could not escape the caregivers and their necessary routine; they became the enemies of his freedom. The independence he had enjoyed since boyhood was gone. His caregivers were impressed by the visitors who came to see Dombrowski, a rainbow spectrum of rich and poor who often unknowingly stayed beyond his endurance. He resented the hint that he was an honored relic.

Dombrowski died on May 2, 1983.[4] He was eighty-six years old. At times, even to his dearest friends, Dombrowski's Christian faith and Socialist values made him a conundrum. He sensed those moments when he tumbled into being the moral authoritarian and regretted them. He knew the social origins of his values; their deep-rooted psychological sources remained a mystery to Dombrowski and made Dombrowski a mystery to some. Those values were his core, they made him a heretic. He died certain that he had steadfastly promoted the Kingdom of God with a businesslike resolve. He was uncertain how, or if, society had profited from his labors.

# Appendix A:
# Chronology
## Life of James A. Dombrowski

| | |
|---|---|
| 1897 | Born Tampa, Florida, January 17. |
| 1902 | Mother dies. |
| 1912 | Father dies. |
| 1915 | Graduates from Hillsborough High School, Tampa. |
| 1917 | Enrolls in Bowman School of Watchmaking and Engraving, Lancaster, Penn. |
| 1917 | Enlists in U.S. Aero Service. |
| 1919 | Discharged from U.S. Aero Service. |
| 1922 | Founds Bayshore Methodist Church, Tampa. |
| 1923 | Graduates from Emory University, *cum laude*. |
| 1923 | Appointed first secretary, Emory Alumni Association, and first editor, *Emory Alumnus*. |
| 1926 | Enrolls in University of California, Berkeley, and is named assistant pastor, Epworth Methodist Church, Berkeley. |
| 1928 | Enrolls in Harvard University. |
| 1929 | Enrolls in Columbia University and Union Theological Seminary. |
| 1929 | Arrested at Elizabethton, Tenn. |
| 1930 | Named Fellow, National Council on Religion in Higher Education. |
| 1931 | Awarded Bachelor of Divinity degree, Union Theological Seminary, *magna cum laude*. |
| 1931 | Named teaching assistant to Dr. Harry F. Ward, Union Theological Seminary. |
| 1933 | Joins staff of Highlander Folk School. |
| 1933 | Awarded Doctor of Philosophy degree, Columbia University. |
| 1936 | Doctoral dissertation published: *The Early Days of Christian Socialism in America*. |
| 1942 | Named executive director, Southern Conference for Human Welfare. |
| 1942 | Marries Ellen Krida, December 5. |

| | |
|---|---|
| 1946 | Founds Southern Conference Education Fund; named first executive director and editor of *The Southern Patriot*. |
| 1948 | Subpoenaed to testify before grand jury, Nashville, Tenn. |
| 1948 | Arrested Birmingham, Ala., for violating Jim Crow segregation law during the Southern Negro Youth Congress. |
| 1954 | Subpoenaed to testify before U.S. Senate Internal Security Subcommittee, New Orleans, La. |
| 1963 | Arrested in New Orleans and charged with subversion. |
| 1963 | *Dombrowski v. Pfister* argued before U.S. Supreme Court. Decision reached in 1965 establishes doctrine of "chilling effect." |
| 1964 | Receives Tom Paine Award, National Emergency Civil Liberties Committee. |
| 1966 | Retires from Southern Conference Education Fund. |
| 1969 | Enrolls in John McCrady Art School, New Orleans. |
| 1971 | Helps found Southern Organizing Committee for Social and Economic Justice. |
| 1972 | Ellen Krida Dombrowski dies, April 26. |
| 1975 | Exhibits oil and watercolor paintings, Earl K. Long Library, University of New Orleans. |
| 1983 | Dies, May 2, New Orleans. |

# Appendix B: From a Mill-Town Jail[1] by James A. Dombrowski

Sherwood Anderson's "Dark Laughter," two pipes, plenty of tobacco—and I can forget that I am lodged in the city jail at Elizabethton, Tennessee—that is, if I turn my back on the evil-looking and foul-smelling bedding, and can generate enough smoke to overcome the odors that lurk in the walls streaked with tobacco juice.

I am in jail as the result of a talk I made last night before a "law and order" meeting at the Chamber of Commerce.

Seated on the edge of the prison bunk, I have plenty of time to think. My education has moved rapidly since I left New York five days ago. The lessons of the past twenty-four hours have been most confusing, and I am almost glad to be in jail, because of the quiet opportunity it affords to think about this new turn in my education.

In the jail, at least, there are few interruptions. In a near-by cell a young chap is spelling out, word for word, a letter from his wife: "If—you—had—listened—to—me—you—would—not—be—in—jail—you—sure—done—me—wrong—I—ain't—coming—back—to—you—till—you—quit—drinking. . . . "

I had a vision of the world tomorrow, when men would seriously apply the ethics of Jesus to a rational ordering of society, and to industry in particular, a vision of the kingdom of God on earth. There had been the hope that the southland, known for its gentler ways of living and now entering upon the initial stages of a great industrial development, would be a pioneer in this spiritualizing of industry.

With the desire to learn at first-hand how my native southland was handling the situation, I had started from New York five days before, using my summer vacation

[1]Reprinted from *The New Republic,* 2 October 1929, pp. 171–72.

to make a tour of a few of the southern mill villages. My lessons thus far prompted only a depressed feeling and a dark picture of the future.

Yesterday in the Elizabethton daily paper there were the usual society notices, but not one word about the strike involving five thousand workers—a third of the population—in a life-and-death struggle. On the front page, however, was the announcement of an open meeting, at the Chamber of Commerce, to organize a league for the better enforcement of the law.

This "law and order" meeting, with its consequences, was to provide the most difficult lesson, up to that time, in my entire career as a student. At eight o'clock, about one hundred business and professional men had gathered in the Chamber of Commerce rooms. There were a few desultory remarks about the enforcement of prohibition and a higher standard of public morals.

It was soon evident, however, that the real business of the evening was, "What can we do with these agitators?" In all of the speeches, which lasted until midnight, there was little or no humor. Men spoke with tense voices. But applause and laughter greeted a doctor when he said, "Now, at last, we have got you preachers where we can use you." Turning to one of the ministers present, he asked, "Did they send machine-guns with missionaries to China?" Just what bearing on the situation this information had was never made plain by the speaker. In tones that quivered with emotion a Sunday School superintendent gave vent to his feelings. He used as an illustration an episode in north Georgia where, he said, a man was found one morning put to death. Across his breast were the words, "in statu quo." This was interpreted as meaning, "I'm in a hell of a fix." A hotel man said that the occasion was one for prayer. This sounded like good advice to a theological student, but the speaker was in disrepute with the audience, for he was shouted down before he could conclude his remarks. He was answered by the next speaker, a Presbyterian minister, and a handsome man, with a well placed voice which one expected to hear give approval to the hotel man's advice, to advocate peace, moderation, to say, "Come, let us reason together." But he said, "The time for prayer is past; when the devil is in your midst, fire upon him." It is unbelievable that he intended his words to strike home as they did, but certainly they were of no avail in stemming the tide of emotion that dominated the meeting. From eight until midnight, these impassioned speeches continued.

It was easy to sympathize with these businessmen. Three months before, their city had been a thriving, prosperous community. The establishing of two huge rayon mills had been the impetus for boom times. Their city had been selected by President Hoover as the one southern city in which to make a campaign speech. The future was golden—until the strike came. Three months of bitter hurling of invectives on both sides, defiant girls walking the streets, dynamiting of water mains, business depression for all, ruin for some. One could pardon them for the intense emotion with which they spoke. But during the evening not one word was said about the injustice of women working ten hours a day for $8.90 a week, about the wage slavery from which the workers were revolting. Which were these men more concerned about: their own losses, or the life-and-death struggle of these five thousand workers?

At this point I asked for the floor. I explained my presence as a student interested in the application of the ethics of Jesus to industry. I spoke of the emphasis, in the teachings of the Prince of Peace, on the sacredness of personalities. Applied to this situation, it meant that human values must be considered above all others. It was a calm, dispassionate statement, spoken with a smile. My training as a student had not prepared me for its effect. I was cross-examined until my life history had been told, without allaying their suspicions. That a student should make a trip at his own expense from New York to Tennessee merely in the interest of his education was incomprehensible to men for whom profit is the only legitimate incentive for the expenditure of time and effort. They must have taken me for a spy, a Red, perhaps a "dangerous agitator." At any rate, following adjournment, I was threatened with personal violence.

The next day, having decided that I had received all of the lessons that Elizabethton offered for the advancement of my education, I started on the road to Asheville. About three miles from town, as I was riding beside a friendly farmer, a party of "law and order" citizens, filling several automobiles, swooped down upon me and carried me off to jail. Looking back at that moment, I cannot suppress a smile, as I remember how large the farmer's eyes were when they laid hold of his passenger's arm and said, "Young man, consider yourself under arrest." No doubt that farmer is spoiled forever as a prospective host of hitch-hikers.

That this gang of men, come to arrest the dangerous student, had no warrant, were outside the city limits, could not show a badge of authority, were unable to tell me with what I was charged, and refused me permission to call a lawyer or to communicate with anyone else for several hours, did not worry these members of the league to encourage "better observance of law."

Later in the day a warrant was read me, charging me with "aiding and abetting in the murder of the chief of police of Gastonia." It was of no consequence that the only time I had been in Gastonia had been four years before.

I hold no ill-will against the men who have been the cause of my arrest. In fact, I feel indebted to them for this valuable part of my education. But, frankly, as I smoke my pipe, seated on the edge of my iron bunk, I am depressed and confused. Before me appears a vision of those young workers with toothpick arms and underfed bodies; of that young father with whom I talked, eating out his heart for a life that seems closed to mill workers forever, a life of books, music, conversation, culture; I hear voices speaking with fierce passion; I see a princely figure of a carpenter blessing his fellow workers with outstretched hand, and saying, "I am come that ye might have life, and that more abundantly."

Yes, I need more time to think of these things. I am grateful that the young fellow in the neighboring cell has finished reading his wife's letter. At least, within the jail, there is peace and quiet.

JAMES A. DOMBROWSKI.

# Notes

## Abbreviations

| | |
|---|---|
| LUAC | Louisiana Joint Legislative Committee on Un-American Activities |
| SCEF | Southern Conference Education Fund |
| SCHW | Southern Conference for Human Welfare |
| SCHWA | Southern Conference for Human Welfare Archives, Hollis Burke Frissell Library, Tuskegee Institute, Tuskegee, Alabama |
| SHC | Southern Historical Collection, University of North Carolina, Chapel Hill, North Carolina |
| SHSW | State Historical Society of Wisconsin, 816 State Street, Madison, Wisconsin |
| USGPO | United States Government Printing Office, Washington, D.C. |

## Introduction

1. Bob Hall, "Georgia Methodism and Coca-Cola" (Atlanta, Ga: Institute for Southern Studies, 1972), n.p. This pamphlet was prepared for the Youth/Young Adult Caucus, United Methodist Church General Convention, Atlanta, 1972. See also Bob Hall, "Journey to the White House: The Story of Coca-Cola," *Southern Exposure* 5, no. 1 (Spring 1977):43–47; Mark K. Bauman, *Warren Akin Candler: The Conservative As Idealist* (New York: Scarecrow, 1981); and Robert F. Wearmouth, *Methodistism and the Working-Class Movements of England, 1800–1850* (London: Epworth Press, 1937).

2. Interview with Hunter Bell, 21 May 1977.

3. Ibid.

## Chapter 1

1. Most biographical material contained herein has been derived from (1) interviews with James A. Dombrowski, carried out by Frank T. Adams on 1–5 May 1976, 25–31 Oct. 1978, 6–9 Dec. 1979, and 5–6 Dec. 1982, all in New Orleans, La; (2) interviews with Dombrowski and his sister, Rose Dombrowsky Stubbs, carried out by Frank T. Adams on 27–30 Dec. 1976, in Tampa, Fla.; and (3) letters from Dombrowski and Stubbs to Frank T. Adams. Tape recordings of the interviews are available at SHSC. These letters are in the collection of Frank T. Adams.

Dombrowski made other personal letters available to Frank T. Adams; these are in Dombrowski Papers being catalogued at SHSW. Still other Dombrowski papers, uncatalogued, form part of SCHWA.

2. Stetson Kennedy, *Palmetto Country* (New York: Duell, Sloan and Pearce, 1942), 31.

3. Karl H. Grismer, *Tampa: A History of the City of Tampa and the Tampa Bay Region of Florida* (St. Petersburg, Fla.: St. Petersburg Printing Co., 1950), 212.

4. Kennedy, *Palmetto Country*, 326.

5. Interview with Dombrowski and Stubbs.

6. Grismer, *Tampa*, 207.

7. Interview with Dombrowski and Stubbs.

8. Ibid.

9. Interview with Dombrowski, 1–5 May 1976.

10. Ibid.

11. Through one prism, Dombrowski's life can be seen as an example of what C. Wright Mills called the sociological imagination, a term explained in his book by the same title, *The Sociological Imagination* (New York: Oxford Univ. Press, 1959). As a child, Dombrowski had a pragmatic intellectual bent. His instinctive artistic inclination and his eventual questioning of the nation's prevailing social and ethnic values also appeared early in his life. When historian Jane Becker of Boston University read this manuscript, she was struck by the congruence of Mills' argument and Dombrowski's life.

12. Ibid.

13. Ibid.

14. Ibid.

15. Interview with Dombrowski and Stubbs.

16. Ibid.

17. Interview with Dombrowski, 1–5 May 1976.

18. *The 1915 Hillsborean*, n.p.

19. Ibid.

20. Interview with Dombrowski, 1–5 May 1976.

21. Woodrow Wilson, quoted in Samuel Eliot Morrison, *The Oxford History of the American People* (New York: Oxford Univ. Press, 1965), 859.

22. Interview with Dombrowski, 1–5 May 1976.

23. Ibid.

24. Ibid.

## Chapter 2

1. Interview with G. Raymond Mitchell, 25 Oct. 1976.

2. Interview with W. Eldridge Freeborn, 25 Oct. 1976.

3. John Knox to Frank T. Adams, 6 July 1976.

4. Interview with Dombrowski, 25–31 Oct. 1978. See also Beth Dawkins Bassett, "Love Without Boundaries," *Emory Alumnus* 60, no. 4 (1984):19–25.

5. George A. Morgan to Frank T. Adams, 26 July 1976.

6. Interview with Dombrowski, 25–31 Oct. 1978.

7. Interview with Freeborn, 25 Oct. 1976.

8. Bassett, "Love," 26.

9. Interview with Dombrowski, 25–31 Oct. 1978. See also John O. Fish, "Southern Methodism and Accommodation of the Negro, 1902–1915," *Journal of Negro History* 55, no. 3 (1970):200–214.

10. Interview with Dombrowski, 25–31 Oct. 1978.

11. Henry W. Blackburn to Frank T. Adams, 22 July 1976.

12. Ernest Cadman Colwell, "Adam and the Sun" (Deland, Fla.: N.p., n.d.), 10 in Frank T. Adams Collection. See also Dr. Louise Lake, "History of Hyde Park methodist Church, Tampa, Florida, 1899–1974." (N.p., n.d.), 13.

13. Ibid.

14. Blackburn to Adams, 22 July 1976.

15. Interview with Dombrowski, 25–31 Oct. 1978.

16. John Knox to Adams, 6 July 1976.

17. David Caute, *The Great Fear: The Anti-Communist Purge Under Truman and Eisenhower* (New York: Simon and Schuster, 1978), 20. Caute's work is free of rhetorical cant. He sets anticommunism in a longer historical span, demonstrating who benefits, and how, through attacks on advocates of civil liberties and democratic rights. See also Irving Howe and Lewis Coser, *The American Communist Party: A Critical History* (New York: Praeger, 1962), 50.

18. Interview with William H. Wilkerson, 25 Oct. 1976.

19. Interview with Eva Knox Evans Witte, 12 Feb. 1978. The sister of John Knox, Eva married Mercer Evans.

20. Interview with Dombrowski, 25–31 Oct. 1978.

21. Ibid.

22. U.S., Executive Branch, National Emergency Council, *Report on the Economic Conditions of the South* (Washington, D.C.: USGPO, 1938). See also George B. Tindall, *The Emergence of the New South, 1913–1945* (Baton Rouge: Louisiana State Univ. Press, 1967), 627. Morton Sosna, *In Search of the Silent South* (New York: Columbia Univ. Press, 1977), esp. 88–104.

23. Interview with Dombrowski, 26–31 Oct. 1978.

24. John Knox to Adams, 26 July 1976.

25. W.E. Freeborn to Adams, 11 July 1976.

26. Interview with G. Raymond Mitchell, 25 Oct. 1976.

27. Bassett, "Love," 8.

28. Ibid., 24.

29. Ibid., 16.

30. Ibid., 24.

31. Interview with Dombrowski, 25–31 Oct. 1978.

## Chapter 3

1. *Atlanta Journal,* 12 June 1929.

2. Interview with Hunter Bell, 21 May 1977. Bell, while remaining upset with Dombrowski, helped me understand the disappointment felt by many of Dombrowski's Emory classmates. Dombrowski, he believed, "threw away" prospects for a brilliant business career.

3. *Atlanta Journal,* 12 June 1929.

4. Interview with Witte, 12 Feb. 1978.

5. *Tampa Times,* 13 June 1929.

6. Interview with Dombrowski and Stubbs.

7. James Anderson Dombrowski, "From a Mill-Town Jail," *New Republic* 60, no. 774 (2 Oct. 1929):171. See also Tom Tippett, *When Southern Labor Stirs* (New York: Jonathan Cape and Harrison Smith, 1931).

8. Eugene P. Link, "A Latter-Day Christian Rebel: Harry F. Ward," *Mid-America: An Historical Review* 56, no. 4 (1974):221. I am indebted to Link for this sketch of Ward. His biography, *Labor-Religion Prophet: The Times and Life of Harry F. Ward* (Boulder, Colo.: Westview Press, 1984), along with the recollections of Dombrowski, Myles Horton, J. King Gordon, and Eva Knox Evans Witte, made this profile of Ward possible.

9. Link, "Latter-Day Christian Rebel," 222. Link founded the Methodist Federation for Social Action in 1907, and it remained an active voice for Christian Socialism within Methodism well into the 1970s. See George D. McClain, "Pioneering Social Gospel Radicalism: An Overview of the History of the Methodist Federation for Social Action," *Radical Religion* 5, no. 1 (1989):10–20.

10. Interview with Dombrowski, 25–31 Oct. 1978.

11. Harvard University Archives to Frank T. Adams, n.d.

12. George A. Morgan to Frank T. Adams, 11 July 1976.

13. W. Aiken Smart to Henry Sloan Coffin, 8 Feb. 1929, Dombrowski Papers.

14. Dombrowski, "From a Mill-Town Jail," 172.

15. Ibid.

16. Ibid.

17. Ibid.

18. Mrs. Raymond R. Paty to Frank T. Adams, 12 Sept. 1976.

19. Dombrowski, "From a Mill-Town Jail," 173.

20. Hall, "Georgia Methodism," n.p.

21. Liston Pope, *Millhands and Preachers: A Study of Gastonia* (New Haven, Conn.: Yale Univ. Press, 1942), 29.

22. Ibid.

23. Fred E. Beal, *Proletarian Journey: A Fugitive from Two Worlds* (New York: Hillman-Curl, 1937), 123–24.

24. Ibid., 129.

25. *Charlotte Observer,* 8 June 1929.

26. Dombrowski, "Gastonia Notes," 18 June, 1929, Dombrowski Papers.

27. Interview with Dombrowski, 25–31 Oct. 1978.

28. Ibid. As has been suggested above, Mills provides one analytical framework in which to understand Dombrowski's life and career. See Mills, *Sociological Imagination.* Also see Peter Clecak, *Radical Paradoxes: Dilemmas of the American Left, 1945–1970* (New York: Harper and Row, 1973).

29. Interview with Dombrowski, 25–31 Oct. 1978.

30. Ibid.

31. Deuteronomy, xv:4.

32. Leviticus, xxv:35–37.

33. Hall, "Georgia Methodism," n.p.

34. Fish, "Southern Methodism and the Negro," 213.

35. Ibid.

36. Hall, "Georgia Methodism," n.p.

37. Link, "Latter-Day Christian Rebel," 222.

38. Interview with Dombrowski, 25–31 Oct. 1978.

39. Hall, "Georgia Methodism," n.p.

40. Interview with Dombrowski, 25–31 Oct. 1978.

41. Link, *Labor-Religion Prophet.* This full-length treatment of Ward's life leaves few aspects of his life and thought untouched, including contradictions. A singular resource which reflects how and through whom Dombrowski matured intellectually.

42. Ibid., 244–49.

43. Interview with J. King Gordon, 8 Feb. 1978.

44. Ibid.

45. Allen Keedy to Frank T. Adams, 10 Aug. 1976.

46. Ibid.

47. Beal, *Proletarian Journey,* 258.

48. Ibid., 193. See also Bill C. Malone, "Protest Music," in *Encyclopedia of Southern Culture,* edited by Charles Reagan Wilson and William Ferris (Chapel Hill: Univ. of North Carolina Press, 1989), 1023.

49. Mercer Evans to Dombrowski, 26 Oct. 1929, Dombrowski Papers.

50. Interview with Dombrowski, 25–31 Oct. 1978.

51. Frank Scarlett to Frank T. Adams, 24 Mar. 1978.
52. Ibid.
53. Interview with Dombrowski, 25–31 Oct. 1978.
54. John C. Bennett to Frank T. Adams, 17 Apr. 1977.
55. John C. Cort, *Christian Socialism* (Maryknoll, N.Y.: Orbis Books, 1988). Cort makes no mention of Ward's significant part in this history.
56. Interview with Myles Horton, 22 Apr. 1977.

## Chapter 4

1. Link, *Labor-Religion Prophet,* 137.
2. Harry F. Ward, "The Russian Question," *Social Service Bulletin,* Methodist Federation for Social Service, Jan.–Feb. 1919, 4.
3. Harry F. Ward, "A Statement by Prof. Harry F. Ward," *Christian Advocate* 94, no. 14 (1919):434.
4. Link, *Labor-Religion Prophet,* 137.
5. Ibid.
6. Ibid., 138.
7. Sherwood Eddy to Dombrowski, 25 Jan. 1931, Dombrowski Papers.
8. Interview with Witte, 12 Feb. 1978.
9. Interview with Dombrowski, 25–31 Oct. 1978. See also Louis Crompton, ed., *The Road to Equality: Ten Unpublished Lectures and Essays by Bernard Shaw* (Boston: Beacon, 1971), xxix.
10. Interview with Witte, 12 Feb. 1978.
11. Dombrowski, "The Education of a Southerner," unpublished ms., 1942, p. 4, Dombrowski Papers. Dombrowski's religious values at this time were also influenced by R.B.Y. Scott, author of *Towards the Christian Revolution* (London: Victor Gollancz, 1937). J. King Gordon authored one chapter in Scott's book. One quotation from an essay by John Line in that book esp. bears on Dombrowski's life: "Religious Radicalism will offer its own version of the occasions for repentance. It will lay on men their responsibility for the acts of a society of which they are a part, and it will bid them repent of all acts and conditions by which society sins against any of its members. The fruit of repentance will be the will to transform these conditions" (62).
12. Dombrowski was slow to be persuaded but, once convinced, could be obdurate. His views about state ownership, as expressed here, persisted much the same throughout his life. Another leading exponent of the Social Gospel, Washington Gladden, opposed Marxist, collectivist socialism, adding: "The subjugation of labor by capital is the first stage in the progress of industry; the second stage is the warfare between capital and labor; the third is the identification of labor and capital by some application of the principle of cooperation." Dombrowski concluded,

no doubt correctly, that he was living in Gladden's second stage. See Washington Gladden, *The Working People and Their Employers* (Boston: Lookwood, Brooks, 1876), 44.

13. Dombrowski, "Education of a Southerner," 4.

14. Ibid., 3.

15. Reinhold Niebuhr, *The Children of Light and the Children of Darkness* (New York: Scribner's, 1944), xiii. My conclusion about Ward is based on Link, *Labor-Religion Prophet*, 141; and on the fact that in the Soviet Union Ward was called "the people's scholar," a description the author first heard Myles Horton use.

16. Interview with Dombrowski, 25–31 Oct. 1978.

17. U.S., Dept. of Justice, FBI, File No. 10–613, James Anderson Dombrowski, p. AT–100–5234. These documents were obtained for the author by attorney Jack Peebles of New Orleans with permission from Dombrowski. As often seems to be the case with government dossiers, in Dombrowski's file considerable unsubstantiated hearsay was recorded by persons whose identity has been masked.

18. James Anderson Dombrowski, "Religion and Vested Interests in the South in the Field of Slavery and the Slave-Trade, from 1619 to 1832," B.D. diss., Union Theological Seminary, Mar. 1931. It should be noted that Niebuhr ministered in Detroit for 13 years before joining the academic world, first at Yale Divinity School and then at Union. In Detroit, he championed the cause of auto workers and migrant African Americans. No doubt his experience influenced Dombrowski's dissertation.

19. Philip S. Foner, ed., *Black Socialist Preacher* (San Francisco: Synthesis, 1983), 261.

20. Ralph Albertson, as quoted in James Anderson Dombrowski, *The Early Days of Christian Socialism in America* (New York: Columbia Univ. Press, 1936), 139. See also Scott, *Towards the Christian Revolution*.

21. Christian Commonwealth Colony, *Social Gospel*, March 1898, as quoted in Dombrowski, *Early Days*, 139. Walter Rauschenbusch, whose views on the Social Gospel were criticised by Niebuhr and others while Dombrowski was at Union, eventually came to have significance for Dombrowski. In the 1970s, as the latter reflected on his life and times, one of Rauschenbusch's arguments in particular made sense. The theologian had argued in *Christianity and the Social Order* (New York: Macmillan, 1907): "Political democracy without economic democracy is an uncashed promissory note, a pot without the roast, a form without substance" (353). Dombrowski became intrigued by the idea of worker ownership.

22. Dombrowski, *Early Days*, 14–15.

23. Ibid., 4–5.

24. Ibid.

25. Stephen Colwell, *New Themes for the Protestant Clergy: Creeds Without*

*Charity: Theology Without Humanity: Protestants Without Christianity; with Notes on the Literature of Charity, Population, Pauperism, Political Economy, and Protestantism* (Philadelphia, 1851), 244. Quoted in Dombrowski, *Early Days,* 33. The title of this work no doubt struck a sympathetic chord in Dombrowski.

26. Dombrowski, *Early Days,* 38.

27. Richard T. Ely, *The Labor Movement in America* (New York, 1886), quoted in Dombrowski, *Early Days,* 58.

28. Dombrowski, *Early Days,* 59.

29. Ibid.

30. Ibid., 180.

31. Ibid.

32. *The Kingdom* [weekly newspaper edited by Herbert W. Gleason], 4 May 1894, quoted in Dombrowski, *Early Days,* 177.

33. Dombrowski, *Early Days,* 148–49.

34. Ibid., 169. Dombrowski's book was reviewed in *The Nation,* 9 Sept. 1939.

35. Dombrowski, *Early Days,* 169.

## Chapter 5

1. Interview with Dombrowski, 25–31 Oct. 1978.

2. Unsigned letter to Wyatt A. Smart, 3 Feb. 1933, Dombrowski Papers.

3. Myles Horton to Dombrowski, ca. Jan. 1933, in Highlander Folk School, Highlander Papers, Box 61, Folder 11. See also Highlander Folk School, "Statement of Purpose," 14 Sept. 1933; and Myles Horton, notes on southern mountain school, Union Theological Seminary, 1929; both in Horton Papers, Box 27. Aimee Isgrig Horton, *The Highlander Folk School: A History of Its Major Programs, 1932–1961* (New York: Carlson, 1988).

4. Interview with Dombrowski, 1–5 May 1976. See also V. Mehta, "The Benefactress," *New Yorker* 77, no. 8 (1988). Ethel Clyde died in 1978.

5. Interview with Dombrowski, 1–5 May 1976.

6. Ibid.

7. Ibid.

8. Ibid.

9. John Dewey, "Internal Social Reorganization After the War," *Journal of Race Development* 8 (1918):395. See also Lawrence A. Cremin, *The Transformation of the School: Progressivism in American Education, 1876–1957* (New York: Vintage, 1964); Martin S. Dworkin, *Dewey on Education* (New York: Teachers College Press, 1959). Among the several organizations formed by Dewey or around his ideas, the Society for Educational Reconstruction still continues the tradition of advocating progressive education.

10. Dewey, "Internal Social Reorganization," 397.

11. Ibid.

12. John Dewey, *Education and the Social Order* (New York: League for Industrial Democracy, 1934), 6.

13. Dewey, "Internal Social Reorganization," 398.

14. Ibid.

15. Ibid.

16. Ibid. See also John Dewey, *Democracy and Education: An Introduction to the Philosophy of Education* (New York: Free Press, 1966), 260. Dewey offers similar views within the context of a discussion of philosophy. For a critique of Dewey's liberalism, see Clarence J. Karier, *Roots of Crisis: American Education in the Twentieth Century* (Chicago: Rand-McNally, 1973).

17. Richard J. Altenbaugh, "Forming the Structure of a New Society Within the Shell of the Old: A Study of Three Labor Colleges and Their Contributions to the American Labor Movement" (Ph.D. diss., Univ. of Pittsburgh, 1980). This unique study sets the histories of three residential adult education centers within the context of American labor history and, deservedly, has been published as a book.

18. Enok Mortensen, *Schools for Life: A Danish-American Experiment in Adult Education* (Solvang, Calif.: Danish-American Heritage Society, 1977), 10–20.

19. Joseph K. Hart, *Light from the North: The Danish Folk Highschools. Their Meaning for America* (New York: Henry Holt, 1926). See also Myles Horton, Denmark trip correspondence, lectures, articles, diaries, notes, and songs, 1931–34, Highlander Papers, Box 41, Folders 16–18.

20. Myles Horton, Denmark trip materials.

21. John Dewey to Dombrowski, 27 Sept. 1933, Dombrowski Papers. See also John Dewey, general correspondence, 1933–1935, Highlander Papers, Box 10, Folder 18.

22. Interview with Myles Horton, 22 May 1977. See also Will W. Alexander to Sherwood Eddy, 26 May 1933, Highlander Collection, Box 5.

23. Donald West, "Knott County, Kentucky: A Study" (B.D. thesis, Vanderbilt Univ., 1931), 87–89.

24. Interview with Myles Horton. See also Myles Horton, "The Community Folk School," in *The Community School,* ed. Samuel Everett, 265–97 (New York: Appleton-Century, 1938). For additional reading on Danish folk high schools as sparks for democratic social change, see Rolland G. Paulston, *Folk Schools in Social Change: A Partisan Guide to the International Literature* (Pittsburgh, Penn.: Univ. of Pittsburgh Press, 1974).

25. As quoted in John Glen, *Highlander: No Ordinary School, 1932–1962* (Lexington: Univ. Press of Kentucky, 1988), 17. Glen's detailed, scholarly work is the measure by which future academic studies of Highlander will be judged. Some persons learn through the use of analytical tools; others use ancedotes. The genius

of Highlander is that both methods are employed. This distinction eludes Glen, who values accumulated details more than context or accuracy. For an equally informative but anecdotal, visual version of this history, see the television program "The Adventures of a Radical Hillbilly," *Bill Moyers' Journal,* program no. 725, 5 June 1981.

26. Myles Horton and Don West to Lillian Johnson, 17 Sept. 1932, Highlander Collection, Box 61. See also Lillian W. Johnson, "Beginnings of the Cooperative Movement in the United States," *Tennessee Union Farmer* 3, no. 4 (Nov. 1947): 5–6.

27. Myles Horton, *The Long Haul: An Autobiography* (New York: Doubleday, 1990), 62–63. Horton, assisted by Judith Kohl and Herb Kohl, tells his own story, characteristically weaving fact and recollection with perceptive analysis, chiefly about himself, learning, and Highlander as an educational institution. See also Frank Adams with Myles Horton, *Unearthing Seeds of Fire: The Idea of Highlander* (Winston-Salem, N.C.: John F. Blair, 1975), 26–27.

28. Adams, *Unearthing Seeds of Fire,* 26–27. See also Glen, *Highlander,* 17.

29. Myles Horton and West to Lillian Johnson, 17 Sept. 1932, Highlander Collection, Box 61.

30. "State Police Hold Suspect at Wilder," *Chattanooga Times,* 25 Nov. 1932. For a longer discussion of how Myles Horton used the strike at Wilder for educational purposes, see Frank T. Adams, "Highlander Folk School: Getting Information, Going Back and Teaching It," *Harvard Educational Review* 42, no. 4 (1972): 497–520. See also Fran Ansley and Brenda Bell, "Strikes in the Coal Camps: Davidson-Wilder, 1932," *Southern Exposure* I (Winter 1974): 113–33.

31. "Teacher Tells Church of Arrest at Wilder," *Knoxville News-Sentinel,* 29 Nov. 1932; "Guard Officer Angered by Charges of 'Horton'" [quotation marks in original], *Chattanooga Times,* 20 Nov. 1932; "Communications, Editor's Note," *Nashville Tennessean,* 1 Dec. 1932.

32. Howard Kester, "A Brief Account of the Wilder Strike," 1 Aug. 1933, in "Annual Report of Howard Kester, Southern Secretary, Annual Conference of the Fellowship of Reconciliation, October 1933," Kester Papers, Reel 1. For a profile of Kester, see also John Egerton: *A Mind to Stay Here: Profiles from the South* (London: Macmillan, 1970), 70–92.

33. Interview with Myles Horton, 22 May 1977. For a full account of the Wilder strike and its significance for an emerging group of white southern radicals, see Anthony P. Dunbar, *Against the Grain: Southern Radicals and Prophets, 1929–1959* (Charlottesville: Univ. Press of Virginia, 1981), 1–20. Dunbar was among the first to document the Social Gospel links among Kester, Dombrowski, Myles Horton, and others.

34. Adams, *Unearthing Seeds of Fire,* 31–32. See misc. newspaper clippings in Highlander Collection, Box 76.

35. Myles Horton, "Strike of the Wilder Miners," 1933, Highlander Collection, Box 76.

36. Kester to Don West, 21 Feb. 1933, Kester Papers, Box 1. Alva W. Taylor, "Building Gains Over the South," *Christian Century* 54 (Sept. 1932):1148. See also Stanley L. Harrison, "The Social Gospel Career of Alva Wilmot Taylor" (Ph.D. diss., Vanderbilt Univ., 1975).

37. Interview with Myles Horton, 22 May 1977.

38. John B. Thompson to Norman Thomas, 23 Feb. 1933, Highlander Papers, Box 27. Also interview with Myles Horton (on slaying of Barney Graham, the union leader), 22 May 1977. "Union Chief Shot in Back, Doctor Says," *Knoxville News-Sentinel*, 2 May 1933; "Slayer of Wilder Strike Chieftain Indicted, on Bond," *Chattanooga Times*, 3 May 1933; "Another Charged With Murdering Barney Graham," 19 May 1933, newspaper clipping, Highlander Papers, Box 76, Folder 17. See also Howard Kester, "A Brief Account of the Wilder Strike," 1 Aug. 1933, Kester Papers, Reel 1.

39. "Don West and Myles Horton Barred from County School Buildings by Order of Chairman," *Cumberland Outlook*, 15 Dec. 1932.

40. Ibid.

41. West to Kester, 15 Feb. 1933, Kester Papers, Box 1.

42. Lillian Johnson to Myles Horton, 8 Dec. 1932, Highlander Collection, Box 16. See also, "Summary of Cash Receipts," June 1932–29 Feb. 1933, Highlander Papers, Box 3.

43. West to Myles Horton, 16 Dec. 1933, Highlander Collection, Box 29, Folder 21. Victoria Byerly is working on a portrait of West, long overdue both because his life was lived as a southerner at odds with society and because of his dedication to a radical vision of adult education. In 1967, he and his wife Constance started the Appalachian South Folklife Center near Pipestem, W.V.

44. Interview with Myles Horton, 22 May 1977. See also Highlander Folk School, "The First Year's Work," ca. Nov. 1932, Highlander Papers, Box 3.

45. Dorothy Thompson recorded the quotation from Billy Thomas in her notes on bugwood strike, 5–29 July and 3 Aug. 1933, Highlander Papers, Box 52. See also Michele Fowlkes Marlowe, "Participation of the Poor: The Southern White in Social Movements" (M.S. thesis, Univ. of Tennessee, 1967).

46. Cumberland Mountain Workers' and Unemployed League, Highlander Papers, Box 52. See also Aimee I. Horton, "The Highlander Folk School" (Ph.D. diss., Univ. of Chicago, 1971).

47. Interview with Myles Horton, 22 May 1977.

48. Michael E. Price, "The New Deal in Tennessee: The Highlander Folk School and Worker Response in Grundy County," *Tennessee Historical Quarterly* 44 (Summer 1984):99–120.

49. Dorothy Thompson, letter, ca. 1933, Dombrowski Papers.

50. Dombrowski letter to contributors, Jan. 1934, p. 4, Dombrowski Papers.

51. "Summary of Expenses—Monteagle and Allardt," 1934, Highlander Papers, Box 3.

52. Members of Highlander's advisory committee in 1934 were Reinhold Niebuhr, Norman Thomas, Arthur Swift, George S. Counts, W.S. Alexander, Sherwood Eddy, Alva Taylor, Joseph K. Hart, William Spofford, and Kirby Page. Dombrowski secured a charter of incorporation for Highlander Folk School from the State of Tennessee on 20 Oct. 1934. Incorporators were Dombrowski, Myles Horton, Hawes, Rupert Hampton, and Malcolm Chisholm, all of whom were the school's board of directors.

53. Interview with Myles Horton, 22 May 1977.

54. Ralph Tefferteller to Frank T. Adams, 25 Jan. 1977.

55. Interview with Myles Horton, 22 May 1977.

56. James A. Dombrowski, "Allardt Diary," 13 Dec. 1933, Dombrowski Papers.

57. Ibid., 17 Dec. 1933.

58. Ibid.

59. Ibid.

60. Ibid.

61. Dombrowski to J. King Gordon, 25 Dec. 1933, Dombrowski Papers.

62. Ibid.

63. Ellen Krida to Dombrowski, 27 Dec. 1933, Dombrowski Papers. Dombrowski saved most if not all of Krida's letters to him. She, on the other hand, destroyed his letters to her, apparently after reading them upon arrival. Only four of his letters to her are known.

64. "Plans for extension work and union contacts, September 1934–September 1935," Highlander Papers, Box 2.

65. Tefferteller to Adams. For a similar view of Dombrowski's role at Highlander Folk School, see Glen, *Highlander*, 90–92.

66. Interview with Dombrowski, 1–5 May 1976.

67. Ibid.

68. Highlander Staff, "To Our Friends of Summerfield and Neighboring Communities," 1934, Highlander Papers, Box 1.

69. Staff meeting minutes, 18 and 25 Mar. 1934, Highlander Papers, Box 2.

70. Interview with Dombrowski, 1–5 May 1976.

71. Ibid. See also "Invitation to Conference of Younger Churchmen of the South," 30 Apr. 1934, Kester Papers, Reel 1; Dunbar, *Against the Grain,* 59–66; and John Starke Bellamy, "If Christ Came to Dixie: The Southern Prophetic Vision of Howard Anderson Kester" (Ph.D. diss., Univ. of Virginia, 1974).

72. Interview with Dombrowski, 1–5 May 1976. See also David Burgess, "The

Fellowship of Southern Churchmen, Its History and Promise," *Prophetic Religion* 13 (Spring 1953):3–11, and Robert F. Martin, "Critique of Southern Society and Vision of a New Order: The Fellowship of Southern Churchmen," *Church History* 52, no. 1 (1979):66–80.

73. Luke 4:8.

74. Thomas B. Cowan, "History of the Fellowship of Southern Churchmen," April 1938, p. 1, Kester Papers.

75. Ibid. See also "Findings: Conference of Younger Churchmen of the South, Monteagle, Tennessee, May 27–29, 1934," Kester Papers, Reel 1.

76. Cowan, "History of the Fellowship," 2.

77. Ibid.

78. Ibid., 3.

79. "Report from Second Annual Conference of Younger Churchmen by Eugene W. Sutherland, Chairman," 6 Dec. 1935, Kester Papers, Reel 1.

80. Interview with Dombrowski, 1–5 May 1976. Revolutionary Policy Committee, "An Appeal to the Membership of the Socialist Party," April 1934, p. 7, Dombrowski Papers.

81. Ibid.

82. James Weinstein, *The Decline of Socialism in America, 1912–1925* (New York: Monthly Review Press, 1967). See also Ira Kipnis, *The American Socialist Movement, 1897–1912* (New York: Columbia Univ. Press, 1952).

83. Interview with Mel Zuck, 3 Dec. 1980.

84. Dombrowski, "Monteagle Diary," 30 Sept. 1934, Dombrowski Papers.

## Chapter 6

1. H.L. Mitchell, *Mean Things Happening in This Land* (Montclair, N.J.: Allanheld, Osmun, 1979).

2. Ibid., 48–50.

3. "Highlander Fling," Mar. 1935, Dombrowski Papers.

4. Ibid.

5. James A. Dombrowski, "Rural Schools for the People," speech at the national convention of the Progressive Education Association, 22 Feb. 1935, Dombrowski Papers.

6. Ibid.

7. Higlander Folk School Summer Report and Summary of Other Educational Activities, Sept. 1933–1934," Highlander Reports, Box 1, Folder 3.

8. Myles Horton, *Long Haul,* 71. For Horton's earlier view of Highlander, himself, and adult education, see Thomas Bledsoe, *Or We'll All Hang Separately: The Highlander Idea* (Boston: Beacon, 1969). Horton prevailed on Bledsoe to write this book but in the end did not find it to his liking.

9. John E. Egerton to Tennessee Manufacturers Association, 28 June 1934, highlander Papers, Box 11, Folder 10. See also Thomas B. Brooks, *Toil and Trouble: A History of American Labor* (New York: Delta Books, 1964), 145.

10. Interview with Dombrowski, 25–31 Oct. 1978. See also *Knoxville Journal,* 28 Mar. 1935.

11. Interview with Dombrowski, 25–31 Oct. 1978.

12. Ibid.

13. "Our Verdict," 21 Jan. 1936, Dombrowski Papers. See also Stanley L. Harbison, "The Social Gospel Career of Alva Wilmot Taylor" (Ph.D. diss., Vanderbilt Univ., 1975). Taylor remained a friend and admirer of Dombrowski all his life, to the distress of some of his former students. The organizations Taylor was affiliated with between 1920 and the 1950s were as diverse as the U.S. Department of Labor, Southern Tenant Farmers Union, Save the Children Federation, and the Progressive Party.

14. Ibid.

15. "Call" (Monteagle, Tenn.: All-Southern Conference on Civil and Trade Union Rights, 4 Feb. 1935), Highlander Papers, Box 31, Folder 14, p. 2. See also Robert F. Martin, "A Prophet's Pilgrimage: The Religious Radicalism of Howard Anderson Kester, 1921–1941," *Journal of Southern History* 48, no. 4 (1982):511–30.

16. Morton Sosna, *In Search of the Silent South,* 143. See also Harvard Sitkoff, "The Emergence of Civil Rights as a National Issue: The New Deal Era" (Ph.D. diss., Columbia Univ., 1975). Sitkoff, starting here and proceeding through his multi-volume published series, earlier than most historians, has traced the civil rights movement's origins to the 1930s. I am indebted to Sitkoff for the important historical framework he has provided.

17. "Legion's Probe of School Discussed by Cook Here," *Chattanooga News,* 6 Apr. 1935.

18. "Call," 1.

19. "Radicals Quit When Put Out of Third Hall," *Chattanooga News,* 27 May 1935. See also Raleigh Crumbliss, "Twas a Famous Victory," *Chattanooga News,* 30 May 1935.

20. Ellen Krida to Dombrowski, 11 May 1935, Dombrowski Papers.

21. Ellen Krida to Dombrowski, 15 May 1935, Dombrowski Papers.

22. "Radicals Quit," *Chattanooga News,* 27 May 1935.

23. Ibid.

24. Ibid.

25. Minutes of the All-Southern Conference for Civil and Trade Union Rights, typescript, 26 May 1935, Highlander Papers, Box 31, Folder 7.

26. Interview with Dombrowski, 25–31 Oct. 1978. See also Raymond Koch and Charlotte Koch, *Educational Commune: The Story of Commonwealth College*

(New York: Schocken, 1972); for a thin sketch, see Sue Thrasher, "Radical Education in the Thirties," *Southern Exposure* 1 (Winter 1974):204–209.

27. Four decades later, both H.L. Mitchell in *Mean Things Happening* and Myles Horton in *Long Haul* managed to ignore one another. Mitchell makes no mention of Dombrowski, Myles Horton, or Highlander. Any mention of Mitchell, Butler, or STFU by Myles Horton escaped notice.

28. Myles Horton, *Long Haul*, 72.

29. Interview with Dombrowski, 25–31 Oct. 1978.

30. Franz Daniel to Dombrowski, 31 May 1935, Dombrowski Papers.

31. "Sunday Condemns U.S. Relief Grant, Denounces Highlander Folk Cooperatives," *Chattanooga Times*, 4 May 1925. See also "Egerton Hits Fund for Reds," *Knoxville Journal*, 31 Mar. 1935; and "Relief Grant to Radical School Stirs Citizenry," *Chicago Daily Tribune*, 26 Mar. 1935.

32. Myles Horton, *Long Haul*, 72.

33. Lillian Johnson to Dombrowski, 22 Jan. 1935, Highlander Papers, Box 16, Folder 18.

34. Interview with Dombrowski, 25–31 Oct. 1978.

35. Ellen Krida to Dombrowski, 6 June 1935, Dombrowski Papers.

36. Ellen Krida to Dombrowski, 13 Feb. 1935, Dombrowski Papers.

37. Ellen Krida to Dombrowski, 8 Feb. 1934, Dombrowski Papers.

38. Ellen Krida to Dombrowski, 17 June 1934, Dombrowski Papers.

39. Ellen Krida to Dombrowski, 7 June 1934, Dombrowski Papers.

40. Ellen Krida to Dombrowski, 28 Dec. 1934, Dombrowski Papers.

41. Ellen Krida to Dombrowski, 2 Sept. 1934, Dombrowski Papers.

42. Arthur Krida to Frank T. Adams, 5 May 1978.

43. Ellen Krida to Dombrowski, 19 June 1934, Dombrowski Papers.

44. Ellen Krida to Dombrowski, 1 May 1934, Dombrowski Papers.

45. Ellen Krida to Dombrowski, 5 Nov. 1935, Dombrowski Papers.

46. Robert P. Ingals, "The Tampa Flogging Case, Urban Vigilantism," *Florida Historical Quarterly* 56, no. 1 (July 1977):13–27.

47. *Tampa Daily Times*, 2, 14 Dec. 1935; *Tampa Morning Tribune*, 2, 3, 13 Dec. 1935.

48. *Tampa Morning Tribune*, 5 Dec. 1935.

49. Ibid.

50. Ibid.

51. Interview with Dombrowski, 1–5 May 1976.

52. Ingals, "Tampa Flogging," 21. See also *Tampa Daily Times*, 16 Dec. 1935.

53. *Tampa Morning Tribune*, 14–24 May 1936.

## Chapter 7

1. Ralph Tefferteller to Frank T. Adams, 24 Jan. 1977.

2. Ibid. See also Bettina Berch, *Radical by Design: The Life and Style of Elizabeth Hawes, Fashion Designer, Union Organizer, Best-Selling Author* (New York: Dutton, 1988), 126–27. No relation to Highlander's Elizabeth Hawes, Elizabeth Hawes the fashion designer, etc., nevertheless was a political activist whom the FBI kept an eye on during the 1930s.

3. David Montgomery, "Some Lessons from Labor History for Our Troubled Times," photocopy, speech given to the Sylvis Society, Cincinnati, Ohio, 14 Oct. 1989, p. 13. See also F. Ray Marshall, *Labor in the South* (Cambridge, Mass.: Harvard Univ. Press, 1967), 176.

4. F. Ray Marshall, *Labor in the South,* 176.

5. James A. Dombrowski, "Journal, 1937" (hereafter referred to as Dombrowski Journal, 1937), p. 2. Dombrowski kept equally detailed journals in 1938, 1939, and 1940. All the journals will be cited by year. All are in Dombrowski Papers.

6. Dombrowski Journal, 1937, p. 2. See also Myles Horton, "Mountain Men," ca. 1937, Highlander Papers, Box 63, Folder 4, p. 5; and "The Highlander Fling," in "WPA Workers To Organize," Sept. 1936, mimeo., Highlander Papers, Box 53, Folder 2, p. 2.

7. *The Finances and Management of Government of Grundy County, Tennessee* (Nashville: Tennessee Taxpayers Association, 1934).

8. Dombrowski to Ethel Clyde, 24 June 1936, Highlander Papers, Box 1, Folder 6.

9. Ibid.

10. "Folk School is Held 'Immoral,' Dangerous," *Chattanooga News,* 6 Feb. 1937, Highlander Papers, Box 53, Folder 2.

11. "WPA Strikers Ask FDR's Aid," *Chattanooga Times,* 12 Mar. 1937.

12. Ibid.

13. "Berry Charges Reds Feed Relief Workers," *Chattanooga News–Free Press,* 13 Mar. 1937.

14. Summary of Activities, Jan.–Oct. 1938, Highlander Papers, Box 1. See also Dombrowski Journal, 1938.

15. Ibid.

16. Dombrowski to Ethel Clyde, 24 June 1936. See also Bea Rich, "Democracy's Dreams in the Hills," *Social Work Today* 8 (Jan. 1941):14.

17. Interview with Dombrowski, 6–9 Dec. 1979. See also Edwin R. Embree and Julia Waxman, *Investment in People: The Story of the Julius Rosenwald Fund* (New York: Rosenwald Foundation, 1949). In May 1933, the Rosenwald Fund sponsored a meeting in Washington, D.C., to discuss the "Economic Status of the Negro."

Dombrowski did not attend, but many of his political allies did, including Will Alexander, Clark Foreman, and Broadus Mitchell. See Dombrowski's typed manuscript, "Fire in the Hole," Dombrowski Papers.

18. Dombrowski, "Fire in the Hole," 5.

19. Ibid., 66–67.

20. Ibid., 119.

21. Ibid., 139.

22. Ibid., 137.

23. Dombrowski Journal, 1938, p. 97.

24. Myles Horton, "Mountain Men," 10–14.

25. "Berry Charges Reds Fed Relief Workers," *Chattanooga News–Free Press*, 13 Mar. 1937. See also "County Highway Commission Gives Its Side of Controversy," *Grundy County Herald*, 19 Jan. 1939.

26. Dombrowski Journal, 1937, p. 6.

27. Ibid., 12.

28. Ibid., 41.

29. Ibid., 42.

30. Ibid., 43.

31. Interview with Dombrowski, 6–9 Dec. 1979.

32. Ibid.

33. Leon Wilson, "The Attack of the Grundy County Crusaders on the Highlander Folk School," mimeo., n.d., SCHWA, Box 145, File 2759. See also Martin Dies, *The Trojan Horse in America* (New York: Dodd, Mead, 1940), 302–361; and Raymond A. Ogden, *The Dies Committee, 1938–1944* (Washington: Catholic Univ. of America Press, 1945).

34. Leon Wilson, "The Attack," 6.

35. "Grundy Group Plans Protest of Folk School," *Nashville Tennessean*, 9 Nov. 1940; "Grundy County Citizens Plan 'Visit' to Folk School," *Chattanooga News–Free Press*, 12 Nov. 1940.

36. Leon Wilson, "The Attack," 2. See also Louisiana, Joint Legislative Committee on Un-American Activities, *Activities of the Southern Conference Education Fund, Inc., in Louisiana* (Baton Rouge: State of Louisiana, 1963), 1:23. 23; and records of Grundy County Crusaders, 1940, Highlander Papers, Box 31, Folders 3 and 4.

37. Lucy Randolph Mason to Frank Porter Graham, 10 June 1937, quoted in John A. Salmond, *Miss Lucy of the CIO: The Life and Times of Lucy Randolph Mason, 1882–1959* (Athens: Univ. of Georgia Press, 1988), 78.

38. Interview with Myles Horton, 22 May 1977. See also James A. Hodges, *New Deal Labor Policy and the Southern Textile Industry, 1933–1941* (Knoxville: Univ. of Tennessee Press, 1986). Chapters 9 and 10, with their inspired epigraphs, were esp. helpful.

39. Interview with Dombrowski, 6–9 Dec. 1979. See also Dombrowski, "Outstanding Achievements in 1937," and Dombrowski, confidential memorandum for the staff, 8 May 1937, both in Highlander Collection, Box 2; Amalgamated Clothing Workers of America Documented History, 1936–38, p. 59, Highlander Papers, Boxes 1, 2, and 64; Walter Galenson, *The CIO Challenge to the ALF: A History of the American Labor Movement, 1935–1941*. (Cambridge, Mass.: Harvard Univ. Press, 1960); and David Brody, *Workers in Industrial America: Essays on the Twentieth-Century Struggle* (New York: Oxford Univ. Press, 1980).

40. Interview with Dombrowski, 6–9 Dec. 1979. Dombrowski and Myles Horton differed sharply on this strategic question; Horton prevailed.

41. Zilphia Horton, "Community Reaction to Negroes at Highlander," ca. 1946, Highlander Papers, Box 15, Folder 14, p. 2.

42. Interview with Dombrowski, 6–9 Dec. 1979. See also Raymond Wolters, *Negroes and the Great Depression* (Westport, Conn.: Greenwood, 1970).

43. Interview with Dombrowski, 6–9 Dec. 1979. John P. Davis of the National Negro Congress, who worked closely with Dombrowski, was a principal organizer of this three-day event, which included many New Deal figures. See also John B. Kirby, *Black Americans in the Roosevelt Era* (Knoxville: Univ. of Tennessee Press, 1980), 161–62; Wolters, *Negroes and the Great Depression*, 354–58; James O. Young, *Black Writers of the Thirties* (Baton Rouge: Louisiana State Univ. Press, 1973).

44. Interview with Dombrowski, 6–9 Dec. 1979.

45. Interview with Dombrowski, 25–31 Oct. 1978.

46. Ibid. See also Lucy Randolph Mason, *To Win These Rights: A Personal Story of the CIO in the South* (New York: Harper and Bros., 1952); and Max Kampelman, *The Communist Party vs. the CIO: A Study in Power Politics* (New York: Praeger, 1957).

47. Interview with Dombrowski, 25–31 Oct. 1978. For later evidence of Dombrowski's effort to apply a united front strategy, see Charles H. Martin, "The Rise and Fall of Popular Front Liberalism in the South: The Southern Conference for Human Welfare, 1938–1948," mimeographed, 1979, Frank T. Adams Collection.

48. Dombrowski to Franz Daniel, 22 May 1987, Highlander Papers, Box 19.

49. Dwight Macdonald to Dombrowski, 4 Aug. 1939, and Dombrowski to Dwight Macdonald, 10 Aug. 1939, Highlander Papers, Box 19.

50. Interview with Myles Horton, 22 May 1977. See also Myles Horton, *Long Haul*.

51. Both Myles Horton and Dombrowski confirmed this version of events.

52. *Nashville Tennessean*, 15–20 Oct. 1939, Highlander Papers, Box 33, or on microfilm.

53. Ibid.

54. Ibid.

55. Interview with Dombrowski, 25–31, Oct. 1978.

56. Leon Wilson, "Summary of Conversation with Mr. Alton [*sic*] Henderson, Tracy City First National Bank, August 1, 1940," Highlander Papers, Box 52. See also Leon Wilson to John J. Lynch, FBI, 1 Oct. 1940, Highlander Papers, Box 31, Folder 7; records of FBI investigation, 1950–51, Highlander Papers, Box 33, Folder 7; and "FBI in the Tennessee Hills," *St. Louis Post Dispatch*, 21 Mar. 1951.

57. Leon Wilson, "Summary of Conversation."

58. Joseph P. Kamp, "The Fifth Column in the South" (New York: Constitutional Educational League, n.d.), Highlander Papers, Box 86, Folder 6. See also American Jewish Congress, New York, N.Y., "Digest of the Anti-Semitic and Democratic Press in the United States," confidential memo, 4 Sept. 1942, pp. 1–5, Highlander Papers, Box 86, Folder 6.

59. Interview with Dombrowski, 25–31 Oct. 1978.

60. Franz Daniel to Dombrowski, 25 Apr. 1941, Dombrowski Papers.

61. Interview with Dombrowski, 25–31 Oct. 1978.

62. "The Attack of the Grundy County Crusaders on the Highland Folk School," 18 Dec. 1940, pp. 1–4, Highlander Papers, Box 33.

63. Leon Wilson, "The Attack of the Grundy County Crusaders on the Highlander Folk School," mimeo., n.d., SCHWA, Box 1435, File 2759. Dombrowski's penchant for saving documents accounts for this citation being found in SCHWA.

64. *Chattanooga News–Free Press*, 14 Nov. 1940. See also "Summary of Meeting Between the Staff of the Highlander Folk School and the Committee from the Grundy County Crusaders, St. Luke's Chapel, Sewanee, Nov. 12, 1940," Highlander Papers, Box 33.

65. "Summary of Meeting, Nov. 12, 1940."

66. *Chattanooga Times*, 18 Nov. 1942.

67. Ibid.

68. *Chattanooga News–Free Press*, 19 Nov. 1940.

69. U.S., Dept. of Justice, FBI, File No. 100-613, James Anderson Dombrowski, p. 3. See also "Dies to Get Evidence on 'Folk School'," *Chattanooga News–Free Press*, 29 Nov. 1940.

70. Ellen Krida to Dombrowski, 13 Apr. 1940, Dombrowski Papers.

71. Dombrowski to Zilla Daniel, 29 July 1940, Dombrowski Papers.

72. Elizabeth Hawes Daniel to Dombrowski, 22 Dec. 1935, Dombrowski Papers.

73. Interview with Myles Horton, 22 May 1977.

74. Ellen Krida to Dombrowski, 11 June 1937, Dombrowski Papers.

75. Ellen Krida to Dombrowski, 23 Feb. 1941, Dombrowski Papers. Sexist attitudes figured in Myles Horton's rupture with Don West. In a letter dated 12 May 1933, West alleged that Horton had ordered West's wife Constance, pregnant with

their first child, out of the house that Highlander had secured from Lillian Johnson, saying, "I'm not going to turn that house into a maternity hospital." Horton, later, did not recall the episode. West letter, Frank T. Adams Collection. See also Leah Langworthy, "Struggles Within Struggles: Women's Experience at the Highlander Folk School," M.A. thesis, Apr. 1990, Carleton College. Frank T. Adams Collection.

76. Ellen Krida to Dombrowski, 14 July 1941, Dombrowski Papers.

77. Ellen Krida to Dombrowski, 12 Dec. 1941, Dombrowski Papers.

78. Dombrowski Journal, 1937, p. 34. Dombrowski Papers.

79. Ibid.

80. Franz Daniel to Dombrowski, 3 Dec. 1939. See also Dombrowski to Franz Daniel, 22 Apr. 1934, Dombrowski Papers.

81. Dombrowski to Franz Daniel, 9 June 1941, Dombrowski Papers.

82. J.B.S. Hardman to Dombrowski, 6 Sept. 1940, Dombrowski Papers.

83. Dombrowski Journal, 1937, n.p., Dombrowski Papers.

84. Ibid.

85. Interview with Dombrowski, 6–9 Dec. 1979. See also Marshall, *Labor in the South; CIO News,* 17 Nov. 1941; and Highlander Executive Council Meeting Minutes, 29 Aug. 1942, Highlander Papers, Box 146.

86. Interview with Dombrowski, 25–31 Oct. 1979 and 6–9 Dec. 1979.

87. Ellen Krida to Dombrowski, 12 Dec. 1941, Dombrowski Papers.

## Chapter 8

1. Virginia Durr, interview with Frank T. Adams, 24 Oct. 1978. See also Interviews with Virginia Durr, Southern Oral History Project, Univ. of North Carolina, Chapel Hill, no. 4007; "The Reminiscences of Virginia Durr," Columbia Univ. Oral History Project; Holinger F. Barnard, ed., *Virginia Foster Durr: Outside the Magic Circle* (University, Ala.: Univ. of Alabama Press, 1985); and Virginia Durr, "Grace and Guts," *Southern Changes* 7, nos. 5–6 (1985):17–20.

2. Durr helped me grasp the extent of Dombrowski's remarkable social skills, esp. with women. Interview with Durr, 24 Oct. 1978.

3. Minutes, Meeting of the SCHW Executive Committee, 2 Aug. 1941, SCHWA.

4. A review of the allegations against Gelders is contained in Thomas A. Krueger, *And Promises to Keep: The Southern Conference for Human Welfare, 1938–1948* (Nashville, Tenn.: Vanderbilt Univ. Press, 1967), 1–6, 76–82. Krueger's study remains the most thorough of this important organization.

5. Salmond, *Miss Lucy,* 153–54, 157, 159.

6. Ibid., 154.

7. U.S., National Emergency Council, *Report on Economic Conditions.* At the

time this research was done, Foreman's papers were in the Trevor Arnett Library, Atlanta University, Atlanta, Ga., unorganized in a filing cabinet and three boxes. Among the loose material was background on the NEC report. W.E.B. DuBois was an important influence on Dombrowski at this time, esp. through an essay: DuBois, "The Position of the Negro in the American Social Order: Where Do We Go from Here?," *Journal of Negro Education* 8 (July 1939):55–70. Here and elsewhere DuBois argued that united class-conscious workers eventually would emancipate labor but that, until that moment of solidarity arrived, race-conscious African Americans would have to build their own institutions and movements to emancipate "the colored race."

8. Interview with Dombrowski, 25–31 Oct. 1978.

9. Gunnar Myrdal, as quoted in Tindall, *Emergence of the New South*, 637. See also Gunnar Myrdal, *An American Dilemma* (New York: Harper and Row, 1962).

10. U.S. National Emergency Council, *Report on Economic Conditions.*

11. Sosna, *In Search of the Silent South*, 95. Sosna argues that the SCHW's decision never to hold another segregated convention was a severe blow from which the organization never recovered. In the minds of Dombrowski and Myles Horton, if that decision had not been taken, the SCHW would have been a waste of time.

12. Ibid.

13. Howard Lee to Frank P. Graham, 4 Nov. 1939, Graham Papers. See also Minutes, Meeting of SCHW Executive Committee, 2 Aug. 1941; Caute, *The Great Fear*, 179; and Frank A. Warren, *Liberals and Communism* (Bloomington: Indiana Univ. Press, 1966).

14. Warren Ashby, *Frank Porter Graham: A Southern Liberal* (Winston-Salem, N.C.: John F. Blair, 1980), 156–68. Ashby gives this issue perhaps more attention than it deserves.

15. Ibid.

16. Ibid.

17. Thompson, like his classmate Dombrowski, remained an activist throughout his life and was dogged by unfounded allegations that he was a Communist.

18. Dombrowski to Ethel Clyde, 25 Jan. 1942, Dombrowski Papers.

19. Dombrowski to Virginia Durr, 10 Mar. 1942, Dombrowski Papers.

20. Dombrowski to Ellen Krida, 12 Mar. 1942, Dombrowski Papers. This is one of four extant letters from Dombrowski to Krida.

21. Dombrowski to Virgina Durr, 17 Mar. 1942, Dombrowski Papers.

22. Interview with Dombrowski, 25–31 Oct. 1978.

23. Ibid. See also Krueger, *Promises to Keep*, 96–102.

24. Interview with Virginia Durr, 24 Oct. 1978.

25. Don H. Doyle, *Nashville in the New South, 1880–1930* (Knoxville: Univ. of Tennessee Press, 1985), 141. See also Lester C. Lamon, *Black Tennesseans, 1900–1930* (Knoxville: Univ. of Tennessee Press).

26. Unless otherwise noted, most quotations in the remainder of this chapter come from SCHW, *Proceedings of the Nashville Convention of the Southern Conference for Human Welfare* (Nashville, Tenn.: n.p., 1942), Dombrowski Papers.

27. J. Edgar Hoover to Marvin H. McIntyre, 7 May 1942, Williams Papers.

28. SCHW, *Nashville Convention Proceedings, 1942.*

29. Ibid.

30. A. Phillip Randolph, speech to the Second National Negro Congress, Oct. 1937, in *Official Proceedings, Second National Negro Congress*, Schomburg Collection, New York Public Library, Harlem Branch.

31. A. Phillip Randolph, "Why Should We March," *Survey Graphic* 2 (Nov. 1942):489.

32. SCHW, *Nashville Convention Proceedings, 1942.*

33. Ibid.

34. Ibid.

35. Ibid.

36. Interview with Dombrowski, 25–31 Oct. 1978.

37. Interview with Virginia Durr, 24 Oct. 1978. See also Barnard, *Virginia Durr*, 123; and Frank McCallister to Clark Foreman, 4 May 1942, Foreman Papers.

38. Roger N. Baldwin to Eleanor Roosevelt, 23 June 1942, Foreman Papers.

39. Eleanor Roosevelt to Roger N. Baldwin, 26 June 1942, Foreman Papers.

40. Dombrowski to Roger N. Baldwin, 27 May 1942, Foreman Papers.

41. Interview with Dombrowski, 25–31 Oct. 1978. See also "Welfare Group Elects Texan," *Nashville Banner*, 22 Apr. 1942; and Krueger, *Promises to Keep*, 102. SCHW, Box 6, has a brief autobiographical outline of Foreman up to this date.

42. Clark Foreman to Roger N. Baldwin, 19 May 1942; see also Dombrowski to Clark Foreman, 25 May 1942; and Roger N. Baldwin to Clark Foreman, 29 May 1942; all in Foreman Papers.

43. Interview with Virginia Durr, 24 Oct. 1978.

44. Interview with Dombrowski, 25–31 Oct. 1978. Clark Foreman to Frank T. Adams, 15, July 1976. For a sympathetic sketch of Foreman's important role in shaping New Deal attitudes toward African Americans, see Kirby, *Black Americans in the Roosevelt Era*, 39–47. See also Wolters, *Negroes and the Great Depression*, 147, for a discussion of how one of Foreman's programs, the National Recovery Act, benefited African Americans only because it did not work as conceived.

45. Interview with Dombrowski, 6–9 Dec. 1979.

46. U.S., Dept. of Justice, FBI, New York File No. 100-41570.

## Chapter 9

1. Interview with Dombrowski, 6–9 Dec. 1979.

2. Ibid. See also Dombrowski to Ellen Krida, 15 May 1943, Dombrowski Papers.

3. Interview with Dombrowski, 25–31 Oct. 1978. See also Charles S. Johnson et al., *Into the Mainstream* (Chapel Hill: Univ. of North Carolina Press, 1947), 5–11.

4. Krueger, *Promises to Keep*, 119–22. See also Ralph J. Bunche, "A Critical Analysis of the Tactics and Programs of Minority Groups," *Journal of Negro Education* 4 (July 1935):308–320.

5. Bunche, "Critical Analysis," 309.

6. Interview with Dombrowski, 25–31 Oct. 1978. See also Clark Foreman to Charles S. Johnson, 13 Aug. 1943, Foreman Papers.

7. Krueger, *Promises to Keep*, 120.

8. Interview with Dombrowski, 25–31 Oct. 1978. See also SCHW, Convention Proceedings, Chattanooga, 14 Apr. 1940, SCHWA, Box 2.

9. Dombrowski Journals, ca. Aug. 1943, Dombrowski Papers. See also Krueger, *Promises to Keep*, 119–21.

10. Dombrowski to Lillian Smith, 16 June 1944, SCHWA.

11. Commission on Interracial Cooperation, *Southern Frontier* (Jan. 43–Dec. 44): 21–26. Between January 1943 and December 1944, the *Southern Frontier* carried solid accounts of the Commission on Interracial Cooperation and its merger with the Southern Regional Council. The last issue was mailed in February 1944 and contained an editorial, "The Curtains Drop on the Old Order." See also Guy B. Johnson, "Southern Offensive," *Common Ground* 4 (Summer 1944):87–93.

12. Lillian Smith, "Address to White Liberals," *New Republic* 111 (Sept. 1944):331–33. See also Lillian Smith, "Southern Defensive—II," *Common Ground* 4 (Spring 1944); 36–42; and J. Saunders Redding, "Southern Defensive—I," *Common Ground* 4 (Spring 1944):43–45. Both authors rebuke the SRC for failing to confront racial issues. Smith went further, suggesting that SRC held "a regressive belief in segregation. "

13. Bound copies of the *Southern Patriot*, vols. 1 and 2, were made available to the author by Anne Braden. Microfilm copies are available from the Social Action Collection, SHSW. See also James A. Dombrowski, "Mobilizing the South for Victory," speech before the National Conference of Social Workers, New Orleans, La., 25–31 May 1942, p. 6, in Dombrowski Papers.

14. Interview with Dombrowski, 25–31 Oct. 1978.

15. *Southern Patriot*, Oct. 1943, SCHWA. See also "Threats to National Unity in the South," n.d., Dombrowski Papers; Krueger, *Promises to Keep*, 107–8; and Sosna, *In Search of the Silent South*, 145.

16. SCHW, Executive Secretary's Report, Jan. 1947, SCHWA, Box 3.

17. Ibid. See also Clark Foreman, "Fascism Has Foot in Door," *PM* 23 Aug. 1946.

18. Foreman, "Fascism." See also *Southern Patriot,* 1945–46.

19. *Southern Patriot,* 1945–46. See also Charles S. Johnson et al., *To Stem This Tide: A Survey of Racial Tension Areas in the United States* (Boston: Pilgrim Press, 1943).

20. Charles S. Johnson et al., *To Stem This Tide.*

21. Interview with Dombrowski, 25–31 Oct. 1978.

22. Ibid. Dombrowski kept a scrapbook of newspaper clippings about the SCHW's work and attacks on the organization in 1945 and 1946; Dombrowski Papers.

23. Dombrowski scrapbook, 1945–46. See also W.E.B. DuBois, "As the Crow Flies," *New York Amsterdam News,* 20 Apr. 1940; and Walter White, quoted in Sosna, *In Search of the Silent South,* 106.

24. DuBois, "As the Crow Flies."

25. "Acme of 'Crust,'" *Chattanooga News–Free Press,* 29 Sept. 1942.

26. John P. Davis to Dombrowski, 27 Jan. 1943. Related letters in SCHW Records, Tuskegee Institute, Box 5.

27. See Guy Johnson, "Southern Offensive." Committee reports from Washington, North Carolina, and Georgia are scattered in SCHWA, Dombrowski Papers, and Foreman Papers.

28. Interview with Dombrowski, 6–9 Dec. 1979.

29. Theodore G. Bilbo to Hugo Black, 26 Mar. 1945, copy in Dombrowski Papers. See also Bobby W. Saucier, "The Public Career of Theodore G. Bilbo" (Ph.D. diss., Tulane Univ., 1971).

30. Theodore G. Bilbo to Dombrowski, 5 Nov. 1945, Dombrowski Papers.

31. Interview with Dombrowski, 6–9 Dec. 1979. See also "Fundraising Appeal," SCHW, n.d., Foreman Papers.

32. Interview with Dombrowski, 6–9 Dec. 1979.

33. U.S., Congress, *Congressional Record* 92, pt. 13:648, and pt. 14:591.

34. "Look Him In The Eye" (Nashville, Tenn.: SCHW, 1945), n.p.

35. U.S., Congress, *Congressional Record* 92, pt. 13:648 and pt. 14:591. See also SCHW news release, 23 Jan. 1946, Dombrowski Papers.

36. "The Truth About Columbia, Tennessee" (Nashville, Tenn.: SCHW, 1946), n.p.; "May Let Off Others in Mink Slide Case," *New York Times,* 4 Nov. 1945.

37. "The Truth About Columbia," n.p.

38. Clark Foreman to Walter White, 20 Apr. 1946, Foreman Papers.

39. Krueger, *Promises to Keep,* 151.

40. "Jury Finishes Questioning of Dombrowski," *Nashville Banner,* 4 June 1946.

41. Ibid.

42. "SCHW Branded Southern Front of Communism," *Nashville Banner*, 19 July 1946.

43. "Communist Daily Worker Comes to Southern Conference for Human Welfare. Here—And Workers Seem to Follow 'Line,' " *Nashville Banner*, 1 Aug. 1946.

44. Interview with Dombrowski, 6–9 Dec. 1979.

## Chapter 10

1. *Southern Patriot*, April 1945, p. 8.
2. Krueger, *Promises to Keep*, 145.
3. Dombrowski to Ethel Clyde, 24 Feb. 1944, Dombrowski Papers.
4. SCHW, "Meeting of the Board of Representatives," SCHW, Minutes, Washington, D.C., 6 Jan. 1945, SCHWA, Box 30.
5. Ibid.
6. Interview with Dombrowski, 6–9 Dec. 1979.
7. SCHW, Executive Secretary's Report, Jan. 1946, SCHWA, Box 3.
8. Interview with Dombrowski, 6–9 Dec. 1979. See also Theodore G. Bilbo to Patricia Murphy Frank, 23 June 1945, Braden Papers.
9. Theodore G. Bilbo to R.M. Newton, 2 Oct. 1945, as quoted in Saucier, "Public Career of Bilbo," 218.
10. Dombrowski, confidential memorandum, n.d., SCHWA, Box 3.
11. Memorandum for the CIO Executive Board, 12 Nov. 1944, SCHWA. See also *New York Times*, 19 Apr. 1946.
12. Paul Christopher to Clark Foreman, 3 May 1946, Foreman Papers.
13. Osceola McKaine to Allen S. Haywood, 14 Apr. 1946, SCHWA, Box 3. See also Haywood to McKaine, 18 Apr. 1948, Dombrowski Papers.
14. Haywood to McKaine, 18 Apr. 1948, Dombrowski Papers.
15. Haywood to McKaine, 18 Apr. 1948. See also "CIO Rejects Powell Support in Drive South," n.d., reprint of report from Washington bureau, *Chicago Defender*, in Foreman Papers; and Krueger, *Promises to Keep*, 139–42.
16. Interview with Dombrowski, 6–9 Dec. 1979.
17. Dombrowski to Board Members, 24 Dec. 1946, Foreman Papers. See also *CIO News*, 18 Mar. 1946, p. 2; 25 Mar. 1946, p. 9; 15 Apr. 1946, p. 6. And see F. Ray Marshall, *The Negro and Organized Labor* (New York: Wiley, 1965), 42–45.
18. Dombrowski to Executive Board, 7 Aug. 1945; Executive Secretary's Report, 12 Sept. 1945; Minutes of the Executive Board, 22–23 Jan. 1946, all in SCHWA, Box 3.
19. Dombrowski recognized that the NAACP's total membership far outstripped the SCHW's nationally. For the South, however, his claim was probably correct.
20. Interview with Dombrowski, 6–9 Dec. 1979. See also "Dombrowski Offices

May Be Moved to New Orleans," *Nashville Banner,* 9 Aug. 1946, and "Mr.
Dombrowski Moves Away," *Nashville Banner,* 27 Nov. 1946.

21. See also "SCHW Assailed in New Orleans," *Nashville Banner,* 17 Nov.
1946. James A. Dombrowski, "The Southern Conference for Human Welfare,"
*Common Ground* 6 (Summer 1946):14–25.

22. "SCHW Assailed in New Orleans," *Nashville Banner,* 17 Nov. 1946.

23. Ibid.

24. FBI Memorandum, 26 Nov. 1946. Collection of Frank T. Adams.

25. Interview with Dombrowski, 6–9 Dec. 1979. See also "Stenographic Report of the New Orleans Convention," Braden Papers; and Krueger, *Promises to Keep,* 152–58.

26. Interview with Dombrowski, 6–9 Dec. 1979.

27. Margaret Fuller to Clark Foreman, 29 Dec. 1946, Foreman Papers.

28. Dombrowski to Tarleton Collier, 10 Dec. 1946, Dombrowski Papers.

29. Interview with Dombrowski, 6–9 Dec. 1979.

30. This direct quotation, other quotations, and the summary of the exchanges
are taken from SCHW, "Meeting of the Board of Representatives," Minutes,
Greensboro, N.C., 5 Jan. 1947, SCHWA. Related correspondence may be found in
Dombrowski Papers, Foreman Papers and SCHWA. See also Krueger, *Promises to
Keep,* 155–58; Sosna, *In Search of the Silent South,* 146–48; and esp. Irwin
Klibaner, "The Southern Conference Educational Fund: A History" (Ph.D. diss.,
Univ. of Wisconsin, 1971), 37–38; and "Minutes, Board of Representatives Meeting," 2 Dec. 1946, Dombrowski Papers.

31. Interview with Dombrowski, 6–9 Dec. 1979. Clark Foreman to Frank T.
Adams, 18 Apr. 1979. My correspondence with Foreman was not entirely productive. For instance, no light was shed on the backgrounds or motives of the persons
he had handpicked for seats on the board.

32. Interview with Virginia Durr, 24 Oct. 1978.

33. Ibid.

34. Ibid.

35. Ibid. See also Aubrey Williams to Ralph McGill, 16 Dec. 1953, Frank T.
Adams Collection.

36. Interview with Dombrowski, 25–31 Oct. 1978.

37. Ibid.

38. Dombrowski to SCHW Board, 6 Dec. 1946. See also Dombrowski to Clark
Foreman, 6 Dec. 1946. Both in Dombrowski Papers.

39. Dombrowski to SCHW Board, 6 Dec. 1946.

40. Interview with Virginia Durr, 24 Oct. 1978; Interview with Myles Horton,
22 May 1977.

41. Myles Horton to Dombrowski, 10 Dec. 1946, Dombrowski Papers. See also
Clark Foreman to Myles Horton, 11 Dec. 1946, Foreman Papers; and interview
with Myles Horton, 22 May 1977.

42. Rebecca M. Gershon to Clark Foreman, 8 Dec. 1946, Foreman Papers.

43. Lucy Randolph Mason to Clark Foreman, 8 Dec. 1946, Foreman Papers.

44. Lewis Jones to Dombrowski, 13 Jan. 1947, Dombrowski Papers. Interview with Lewis Jones, 1–2 Nov. 1978.

45. Virginia Durr to Dombrowski, ca. 15 Dec. 1946, Dombrowski Papers. See also Mary Price Adamson to Frank T. Adams, 15 Sept. 1976. During my interview with Adamson in California, she candidly fleshed out this history.

46. Interview with Dombrowski, 25–31 Oct. 1978. See also Krueger, *Promises to Keep*, 154–57.

47. SCHW, Minutes of the Board of Representatives, 5 Jan. 1947, Dombrowski Papers.

48. Ibid.

49. Ibid.

50. Ibid.

51. Ibid.

52. Ibid.

53. Ibid.

54. Ibid.

55. Ibid.

56. Ibid.

57. Ibid.

58. Ibid. Interview with Dombrowski, 25–31 Oct. 1978.

59. Clark Foreman to Dombrowski, 10 Apr. 1947, Foreman Papers.

60. Dombrowski to Daniel Weitzman, 29 May 1947, Dombrowski Papers.

### Chapter 11

1. Interviews with Dombrowski, 25–31 Oct. 1978 and 6–9 Dec. 1979. Three additional primary sources provide the basis for this chapter: SCHW, Board of Representatives, "Minutes of Meeting," Birmingham, Ala., 19 Apr. 1947; SCHW, "Administrative Committee, Minutes of Meeting," Washington, D.C., 21 June 1947; and SCHW, "Report of the Administrator to the Board," Richmond, Va., 12 July 1947—all in SCHW Papers, Box 6.

2. Henry Fowler to Dombrowski, 27 Apr. 1947, Dombrowski Papers.

3. SCHW Board Minutes, 19 Apr. 1947, SCHWA, Box 6.

4. U.S., Congress, House of Representatives, Committee on Un-American Activities, *Report on the Southern Conference for Human Welfare*, 80 Cong., 1st Sess. (Washington, D.C.: USGPO, 1947). See also Walter Gellhorn, "Report on a Report of the House Committee on Un-American Activities," *Harvard Law Review* 60 (Oct. 1947):1193–1234; and "Resolution, Meeting of the Board of the SCHW," Richmond, Va., 21 Nov. 1947, SCHWA.

5. SCHW, Administrative Committee Minutes, 21 June 1947.

6. *New Orleans States* articles and related materials from the Young Men's Business Club, SCHWA, Box 1.

7. SCHW, Administrator's Report to Board, 12 July 1947. Interview with Dombrowski, 25–31 Oct. 1978, SCHW Papers.

8. Interview with Dombrowski, 25–31 Oct. 1978.

9. Ibid.

10. Ibid.

11. Ibid.

12. Lucy Randolph Mason to Dombrowski, 22 Apr. 1947, SCHWA.

13. Ibid.

14. Interview with Dombrowski, 25–31 Oct. 1978.

15. Ibid.

16. Interview with Virginia Durr, 24 Oct. 1978.

17. Interview with Dombrowski, 25–31 Oct. 1978. See also Krueger, *Promises to Keep,* 189–91.

18. SCHW, Board, "Resolution," 21 Nov. 1947, SCHWA.

19. Interview with Virginia Durr, 25 Oct. 1978.

## Chapter 12

1. American Civil Liberties Union, *In Times of Challenge: U.S. Liberties, 1946–47,* 4. See also Caute, *Great Fear.* 101, 112, 169–70, 269, 271–72.

2. Caute, *Great Fear,* loc. cit.

3. As quoted in Dombrowski Journal, 1947, Dombrowski Papers.

4. Aubrey Williams, "Memoirs," Williams Papers, Box 44, n.p.

5. Dombrowski to subscribers, *Southern Patriot,* 30 Aug. 1947.

6. Ibid.

7. Dombrowski to Frank T. Adams, 24 Apr. 1979.

8. Dombrowski, Notes, 5 Aug. 1947, n.p., Dombrowski Papers. See also *Southern Patriot,* August 1947.

9. Dombrowski to Frank T. Adams, 24 Apr. 1979.

10. Ibid.

11. Aubrey Williams, "Memoirs." See also Joseph P. Lash, *Eleanor and Franklin* (New York: American Library, 1971), 670; and Klibaner, "The Southern Conference Educational Fund," 163.

12. John Salmond, *A Southern Rebel: The Life and Times of Aubrey Willis Williams, 1890–1965* (Chapel Hill: Univ. of North Carolina Press, 1983). U.S., Congress, Senate, *Nomination of Aubrey W. Williams: Hearings before the Committee on Agriculture and Forestry,* 79th Cong., 1st sess., 1945.

13. Interview with Dombrowski, 5–6 Dec. 1982.

14. Aubrey Williams to Eleanor Roosevelt, 12 May 1954, Williams Papers, Box 38.

15. Interview with Dombrowski, 5–6 Dec. 1982.

16. Saucier, "Public Career of Bilbo."

17. *Nashville Tennessean,* 23 June 1947, and *Pascagoula (Miss.) Chronicle Star,* 28 July 1946.

18. Dombrowski, Notes, 4 Aug. 1947, n.p., Dombrowski Papers. See also Clarice T. Campbell and Oscar Allen Rogers, Jr., *Mississippi: The View From Tougaloo* (Jackson: Univ. Press of Mississippi, 1979), 186.

19. Interview with Dombrowski, 5–6 Dec. 1982.

20. Ibid.

21. Ibid.

22. Ibid.

23. Dombrowski to Ethel Clyde, 12 Aug. 1947, Dombrowski Papers.

24. Interview with Dombrowski, 5–6 Dec. 1982.

25. Ibid.

26. Ibid.

27. Ibid. See also *Southern Patriot,* Oct. 1947.

28. *Southern Patriot,* Oct. 1947.

29. Dombrowski to Mary Price, 19 Oct. 1947, Dombrowski Papers.

30. Edith and Neth Bower to Dombrowski, 3 Jan. 1948, Dombrowski Papers.

31. John B. McDaniel, quoted in William Bryan Crawley, Jr., *Bill Tuck: A Political Life in Harry Byrd's Virginia* (Charlottesville: Univ. of Virginia Press, 1979), 142.

32. Associated Press, quoted in Dombrowski Notes, 4 Aug. 1947, Dombrowski Papers.

33. Ibid.

34. Dombrowski, Memo to Board of Directors of the SCEF, Oct. 1947, Dombrowski Papers.

35. Sen. Strom Thurmond, 25 quoted in Dombrowski Notes, 4 Aug. 1947, Dombrowski Papers.

36. Ibid.

37. Wilson Record, *Race and Radicalism: The NAACP and the Communist Party in Conflict* (Ithaca, N.Y.: Cornell Univ. Press, 1964), 97. Record presents a thorough, balanced analysis of the relationships between these often intertwined organizational histories.

38. Interview with Modjeska Simkins, 15 June 1977.

39. Ibid.

40. Interview with Dombrowski, 5–6 Dec. 1982.

41. Ibid.

42. Interview with Simkins, 15 June 1977.

43. Ibid.

44. Ibid.

45. "Senator Protests Arrest," *Birmingham News,* 6 May 1948. See also *Daily Worker,* 6 May 1948.

46. Interview with Simkins, 15 June 1977.

47. Ibid.

48. *Birmingham News,* 12 June 1948.

49. *Daily Worker,* 13 June 1948.

50. Ibid.

51. Record, *Race and Radicalism,* 97.

52. Dombrowski to Aubrey Williams, 1 Nov. 1948, Williams Papers.

53. *New York Times,* 21 Nov. 1948.

54. Jennings Perry, "Declaration of Civil Rights," SCHWA.

55. *New York Times,* 21 Nov. 1948.

56. Dombrowski to Ethel Clyde, 7 Dec. 1948.

57. Ibid.

## Chapter 13

1. See John P. Davis, *The American Negro Reference Book* (Englewood Cliffs, N.J.: Prentice-Hall, 1967), 49.

2. John P. Davis, *American Negro,* 498–99. See also *Plessy v. Ferguson,* 163 U.S. 537; and Jack Greenberg, *Race Relations and American Law* (New York: Columbia Univ. Press, 1959).

3. John P. Davis, *American Negro,* 49.

4. Reinhold Niebuhr, *Moral Man and Immoral Society* (New York: Scribner's, 1932).

5. Ibid. See also Richard Wrightman Fox, *Reinhold Niebuhr: A Biography* (New York: Pantheon, 1986); and Christopher Lasch, *In These Times,* 26 Mar. 1986, p. 13.

6. Lasch, *In These Times,* 26 Mar. 1986.

7. Ibid.

8. Ibid.

9. Ibid.

10. Irwin Klibaner, *Conscience of a Troubled South: The Southern Conference Educational Fund, 1946–1966* (Brooklyn, N.Y.: Carlson, 1989). Klibaner's scholarship and analysis are invaluable.

11. Interview with Dombrowski, 5–6 Dec. 1982.

12. *Southern Patriot,* May 1948.

13. Redding S. Sugg, Jr., and George Hilton Jones, *The Southern Regional Education Board: Ten Years of Regional Cooperation in Higher Education* (Baton Rouge: Louisiana State Univ. Press, 1960), 11–14.

14. James A. Dombrowski, "The Regional School Plan," *New World Commentator* 2 (Dec. 1949):6–10.

15. *Southern Patriot,* Sept. 1949.

16. SCEF, Minutes, 6 Nov. 1949, p. 3, SCHWA, Box 5.

17. Aubrey Williams to John E. Ivey, Jr., 6 Mar. 1950, Williams Papers.

18. Ibid.

19. John E. Ivey, Jr., to Aubrey Williams, 1 Mar. 1950, Williams Papers, Box 39.

20. SCEF, Minutes, 6 Nov. 1949.

21. Ibid.

22. Dombrowski to Mary McLeod Bethune, 26 Nov. 1949, Dombrowski Papers.

23. *Atlanta Constitution,* 26 Feb. 1950.

24. Ibid.

25. Dombrowski, Report to the SCEF Board of Directors, 27 Apr. 1951, Dombrowski Papers.

26. Albert Einstein, as quoted in *Southern Patriot,* April 1950.

27. Ibid.

28. Ibid.

29. Dombrowski, Report to SCEF Board of Directors, 27 Apr. 1951, Dombrowski Papers.

30. Judge Charles Markell, as quoted in Sugg and G.H. Jones, *Southern Regional Board,* 46.

31. Dombrowski, Report to SCEF Board of Directors, 27 Apr. 1951, Dombrowski Papers.

32. Dombrowski organized 18 lawyers from each southern state to file an *amicus curiae* brief on behalf of Sweatt before the U.S. Supreme Court; *Southern Patriot,* Jan. 1950.

33. Dombrowski, Report to SCEF Board of Directors, 27 Apr. 1951, Dombrowski Papers.

34. Interview with Dombrowski, 5–6 Dec. 1982. See also Daniel Rosenberg, *New Orleans Dockworkers: Race, Labor, and Unionism, 1892–1923* (Albany: State Univ. of New York Press, 1988).

35. *Southern Patriot,* Jan. 1951.

36. *Southern Patriot,* Apr. 1951.

37. Dombrowski, Report to SCEF Board of Directors, 27 Apr. 1951, p. 3, Dombrowski Papers. See also Dombrowski to Ethel Clyde, 13 Mar. 1951, Dombrowski Papers. The sequence here attests to Dombrowski's penchant for finding funds before launching a campaign.

38. *Southern Patriot,* Apr. 1951.

39. Interview with Dombrowski, 5–6 Dec. 1982.

40. *Southern Patriot,* Dec. 1951.

41. Ibid.

42. Ibid.

43. Ibid.

44. *Southern Patriot,* Jan. 1951.
45. Dombrowski to Ethel Clyde, 13 Mar. 1951, Dombrowski Papers.
46. Interview with Dombrowski, 6–9 Dec. 1979.
47. *Memphis Commercial Appeal,* 6 Apr. 1952.
48. Dombrowski, Memorandum to Members of the Board, SCEF, 21 July 1952, Dombrowski Papers.
49. Ibid.
50. Dombrowski to Ethel Clyde, 2 Oct. 1952, Dombrowski Papers.
51. Interview with Dombrowski, 6–9 Dec. 1979.
52. *Vieux Carre Courier,* 2–10 Feb. 1962.
53. *Southern Patriot,* Jan. 1953.
54. Dombrowski to E.D. Sledge, 2 Aug. 1953, Dombrowski Papers.
55. Ibid.
56. SCEF, press release, n.d., Dombrowski Papers.

## Chapter 14

1. Interview with Dombrowski, 6–9 Dec. 1979. Subpoena for Aubrey Williams is in Williams Papers, Box 41. See also Klibaner, *Conscience of a Troubled South,* 73; and Salmond, *A Southern Rebel,* 229. The date of this event is in dispute. Klibaner writes that the subpeona was handed to Williams on 5 Mar. Salmond writes that the date was 6 Mar. Dombrowski recalled 5 Mar.
2. *Southern Patriot,* Feb. 1954. See also Robert E. Griffith, *The Politics of Fear: Joseph R. McCarthy and the Senate* (Lexington: Univ. Press of Kentucky, 1970).
3. Interview with Dombrowski, 6–9 Dec. 1979. See also Minutes, SCEF Board of Directors, 7 Feb. 1954, Dombrowski Papers.
4. Interview with Dombrowski, 6–9 Dec. 1979.
5. *Southern Patriot,* Feb. 1954.
6. Klibaner, *Conscience of a Troubled South,* 74–75.
7. Aubrey Williams to Dombrowski, 7 Mar. 1954, Williams Papers.
8. Aubrey Williams to Eleanor Roosevelt, 12 May 1954, Williams Papers.
9. Aubrey Williams to Dombrowski, 7 Mar. 1954, Williams Papers. See also Aubrey Williams to Benjamin Mays, 5 Mar. 1954, Williams Papers, Box 38.
10. Interview with Virginia Durr, 24 Oct. 1978. See also Barnard, *Virginia Durr: Outside the Magic Circle,* 254–73 *passim,* 295, 297, 312, 314.
11. Interview with Dombrowski, 6–9 Dec. 1979.
12. Interview with Myles Horton, 22 May 1977. See also Myles Horton, "Statement in connection with hearings before Subcommittee on Internal Security, New Orleans, Louisiana," 18–20 Mar. 1954, Highlander Papers, Box 33.
13. Aubrey Williams, "Memoirs."
14. Ibid.

15. Aubrey Williams to Clarence Mitchell, Feb. 8, 1954, Williams Papers, Box 44.

16. Aubrey Williams to Mary McLeod Bethune, 7 Mar. 1954, Williams Papers, Box 44.

17. Aubrey Williams, "Memoirs."

18. *Southern Patriot* Apr. 1954.

19. "The Congressional Inquisition Moves South," *I.F. Stone's Weekly,* 27 Mar. 1954. See also "The Witch Trial at New Orleans," *Alabama Journal,* 25 Mar. 1954; and "Battle of New Orleans—Eastland Meets His Match," *Nation,* 3 Apr. 1954.

20. Interview with Dombrowski, 6–9 Dec. 1979 and 5–6 Dec. 1982.

21. U.S., Congress, Senate, Committee of the Judiciary, Subcommittee to Investigate the Administration of the Internal Security Act and Other Internal Security Laws, Transcript, Hearings, New Orleans, La., 18–19 Mar. 1954, 3 vols. 1–3. Hereafter referred to as Internal Security Hearings. P. I:3.

22. Ibid., I:20. See also "Congressional Inquisition Moves South."

23. Internal Security Hearings, 1:80.

24. Ibid., 1:111.

25. "Congressional Inquisition Moves South."

26. Interview with Virginia Durr, 24 Oct. 1978.

27. Ibid.

28. Internal Security Hearings, 2:203–239.

29. Interview with Dombrowski, 25–31 Oct. 1978. See also "Congressional Inquisition Moves South."

30. "Congressional Inquisition Moves South."

31. Ibid.

32. *New Orleans Item,* 21 Mar. 1950.

33. Interview with Dombrowski, 25–31 Oct. 1978.

34. Ibid. See also: Internal Security Hearings, 2:223–24; "Black's Relative Is Linked to Reds," *New York Times,* 19 Mar. 1954; "Ex-Communist Names Sister-In-Law of Black As Party Aide," *Washington Star,* 19 Mar. 1954.

35. "Congressional Inquisition Moves South."

36. Interview with Virginia Durr, 24 Oct. 1978.

37. Petition to Sen. William Langer, U.S. Senate Judiciary Committee, n.d., Dombrowski Papers. See also Aubrey Williams, "Memoirs," and Aubrey Williams to Eleanor Roosevelt, 12 May 1954, Williams Papers, Box 38.

38. Aubrey Williams, "Memoirs." See also Aubrey Williams to Lyndon B. Johnson, 5 Apr. 1954, Williams Papers.

39. Award to *Southern Patriot,* Lincoln Univ., Jefferson City, Mo., 22 Apr. 1954.

40. John P. Davis, *American Negro,* 373–75. See also Richard Kluger, *Simple Justice* (New York: Random House, 1975), and William H. Chafe, *Civilities and*

*Civil Rights: Greensboro, North Carolina, and the Black Struggle for Freedom* (New York: Oxford Univ. Press, 1980).

41. As quoted in Klibaner, *Conscience of a Troubled South*, 105.

42. *Richmond Times Dispatch*, 24 June 1954. See also Robert C. Smith, *They Closed Their Schools* (Chapel Hill: Univ. of North Carolina Press, 1965).

43. U.S., Dept. of Justice, FBI, File AT-100-5234, 6 Feb. 1954.

44. *Southern Patriot*, Oct. 1954.

45. *Southern Patriot*, Jan. 1955.

46. *Houston Post*, 18 May 1955.

47. *New York Times*, 26 June 1956.

48. *New Orleans Times Picayune*, 6 Aug. 1956.

49. Interview with Dombrowski, 6–9 Dec. 1979.

50. Aubrey Williams to Lillian Smith, 17 Dec. 1954, Williams Papers, Box 39.

51. Interview with E.D. Nixon, 22 Aug. 1977.

52. Albert W. Barnett to Roy Wilkins, 4 Dec. 1956, Dombrowski Papers.

53. Ibid.

54. Record, *Race and Radicalism*, 164.

55. Roy Wilkins to Albert E. Barnett, 4 Feb. 1957, and Barnett to Wilkins, 11 Feb. 1957, both in Dombrowski Papers.

56. Aubrey Williams to Albert E. Barnett, 1 Aug. 1957, Williams Papers, Box 39.

57. Alfred A. Maund to Dombrowski, 31 July 1957, and Dombrowski to Maund, 2 Aug. 1957, Dombrowski Papers. See also Louisiana, Legislature, Joint Legislative Committee on Un-American Activities, "Activities of the Southern Conference Educational Fund, Inc., in Louisiana," Report No. 6, pt. 3, 19 Jan. 1965. Hereafter referred to as LUAC, Report.

58. Aubrey Williams to Dombrowski, 18 Feb. 1956, Dombrowski Papers.

59. Interview with Dombrowski, 6–9 Dec. 1979. See also Record, *Race and Radicalism*, 203–214.

## Chapter 15

1. Interview with Rev. Fred. L. Shuttlesworth, 6 Nov. 1979.

2. "Kentucky Rewards Its Good Samaritan," *Packinghouse Worker*, Oct. 1955. See also news release from Wade Defense Committee, 9 May 1957, Dombrowski Papers.

3. As quoted in *Southern Patriot*, Oct. 1953.

4. Interview with Anne Braden, 5–6 Nov. 1979. See also Anne Braden, *The Wall Between* (New York: Monthly Review Press, 1958).

5. Interview with Anne Braden, 5–6 Nov. 1979.

6. Ibid. In this respect, Dombrowski's thinking paralleled theologian Karl

Barth's line of reasoning. In 1957, Barth scorned Niebuhr's strident anticommunism: "Anti means against. God is not against, but for men. The communists are men too. God is also for the communists. So a Christian cannot be against the communists but only for them. To be for the communists does not mean to be for communism." Karl Barth, *Christian Century* 74 (Mar. 1959):335.

7. "Charge Petition Link With Suspect Fund," *New Orleans Item,* 25 Feb. 1957.

8. Ibid.

9. "Early SCHW Supports Tell of Riff; Tolerated Help of Known Commies," *New Orleans States-Item,* 20 May 1957.

10. *Southern Patriot,* Feb. 1956.

11. *Southern Patriot,* Oct. 1956.

12. James A. Dombrowski, "School Desegregation in the South: A Review and an Analysis," Oct. 18 1957, mimeo., Dombrowski Papers.

13. *Southern Patriot,* Oct. 1957.

14. Aubrey Williams to Dombrowski, 24 Oct. 1957, Braden Papers, Box 17, Folder 5. See also Salmond, *Southern Rebel,* 247–51.

15. Aubrey Williams to Dombrowski, 24 Oct. 1957.

16. As quoted in *Southern Patriot,* Feb. 1959.

17. James M. Nabrit, Jr., "Summary of Reports on Voting Restrictions in Southern States," 27 Apr. 1957, Dombrowski Papers. See also Margaret Price, *The Negro and the Ballot in the South* (Atlanta, Ga.: Southern Regional Council, 1959).

18. During this trip, which began on 13 Mar. 1958 and ended on 2 Apr. 1958, Dombrowski typed notes on each day's events. Dombrowski Papers.

19. Ibid., n.p.

20. Aubrey Williams, "Report from the South," mimeo., 27 Apr. 1957, Dombrowski Papers.

21. Ibid.

22. Nabrit, "Summary of Reports on Voting."

23. As quoted in William Bryan Crawley, Jr., *Bill Tuck: A Political Life in Harry Byrd's Virginia* (Charlottesville: Univ. of Virginia Press, 1979), 142.

24. See Internal Security Hearings.

25. Dombrowski to Ethel Clyde, 24 July 1958, Dombrowski Papers.

26. Dombrowski Notes, 6 Aug. 1958, Dombrowski Papers.

27. Ibid.

28. Ibid.

29. "An Open Letter to the U.S. House of Representatives," *Washington Post and Times-Herald,* 31 July 1958.

30. Dombrowski Notes, 6 Aug. 1958, Dombrowski Papers. See also interview with Anne Braden, 5–6 Nov. 1979. Braden's book, *The Wall Between,* was published 8 days before the Atlanta hearings opened.

31. *Los Angeles Tribune,* 11 July 1958.

32. Ibid. See also *Southern Patriot,* Sept. 1958, and Walter Goodman, *The Committee* (Baltimore, Md.: Penguin, 1969), 420.

33. Interview with Shuttlesworth, 6 Nov. 1978.

34. Jared Joseph Spaeth, "*Braden v. United States:* A Constitutional Case History," M.A. thesis, Butler Univ., 1968, p. 76.

35. Dombrowski Notes, 1 May 1961, Dombrowski Papers.

36. Ibid.

37. *New York Times,* 21 Jan. 1961.

38. Frank T. Adams, *Unearthing Seeds of Fire,* 89.

39. Frank T. Adams, ed., *Just Schools: A Special Report Commemorating the 25th Anniversary of the Brown Decision* (Chapel Hill, N.C.: Institute for Policy Studies, 1979), 56. See also Louisiana, State Advisory Committee on Civil Rights, *The New Orleans School Crisis,* 1961.

40. Dombrowski Notes, 30 Mar. 1961, Dombrowski Papers. See also *Miami Herald,* 31 May 1961.

41. *New York Times,* 22 May 1961. See also Dombrowski Notes, 24 May 1961, Dombrowski Papers.

42. Interview with E.D. Nixon, 22 Aug. 1977.

43. Interview with Dombrowski, 25–31 Oct. 1978.

44. As quoted in Dombrowski Notes, 24 May 1961, Dombrowski Papers.

45. Ibid.

46. Ibid.

47. Ibid. See also *New Orleans Times Picayune,* 22 May 1961.

48. Dombrowski to Ethel Clyde, 13 Aug. 1961, Dombrowski Papers.

49. See Klibaner, *Conscience of a Troubled South,* 177–98. Political realities forced this strategy on the SCEF, but circumstances proved fortuitous from Dombrowski's vantage point.

50. Wyatt Tee Walker to Southern Christian Leadership Conference Affiliates, 6 Nov. 1961, Braden Papers, Box 13.

51. Ibid.

52. Carl Braden to John M. Coe, 31 May 1962, Braden Papers, Box 35.

53. James Foreman to Dombrowski, 16 June 1962, Braden Papers, Box 35.

54. Robert Moses to Dombrowski, Nov. 1961, Braden Papers, Box 47.

55. Dombrowski to Robert Zellner, 13 June 1961, Dombrowski Papers. See also LUAC, Report 5, pt. 2, Exhibit 46, p. 102.

56. Aubrey Williams to Anne Braden, 14 May 1961, Dombrowski Papers.

57. See "Report of John Robert Zellner on White Student Project (School Year 1961–62)," 19 May 1962, Dombrowski Papers.

58. Interview with Dombrowski, 25–31 Oct. 1978 and 5–6 Dec. 1982. See also Branch, *Parting the Waters,* 509–512.

59. Howard Zinn, *SNCC: The New Abolitionists* (Boston: Beacon, 1964), 72–75, 170, 192.

60. Dombrowski Notes, 9 Mar. 1962, Dombrowski Papers.

61. Ibid.

62. Interview with Dombrowski, 5–6 Dec. 1982. See also Zinn, *SNCC*.

63. Dombrowski Notes, 10 Nov. 1962, Dombrowski Papers.

64. Interview with Shuttlesworth, 6 Nov. 1978. See also Aldon D. Morris, *The Origins of the Civil Rights Movement: Black Communities Organizing for Change* (New York: Free Press, 1984), 229–74.

65. Morris, *Origins*, 229–74.

66. Ibid.

67. Ibid.

68. *Southern Patriot*, May 1963. See also Dombrowski Notes, 24 Apr. 1963, Dombrowski Papers.

69. Dombrowski Notes, 24 Apr. 1963.

70. *Southern Patriot*, May 1963. See also Branch, *Parting the Waters*, 673–795.

71. Interview with Dombrowski, 5–6 Dec. 1978.

72. Interview with Shuttlesworth, 25–31 Oct. 1978. See also Record, *Race and Radicalism*, 185.

73. For one version of why Baker left SCLC, see William Kunstler, *Deep in My Heart* (New York: William Morrow, 1966), 101. For another, see Morris, *Origins*. For Salter's experiences in Jackson, Miss., before he joined the SCEF, see John R. Salter, Jr., *Jackson, Mississippi: An American Chronicle of Struggle and Schism* (Hicksville, N.Y.: Exposition Press, 1979).

## Chapter 16

1. *New Orleans Times-Picayune*, 5 Oct. 1963.

2. James A. Dombrowski, "The Argosy and Agony of the Raids," typed notes, 4 and 5 Oct. 1963, Dombrowski Papers.

3. The Subversive Activities and Communist Control Act, Louisiana Revised Statute 14, Section 358, et seq.

4. Dombrowski, "The Argosy and Agony."

5. Ibid. See also Arthur Kinoy, *Rights on Trial: The Odyssey of a People's Lawyer* (Cambridge, Mass.: Harvard Univ. Press, 1983), 209–255.

6. Interview with Kinoy, 4 Nov. 1984.

7. *New Orleans Times-Picayune*, 6 Oct. 1963.

8. *New Orleans Times-Picayune*, 5 Oct. 1963.

9. Dombrowski, "The Argosy and Agony." See also *New Orleans Times-Picayune*, 5 Oct. 1963.

10. Dombrowski, "The Argosy and the Agony."

11. *National Guardian,* 30 Mar. 1977.See also Darlene Clark Hine, ed., *Black Women in American History* (Brooklyn: Carlson, 1989), vols. 5, 8, and 16. For a compassionate essay on Hamer's life, see John Egerton, *A Mind to Stay Here: Profiles from the South* (New York: Macmillan, 1981).

12. Dombrowski, "The Argosy and Agony."

13. Kinoy, *Rights on Trial,* 218–20.

14. Interview with Dombrowski, 5–6 Dec. 1978. See also Jack Peebles, "The Dombrowski Case," *Guild Practitioner* 33, no. 33 (1976):89–101.

15. Interview with Dombrowski, 5–6 Dec. 1978.

16. Ibid.

17. *New Orleans Times-Picayune,* 26 Oct. 1963. See also Peebles, "Dombrowski Case," 95.

18. Interview with Dombrowski, 5–6 Dec. 1978.

19. Ibid. See also Peebles, "Dombrowski Case," 94.

20. Peebles, "Dombrowski Case," 94.

21. Ibid.

22. Bradley R. Brewer, "*Dombrowski v. Pfister:* Federal Injunctions Against State Prosecutions in Civil Rights Cases—A New Trend in Federal-State-Judicial Relations," *Fordham Law Review* 34, no. 1 (1965):78.

23. *Southern Patriot,* Sept.–Nov. 1963, *passim.*

24. Interview with Dombrowski, 5–6 Dec. 1979. See also *New Orleans Times-Picayune,* 9 Nov. 1963.

25. Dombrowski to Ethel Clyde, 7 Nov. 1963, Dombrowski Papers.

26. Dombrowski to Ethel Clyde, 28 Nov. 1963, Dombrowski Papers.

27. Dombrowski to Ethel Clyde, 20 Nov. 1963, Dombrowski Papers.

28. Marjory Collins, "Witch Hunt Southern Style," *Minority of One,* May 1964, p. 19.

29. Interview with Dombrowski, 5–6 Dec. 1979. See also Brewer, "*Dombrowski v. Pfister*"; and W. William Hodes, "*Dombrowski v. Eastland*—A Political Compromise and Its Impact," *Rutgers Law Review* 22, no. 1 (1967):137–66.

30. Hodes, "Dombrowski v. Eastland," 139.

31. See Transcript of Record, *Dombrowski v. Eastland,* 387 U.S. 82 (1967).

32. Ibid.

33. *Kilbourn v. Thompson,* 103 U.S. 168, 204 (1880), quoted in Hodes, 151.

34. *Dombrowski v. Burbank,* 358 F 2d 821 (D.C. Cir. 1966).

35. Hodes, "Dombrowski v. Pfister," 162.

36. Peebles, "Dombrowski Case," 97–99.

37. Ibid.

38. LUAC, "Activities of the Southern Conference Educational Fund, Inc., in Louisiana," Report 5, pt. 3, 1963–64, p. 104.

39. Interview with Dombrowski, 6–9 Dec. 1979. See also James A. Dom-

browski, "Civil Rights and Civil Liberties in the South—1964," speech delivered at Unitarian-Universalist Fellowship, Los Angeles, 1964, Braden Papers, Box 34.

40. Dombrowski, "Civil Rights and Civil Liberties."

41. Ibid. See also Salmond, *Southern Rebel*, 283–84.

42. *Dombrowski v. Pfister*, 380 U.S. 479 (1965). See also Frank L. Maraist, "Federal Injunctive Relief Against State Court Proceedings: The Significance of Dombrowski," *Texas Law Review* (Feb. 1970):562.

43. Arthur Kinoy, "Brief Remarks on *Dombrowski v. Pfister*—A New Path in Constitutional Litigation?" *Guild Practitioner* 26, no. 1 (1967):7–8.

44. Peebles, "Dombrowski Case," 101.

### Epilogue

1. Dombrowski to Ethel Clyde, 27 Apr. 1972, Dombrowski Papers.

2. New Orleans *States-Item*, 20 Oct. 1976.

3. Interview with Dombrowski, 5–6 Dec. 1978. See also Klibaner, *Conscience of a Troubled South*, 40.

4. John S. Rosenberg, "Jim Dombrowski," *Nation*, 28 May 1983, p. 659. An obituary.

# Bibliography

## I. Unpublished Sources

### A. MANUSCRIPT COLLECTIONS

Carl and Anne Braden Papers, State Historical Society of Wisconsin, Madison, Wisc. Referred to as Braden Papers.

James A. Dombrowski Papers, State Historical Society of Wisconsin, Madison, Wisc. Referred to as Dombrowski Papers.

Mercer G. Evans Papers, Southern Historical Collection, University of North Carolina, Chapel Hill, N.C. Referred to as Evans Papers.

Clark Foreman Papers, Trevor Arnette Library, Atlanta University, Atlanta, Ga. Referred to as Foreman Papers.

Frank Porter Graham Papers, Southern Historical Collection, University of North Carolina, Chapel Hill, N.C. Referred to as Graham Papers.

Highlander Papers, Social Action Collection, State Historical Society of Wisconsin, Madison, Wisc. Referred to as Highlander Papers.

Myles Horton Papers, Highlander Research and Education Center, New Market, Tenn. Referred to as Horton Papers.

Howard Anderson Kester Papers, Southern Historical Collection, University of North Carolina, Chapel Hill, N.C. Referred to as Kester Papers.

Lucy Randolph Mason Papers, Manuscript Division, Duke University, Durham, N.C. Referred to as Mason Papers.

Southern Conference for Human Welfare Archives, Hollis Burke Frissell Library, Tuskegee Institute, Tuskegee, Ala. Referred to as SCHWA.

Southern Regional Council Archives, Southern Regional Council, Atlanta, Ga.

Aubrey Williams Papers, Franklin D. Roosevelt Library, Hyde Park, N.Y. Referred to as Williams Papers.

### B. OTHER UNPUBLISHED MATERIAL

Allred, William C., Jr. "The Southern Regional Council, 1943–1961." M.A. thesis, Emory University, 1966.

Beck, John P. "Highlander's Junior Union Camps, 1940–1944: Workers' Children and Working Class Culture." Paper delivered at the Fourth Southern Labor Studies Conference, 1 October 1982, Frank T. Adams Collection.

Belles, A. Gilbert. "The Julius Rosenwald Fund: Efforts in Race Relations, 1928–1948." Ph.D. dissertation, Vanderbilt University, 1972.

Berman, Daniel M. "The Political Philosophy of Hugo Black." M.A. thesis, Rutgers University, 1957.

Burrows, Edward F. "The Commission on Interracial Cooperation, 1919–1944: A Case Study in the History of Interracial Movements in the South." Ph.D. dissertation, University of Wisconsin, 1955.

Dombrowski, James A. "Religion and Vested Interests in the South in the Field of Slavery and the Slave-Trade, From 1819 to 1832." M.A. thesis, Union Theological Seminary, 1931.

————. "Fire in the Hole." Manuscript, in Frank T. Adams Collection.

Douty, Kenneth. "The Southern Conference for Human Welfare: A Report." N.d. Foreman Papers, Trevor Arnette Library, Atlanta University, Atlanta, Ga.

Evans, Mercer G. "History of the Organized Labor Movement in Georgia." Ph.D. dissertation, University of Chicago, 1929.

Gordon, J. King. "A Christian Socialist in the 1930s." N.d. Manuscript, in Frank T. Adams Collection.

Kester, Howard. "Autobiography." Tennant Farmers Union Papers, Southern Historical Collection, University of North Carolina, Chapel Hill, N.C.

Kifer, Allen F. "The Negro Under the New Deal, 1933–1941." Ph.D. dissertation, University of Wisconsin, 1961.

Klibaner, Irwin. "The Southern Conference Educational Fund: History." Ph.D. dissertation, University of Wisconsin, 1971.

Langworthy, Leah. "Struggles Within Struggles: Women's Experience at the Highlander Folk School." M.A. thesis, Carleton College, 1990.

Martin, Charles H. "The Rise and Fall of Popular Front Liberalism in the South: The Southern Conference for Human Welfare, 1938–1949." Paper presented at the Annual Meeting of the Organization of American Historians, 1979, New Orleans, La.

Montgomery, David. "Some Lessons from Labor History for Our Troubled Times." Speech given to the Sylvis Society, Cincinnati, Ohio, 14 October 1989.

Saucier, Bobby W. "The Public Career of Theodore G. Bilbo." Ph.D. dissertation, Tulane University, 1971.

Spaeth, Jared Joseph. "*Braden v. United States:* A Constitutional Case History." M.A. thesis, Butler University, 1968.

Williams, Aubrey. "A Southern Rebel." Aubrey Williams Papers, Franklin D. Roosevelt Library, Hyde Park, N.Y.

## II. Published Sources

### A. NEWSPAPERS AND PERIODICALS

*Atlanta Constitution*
*Atlanta Journal*
*Atlantic Monthly*
*Birmingham News*
*Charlotte (N.C.) Observer*
*Chattanooga News–Free Press*
*Christian Century*
*Commentary*
*Common Ground*
*Commonweal*
*Daily Worker*
*Emory Alumnus*
*Grundy County (Tenn.) Herald*
*Guild Practitioner*
*Knoxville (Tenn.) Journal*
*Labor and Nation*
*Memphis Commercial Appeal*
*Nashville Banner*
*Nashville Tennessean*
*Nation*
*National Guardian*
*Negro Digest*
*New Republic*
*New Orleans Item*
*New Orleans Times-Picayune*
*New York Times*
*Norfolk (Va.) Virginian-Pilot*
*Phylon*
*Radical America*
*Religious Education*
*Reporter*
*Richmond (Va.) Times-Dispatch*
*Social Forces*
*Southern Exposure*
*Southern Patriot*
*Tampa (Fla.) Daily Times*
*Tampa (Fla.) Morning Tribune*
*Vieux Carre Courier*

B. LEGAL DOCUMENTS

*Braden v. United States*, 365 U.S. 431 (1961).
*Dombrowski v. Burbank*, 358 F. 2d 821, 824 (D.C. Cir. 1966).
*Dombrowski v. Eastland*, 387 U.S. 82 (1967).
*Dombrowski v. Pfister*, 380 U.S. 479 (1965).

C. PUBLIC DOCUMENTS

Louisiana, Legislature, Joint Committee on Un-American Activities. *Activities of the Southern Conference Educational Fund, Inc., in Louisiana*, Report No. 4, part 1, 19 Nov. 1963.

U.S., Congress, House of Representatives, Committee on Un-American Activities. *Hearings Regarding Communist Infiltration of Minority Groups*. 81st Congress, 1st Session, July 1949.

————. *100 Things You Should Know About Communism*. House Document No. 136. N.d.

————. *Colonization of America's Basic Industries by the CPUSA*. Washington, D.C., 3 September 1954.

————. *Cumulative Index to Publications of the Committee on Un-American Activities, 1938–1954*. Supplement, 1955–60. Washington, D.C.: U.S. Government Printing Office, 1962.

————. *Report on the Southern Conference for Human Welfare*, 1947.

U.S., Congress, Senate, Committee on Agriculture and Forestry. *Hearings on the Nomination of Aubrey W. Williams To Be Administrator, Rural Electrification Administration*. 79th Congress, 1st Session, 1945.

U.S., Congress, Senate, Committee on Education and Labor. "Private Police Systems, Harlan County, Kentucky." In *Violations of Free Speech and Rights of Labor*. 76th Congress, 1st Session; Report 6, part 2.

U.S., Congress, Senate, Committee on Manufactures. *Working Conditions in the Textile Industry in North Carolina, South Carolina and Tennessee*. 71st Congress, 1st Session, 1930. Senate Report 28, vols. A and B.

U.S., Congress, Senate, Committee on Rules and Administration. *Hearings on H.R. 29: An Act Making Unlawful the Requirement for the Payment of a Poll Tax as a Prerequisite to Voting in a Primary or Other Election for National Offices*. 1948.

U.S., Congress, Senate, Committee on the Judiciary, Subcommittee to Investigate the Administration of the Internal Security Act and Other Internal Security Laws. *Hearings*. 18 and 19 March 1954, New Orleans, La. 3 vols.

————. *Hearings*. 18 and 19 March 1954. Stenographic transcript, vols. 1–3. Washington, D.C.: Alderson Reporting Company.

U.S., Congress, Senate, Subcommittee on the Judiciary. *Hearings on Poll Taxes*. 77th Congress, 2d Session, 1942.

U.S., National Emergency Council. *Report on the Economic Conditions of the South.* 1938.

U.S., President's Committee on Civil Rights. *To Secure These Rights: Report of the President's Committee on Civil Rights.* New York: Simon and Schuster, 1947.

## D. ARTICLES

Aptheker, Herbert, "Communism and Truth." *Masses and Mainstream* 6, no. 2 (1953):111–21.

Beecher, John. "The Sharecroppers' Union in Alabama." *Social Forces* (October 1934):64–124.

Bendiner, Robert. "Surgery in the CIO." *Nation* 199, no. 20 (12 November 1949):123–25.

Bornet, Vaughn D. "Historical Scholarship, Communism, and the Negro." *Journal of Negro History* 37 (July 1952):302–324.

Braden, Anne. "House Un-American Activities Committee: Bulwark of Segregation." Louisville, Ky.: Southern Conference Educational Fund, 1964.

———. "A View from the Fringes." *Southern Exposure* 9, no. 1 (1981):68–74.

Braden, Carl. "Dynamite Was Fear." *Nation* 183 (8 December 1956):149.

Brewer, Bradley R. "*Dombrowski v. Pfister:* Federal Injunctions Against State Prosecutions in Civil Rights Cases—A New Trend in Federal-State Judicial Relations." *Fordham Law Review* 34, no. 1 (1965):71–79.

Carter, Hodding. "A Wave of Terror Threatens the South." *Look,* 22 March 1955.

Cartwright, Colbert S. "Lesson from Little Rock." *Christian Century* 74, no. 40 (1957):1193–94.

Collins, Marjory. "Witch Hunt Southern Style." *Majority of One,* May 1964, 18–20.

Degler, Carl N. "The Negro in America—Where Myrdal Went Wrong." *New York Times Magazine,* 7 December 1969.

Dethloff, Henry G., and Robert R. Jones. "Race Relations in Louisiana, 1877–1898." *Louisiana History* 9, no. 4 (1968):301–25.

Dinnerstein, Leonard. "The Senate's Rejection of Aubrey Williams as Rural Electrification Administrator." *Alabama Review* 21, no. 2 (1966):133–42.

Dombrowski, James A. "Attitudes of Southern University Professors Toward the Elimination of Segregation in Graduate and Professional Schools in the South." *Journal of Negro Education* 19, no. 1 (Winter 1950):118–33.

———. "From a Mill-Town Jail." *New Republic* 60 (2 October 1929):171–72.

———. "The New South on the March." *Nation,* 3 March 1954.

———. "The Southern Conference for Human Welfare." *Common Ground* 6 (Summer 1946):14–25.

Donner, Frank J. "Hoover's Legacy. *Nation* 218 (1 June 1974):119–20.

———. "The Informer." *Nation* 178, no. 15 (10 April 1954):298–309.

Dunjee, Roscoe. "'Tis the Set of the Soul." *Crisis* 63 (January 1956):25–26, 90.
———. "Are Dixie Race Relations Improving?" *Negro Digest* 6 (April 1948):52–57.

Fein, Leonard J. "The Limits of Liberalism." *Saturday Review* 53 (20 June 1970):82–85.

Fish, John O. "Southern Methodism and Accommodation of the Negro, 1902–1915." *Journal of Negro History* 55 (July 1970):200–214.

Fishel, Leslie H. Jr. "The Negro in the New Deal Era." *Wisconsin Magazine of History* 48 (Winter 1964–65):111–26.

Foreman, Clark. "The Decade of Hope." *Phylon* 12 (1951):137–50.

Frantz, Laurent B. "H-Bomb for Unions—The Butler Bill," *Nation* 177, no. 22 (29 November 1953):126–27.

Gellhorn, Walter. "Report on a Report of the House Committee on Un-American Activities," *Harvard Law Review* 60 (October 1947):1193–1234.

Handlin, Oscar. "Civil Rights After Little Rock: The Failure of Moderation." *Commentary* 24 (November 1957):392–96.

Harding, Vincent. "A Beginning in Birmingham." *Reporter* 28 (6 June 1963):13–19.

Harlan, Louis R. "The Southern Education Board and the Race Issue in Public Education." *Journal of Southern History* (May 1957).

Harris, Richard. "Annals of Law," parts 1–3. *New Yorker* 51 (3, 10, 17 November 1975).

Hodes, W. William. "*Dombrowski v. Eastland*—A Political Compromise and Its Impact." *Rutgers Law Review* 22, no. 1 (1967):137–66.

Hutson, A.C., Jr. "The Coal Miners' Insurrection of 1891 in Anderson County, Tennessee." *East Tennessee Historical Society Publications* 7 (1935):103–121.
———. "The Overthrow of the Convict Lease System in Tennessee." *East Tennessee Historical Society Publications* 8 (1936):82–103.

Kinoy, Arthur. "Brief Remarks on *Dombrowski v. Pfister*—A New Path in Constitutional Litigation?" *Guild Practitioner* 26, no. 1 (1967):7–9.
———. "The Constitutional Right of Negro Freedom Revisited: Some First Thoughts on *Jones v. Alfred H. Mayer Company.*" *Rutgers Law Review* 22, no. 3 (1966):321–27.

Kirby, Phil. "The Legion Blacklist." *New Republic,* 18 June 1952.

Lifschultz, Lawrence. "The Great Depression Revisited." *Economic and Political Weekly* 24, no. 3 (21 January 1989):138–41.

Mandel, Bernard. "Samuel Gompers and the Negro Workers, 1886–1914." *Journal of Negro History* 40, no. 1 (1955):34–60.

Maraist, Frank L. "Federal Injunctive Relief Against State Court Proceedings: The Significance of Dombrowski." *Texas Law Review* 48, no. 3 (February 1970):535–51.

Mathews, Donald R., and James W. Prothro. "Political Factors and Negro Voter Registration in the South." *American Political Science Review* 57 (1963):355–67.

Maund, Alfred. "Aubrey Williams: Symbol of a New South." *Nation* 177 (10 October 1953):289–90.

Mays, Benjamin E. "Church and Racial Tensions." *Christian Century* 71 (8 September 1954):1068–69.

———. "Negroes and the Will to Justice." *Christian Century* 69 (October 1942):1316–18.

Meier, August, and Eliott Rudwick. "The Boycott Movement Against Jim Crow Streetcars in the South, 1900–1906." *Journal of American History* 51 (March 1969):756–75.

Meyers, Frederic. "The Knights of Labor in the South." *Southern Economic Journal* (April 1940):20–21.

Milton, George Fort. "The South Fights the Unions." *New Republic* 59 (10 July 1929):202–203.

Mitchell, Broadus. "Labor Unions and Churches." *Christian Century* 62 (November 1946):1369–71.

———. "The Broad Meaning of the CIO Organizing Drive in the South." *Labor and Nation* (April–May 1946):131–35.

———. "The Present Situation in the Southern Textile Industry." *Harvard Business Review* 8, no. 3 (April 1930):296–306.

Morris, Aldon D. "Black Southern Student Sit-In Movement: An Analysis of Internal Organization." *American Sociological Review* 46 (December 1981):755–67.

Nabritt, James M., Jr. "Future of the Negro Voter in the South." *Journal of Negro Education* 26, no. 3 (1957):418–23.

Nixon, H.C. "The New Deal and the South." *Virginia Quarterly Review* 19 (Summer 1943):321–33.

———. "The South After the War." *Virginia Quarterly Review* 20 (Summer 1944):321–34.

Oppenheimer, Martin. "The Southern Student Movement: Year I." *Journal of Negro Education* 33 (1964).

Osofsky, Gilbert. "Progressivism and the Negro: New York, 1900–1915." *American Quarterly* 16, no. 2, pt. 1 (Summer 1964):153–168.

Peebles, Jack. "The Dombrowski Case." *Guild Practitioner* 33, no. 3 (1976):89–93.

Perry, Jennings. "Hillbilly Justice in Tennessee." *New Republic* 109 (19 July 1943):68–70.

———. "Sedition in Louisville: The Braden Affair." *Nation* 180 (15 January 1955):43–44.

Ratchford, B.U. "Economic Aspects of the Gastonia Situation." *Social Forces* 8, no. 3 (March 1930):359–67.

Rosenberg, John S. "Jim Dombrowski." *Nation,* 28 May 1983.

Sedler, Robert Allen. "The Dombrowski-Type Suit as an Effective Weapon for Social Change: Reflections from Without and Within," part 1. *Kansas Law Review* 18, no. 2 (1970):237–76.

Shelton, Willard. "Paul Crouch, Informer." *New Republic,* 9 July 1954, 7–9.

Thrasher, Sue, and Leah Wise. "The Southern Tenant Farmers' Union." *Southern Exposure* 1, nos. 3 & 4 (1974):26–30.

Washington, Booker T. "The Negro and the Labor Unions." *Atlantic Monthly,* June 1913, 756–67.

Webber, Charles C. "A Worker's Education: Program for First Rate Citizenship." *Religious Education* 43 (September-October 1948):242–96.

Wells, Dave, and Jim Stodder. "A Short History of New Orleans Dockworkers." *Radical America* 10, no. 1 (1976):32–38.

Transcript. "Today Show." National Broadcasting Company, WNBC-TV, and NBC-TV Network, 27 September 1963.

## E. BOOKS

Adamic, Louis. *From Many Lands.* New York: Harper and Brothers, 1939.

Adler, Selig. *The Isolationist Impulse.* New York: Abelard-Schuman, 1957.

Agee, James, and Walker Evans. *Let Us Now Praise Famous Men.* Boston: Houghton Mifflin, 1941.

Allport, Gordon. *The Nature of Prejudice.* Boston: Beacon, 1955.

American Civil Liberties Union. *In Times of Challenge: U.S. Liberties, 1946–1947.* New York: ACLU, August 1947.

————. *Liberty Is Always Unfinished Business.* 36th Annual Report of the ACLU, 1 July 1955. New York: American Civil Liberties Union, 1955.

Aptheker, Herbert. *American Negro Slave Revolts.* New York: International Publishers, 1943.

Ashby, Warren. *Frank Porter Graham: A Southern Liberal.* Winston-Salem: John F. Blair, 1980.

Auerbach, Jerold S. *Labor and Liberty: The LaFollette Committee and the New Deal.* Indianapolis: Bobbs-Merrill, 1966.

Bailey, Kenneth K. *Southern White Protestantism in the Twentieth Century.* New York: Harper and Row, 1964.

Baker, Roscoe. *The American Legion and American Foreign Policy.* New York: Bookman, 1954.

Bardolph, Richard. *The Negro Vanguard.* New York: Vintage, 1956.

Barnard, Hollinger F., ed. *Virginia Foster Durr: Outside the Magic Circle.* University, Ala.: University of Alabama Press, 1985.

Bartley, Numan V. *The Rise of Massive Resistance: Race and Politics in the South During the 1950s.* Baton Rouge: Louisiana State University Press, 1969.

Bartley, Numan V., and Hugh D. Graham. *Southern Politics and the Second Reconstruction.* Baltimore, Md.: Johns Hopkins University Press, 1975.

Beal, Fred E. *Proletarian Journey: A Fugitive from Two Worlds.* New York: Hillman-Curl, 1937.

Beck, Carl. *Contempt of Congress: A Study of the Prosecutions Initiated by the Committee on Un-American Activities, 1945–1957.* New Orleans: Hauser Press, 1959.

Belfrage, Cedric. *The American Inquisition, 1945–1960.* Indianapolis: Bobbs-Merrill, 1973.

————. *The Frightened Giant.* London: Secker & Warburg, 1957.

Bentley, Eric, ed. *Thirty Years of Treason: Excerpts from Hearings Before the House Committee on Un-American Activities, 1938–1968.* New York: Viking, 1971.

Berlin, Ira. *Slaves Without Masters.* New York: Random House, 1974.

Berman, William C. *The Politics of Civil Rights in the Truman Administration.* Columbus: Ohio State University Press, 1970.

Bernstein, Barton J., ed. *Politics and Policies of the Truman Administration.* Chicago: University of Chicago Press, 1970.

Bernstein, Michael. *The Great Depression: Delayed Recovery and Economic Change in America, 1929–1939.* Cambridge, England: Cambridge University Press, 1989.

Boyle, Sarah Patton. *The Desegregated Heart.* New York: William Morrow and Company, 1962.

Braden, Anne. *The Wall Between.* New York: Monthly Review Press, 1958.

Branch, Taylor. *Parting the Waters: America in the King Years, 1954–63.* New York: Simon and Schuster, 1988.

Brody, David. *Workers in Industrial America.* New York: Oxford University Press, 1980.

Brooks, Thomas. *Walls Come Tumbling Down: A History of the Civil Rights Movement, 1940–1970.* Englewood Cliffs, N.J.: Prentice-Hall, 1974.

Buckley, William F., Jr., and Brent L. Bozell. *McCarthy and His Enemies.* Chicago: Henry Regnery, 1954.

Buckley, William F., Jr., and editors of the *National Review. The Committee and Its Critics: A Calm Review of the House Un-American Activities Committee.* New York: Putman, 1962.

Burr, Nelson R. "A Critical Bibliography of Religion on America," parts 1 and 2. In *Religious Life in America,* edited by James Ward Smith and A. Leland Jamison. Princeton, N.J.: Princeton University Press, 1961.

Carson, Clayborne. *In Struggle: SNCC and the Black Awakening of the 1960s.* Cambridge, Mass.: Harvard University Press, 1981.

Casdorph, Paul D. *Republicans, Negroes, and Progressives in the South, 1912–1926.* University, Ala.: University of Alabama Press, 1981.

Cayton, Horace R., and George S. Mitchell. *Black Workers and the New Unions.* Chapel Hill: University of North Carolina Press, 1939.

Clapman, H. H. *The Iron and Steel Industries of the South.* University, Ala.: University of Alabama Press, 1953.

Colwell, Stephen. *New Themes for the Protestant Clergy: Creeds Without Charity; Theology Without Humanity; Protestants Without Christianity; with Notes on the Literature of Charity, Population, Pauperism, Political Economy, and Protestantism.* Philadelphia, 1851.

Cook, Thomas. *Democratic Rights Versus Communist Activity.* Garden City, N.Y.: Doubleday, 1954.

Cort, John C. *Christian Socialism: An Informal History.* Maryknoll, N.Y.: Orbis Books, 1988.

Couch, W. T., ed. *Culture in the South.* Chapel Hill: University of North Carolina Press, 1934.

Cushman, Robert E. *Civil Liberties in the United States.* Ithaca, N.Y.: Cornell University Press, 1956.

Danhof, Clarence H. "Four Decades of Thought on the South's Economic Problems." In *Essays in Southern Economic Development,* edited by Melvin L. Greenhut and W. Tate Whitman. Chapel Hill: University of North Carolina Press, 1964.

Davis, John P. *The American Negro Reference Book.* Englewood Cliffs, N.J.: Prentice-Hall, 1967.

Degler, Carl N. *The Other South: Southern Dissenters in the Nineteenth Century.* New York: Harper and Row, 1974.

Deutcher, Isaac. *Heretics and Renegades.* London: Jonathan Cape, 1955.

Dies, Martin. *The Trojan Horse in America.* New York: Dodd, Mead, 1940.

Dombrowski, James A. *Early Days of Christian Socialism in America.* New York: Columbia University Press, 1936.

DuBois, W.E.B. *Autobiography.* New York: International Publishers, 1968.

———. *Some Efforts of American Negroes For Their Own Social Betterment.* Atlanta University Publications, No. 3. Atlanta, Ga.: Atlanta University Press, 1898.

Dunbar, Anthony P. *Against the Grain: Southern Radicals and Prophets, 1929–1959.* Charlottesville: University Press of Virginia, 1981.

Dunham, Barrows. *The Artist in Society.* New York: Marzani & Munsell, 1960.

———. *Heroes and Heretics: A Political History of Western Thought.* New York: Knopf, 1964.

———. *Ethics Dead and Alive.* New York: Knopf, 1971.

Dunn, Hampton. *Yesterday's Tampa.* Miami, Fla.: E.A. Seaman, 1975.

Dunne, William F. *Gastonia, Citadel of the Class Struggle in the New South*. New York: Workers Library for the National Textile Workers Union, 1929.

Egerton, John. *The Americanization of Dixie: The Southernization of America*. New York: Harper's Magazine Press, 1974.

Embree, Edwin R., and Julia Waxman. *Investment in People: The Story of the Julius Rosenwald Fund*. New York: Rosenwald Fund, 1949.

Foner, Philip S. *American Socialism and Black Americans: From the Age of Jackson to World War II*. Westport, Conn.: Greenwood, 1977.

————. *Organized Labor and the Black Worker*. New York: International Publishers, 1982.

Foner, Philip S., and Ronald L. Lewis, eds. *The Black Worker*, vol. 4. Philadelphia: Temple University Press, 1979.

Foreman, Clark. *Environmental Factors in Negro Elementary Education*. New York: Norton, 1932.

————, with Rauschenbush, Joan. *The New Internationalism*. New York: Norton, 1934.

————. *Total Defense*. New York: Doubleday Doran, 1940.

Forman, James. *The Making of Black Revolutionaries*. New York: Macmillan, 1972.

Franklin, John Hope. *From Slavery to Freedom*. New York: Knopf, 1968.

Frazier, E. Franklin. *The Negro Church in America*. New York: Schocken, 1963.

Garrow, David J. *Protest at Selma: Martin Luther King, Jr., and the Voting Rights Act of 1965*. New Haven: Yale University Press, 1978.

Gaston, Paul M. *The New South Creed: A Study in Southern Mythmaking*. New York: Knopf, 1970.

Gellhorn, Walter, ed. *The States and Subversion*, Ithaca, N.Y.: Cornell University Press, 1952.

Glen, John M. *Highlander: No Ordinary School, 1932–1962*. Lexington: University Press of Kentucky, 1988.

Goldman, Eric. *Rendezvous with Destiny*. New York: Vintage, 1956.

Goodman, Walter. *The Committee: The Extraordinary Career of the House Committee on Un-American Activities*. New York: Farrar, Straus and Giroux, 1968.

Goodwyn, Lawrence. *Democratic Promise: The Populist Moment in America*. New York: Oxford University Press, 1976.

Greenberg, Polly. *The Devil Has Slippery Shoes*. London: Collier-Macmillan, 1969.

Grismer, Karl H. *Tampa: A History of the City of Tampa and the Tampa Bay Region of Florida*. St. Petersburg, Fla.: St. Petersburg Printing Co., 1950.

Harding, Vincent. *There Is a River: The Black Struggle for Freedom in America*. New York: Vintage, 1963.

Hellman, Lillian. *Scoundrel Time*. Boston: Atlantic–Little, Brown, 1976.

Hobsbawm, E.J. *Labouring Men: Studies in the History of Labor*. New York: Basic, 1964.

Hodges, James A. *New Deal Labor Policy and the Southern Cotton Textile Industry, 1933–1941*. Knoxville: University of Tennessee Press, 1986.

Hofstadter, Richard. *The Paranoid Style in American Politics and Other Essays*. London: Jonathan Cape, 1966.

Holt, Rackham. *Mary McLeod Bethune: A Biography*. Garden City, N.Y.: Doubleday, 1964.

Horton, Myles, with Judith Kohl and Herb Kohl. *The Long Haul: An Autobiography*. New York: Doubleday, 1989.

Johnson, Charles S., et al. *To Stem This Tide: A Survey of Racial Tension Areas in the United States*. Boston, 1943.

———. *Into the Mainstream*. Chapel Hill: University of North Carolina Press, 1947.

Kampelman, Max. *The Communist Party vs. the CIO*. New York: Praeger, 1957.

Kempton, Murray. *Part of Our Times: Some Monuments and Ruins of the Thirties*. New York: Delta, 1967.

Kennedy, Stetson. *Palmetto Country*. New York: Duell, Sloan and Pearce, 1942.

Kester, Howard. *Revolt Among the Sharecroppers*. New York: Covici-Fried, 1935.

Key, V.O. *Southern Politics in the State and Nation*. New York: Vintage, 1949.

Killian, Lewis. *The Impossible Revolution, Phase II: Black Power and the American Dream*. New York: Random House, 1975.

Kinoy, Arthur. *Rights on Trial: The Odyssey of a People's Lawyer*. Cambridge, Mass.: Harvard University Press, 1983.

Kirby, John B. *Black Americans in the Roosevelt Era: Liberalism and Race*. Knoxville: University of Tennessee Press, 1980.

Krueger, Thomas A. *And Promises to Keep: The Southern Conference for Human Welfare, 1938–1948*. Nashville, Tenn.: Vanderbilt University Press, 1968.

Kunstler, William. *Deep in My Heart*. New York: William Morrow, 1966.

Lasch, Christopher. *The Agony of the American Left*. London: Andre Deutch, 1970.

———. *The New Radicalism in America, 1889–1963*. New York: Vintage, 1965.

Lemert, Ben F. *The Cotton Textile Industry of the Southern Appalachian Piedmont*. Chapel Hill: University of North Carolina Press, 1933.

Link, Eugene P. *Labor-Religion Prophet: The Times and Life of Harry F. Ward*. Boulder, Colo.: Westview Press, 1984.

Logan, Rayford, ed. *What the Negro Wants*. Chapel Hill: University of North Carolina Press, 1945.

Macdonald, Dwight. *Henry Wallace: The Man and the Myth*. New York: Vanguard Press, 1948.

McAdam, Doug. *Freedom Summer*. New York: Oxford University Press, 1988.

Markmann, Charles L. *The Noblest Cry: A History of the American Civil Liberties Union.* New York: St. Martin's Press, 1965.

Marshall, F. Ray. *Labor in the South.* Cambridge, Mass.: Harvard University Press, 1967.

————. *The Negro and Organized Labor.* New York: John Wiley and Sons, 1965.

Mason, Lucy Randolph. *To Win These Rights.* New York: Harper, 1952.

Mays, Benjamin E. *Born to Rebel.* New York: Charles Scribner's Sons, 1971.

Mazlish, Bruce. *The Revolutionary Ascetic: Evolution of a Political Type.* New York: Basic, 1976.

Meier, August, and Eliott Rudwick. *CORE: A Study in the Civil Rights Movement, 1942–1968.* New York: Oxford University Press, 1973.

————. *Along the Color Line.* Urbana: University of Illinois Press, 1976.

Miller, Robert Moats. *American Protestantism and Social Issues, 1919–1939.* Chapel Hill: University of North Carolina Press, 1958.

Mitchell, Broadus. *The Rise of Cotton Mills in the South.* Baltimore, Md.: Johns Hopkins University Press, 1921.

————, and George S. Mitchell. *Industrial Revolution in the South.* Baltimore: Johns Hopkins University Press, 1930.

Mitchell, H.L. *Mean Things Happening in This Land: The Life and Times of H. L. Mitchell, Cofounder of the Southern Tenant Farmers Union.* Montclair, N.J.: Allanheld, Osmun, 1979.

Morris, Aldon D. *The Origins of the Civil Rights Movement: Black Communities Organizing for Change.* New York: Free Press, 1984.

Morrison, Samuel Eliot. *The Oxford History of the American People.* New York: Oxford University Press, 1965.

Myrdal, Grunnar, with Richard Sterner and Arnold Rose. *An American Dilemma.* New York: Harper, 1944.

Nixon, H.C. *Forty Acres and Steel Mules.* Chapel Hill: University of North Carolina Press, 1938.

Odum, Howard W. *Southern Regions of the United States.* Chapel Hill: University of North Carolina Press, 1936.

Ogden, Raymond A. *The Dies Committee: A Study of the Special House Committee for the Investigation of Un-American Activities, 1938–1944.* Washington: Catholic University of America Press, 1945.

Osofsky, Gilbert. *The Burden of Race: A Documentary History of Negro-White Relations in America.* New York: Harper and Row, 1967.

Perry, Jennings. *Democracy Begins at Home: The Tennessee Fight on the Poll Tax.* Philadelphia: J.B. Lippincott, 1944.

Pleasants, Julian M., and Augustus M. Burns, III. *Frank Porter Graham and the 1950 Senate Race in North Carolina.* Chapel Hill: University of North Carolina Press, 1990.

Piven, Frances F., and Richard A. Cloward. *Poor People's Movements: How They Succeed. Why Some Fail.* New York: Vintage, 1979.

Pope, Liston. *Millhands and Preachers: A Study of Gastonia.* New Haven: Yale University Press, 1942.

Preston, William, Jr. *Aliens and Dissenters: Federal Suppression of Radicals, 1903–1933.* Cambridge, Mass.: Harvard University Press, 1963.

Price, Margaret. *The Negro and the Ballot in the South.* Atlanta, Ga.: Southern Regional Council, 1959.

Record, Wilson. *The Negro and the Communist Party.* Chapel Hill: University of North Carolina Press, 1951.

———. *Race and Radicalism.* Ithaca, N.Y.: Cornell University Press, 1964.

Roosevelt, Eleanor. *This I Remember.* New York: Harper Brothers, 1949.

Roy, Ralph Lord. *Communism and the Churches.* New York: Harcourt, Brace and World, 1960.

Salter, John R., Jr. *Jackson, Mississippi: An American Chronicle of Struggle and Schism.* Hicksville, N.Y.: Exposition Press, 1979.

Salmond, John A. *A Southern Rebel: The Life and Times of Aubrey Willis Williams, 1890–1965.* Chapel Hill: University of North Carolina Press, 1983.

———. *Miss Lucy of the CIO: The Life and Times of Lucy Randolph Mason, 1882–1959.* Athens: University of Georgia Press, 1988.

Schmidt, Karl. *Henry A. Wallace: Quixotic Crusade, 1948.* Syracuse, N.Y.: Syracuse University Press, 1960.

Scott, R.B.Y., ed. *Toward the Christian Revolution.* London: Victor Gollancz, 1937.

Shannon, David. *The Socialist Party of America.* New York: Macmillan, 1955.

Sitkoff, Harvard. *A New Deal for Blacks.* New York: Oxford University Press, 1978.

Skaggs, William H. *The Southern Oligarch: An Appeal in Behalf of the Silent Masses of Our Country Against Despotic Rule of the Few.* New York: Devin-Adair, 1924.

Smith, Lillian. *Strange Fruit.* New York: Reynal and Hitchcock, 1944.

———. *Killers of the Dream.* New York: Norton, 1949.

Sosna, Morton. *In Search of the Silent South: Southern Liberals and the Race Issue.* New York: Columbia University Press, 1977.

Spero, Sterling D., and Abram L. Harris. *The Black Worker.* New York: Columbia University Press, 1931.

Sterne, Emma Gelders. *Mary McLeod Bethune.* New York: Knopf, 1957.

Stone, I.F. *The Best of I.F. Stone's Weekly.* London: Penguin, 1973.

———. *The Truman Era.* London: Turnstile Press, 1953.

———. *The Haunted Fifties.* New York: Random House, 1963.

Strobell, G. H. *Appeal to Reason.* Girard, Kansas: N.p., 1917.

Sugg, Redding S., Jr., and George Hilton Jones. *The Southern Regional Education Board: Ten Years of Regional Cooperation in Higher Education.* Baton Rouge: Louisiana University Press, 1960.

Swanberg, W.A. *Norman Thomas: The Last Idealist.* New York: Charles Scribner's Sons, 1976.

Sweet, William Warren. *Methodism in American History.* New York: Abingdon, 1954.

Taylor, Alva W. *Christianity and Industry in America.* New York: Friendship Press, 1933.

Tillich, Paul. *The Socialist Decision.* New York: Harper and Row, 1977. Translated by Franklin Sherman from the original, *Die socialistische Entscheidung.* Potsdam: Alfred Protte, 1933.

Tindall, George B. *The Emergence of the New South, 1930–1945.* Baton Rouge: Louisiana State University Press, 1967.

Tippett, Tom. *When Southern Labor Stirs.* New York: Jonathan Cape and Harrison Smith, 1931.

Tugwell, Rexford G. *The Democratic Roosevelt.* Garden City, N.Y.: Doubleday, 1957.

Wearmouth, Robert F. *Methodistism and the Working-Class Movements of England, 1800–1850.* London: Epworth Press, 1937.

Williams, Aubrey W. *Work, Wages, and Education.* Cambridge, Mass.: Harvard University Press, 1940.

Wolfenstein, E. Victor. *The Revolutionary Personality: Lenin, Trotsky, Gandhi.* Princeton, N.J.: Princeton University Press, 1967.

Woodward, C. Vann. *Origins of the New South.* Baton Rouge: Louisiana State University Press, 1951.

———. *The Strange Career of Jim Crow.* New York: Oxford University Press, 1955.

Wynes, Charles E., ed. *Forgotten Voices: Dissenting Southerners in an Age of Conformity.* Baton Rouge: Louisiana State University Press, 1967.

Yellen, Samuel. *American Labor Struggles.* New York: Harcourt, Brace, 1936.

# Index

Abernathy, Reverend Ralph, SCLC leader, opposes SCEF role in Montgomery bus boycott, 236; invites Dombrowski to speak at rally, 251–52; ignores red-baiting, 254

Adams, Charles, Grundy labor candidate, elected, 108

Addams, Jane, founder of Hull House, 29, 50

Aderholt, O. F., Gastonia chief of police, killed, 33

aesthetics, of Dombrowski, 3; as a child, 11–12; enrolls at Bowman School of Watchmaking and Engraving, 14; first classes, 34, 36, 72; organizers as artists, 80, 95–96; use of art in social change, 212–13; turns to art study, 286–87; art distribution, 287

AFL-CIO, puts SCEF on subversive list, 237

*Afro-American,* weekly newspaper, 214; defends SCEF during Eastland probe, 225–26

Ainsworth, U.S. District Judge Robert A., rules in Dombrowski case, 270–71

Alabama Christian Movement for Human Rights, Shuttlesworth founds after NAACP outlawed, 239; launches desegregation drive, 258–61

Albertson, Ralph, founds Christian Commonwealth Colony, 54–56

Alexander, Colonel Frederick B., Louisiana Joint Legislative Committee on Un-American Activities, on SCEF raid, 263

Alexander, Will W., executive director, Commission on Interracial Cooperation, introduces Horton and West, 64; on Highlander advisory committee, 71, 90, 146, 150

All-Southern Conference for Civil and Trade Union Rights, attempted united front, routed from Chattanooga, 89–95; assailed by Daniel, 94; assessed by Dombrowski, 102–103

Allen, Woody, film *The Front* shown at fete, 284

Altgeld, Joseph, 54

Amalgamated Clothing Workers of America, Knoxville leader attacks

Amalgamated Clothing Workers of
America (*cont.*)
Dombrowski, Hawes as communists, 74, 84; sends student to Highlander, 89; joins TWOC drive, 117
Amburn, Sam, zinc miner, at Highlander, 89
American Association for the Preservation of State Government and Racial
Integrity, segregationist group, 235
American Association of University
Professors, New Orleans chapter,
backs SCEF, 271
American Civil Liberties Union,
founded by Ward, 28; defends
Dombrowski in Elizabethton, 31,
90; offers reward in Tampa vigilante
case, 102; decries anti-communist
hysteria, 186; defends Braden on sedition charge, 240–41; files brief in
*Dombrowski v. Pfister,* 273–74,
279; of Louisiana, honors Anne
Braden, Dombrowski, Virginia Durr,
284
American Economics Association,
founded by Christian Socialist, 53
American Federation of Hosiery
Workers, joins TWOC drive, 117
American Federation of Labor, spurns
bugwood strikers, 69; split with
CIO discussed, 84; limits political
role, 105; impeaches Georgia officer,
117; attacks TWOC drive, 127, 142;
leaders query Dombrowski, 127–28
American Legion, in Chattanooga,
89–95; Dombrowski a member of
Willard Straight Post, 91; of Louisiana attacks SCHW, 169
American Medical Society, SCEF poll
on hospital segregation policies,
215–17

American Peace Mobilization, united
front founded by Ward, to counter
attacks on Roosevelt, 135
Anderson, Nels, WPA official, settles
Grundy dispute, 114–15
Andrews, Bishop James O., early
Emory leader, slave ownership controversial, 37
Anglicans, in Colonial Virginia and
slavery, subject of Dombrowski
study at Union, 49
anti-communism, x; Dombrowski target of attack, 3, 24, 31, 186–87; at
Union Theological Seminary, 42;
Methodists attack on Ward, 44–45;
directed toward Highlander, 74, 86–
87, 90–94, 106–109, 112, 115–17,
122–25; by Tampa vigilantes, 100–
103; against unions, 129–30; as a
mask for segregation, aimed at
SCHW, 135–36, 138–40, 145–46,
156–58, 166; and at SCEF, 210–11,
218, 224–32, 236–38, 241–42,
246–49, 267–68
Arens, Richard, anti-communist congressional lawyer, at Eastland hearing, 226–32; at HUAC hearing with
Braden, 246–48
Argrow, Reverend W. Waldermar, marries Dombrowski and Krida, 149
Arnall, Ellis, Georgia governor, backed
by SCHW, 157; attends SCHW convention, 170
Associated Press, reports Dombrowski
arrest, 27; Southerners denounce
civil rights report, 195; ignores
SCEF civil rights call, 202
*Atlanta Constitution,* 145; attacks
Dombrowski, SCEF education meeting, 210; refuses SCEF ad attacking
HUAC, 247

*Atlanta Journal, The,* 27

Avery, Maltheus R., African American refused hospital care, dies, 214

Baker, Ella J., resigns as SCLC executive director, joins SCEF, 260, 271

Baldwin, Roger, head of American Civil Liberties Union, 90; seeks SCHW red purge, 143–45

Bancroft, Frank C., edits *The Southern Patriot,* 153, 178

Baptiste, Reverend L. T., sponsors All-Southern Conference for Civil and Trade Union Rights, 90

Barbee, William, Freedom Rider, beaten in Montgomery, 253

Barker, Richard, FBI agent, investigates Highlander, 115–16

Barnett, Dr. Albert E., Methodist minister and professor, aids Wilder strikers, 67; urges SCEF role in civil rights coalition, 236–38; opposes HUAC fight, 248

Barr, John U., Louisiana Dixiecrat, attacks SCEF, 210

Bates, L. C. and Daisy, Little Rock integration leaders, Dombrowski visits, 242–43

Beal, Fred, Gastonia strike organizer, 32; convicted of murder, 40

Beaty, Alec, Socialist Highlander supporter, 72

Bedow, Noel, steelworker, on race issues at SCHW meeting, 142

Belfrage, Cedric, author and Dombrowski friend, 284

Bell, Hunter, Atlanta editor and Dombrowski classmate, 27–28; denies Coca-Cola segregated machines, 219

Bellamy, Edward, author and Christian Socialist, 52

Bender, Reverend William, founder of Mississippi NAACP, heads vote drive, 191

Bennett, John, Dombrowski classmate at Union, 42–43

Bernays, Edward L., public relations pioneer, gives Dombrowski tips, 192–93, 207

Berry, Colonel Harry S., Tennessee WPA director, attacks Highlander, 106–15

Bethune, Mary McLeod, founder, Bethune-Cookman College, joins New Deal, 134; given SCHW award, 140, 143–44; heads SCHW membership drive, 164–69; role in Dombrowski SCHW ouster try, 174–77; resigns from SCHW, 179, 189, 210, 213, 225, 281; police seize photo, 263

Better Business Bureau of New Orleans, badgers SCEF out offices, 210

Biddle, Francis, New Deal official, attends SCHW meeting, 138

Bilbo, Senator Theodore G., attacks SCHW, 156–57, 165; filibusters FEPC, 186; dies amidst investigation, 190–91

Bingham, Barry, publisher and onetime SCHW leader, blasts Bradens for house sale, 240

*Birmingham News,* carries SCHW ad, 154; reports on SNYC trial, 200

*Birmingham World, The,* 90

Bittner, Van A., CIO official, attacks SCHW, 166–67

Black, Hugo, U.S. Supreme Court Justice, brother-in-law of Virginia Durr, 132, 184; given SCWH award, 135;

Black, Hugo (*cont.*)
  Bilbo reminds of early Ku Klux Klan
    membership, 156; target of Eastland
    New Orleans probe, 224–32; ab-
    stains in *Dombrowski v. Eastland,*
    273
black power, SCEF views toward, 2–3;
  Dombrowski learns from A. Phillip
  Randolph, 141; splits SCEF after
  Dombrowski leaves, 281–82
Blackburn, Henry W., Dombrowski
  fraternity brother, 22
Bliss, W. D. P., Christian Socialist, in-
  fluences Dombrowski, 52
Block, Doris S., American Youth for a
  Free World, arrested with
  Dombrowski in Birmingham, 197–
  201
Block, Emmanuel, attorney, defends
  Dombrowski in Birmingham, 197
Bower, Edith, and Neth, SCEF con-
  tributors, 194
Bowman, Dr. Leroy, early influence on
  Ethel Clyde, 61
Boykin, S. Frank, Coca-Cola official,
  1–4, 24–25
Braden, Anne, begins long career as
  segregation foe, 240–41; joins
  SCEF, 241; in vote drive, 244–46;
  defies HUAC subpoena, 246–47; re-
  cruits Zellner, 255, 271, 282
Braden, Carl, jailed for selling house to
  African-American veteran, 240–41;
  joins SCEF, 241; in vote drive, 244–
  46; defies HUAC and is jailed, 246–
  50; paroled, 254; aids SNCC fund
  drive, 254–55, 271, 282
Bradford, Gaines T., African-American
  publisher, sponsors All-Southern
  Civil and Trade Union Rights Conference, 90–91

Brener, Milton E., New Orleans at-
  torney, defends Dombrowski, 269
Brennen, William, U.S. Supreme Court
  Justice, writes *Dombrowski v. Pfister*
  decision, x, 275–76
Brookwood Labor College, 62; Hawes
  at, 68–69
"Brotherhood, The," Emory class-
  mates of Dombrowski, 1, 21–22,
  28, 36, 276, 279. *See also* fraternity
Brown, Charlotte Hawkins, North
  Carolina educator, role in
  Dombrowski SCHW ouster try, 176
Brown, Will L., Dombrowski neighbor
  in Monteagle, 80
*Brown v. Board of Education,* decision
  pending, 223; reaction after ruling,
  232–38, 240
Broyles, Reverend L. M., influenced
  young Dombrowski, 14–18, 20
Browder, Earl, Communist Party
  leader, jailed, 140
Bryan, Horace, jailing protested, 92
Buchanan, Nell, courted by
  Dombrowski, 25
Bunche, Dr. Ralph, African-American
  sociologist, appointed to New Deal,
  151
Burbank, Luther, sends trees to
  Christian Commonwealth Com-
  munity, 50
Burnham, Louis, a founder of the
  Southern Negro Youth Congress,
  helps start *The Southern Patriot,*
  152; role during Birmingham ar-
  rests, 196–201
Burns, John McDougal, reporter, red-
  baits Highlander, 121–22
Burns, Lee, sponsor of All-Southern
  Conference for Civil and Trade
  Union Rights, 90

Burns, Tommy, union speaker at Highlander, 84

Butler, J. R., Southern Tenant Farmer's Union organizer, 81

Butler, John, informer, testifies in New Orleans, 228–30

Buttrick, Bill, teaches economics at Highlander, 84, 123–24

Cable, George Washington, admired by Dombrowski, 214

Camp, Col. Lindley W., Georgia State Guard leader, defies "race-mixing," 154

Campbell, John C., Folk School, Hawes at, 69; differs with Highlander, 93

Candler, Asa G., Coca-Cola Company founder, Emory University benefactor, 1–4, 18–20, 25; views on education and christianity, 36–37, 278

Candler, Bishop Warren Akin, Emory leader, organizes merger, 18

Candler School of Theology, Dombrowski studies at, 25

capitalism, Dombrowski's view of, 3, 12–14, 23–24, 30–32, 36–37, 42, 47–48, 50–56, 78–79, 82, 282–83, 286–87, 291–94

Carey, James, attends SCHW conference, 138

Carothers, Sam, secretary, SCHW committee in Louisiana, 178

Champion, Edna, student at Highlander, 89

Chaney, James, civil rights worker, murdered in Mississippi, 275

Charity, Ruth Harvey, Danville attorney, leads civil rights campaign, 271

Charlotte News, The, condemns civil rights report, 195

Charlton, Judge Louise, chairs first SCHW convention, 135

Chattanooga Free Press, The, red-baits Highlander, 125; attacks Dombrowski, 155

Chattanooga News-Free Press, The, reports on All-Southern Conference for Civil and Trade Union Rights, 91–92

Cheek, Cordie, African-American youth, lynched, 159

Chicago Defender, The, 225

"chilling effect," 3; phrase coined in Supreme Court ruling, 275–76

Christian charity, Southern Methodist view of, 19–22, 32, 36–37; solidarity preferred to, 34, 113–14, 279

Christian Commonwealth Colony, the Kingdom of God in Georgia, 50–56

christian ethics, of Dombrowski, See theology

Christian Labor Union, founded in Boston, 52, 55

Christian Socialism, Dombrowski identified with, 2, 28–30, 35, 37–39, 46–48, 50–56, 60, 102–103, 137, 171, 182–83, 276, 279–81, 286–88

Christopher, Paul, Textile Workers Organizing Committee leader, backs Highlander, 112, 124; aids Dombrowski with SCHW, 137; role in Dombrowski SCHW ouster move, 175–77

Church of All Nations, Dombrowski manages forums, 43

Citizens Committee to Preserve American Freedom, formed to oppose HUAC, 246

civil liberties and civil rights,
    Dombrowski sees as one, ix–xi, 2–
    3, 102–103, 172–73, 182–83, 226,
    248, 254, 276, 281–82
Clement, Dr. Rufus E., African-
    American educator, urges wartime
    SCHW race policy, 155
Clyde, Ethel, benefactress, 60–61, 71,
    76; underwrites *People of the Cum-
    berlands* filming, 105, 108;
    Dombrowski seeks loan for SCHW,
    137, 145, 192–93; posts bond dur-
    ing *Birmingham* arrests, 197; backs
    drive to desegregate hospitals, 214–
    17; hears SCEF woes, 218–19; at-
    tends Eastland hearings, 226–30,
    246; pays SCEF legal fees, 272, 284
coalfield convict labor wars, described
    in Dombrowski oral history, "Fire in
    the Hole," 2, 109–11
Coca-Cola Company, founder tries to
    hire Dombrowski, 1, 18, 20, 56;
    SCEF decries "segregated" machine,
    219–21, 278
Cocke, Judge J. Bernard, dismisses
    Dombrowski arrest charges, 269–70
Coe, George A., pragmatist educator,
    38
Coffin, Henry Sloan, Union Theologi-
    cal Seminary president, under at-
    tack, 29; hires Harry Ward and
    Reinhold Niebuhr, 39
Cold War, x; "bolshevism," feared
    among liberals, 42–43, 140; Tru-
    man orders government red purge,
    186–87, 284. *See also* anti-
    communism
Collier, Tarleton, SCHW leader,
    Dombrowski tells of ouster try, 171–
    72

Collins, Addie Mae, African-American
    teenager, killed in Birmingham
    church blast, 260
Colmer, Representative William M.,
    campaigns in Mississippi, 191
Columbia, Tenn., police riot in Mink
    Slide, 158–62
Colwell, Edwin, Dombrowski class-
    mate at Emory, 20
Colwell, Ernest C., Dombrowski class-
    mate at Emory, 20–21
Colwell, Stephen, Christian Socialist
    who sided with labor, 52–53, 55
Commission on Interracial Coopera-
    tion, created by YMCAs, 64, 71, 90,
    143, 146, 150
Committee of Southern Churchmen,
    77–80, 90. *See also* Younger
    Churchmen of the South and Com-
    mittee of Southern Churchmen
Commonwealth College, labor college,
    at odds with Highlander, 93
communism, Dombrowski views on, 3,
    42, 44–48, 78–80, 94, 113–14,
    121, 129, 138–39, 222–28, 238,
    267–68, 282–83
Communist Youth Organization,
    Highlander secretary a member of,
    128
Communist Party, 90; united front pol-
    icy, 94; Birmingham Communist
    Party, participates in first Southern
    Conference for Human Welfare con-
    vention, 128; organizes veterans,
    205, 224, 228, 229
Conference on Discrimination in
    Higher Education, sponsored by
    SCEF, 210–12
Congress of Industrial Unions, 84;
    backs Roosevelt, 105; launches

Southern organizing drive, 117–22; split grows with Highlander, 119–30, 142; endorses SCHW, 166; opens postwar drive with attack on SCHW, 166–67, 170; few leaders back SCEF rights conference, 201

Connor, Eugene "Bull," enforces Jim Crow laws at SCHW meeting, 135; causes split in SCHW, 164, 198, 258–59

Constitutional Educational League, anti-communist group, publishes tract, 122

Cooper, Governor Prentice, Tennessee leader, aids Highlander, 124

Couch, Wiley, Tennessee official, chases Reds, 92

Cox, Representative Eugene, claims Russia behind civil rights drive, 196

Cox, Florence and Will, an aunt and uncle, 10–13

Cox, Helen and Roy, Dombrowski's cousins, 10–13

Crisis, The, Voice of the National Association for the Advancement of Colored People, 78; reports on Coca-Cola machine, 219

Crouch, Bob, Grundy labor candidate, elected, 108

Crouch, Paul, congressional informer, testifies at Eastland probe, 229–32

Crumbless, Raleigh, American Legionnaire and foe of communism, attacks conference, 90–95

Crump, Ed, Memphis political boss, called by Roosevelt, 139

Cumberland Mountain Workers' and Unemployed League, bugwood cutter's organization, 69–71, 83

Current, Gloster, NAACP director of branches, red-baits SCEF, 260

Daily Worker, Communist Party newspaper, 161

Daniel, Franz, Dombrowski classmate at Union, 40–43; Socialist Party organizer, 43; Amalgamated Clothing Workers' Union organizer, 82; critical of Dombrowski, 94; HUAC investigates, 115; joins TWOC drive, 117, 123; severs ties with Highlander, 128

Daniels, Jonathan, publisher, attends SCHW meeting, 138

Danish Folk High Schools, origins described, 61–64. See also Highlander

Darby, Reverend H. D., African American, fights for vote in Mississippi, 244

Daughters of America, red-bait Highlander, 123

Daves, Dr. J. Herman, defies Jim Crow laws at Highlander, 76, 119–20

Davis, John P., executive secretary, National Negro Congress, SCHW leader, 138; debates race, 142–43; at founding of The Southern Patriot, 152; on wartime racial policies, 155

Dawn, The, radical religious publication, 52

Debs, Eugene, Socialist presidential candidate, 23–24, 54

"Declaration of Civil Rights," SCEF resolve, signed at Monticello, 201–202

DeHart, Reverend William Wilson, Dombrowsky family minister, 10

Demarest, Henry, early American Christian Socialist, 52

democratic control of industry,
Dombrowski goal, 28, 47–49, 50–
55, 62, 76–78, 89–94, 281, 286

Democratic Party, 2, 105; primaries in
Grundy, 108–109; white-only primary outlawed, 185; Southerners argue Roosevelt policies, 135, 170;
divides over Wallace candidacy, 184;
Southern Democratics filibuster
FEPC, deny William REA post, 189;
Hamer denied convention seat,
268

Derricotte, Juliette, dies after being refused treatment, 214–15

Devane, Judge Dozier, Tampa neighbor, 31

Dewey, Dr. John, 34, 38; views contrasted with Ward, 61–63; endorses
Highlander, 62–63, 65; on Highlander advisory board, 71, 79, 83;
defends Highlander against red-
baiting, 107

Dewey, Dr. Malcolm H., founds Emory
Glee Club, 19–20

Diamond, Dion, Howard University
student, meets Dombrowski, 252;
jailed in McComb, 256–57

Dies, Congressman Martin, chair of
HUAC, investigates Highlander,
115–23, 140, 225

Dillon, Walter E., Washington attorney,
defends Dombrowski, 269

Dixiecrats, Southern Democrats, bolt
party, 195–96; defeated at polls,
201

Dixon, Governor Frank, Alabama governor, halts contract over race, 154

Dobbs, John Wesley, grand master of
Georgia Prince Hall Masons, defends SCEF, 225–26, 233–34

Dobbs, Malcolm, headed SCHW in Alabama, laid off, 178

Dodge, Reverend Witherspoon, SCHW
organizer, 166

Dombrowski, Eugene, cousin, 12–13,
22

Dombrowski, James Anderson, early
childhood, 5–14; academic career,
12–15, 18–26, 19–41, 44–56;
founds Methodist church, 20; assistant pastor, 26; arrests, 27–32,
197–200, 262–66; changes spelling
of name, 28; joins Highlander, 70–
76; probes by Dies, 115–23; appointed to SCHW, 132–34; grand
jury investigates, 160–61; founds
SCEF, 182–87; probes by Eastland,
223–33; probes by HUAC, 246–48;
LUAC raid and Supreme Court test,
262–76; death of, 287

Dombrowski, Mathilde Harmon, pa-
ternal grandmother, 4–13

Dombrowski v. Eastland, alleged SCEF
lists seized illegally, 270–71, 273

Dombrowski v. Pfister, alleged First
Amendment rights violated by raid,
x, 3, 273–76

Dombrowsky, Albert, brother, 7–11

Dombrowsky, Daisy, sister, 5–13; estranged from Dombrowski, 100–
103

Dombrowsky, Isabella Elizabeth,
mother, 5–9

Dombrowsky, Rose, sister, 5–13; angered by report, 27–28; estranged
from Dombrowski, 100–103

Dombrowsky, William John, father, 5–
13

Douglas, Senator Paul, backs SCEF after Eastland hearing, 232

Douglass, Frederick, author and aboli-
tionist leader, quoted, 206, 286
Dred Scott case, U.S. Supreme Court
decision on slavery, 203–204
Dubinsky, David, Socialist Party and
labor leader, 79
DuBois, W. E. B., African-American
scholar, 196
Duncan, Elizabeth, Emory alumni sec-
retary, 70–71
Durham, Reverend Plato T., evangelist,
22; theology contrasted with Harry
Ward, 32
Durham Statement, African-American
policy resolve, 150–51
Durr, Clifford, attorney, director,
Federal Communications Commission, 132; urges wife to spurn Progressive Party bid, 184; during
Eastland hearings, 225–33; car destroyed by mob, 252
Durr, Virginia, encourages
Dombrowski to lead SCHW, 132–
33, 137; backs Dombrowski in
SCHW ouster try, 174; runs for governor of Virginia, 184; quoted on accomplishments of SCHW, 184–85;
closes SCHW, 184; defies Eastland,
222–33; at civil rights rally, 251–52

Eastland, Senator James O., Mississippi political leader, attacks
African-American soldiers, 157–58;
ridicules Dombrowski name, 158;
filibusters FEPC, 186; during New
Orleans SCEF hearings, 223–33;
charges Reds brainwash Supreme
Court, 233; hearings harm SCEF,
236–38, 242; subpoenas SCEF records, 270–71

Eddy, Dr. Sherwood, missionary and
reformer, asks Dombrowski to organize 1932 European tour, 45–49; on
Highlander advisory board, 71
Edens, Hollis, Dombrowski classmate,
25
"education for empowerment," 2
education, Dombrowski views on, 29,
32, 34–37, 56, 60, 62–64, 71, 81–
89, 207, 278–80
Egerton, John E., Tennessee manufacturer attacks Highlander, 86–87,
95
Einstein, Dr. Albert, praises SCEF
school stand, 211
Eisenhower, General Dwight D., defends African-American soldiers,
158
Elizabethton, Tenn., scene of 1929
strike, 1, 27–32; impact on
Dombrowski, 31–32
Ellis, U.S. Judge Frank B., rules against
Dombrowski, 272
Ely, Richard, influential Christian Socialist author and economist, 38,
52–54
Embree, Edwin R., president, Rosenwald Fund, 120
Emory Alumni Association, organized
by Dombrowski, 24–26
Emory Glee Club, 1; Dombrowski role
in, 25–26, 27
Emory University, founding, 1, 18–25,
278–79
Enestvedt, Odean, Highlander student,
89
evangelism, 1; for commercial ends,
20; of "The Brotherhood," 20–23;
Dombrowski as evangelist, 30–31,
187–89, 291–94

Evans, Eva Knox, teacher on European
    tour, 46–47
Evans, Mercer, hazed at Emory, 23; in-
    fluence on Dombrowski, 23–24;
    coauthors Report on the Economic
    Conditions of the South, 24, 27, 41,
    134; under fire at Emory, 46
Executive Order 9835, issued by Presi-
    dent Truman, starts federal loyalty
    list, 186

Fair Employment Practices Commis-
    sion, New Deal agency, 143, 152–
    53, 158
Farmers Holiday Association, sends
    members to Highlander, 89
Farris, Dee, Highlander student, 70
Faulk, John Henry, radio personality,
    hosts Wallace bid rally in Texas, 180
Federal Bureau of Investigation, inves-
    tigates Highlander, 115–16; agent
    reports on vigilante meeting, 125;
    reports on SCHW "race mixing,"
    140; puts Dombrowski on
    "custodial detention" list, 147,
    229; trails Dombrowski, 234, 244;
    not told about SCEF police raid,
    267
Federal Shorthand Reporters Associa-
    tion, alleged subversive group, 223
Fentress Coal and Coke Company,
    owned Wilder mines, 66
Field, Marshall, department store
    owner, backs Williams publication,
    189; asked to back drive to desegre-
    gate medical schools, 216
First Amendment, importance to
    Dombrowski, x, 3, 224–26, 247,
    267–68, 273–76, 281
Fisher, Margaret, Georgia SCHW
    leader, 157

Fleming, Will, store clerk, starts Mink
    Slide riot, 158
Florida Investment Company, racist
    advertisement, 7
Foreman, Clark H., New Deal advisor,
    120; coauthors Report on the Eco-
    nomic Conditions of the South, 134,
    137; race views prevail at SCHW,
    143; elected SCHW president, 145–
    47; moves to oust Dombrowski,
    170–77; closes SCHW, 184
Foreman, Reverend Lloyd, forced to
    hide family, 250–51
Foreman, Pamela Lynn, attends de-
    segregated school, 250–51
Forey, Edward, National Maritime
    Union member, at SNYC meeting,
    197
Forman, James, SNCC leader, praises
    SCEF, 254–55
Fowler, Henry, SCHW leader in Vir-
    ginia, resigns, 179
Fox, Mary, League for Industrial De-
    mocracy staffer, 101
Frank, Lou, edits, The Southern Pa-
    triot, 153, 158
Frantz, Laurent, lawyer, coauthors
    Mink Slide report, 159–62
Frantz, Marge Gelders, daughter of
    SCHW founder, joins Dombrowski
    at SCHW, 137–38, 153, 159
fraternity, importance to Dombrowski,
    1–4, 18, 19–25, 34, 40–43, 91,
    170–72, 182–84, 213–14, 223–24,
    226, 279
Frazier, Dr. E. Franklin, dismisses
    "Negro education," 211
Freedom Riders, beaten in Montgom-
    ery, 251–53
Fuller, Helen, at founding of The
    Southern Patriot, 152

Fuller, Margaret, leader of SCHW in Georgia, 170

Fults, Jim, Grundy labor candidate, elected, 108

Fund for the Republic, headed by Robert M. Hutchins, 192; regards SCEF as communist, 237

Gach, Frederick and Anna, witness Freedom Riders beaten, 253

Gaines, Lloyd L., ordered admitted to Missouri law school, 207–208

Gardner, O. Max, Governor of North Carolina, 33

Garrison, District Attorney James, delays Dombrowski trial, 272–73

Gelders, Joseph, Alabama activist, founds SCHW, 133–35

Gentilly Citizen's Council, segregationist group, warned of SCEF, 241

George, Henry, author, influences Dombrowski, 29, 52

George, Senator Walter, Georgia Roosevelt foe, defeats Foreman bid, 146

Georgia SCHW Committee, in election fight, 157; voter drive, 164

Gershon, Rebecca M., SCHW leader, opposes Dombrowski ouster, 173–75

Gladden, Washington, Social Gospel advocate, 38, 286

Godwin, Governor Mills, Virginia segregationist, coins phrase, 235

Goldstein, Dr. Benjamin B., defends Scottsboro Boys, 77

Gomillion, Dr. Charles G., Tuskegee dean, at SCEF vote meet, 245; suit, *Gomillion v. Lightfoot,* seeks end to gerrymandering in Alabama, 245

Goodman, Andrew, civil rights worker, murdered in Mississippi, 275

Gordon, J. King, Dombrowski classmate at Union, 40–44, 73

Graham, Barney, leader of Wilder strike killed, 66–68

Graham, Dr. Frank Porter, president SCHW and University of North Carolina, appoints Dombrowski to SCHW post, 133, 135; resigns from SCHW, 136, 139; probes for Reds in SCHW, 145–46, 168; SCEF advisor, 195

Grant, Edmonia K., African American, joins SCHW staff, 179

Gray, John, pragmatist philosopher, 38

Green, Percy, Mississippi editor, at vote drive, 191; aids Williams, 233

Green, William, president, AFL, attacks CIO drive, 127

Gruening, Ernest, editor, sparks Emory fight, 46

Grundtvig, Bishop N. S. F., envisioned Danish folk high schools, 61–62

Grundy County Crusaders, attack Highlander, 122–25

Grundy Parent-Teachers Association, red-baits Highlander, 123

"half and half" agreements, New Orleans dock labor contracts, Dombrowski learns about, 213–14, 281

Hall, Birmingham City Judge Oliver, rules on SNYC arrests, 200–201

Hall, Rob, Communist Party leader, Dombrowski withdraws invitation to SCHW meeting, 138–39

Hamer, Mrs. Fannie Lou, Mississippi Freedom Democratic Party leader, denied seat at Democratic Party meeting, 268

Hamilton, Dr. Charles G., polls Mississippi school teachers for SCEF, 234

Hampton, E. L., coal company stockholder, attacks Highlander, 123

Hampton, Rupert, Highlander music teacher, 70

Handy, Charles, student at Highlander, 89; TWOC organizer, 117

Hanley, Frank, artist, creates SCEF desegregation booklet, 213

Hansberry, William, Dombrowski brother-in-law, 13

Hardman, J. B. S., Amalgamated Clothing Workers leader, warns Dombrowski on united front, 128–29

Harlan, Supreme Court Justice John Marshall, dissents in Jim Crow decision, 203–204

Hart, Joseph K., advocate of folk high schools, 63–64

Hawes, Elizabeth (Zilla) Daniel, starts Highlander career, 68–69; organizes union local in Knoxville, 74; signs call for military Socialist Party, 78–80; red-baited, 86–87, 96, 101; HUAC investigates, 115; joins TWOC drive, 117, 125–26; critical of Dombrowski, 126; severs ties with Highlander, 128, 279–80

Haymarket riot, 52

Haywood, Allan S., CIO vice president, criticized by SCHW, 166–67

Hearst, William Randolph, 9

Henderson, Alvin, Grundy banker, attacks Highlander, 116

Henderson, Lewis, Dombrowski friend, 182–84

Henry, Aaron, African-American leader in Mississippi, visited by Dombrowski, 244

Herndon, Angelo, Communist organizer, 68

Herrmann, Susan, witnesses Freedom Riders beaten, 251

Herron, George D., Christian Socialist minister, 51, 53–55

Highlander Folk School, early description, 2, 43, 59, 62–71; under attack, 66–68, 74, 89–93, 108–18, 121–30; Dombrowski role at, 71, 74–76, 85–86, 104–105, 114–17; African Americans attend, 76, 119–20; described to Progressive educators, 81–86; staff joins TWOC drive, 117–19; seeks to quit administration, 119, 125–27; Dombrowski, Horton split, 129–33

Hill, Senator Lester, backs SCEF after Eastland hearing, 232

Hillman, Sidney, labor leader, accused as communist, 123

Hitler, Adolph, emerging threat to democracy, 46, 112

Holt, Dr. Hamilton, Rollins College president, speaks at voting rights rally, 179

Hoover, President Herbert, campaigns in Elizabethton, 29

Hopkins, Harry, New Deal official, accused by HUAC, 115; Williams worked for in agency, 189

Horton, Myles, a founder of Highlander Folk School, 2; at Union Theological Seminary, 40–43; recruits Dombrowski, 59–60; arrested in Wilder strike, 67; does not sign call for militant Socialist Party, 79–80, 90; educational views, 95; ill. 96; organizer for TWOC, 117–21; critical of TWOC, 121; in auto accident, 121–22; and Dombrowski split, 125–33; votes to oust

Dombrowski from SCHW, 170–73; closes SCHW, 184; subpoenaed by Eastland in red-hunt, 222–33, 279–80

Horton, Zilphia Johnson, musician, wife of Myles, teaching music at Highlander, 84; organizer for TWOC, 117–19; in auto accident, 121–22

House Committee on Un-American Activities, probes Highlander, 115–23, 148; condemns SCHW, 180–81, 242

Huberman, Leo, attends premier of Highlander film, 105

Hulbert, Hilda, Highlander librarian, 80

Humphrey, Senator Hubert H., backs SCEF after Eastland probe, 232

Hutchins, Dr. Robert M., chancellor, University of Chicago, meets with Dombrowski, 192

Ickes, Harold, New Deal official, accused by HUAC, 115, 151

Institute on Non-Violence and Social Change, Montgomery bus boycott center, fears SCEF ties, 235–36

International Hod Carriers and the Builders and Common Laborers' Union of America, Grundy WPA workers affiliate, 106

International Ladies Garment Workers, Local 122 sends member to Highlander, 89; joins TWOC drive, 117

Interracial Hospital Movement, leads desegregation effort in Kentucky, 216

Ivey, John E., Jr., director, Southern Regional Conference Board, refuses to debate Williams, 209–10

Jackson, John, Louisiana state attorney, before U.S. Supreme Court, 274

James, Dean Flemming, University of the South theologian, 124

James, Henry, protects Freedom Rider, 252–53

James, William, author, 38

Jenner, Senator William, chair, Senate Internal Security Committee, announces SCEF probe, 222–23

Jim Crow, Dombrowski's struggle with American racism, 7, 19–20, 36–37, 76–78, 81–82, 100–103, 129–30, 137, 141–42, 148–49, 150–62, 196–202, 219–20; birth of legal doctrine, 203–204

Johnson, Dr. Charles S., SCHW leader, signs Durham Statement, 150–51, 179

Johnson, Dr. Lillian, Highlander benefactress and social activist, 65–68; deeds property to Highlander, 95, 124

Johnson, Guy, North Carolina professor, a founder of Southern Regional Council, 152

Johnson, Lyndon B., hired by Williams for New Deal job, 189; backs SCEF after Eastland hearing, 232; urged to call off HUAC probe, 247

Johnson, Thomas, Georgia lawyer, defends Dombrowski in Birmingham, 197–201

Jones, Reverend Ashton, jailed after trying to desegregate Atlanta church, 272

Jones, Dr. Lewis, Tuskegee Institute sociologist, backs Dombrowski in SCHW ouster try, 173–74

Junior Chamber of Commerce of New Orleans, asks city to oust SCHW, 181

Junior Order of United American Mechanics, red-baits Highlander, 123

Kagawa, Dr. Toyohiko, Japanese Christian Socialist, speaks to Highlander students, 88–89
Kamp, Joseph P., anti-communist publisher, attacks Highlander, 122
Kant, Immanuel, influence on Dombrowski, 282–83
Kazan, Elia, films *People of the Cumberlands*, film on Wilder strike, 105, 126
Kennedy, President John F., sworn in as president, 249–50
Kennedy, Attorney General Robert, orders marshals to Montgomery, 252
Kester, Alice, social activist, aids Wilder strikers, 67
Kester, Howard "Buck," southern secretary, Fellowship of Reconciliation, aids Wilder strikers, 67–69; early interracial organizing, 76–79, 81; and Dombrowski split, 89–93, 134
Kilby, C. H., Grundy banker, attacks Highlander, 116; organizes vigilantes, 123–26
Kilgore, Alf, Dombrowski neighbor in Monteagle, 80
King, Reverend Ed, helps organize Mississippi Freedom Democratic Party, 268
King, Reverend Martin Luther, starts Montgomery bus boycott with Nixon, 235–36; compares attack on Freedom Riders to Hitler, 252; ignores red-baiting, 254; linked to SCEF, 266–67
Kingdom of God, The, Dombrowski's concept of, 3, 28–29, 30, 47–48, 282–83, 287–88. *See also* Appendix B, 291–94

*Kingdom, The,* radical religious publication, 52
Kinoy, Arthur, National Lawyers Guild attorney, ix–xi; defends Dombrowski after police raid, 266–76
Knebel, Fletcher, reports on All-Southern Conference on Civil and Trade Union Rights rout, 91–92
Knight, H. L., 9
Knight, Peter O., 9
Knights of Columbus of New Orleans, wants city to oust SCHW, 181
Knights of Labor, organize in Grundy, 109–11
Knox, John, Dombrowski classmate at Emory, 18–24, 46
Koeninger, Dr. Rupert C., sociologist, speaks at SCEF school conference, 234–35
Kohn, John P. Jr., Montgomery lawyer, defends Virginia Durr, 226–30
Kold, Kristen, founds first folk school, 63, 126
Krida, Arthur, Dombrowski brother-in-law, 41
Krida, Ellen, meets Dombrowski, 41–43, 46, 49–50, 57; fails to persuade Dombrowski to stay in New York, 60–63, 73; fears for Dombrowski's safety, 91; views depicted, 95–100, 115; urges Dombrowski to quit Highlander, 125–31, 136–38; marries Dombrowski, 149–50; harassed in Nashville, 162; health declines, 217; attends Eastland hearings, 226; police hold at gunpoint, 264–65; death of, 283–84
Ku Klux Klan, Bilbo a member of, 156; revives, 186; threaten Birmingham meeting, 197–98, 233, 235, 255
Kunstler, William, civil rights attorney,

defends Dombrowski after police raid SCEF, 266–76

labor movement, Dombrowski views of and work with, 2, 29–34, 51–54, 60, 62, 71, 74, 76, 82–87, 89, 94, 104–15, 117–21, 127–30, 141, 164, 166–67, 213–14, 254, 280
Labor's Political Conference, Grundy WPA workers, elect county officials, 106–108; defeated and disbands, 112–14
Lady Astor, hosts Emory Glee Club, 25; introduces Dombrowski to George Bernard Shaw, 46
Lamb, Edna, speaks at Highlander, 84
Lassiter, Louise, disqualified to vote in North Carolina, 245
Lawrence, Alton, Dombrowski's predecessor at the SCHW, 136; helps start *The Southern Patriot,* 152; linked to communists by informer, 229
Leadership Conference on Civil Rights, denies SCEF affiliation, 236–38, 253
League for Industrial Democracy, 40, 61
League of American Writers, Communist group, invited to Highlander, 121
Lee, Algernon, Socialist Party leader, 79
Lee, Herbert, Mississippi farmer, killed for vote try, 256
Lee, Howard, director of SCHW, red-baited and resigns, 135–36
Lerner, Max, attends premier of Highlander film, 105
Lewis, John L., president, United Mine Workers, accused as communist, 123; backs SCHW, 136, 151

Lilienthal, David E., New Deal official, at SCHW meeting, 138
Lincoln University School of Journalism, honors Dombrowski after Eastland attack, 232
Long, Earl K., Library, exhibits Dombrowski's art, 287
Louisiana Joint Legislative Committee on Un-American Activities, 263–76, 286
Louisville Courier Journal, hires Dombrowski ally, 217; denounces Braden house sale, 240
Love, Bishop Edgar A., gives keynote address at SCEF vote meeting, 245

McCallister, Frank, Socialist Party leader, helps Dombrowski defend Tampa vigilante victims, 101–103; seeks SCHW Red purge, 143–44
McCarthy, Senator Joseph, red-hunt gets attention, 218, 224, 284; McCarthyism, 267, 278
McCready, Ester, barred from Maryland nursing school, 212
McCullers, Carson, novelist, impact on Dombrowski, 148
McDaniel, John B., Virginia Democrat, attacks civil rights report, 195
McDew, Charles, SNCC volunteer, beaten and jailed in McComb, 256–57
MacDonald, James Ramsey, British Labor Party leader, 46
McGill, Ralph, attacks Dombrowski, SCEF, 210–11
McGovern, Phil, Grundy anti-labor candidate, loses, 108
McKaine, Osceola, African-American editor and SCHW staff, critical of CIO race policy, 166–67, 171, 174

McKinley, President William, declares
war on Spain, 9

McMichael, Jack, American Youth
Congress leader, Dombrowski withdraws invitation to SCHW meeting,
138–39

McNair, Denise, African-American
child, killed in Birmingham church
blast, 260

MacTaggart, Helena, Dombrowski
sister-in-law, 42

MacTaggart, Robert, Dombrowski
brother-in-law, 42

McWilliams, Joe, "the Christian Mobilizer," racist crusader, 187

*Maine,* battleship sunk, 9

Mann, Floyd, Alabama public safety
director, 253

Maples, Sam, Smoky Mountain musician, 104

Markell, Judge Charles of Maryland
Court of Appeals, orders nursing
school desegregated, 212

Marshall, Thurgood, NAACP lawyer,
praises SCHW, 163

Marshall Fund, promises SCHW
funds, 137; backs reform groups,
144–45

Martin, Walker, Highlander student,
70

Martinet, Louis A., Society, African-
American legal group, works with
SCEF, 262, 271

Marx, Karl, 29; marxism, 2; Soviet
marxism, 33; influence on
Dombrowski through Ward, 38–43;
described by George Bernard Shaw,
46; Niebuhr break with, 205–206;
Dombrowski view of, 282

Mason, Lucy Randolph, joins TWOC
drive, 117; backs Gelders on SCHW,

134, 140; opposes Dombrowski
SCHW ouster, 175–76; proposes
idea for SCEF, 182–83, 187, 280–
81

Maund, Al, writer and long-time
friend of Dombrowski, 153; fired by
New Orleans paper, 217–18; learns
SCEF on AFL-CIO subversive list,
237; helps SCEF after raid, 271

May, Mortimer, textile manufacturer,
debates race, 142

Mays, Dr. Benjamin E., Morehouse
College president, joins SCEF, 182,
188, 190; quits SCEF, 225–30, 281

Mead, George Herbert, influence on
Ward, 38

Meiklejohn, Alexander, Dombrowski
teacher, 28

Melish, Reverend W. Howard, raises
funds for SCEF, 254

Memphis *Commercial Appeal,* red-
bait attack on SCEF, 218

Meredith, James, enrolled at University
of Mississippi, 255

Metcalf, Reverend Walter, eulogizes
vigilante Tampa victims, 101–102

Methodist Federation for Social Action, founded by Harry S. Ward, 28,
188, 279

Miller, Pink, veteran killed during
strike, 81

Mine, Mill and Smelter Workers
Union, Local 188 sends members to
Highlander, 89; linked to commu-
nists by informer, 229

Mississippi Freedom Democratic Party,
betrayed by Democratic Party, 268,
275

Mitch, William, United Mind Workers
leader, 137, 179; resigns from
SCHW, 184

Mitchell, Clarence, NAACP legislative director, 225–26

Mitchell, G. Raymond, Dombrowski classmate at Emory, 18–23

Mitchell, George, SCHW leader, opposes Dombrowski SCHW ouster, 175

Mitchell, H. L., a founder of Southern Tenant Farmer's Union, 81; sponsors All-Southern Trade Union and Civil Rights Conference, 90; clashes with Horton, 93; seeks SCHW Red purge, 144–45

Mitchell, James B. "Jimmy," Dombrowski classmate at Emory, 20

Modern Democrats, Tampa socialists tarred and beaten, persecuted, 100–103

Moore, Ashley, Smoky Mountain banjoist, 104

Moore, William L., postman killed on civil rights march, 259–60

Morgan, George A., Dombrowski classmate at Emory and Harvard, 29

Morningside Heights Branch of the Socialist Party, Dombrowski joins, 40–43

Moses, Robert, SNCC volunteer, registers voters, 256

Muste, A. J., dean, Brookwood Labor College, speaks with Dombrowski, 40

Myrdal, Gunnar, sociologist, quoted, 134, 151

Nabrit, Dr. James M. Jr., Howard University law professor at SCEF vote meeting, 246

Nance, A. Steve, heads TWOC Deep South drive, 117

Nashville Banner, The, SCHW foe, 161, 169

Nashville Tennessean, red-baits Highlander, 121–22; warns Dombrowski of raid, 123, 142

Nathan, Dr. Otto, at Braden sentencing, 249

Nation, The, editor causes Emory controversy, 46

National Association for the Advancement of Colored People, invited to SCHW conference, 138; joins SCHW on Mink Slide case, 158–60; New Orleans branch refuses Dombrowski membership, 238; organizes veterans, 205; NAACP Legal Defense Fund, 274; outlawed in Alabama, 239; red-baits SCEF, 236, 260; Legal Defense Funds files brief in Dombrowski v. Pfister, 274

National Committee Against Discrimination of the Association of Interns and Medical Students, hears Williams, 216

National Committee for the Defense of Political Prisoners, Joseph Gelders southern secretary, 133

National Conference on the Economic Crisis and the Negro, at Howard University, 120

National Council on Religion in Higher Education, names Dombrowski a Fellow, 43

National Labor Relations Board, Nashville hearing, 129

National Lawyers Guild, aides civil rights lawyers, 257; New Orleans meeting, 262–68

National Negro Congress, organized, 120; views on New Deal, 141–42

National Student Association, 255

National Textile Workers' Union, aids
    Gastonia strikers, 32–33, 40–41
National Youth Administration, New
    Deal agency, 134, 143, 189
Neff, L. W., Methodist publisher, 57
Nelson, A. James, president of Young
    Men's Business Club of New Or-
    leans, attacks SCEF at Eastland hear-
    ing, 227
New Deal, social causes for, 105
New Orleans Item, prints series dis-
    crediting SCEF, 242
New Orleans Medical Association,
    SCEF polls on integration, 235
New Orleans school desegregation,
    250–51
New Orleans States, series attacks
    SCHW, 181
New Orleans States-Item, lauds "re-
    tired" Dombrowski, 284
New Orleans White Citizen's Council,
    threatens integration advocates,
    250–51
New Republic, The, Dombrowski pub-
    lishes essay, "From a Mill-Town
    Jail," 40; reports on Tampa vigilante
    case, 102, 153. See also Appendix B,
    291–94
New York Times, The, carries photo of
    young Dombrowski, 12; covers Mink
    Slide police riot, 160; reports on
    SCEF civil rights resolve, 202; re-
    ports SCEF medical poll, 235
Niebuhr, Reinhold, joins Union Theo-
    logical Seminary, 39; described, 40;
    views on Marxism, 48, 205–206; on
    Highlander advisory board, 71;
    speaks at founding of Younger
    Churchmen of the South, 77–78; de-
    fends Highlander against red-
    baiting, 107; cycle of violence, 205–
    207; signs petition for SCEF, 232

Nightingale, Reverend Abram, a Con-
    gregational minister, aids Horton,
    67
Nix, Congressman Robert C., votes
    against Braden indictment, 248
Nixon, E. D., Alabama African-
    American leader, aids Williams,
    233; organizes Montgomery bus
    boycott, 235–36; withdraws
    Williams invitation, 236

Oakley, Harvey, Smoky Mountain
    guitarist, 104
Oakley, Wiley, Smoky Mountain story-
    teller, 104
Odum, Dr. Howard W., at Emory, 19;
    founds Southern Regional Council,
    150–52
Oliver, Reverend C. Herbert, arrested
    with Dombrowski in Birmingham,
    196–201
O'Neal, James, Socialist Party leader,
    79

Page, Kirby, newspaper editor, 77
Palfi, Marion, photographer, mounts
    SCEF exhibit, 213
Palmer, Attorney General A. Mitchell,
    organizes nationwide arrests of
    "radicals," 22–23
Pandit, Madame Jijaya, honored by
    SCEF, 213
Parade, TWOC magazine,
    Dombrowski edits special issue, 120
Park, Robert E., sociologist, Horton a
    student of, 59
Parsons, Lucy, 54
Patterson, Dr. Franklin, African-
    American leader, urges SCHW war-
    time policies, 155
Pate, John, speaks at Highlander, 84

Paty, Adelaide, wife of Raymond Paty, 31

Paty, John, lawyer represents Dombrowski in Elizabethton, 31

Paty, Raymond, Dombrowski fraternity brother, 31

Payne, Taylor, Highlander student, 89

Peebles, Jack, New Orleans attorney, defends Dombrowski after police raid SCEF, 266–76

*People of the Cumberlands,* film on Wilder strike premiers, 104–105; stirs argument in Grundy, 111–12

Pepper, Senator Claude, attends SCHW convention, 170

Perez, Judge Leander H., Louisiana segregationist, warns of SCEF red threat, 241–42

Perkins, Frances, New Deal official, accused by HUAC, 115

Perry, Jennings, Tennessee editor, drafts vote resolve, 142; drafts SCEF civil rights resolve, 201–202

Pfister, Representative James H., chair, Louisiana Joint Legislative Committee on Un-American Activities, orders SCEF police raid, 266–67; ensuing legal snarl, 267–74; defeated in reelection bid, 272

*Pittsburgh Courier,* reports on Coca-Cola machine, 219

Plessy, Homer Adolph, a "colored" man, challenges Jim Crow doctrine, 203–204, 214

*PM,* New York newspaper, covers race conflict, 154

Poteet, Ewing, fired by New Orleans newspaper for alleged ties to SCEF, 241

Poulnot, Eugene F., flogged by Tampa vigilantes, 101–102

Powell, Representative Adam Clayton, attacked by CIO official, 166

President's Commission on Civil Rights, Truman era rights agency, opposition to, 186

Price, Branson, headed SCHW in North Carolina, 166–67; role in Dombrowski ouster, 171

Price, Mary, SCHW fundraiser, 167

Progressive Education Association, Dombrowski speaks at, 81–84, 207

Progressive Party, SCHW backs candidates, 180–85, 195–98

property, Dombrowski attitude toward, 14, 19, 24, 47–48, 50, 61–62, 141, 219, 240, 287

Prugh, Benton, studied cooperatives at Highlander, 89

Prouty, Charles, Highlander student, 89

Pulitzer, Joseph, 9

Rainey, Dr. Homer Price, Texas university president, forced to quit SCHW, 145

Randolph, A. Philip, head of Brotherhood of Sleeping Car Porters, founder of National Negro Congress, 120; views on New Deal, 141–42, 189

Raper, Arthur, director, Commission on Interracial Cooperation, speaks on race at Highlander, 120

Rauschenbusch, Walter, Social Gospel advocate, 38

Reid, Dr. Ira DeA., African-American educator, debates race, 142–43

Relief Workers Union, strikes WPA in Grundy, 81–83, 87; take-over of Grundy offices, 112–15

*Report on the Economic Conditions of the South,* 24, 134

Republican Party, 29, 185, 186

revolution, Dombrowski's views on, 44–48, 51, 72, 282

Revolutionary Policy Committee for Socialists, young turks urge Socialist Party militancy, 78–80

*Richmond Times-Dispatch, The,* opposes Southern Regional Education Board, 208

Roberts, Carl, Grundy banker, attacks Highlander, 116

Robertson, Carole, African-American teenager, killed in Birmingham church blast, 260

Robeson, Paul, first Southern concert, 138–40

Rodman, Samuel, SCHW leader, backs move to oust Dombrowski, 177

Rogers, Jack N., chief counsel, Louisiana Joint Legislative Committee on Un-American Activities, 267–74

Rogers, Sam, flogged by Tampa vigilantes, 101–103

Rogers, Ward, jailed for literacy teaching, 81

Rollins, J. Lewis, Grundy labor candidate for school superintendent, 108

Roosevelt, Eleanor, hosts Highlander film screening, 104–105; gift to Highlander causes stir, 115–16; linked to communists, 122–23; on SCHW panel with Horton, 134; mediates SCHW Red purge dispute, 144; defends Mink Slide citizens, 160; sends message to SCHW, 169; hears about Dombrowski from Williams, 190; dances with Dombrowski, 213, 224; signs petition for SCEF, 232; photo seized by police, 263

Roosevelt, President Franklin D., backs SCHW, 2–3, 72, 133–34, 139–40; policies debated, 77–79; WPA strikers wire, 107–108; declares WWII, 132; race policies debated, 141–43; death felt at SCHW, 163–64

Roosevelt, Congressman James, spurns plea to stop HUAC hearing, 247

Roosevelt, Theodore, in Tampa, 10

Rosenwald Fund, supports Dombrowski oral history, 109; supports National Negro Congress, 120

Royce, Josiah, influence on Ward, 38

Salter, John R. Jr., Tougaloo sociologist, joins SCEF after Jackson sit-ins, 260, 268; help organize Mississippi Freedom Democrats, 271

Schaff, Monroe, Tennessee Legionnaire, attacks SCHW, 160–61

Schwerner, Michael, civil rights worker, murdered in Mississippi, 275

Shaw, George Bernard, author, meets Dombrowski, 46

Sheiner, Leo, Miami lawyer, subpoenaed by Eastland, 227–28

Shlafrock, Leo, Miami builder, subpoenaed by Easthand, 227–28

Shoemaker, Joseph, killed by Tampa vigilantes, 100–103

Shores, Arthur, Alabama civil rights lawyer, defends Dombrowski in Birmingham arrest, 197–201

Shuttlesworth, Reverend Fred, Birmingham African-American leader, 3; house bombed, 239–40, 242; joins SCEF as president, 248–49; arrested 257–58; launches Birmingham desegregation drive, 258–

61; ignores NAACP red-baiting of SCEF, 260; SCEF police raid, 266

Shuttlesworth, Ruby, wife of minister, stabbed at school, 242

Siegenthaler, John, Kennedy aide, clubbed in Montgomery, 253

Simkins, Modjeska, South Carolina SCHW leader, role in Dombrowski ouster try, 176; at Taylor arrest, 196–201

Skinner, Annie Sully, Dombrowski maternal grandmother, 7

Skinner, James F., Dombrowski maternal grandfather, 7

Sledd, Andrew, fired from Emory, 37

Sloan, Federal Judge Boyd, sentences Braden and Wilkinson, 248

Smart, W. Aiken, Emory dean, 29

Smith, Benjamin E., New Orleans lawyer, x; at Eastland hearing, 226–31, 257; during SCEF police raid, 261–69; impact on life, 274

Smith, Gerald L. K., founder, American Nationalists' Committee, 187

Smith, Lillian, author and segregation foe, critical of Southern Regional Council, 152; quits SCHW, 164; accused of red-baiting by Williams, 236

Social Creed, Christian Socialism statement authored by Harry Ward, 39

Social Gospel, 37–38, 51–52

Social Gospel, The, magazine published by Christian Commonwealth Colony, 50

socialism, Dombrowski view of. See capitalism; civil liberties and civil rights; fraternity; The Kingdom of God; theology

Socialist Party, Dombrowski relations with, 3, 23–24, 40, 43, 78–79, 85, 96, 101–103, 143–44, 282

Sourwine, J. G., chief counsel, Senate Internal Security Subcommittee, confiscates SCEF records, 270–71, 273

Southern Christian Leadership Conference, works with SCEF, 253–61; communist allegations, 274

Southern Conference Education Fund, 2–3; founded as arm of SCHW, 167–68; Dombrowski "assigned to," 172–77; takes over The Southern Patriot, 181; single focus strategy, 182–83; survives SCHW, 184; major campaigns against Jim Crow, 190–92, 193–96, 196–200, 201–202, 207–10, 214–17, 219–21, 244–45, 251–61; adopts propaganda techniques, 192–93; IRS revocation, 210–12, 218; office move forced, 210; split over Eastland hearings, 224–26; Eastland harms, 236–38; new leaders, 239–40, 248, 260; HUAC hearings, 246–49; police raid, 262–68; court battle, 268–80; split over black power, 281–82; Dombrowski "retires," 286

Southern Conference for Human Welfare, 2, 128; allegations of communist influence, 128, 135, 143–46, 160–62, 180–81; Dombrowski takes over, 132–37; founding, 133–35; role of African Americans, 134, 137–43, 146, 164, 170; ties to New Deal, 134–36, 138–39, 141, 155, 170; Foreman elected president, 145; reaction to Durham Statement, 150–51; vies with SRC, 151–52; Smith criticism of, 152; forms The Southern Patriot, 152–53; state

Southern Conference for Human Welfare (*cont.*)
committees, 155; Southern senators attack, 156–58, 165; Mink Slide tragedy, 158–60; wartime policies debated, 163–65; South's largest interracial group, 164–68; IRS attacks, 165; CIO split, 166–67; Dombrowski and Foreman split, 170–77; last meeting, 176, 184, 187, 190, 191, 197, 279–80; Wallace campaign, 180

Southern Electoral Reform League, mentioned as socialist, 144

*Southern Farm and Home,* magazine bought by Williams, 189; publication sold after Eastland attacks, 243

Southern Governor's Conference, seeks to thwart school desegregation, 209

Southern liberals, dilemmas of, 148–49

Southern Methodists, 1, 4, 9, 36–37, 255, 278

Southern Negro Youth Congress, founded by Communist Party, on subversive list, 196; arrests at Birmingham meeting, 196–201

*Southern Patriot, The,* founded, 152–55; uses during WWII, 152; postwar anti-Jim Crow campaigns, 187–88, 192–202; segregation in higher education, 207–209; segregation in health, 214–17; Coca-Cola campaign, 219–21; wins award for reports on school desegregation, 232; on voting rights, 245

Southern Regional Council, founded, 150–52; vies with SCHW, 164

Southern Regional Educational Board, founded to thwart desegregation, 208–12; attacked by SCEF, 208–10

Southern Sociological Society, polled by SCEF, 208–209

Southern States Industrial Council, attacks Highlander, 87

Southern Summer School for Women Workers, Dombrowski critical of, 93

Southern Tenant Farmer's Union, 81, 144–45

Spaulding, C. C., African-American business leader, signs Durham Statement, 151

Sprinkle, Reverend Henry, kept from All-Southern Conference for Civil and Trade Union Rights, 92

Stalin, Joseph, 47, 196

Stalinism, 42, 47–48, 279

State Defenders of State Sovereignty and Individual Liberties, segregationist group, 235

State of Louisiana, apologizes to Dombrowski for arrest, 286

Stembridge, Jane, proposes joint SNCC-SCEF project, 255

Stephenson, Gladys, African-American housewife, slapped by store clerk, 158–59

Stephenson, James, African-American veteran, hits clerk, 158–59, 163

Stevens, Judge J. Morgan, Mississippi Methodist, signs ad hitting race violence, 154–55

Stewart, Supreme Court Justice Potter, upholds convictions of Braden, Wilkinson, 249

Stockton, Joe Kelly, supports Highlander, 71–73, 80, 99

Stockton, Kate Bradford, supports Highlander, 71–73; reads poetry to Krida, 99–100

Stoval, Lyle C., Chattanooga Legion-

naire, red-baits Highlander, 107–
108
Streator, George, African-American
editor, decries South's racism, 78
Strong, Josiah, prominent Social Gospel advocate, 38
Student Non-Violent Coordinating
Committee, cooperates with SCEF,
253–61; alleged to control by reds,
274
Students for Democratic Society, 255
Sutherland, Eugene and Margaret,
study cooperative at Highlander, 89
Sweatt, Herman, challenges Texas law
school race barriers, 207, 212
Sweet, Fred, labor editor, helps start
*The Southern Patriot,* 152–53
syndicalism, short-lived in Grundy,
105–109

Talleferro, T. C., Tampa neighbor, 9
Talmadge, Eugene, Georgia governor,
SCHW political foe, 157; debates
Williams, 223
Talmadge, Herman, Georgia governor,
named by legislature, 157, 211
*Tampa Times, The,* reports
Dombrowski's arrest, 27
Tawney, R. H., writing influenced
Dombrowski, 29
Taylor, Dr. Alva W., professor of
Christian Social Ethics, West teacher,
64; aids Wilder strike relief, 67–69;
on Highlander advisory board, 71,
76, 88; defends Highlander against
red-baiting, 107, 124; aids
Dombrowski with SCHW, 137;
back Dombrowski in SCHW ouster
fight, 176
Taylor, Senator Glen, Wallace running

mate, arrested in Birmingham, 196–
201, 240
Tefferteller, Ralph, musician, joins
Highlander, 74; develops cultural
program, 88; at White House, 104;
parttime role in TWOC, 117–19;
leaves Highlander, 126, 213
Temporary Commission on Employee
Loyalty, Truman era red-hunting
agency, 196
Tennessee Coal and Iron, starts convict
leasing, 109–11; suspected of
launching HUAC probe of Highlander, 116; fights union drive in Birmingham, 133
Tennessee State Highway Patrol, repor-
tedly investigates Highlander, 107
Tennessee Valley Authority, 69, 138,
170
Terry, James H., United Mine Workers
official, discusses race at Highlander,
120
Textile Workers Organizing Committee (TWOC), 84; split over race,
129–30
theology, of Dombrowski, 2, 14, 19–
22, 28–29, 32, 36, 42–43, 47–48,
50–56, 182, 282–83, 288. *See also*
Appendix B, 291–94; "Brotherhood, The"; fraternity; Kingdom of
God, The
Thomas, Henry, organizes bugwood
strike, 69–71
Thomas, Representative J. Parnell,
chair of HUAC, condemns SCHW,
180
Thomas, Norman, helps Dombrowski,
60; speaks at Wilder strike rally,
69; on Highlander advisory board,
71; split in Socialist Party, 79–

Thomas, Norman (*cont.*)
80, 101; defends Highlander,
107
Thomas, Roy, Grundy labor candidate,
nominate, 108; salary cut by state,
112
Thompson, Dorothy, teaches music at
Highlander, 68; works with bug-
wood strike, 69–71, 88
Thompson, Reverend John B.,
Dombrowski classmate at Union,
40–43; joins Highlander, 68; president of SCHW, 136; votes to oust
Dombrowski from SCHW, 170–
71
Thurmond, J. Strom, South Carolina
governor, decries racial desegregation, 186; bid for president defeated,
196–201
Tipton, A. C., attorney, defends
Dombrowski in Elizabethton, 31
Tobias, Dr. Channing, African-
American YMCA leader, defends
Mink Slide citizens, 160; SCEF advisor, 195
Tolstoi, Leo, corresponded with
Christian Commonwealth Community, 50
totalitarianism, Dombrowski opposition to, ix, 3, 48, 109–11, 147, 154,
206, 277–78, 286
Trapolin, Ivor A., New Orleans anti-
communist, attacks SCHW, 169; testifies at Eastland probe, 227
Trawich, Robert, Alabama lawyer, defends Dombrowski in Birmingham,
197–201
Trentham, Long John, Smoky Mountain fiddler, 104
Trosclair, Major Presley J., New Orleans policeman, on SCEF raid, 263

Truet, Will, organizes Gastonia strike,
32
Truman, President Harry S., ignores
SCHW, 163; corresponds with
Dombrowski, 169–70; rankled by
Wallace bid, 180; issues loyalty oath
order, 186, 196; Commission on
Civil Rights, 187, 195–96
Tuck, Congressman William M., Virgi-
nian fights desegregation, 246
Tureaud, A. P., New Orleans attorney,
defends Dombrowski, 269

Union Theological Seminary,
Dombrowski a student at, 28–59;
names Dombrowski 1931 Traveling
Fellow, 43
united front strategy, Dombrowski be-
lief in and use of, ix, 2–3, 76–80,
89–94, 102–103, 129–30, 137–38,
170–71, 182, 196–200, 201–202,
213–14, 251–55, 278–79, 281–82
United Garment Workers of America,
Local 145 members at Highlander,
89
United Mine Workers, strike in Wilder,
66; organize Grundy locals, 111;
Local 5881 attacks Highlander, 123
United Nations, 168
United Negro and Allied Veterans of
America, founded by Communist
Party, 205
United Press International, reports on
HUAC hearing, 247
United Rubber Workers Union, leader
speaks at Highlander, 84; joins
TWOC drive, 117
University of Arkansas Law School,
admits African-Americans, 209
University of California at Berkeley,
Dombrowski enrolls, 28

University of Delaware, desegregation plan, 208–209

University of Maryland School of Nursing, ordered to admit African American, 212

University of Missouri Law School, ordered to admit African-Americans, 207

University of Oklahoma, ordered to desegregate, 208–209

University of Texas Law School, African-American enrolled in basement school, 207

U.S. Civil Rights Commission, lobbied by Dombrowski, 246

U.S. Customs, detain Dombrowski for Soviet posters, 49; detention used in red-baiting, 86–87; recounted in Eastland probe, 227

U.S. Senate Internal Security Subcommittee, investigates SCEF, 222–33

U.S. Supreme Court, x, 3; ruling creates Jim Crow doctrine, 203–204; orders professional schools desegregated, 207–12; Dombrowski comments on, 211; Brown case pending, 223; upholds convictions of Braden, Wilkinson, 248–49; hears Dombrowski cases, 273–76

U.S. Treasury Department, Internal Revenue Service, grants Highlander exempt status, 116; threatens SCHW tax exempt status, 165–67; revokes SCEF exempt status, 210–18

Vance, Rupert, attends SCHW conference, 138

Vaughn, Dolph, blacklisted Grundy miner, joins Highlander staff, 106; organizes Grundy WPA workers, 106–15; defends Highlander, 122

Veblen, Thorsten, 29

Veterans of Foreign Wars, in Grundy, attack Highlander, 123–24

vigilantism, against Dombrowski, 30–32, 160–62, 169, 181, 218–19, 263–69; against Highlander, 90–92, 121–25; in Tampa, 100–103; at Emory, 23; against New Orleans school integration, 250–51; against Freedom Riders, 251–52

voting, voting rights, Dombrowski suffrage efforts, 78, 100–101, 104–11, 137, 164, 167–68, 179, 188, 190–92, 212, 243–46, 268, 280

Walker, James R. Jr., lawyer jailed for defending client's vote try, 245

Walker, Mayor Jimmy, hears Emory Glee Club, 25

Walker, Reverend Wyatt Tee, King aide, ignores SCEF red-baiting, 254

Wall Street Journal, The, 243

Wallace, Governor-elect George, orders Zeller arrest, 256; as governor, accuses Dombrowski, Bradens, 267

Wallace, Henry, New Deal secretary of commerce, accused as communist, 123; bids for presidency with SCHW backing, 180–85; campaign, 196–201

Walter, Representative Frances, chair, HUAC, 247

Waltzer, Bruce, New Orleans attorney, arrested in SCEF raid, x, 265–69; impact on life, 274

war and violence, Dombrowski's views on, 15–17, 30–31, 47–48, 71–72, 78–80, 109–11, 147–49, 204–206, 286

Warburg, James P., banker, backs
  Williams publication, 189
Ward, Daisy, wife of Harry Ward, 44
Ward, Dr. Harry F., Dombrowski
  meets at lecture, 28; as Dombrowski
  mentor, 28–59, 79; contrasts with
  Methodists, 32, 37–39; formulates
  Methodist Social Creed of the
  Churches, 39, 42; denied tenure at
  Boston University School of Theology, 39; differs with Niebuhr, on
  theology, 39–42; makes controversial visit to Soviet Union, 44–45;
  critical of Social Gospel, 51–56; on
  economic control, 61–62; repudi-
  ates dictatorship of proletariat, 79–
  80, 279; differs with Niebuhr, on violence, 205–206. See also American
  Civil Liberties Union; American
  Peace Mobilization; Methodist
  Federation for Social Action; united
  front strategy
Waring, District Judge J. Waites, honored by SCEF, 188, 213
Washington Post, The, prints SCEF ad
  attacking HUAC, 247–48
Weaver, Robert A., African-American
  economist, New Deal official, 146
Weber, Max, 29
Weber, Palmer, CIO official, role in
  Dombrowski SCHW ouster, 171
Weitzman, Daniel, SCHW leader,
  backs effort to oust Dombrowski,
  177
Wesley, Cynthia, African-American
  teenager, killed in Birmingham
  church blast, 260
Wesley, John, founder of Methodism
  quoted, 32, 38
West, Don, a founder of Highlander
  Folk School, 2, 59; meets Horton,
  63–67; splits with Horton, 68, 70

West, Elsie, Highlander drama teacher,
  70
West, U.S. Judge E. Gordon, rules
  against Dombrowski, 272
White, Mildred, Highlander student,
  alleged to be communist, 231
White, Walter, director, NAACP, forms
  Mink Slide defense committee with
  SCHW, 160–62; attends SCHW
  conference, 170
White Citizens Council, formed by
  Mississippi businessmen, 233, 235
Whitehead, Albert North,
  Dombrowski studies with, 29
Whitney fund, promises SCEF funds,
  137
Wiggins, Ella May, worker's song
  leader, killed in Gastonia, 41
Wilkerson, William "Wee Willie," at
  Emory Alumni Association, 25
Wilkins, Josephine, influential Geor-
  gian, proposed SCHW reorganize,
  167–68
Wilkins, Roy, NAACP leader, opposes
  SCEF role in civil rights coalition,
  236–38, 253
Wilkinson, Frank, HUAC foe, at Atlanta hearing, 246–48; jailed with
  Braden, 249–50; paroled, 254
Williams, Aubrey, founds SCEF with
  Dombrowski, 2–3, 182–90; heads
  National Youth Administration,
  hires Mary McLeod Bethune, 134,
  140; role in Dombrowski SCHW
  ouster try, 175–77, 181; refused
  confirmation to REA, 189, 195;
  reads SCEF civil rights resolve, 201–
  202; pressures hospitals to desegregate, 216; subpoenaed by Eastland,
  222–33; debates Talmadge, 223;
  enlists African-American aid to keep
  magazine alive, 233; fears SCEF

harmed by Eastland, 237–38; sells magazine, 243; at civil rights rally, 252–53; dies of cancer, 275

Williams, Reverend Claude C., jailing protested, 92

Willie, Major Russell, Louisiana state policeman, on SCEF raid, 263

Willis, Congressman Edwin, chairs HUAC probe, 247–48

Wilson, Leon, Highlander staff, defends school, 122

Wilson, President Woodrow, declares war, 15

Wisdom, U.S. Judge John Minor, rules for Dombrowski, 272

Wood, Robert C., secretary, International Labor Defense Committee, sponsors All-Southern Civil and Trade Union Rights Conference, 90

Woodbey, Reverend George Washington, former slave and Christian Socialist minister, 50

Wolfe, J. August, influences young Dombrowski, 12, 36

Work Peoples' College, 62

Work Progress Administration, struggles in Grundy, 81, 105–15; occupy Grundy offices, 112–15

Workers' Defense League, defends Tampa vigilante victims, 101

workers' education, 2; at Highlander Folk School, 57–80; theory and methods described by Dombrowski, 81–89

Workers' Folk School, at Esbjerg, Denmark, 64

*World Tomorrow, The,* progressive tabloid, 77

Wright, Mrs. Ada, mother of Scottsboro Boy, 77

Wyland, Reverend Ben F., leads interrogationists in Tampa, 245

Young, P. B., African-American publisher, signs Durham Statement, 151

Young Men's Business Club of New Orleans, attacks SCHW, 169

Younger Churchmen of the South, organized by Dombrowski and Kester, 77–80; hold second meeting, 78, 90. *See also* Fellowship of Southern Churchmen and Committee of Southern Churchmen

Zellner, Robert, Alabama student, joins SNCC staff, 255; visits southern campuses, 255–56; beaten and jailed in McComb, 256–57; splits in SCEF, 282